American Philosophical Society

Transactions of the American Philosophical Society

Held at Philadelphia, for Promoting Useful Knowledge. Volume II

American Philosophical Society

Transactions of the American Philosophical Society
Held at Philadelphia, for Promoting Useful Knowledge. Volume II

ISBN/EAN: 9783337008260

Printed in Europe, USA, Canada, Australia, Japan

Cover: Foto ©Thomas Meinert / pixelio.de

More available books at **www.hansebooks.com**

TRANSACTIONS

OF THE

AMERICAN

PHILOSOPHICAL SOCIETY,

HELD AT

PHILADELPHIA,

FOR PROMOTING

USEFUL KNOWLEDGE.

VOLUME II.

PHILADELPHIA:

PRINTED AND SOLD BY *ROBERT AITKEN*, AT POPE's HEAD
IN MARKET STREET.

M.DCC.LXXXVI.

ADVERTISEMENT.

THE peculiar circumftances of America, fince the publication of the firft volume of the Tranfactions of this Society, will be a fufficient apology for the long delay in publifhing a fecond. The Society having, however, refumed their former labours in promoting ufeful knowledge, which were necefffarily fufpended during the late war: and finding themfelves in poffeffion of materials more than fufficient for a fecond volume of Tranfactions, appointed a Committee to felect fuch pieces as might be moft proper for that purpofe : The Committee have made that felection, which is here offered to the public. Several pieces ftill remain worthy of publication, which will probably appear in a future volume.

It

It may not be amifs in this place to infert the Rules which the Society have adopted for the direction of their Committees in the choice of papers for publication.

FIRST, " That the grounds of the Com-
" mittee's choice of papers for the prefs, fhould
" always be the importance or fingularity of
" the fubjects, or the advantageous manner of
" treating them, without pretending to an-
" fwer, or to make the fociety anfwerable,
" for the certainty of the facts, or propriety
" of the reafonings, contained in the feveral
" papers fo publifhed, which muft ftill reft on
" the credit or judgment of their refpective
" authors.

SECONDLY, " That neither the Society, nor
" the Committee of the prefs, do ever give
" their opinion as a body, upon any paper
" they may publifh, or upon any fubject of
" Art or Nature that comes before them."

LAWS

LAWS AND REGULATIONS,

OF THE

American PHILOSOPHICAL SOCIETY

HELD AT *PHILADELPHIA*, FOR PROMOTING

USEFUL KNOWLEDGE.

TWO focieties having formerly fubfifted in Philadelphia, whofe views and ends were the fame, viz. " *the advancement of ufeful knowledge,*" it was judged that their union would be of public advantage; and they were accordingly united *January* 2d, 1769, by a certain *Fundamental Agreement;* the chief *Articles* of which are,

Firft, That the name of the *United Society* fhall be *The American Philofophical Society, held at Philadelphia, for promoting ufeful Knowledge.*

Secondly, That there fhall be the following officers of the fociety, viz. one *Patron,* one *Prefident,* three *Vice-Prefidents,* one *Treafurer,* four *Secretaries,* and three *Curators.*

Thirdly, That all the above officers fhall be chofen annually by ballot, at the firft meeting of the Society in January; excepting only that inftead of electing a Patron, the Governor of the Province be requefted to be Patron.

Other Laws were to be made by the *United Society;* and accordingly the following LAWS, &c. were paffed *February* 3d, 1769.

I. *Of the annual Payments to be made by Members.*

Every Member of this Society fhall fubfcribe *Ten Shillings* yearly, to be applied by the Society to fuch purpo-

fes

fes as they fhall direct; and no Member fhall be intitled
to a vote in the annual election of officers, unlefs it appears that he has paid into the hands of the Treafurer,
the fubfcription of the preceding year, and all former
arrears, if any there were.

Every Member hereafter to be chofen, agreeable to the
Laws of this Society, fhall pay *Ten Shillings* admiffion money, and alfo fubfcribe for the yearly payment of *Ten
Shillings*, before he is intitled to have any vote in the bufinefs of the Society at their meetings.

II. *Of the Election of Members.*

The election of new Members fhall be by ballot, and
that only on the third Friday in the months of January,
April, July and October; and in order to fuch election at
leaft twenty Members muft be prefent.

Any Member may, at any meeting, propofe fuch perfon or perfons, as he thinks proper to be a Member or
Members of this Society; but no perfon fhall be ballotted
for, unlefs his name, together with the name or names of
the Member or Members who propofed him, has been fixed up by the Secretaries for the view of the Society, at
the two meetings preceding the time of election. Nor
fhall any perfon be deemed duly chofen unlefs three-fourths
of the votes of the whole Members be in his favour.

III. *Of the Officers, and manner of their election.*

The election of fuch Officers as are to be chofen in this
Society, fhall be on the firft Friday in January every year,
by ballot or written ticket, between the hours of two and
five in the afternoon, at fuch place in this city as fhall be
fixed by the Society at their previous meeting on the third
Friday in December every year; of which notice fhall be
given in the Gazette, or fuch other public papers as the
Society

Society shall order, at least one week before the day of election.

Before opening the election, the company that shall be met at half an hour after two, shall appoint three Members of the Society as judges of the election, and also two clerks or secretaries, for taking down the names of the voters. And in case of an equality of votes for any Officer, after casting up the ballots, the decision shall be by lots, to be drawn by one of the judges.

IV. *Of the President.*

The President is to preside at all meetings, to preserve order, to regulate the debates, and to state and put questions, agreeable to the sense and intention of the Members.

V. *Of the Vice-Presidents.*

In the absence of the *President*, his duty shall devolve on the *Vice-Presidents*, so that they shall preside alternately at meetings. But if the Vice-President, whose turn it is to preside at any meeting, should be absent, his place shall be supplied by any of the other Vice-Presidents, who shall be present, according as he may be next in turn. If only one Vice-President be present, he shall of course preside; and if neither the President, nor any Vice-President be present, the Members met, shall appoint one of their number to take the chair for that meeting.

VI. *Of the Treasurer.*

The *Treasurer* shall receive the subscriptions of the Members, and all other monies that may become due to the Society, and shall pay the same agreeable to their orders, certified to him by the President, Vice-President or Member, who was in the chair when the order was made.

The

The Treasurer shall keep a regular account of all monies received and paid by him as aforesaid; and once every year, or oftener if required by the Society, he shall render an account to them of the stock in his hands, and the disbursements made by their order, and shall deliver up to his successor the books and all papers belonging to them, together with the balance of cash in his hands. And for the faithful discharge of his trust, he shall, before he enters on his office, give bond and security to the President and Vice-Presidents, in double the sum which they, or any three of them, shall judge he may probably become entrusted with during his said office.

VII. *Of the Secretaries.*

The *Secretaries* shall so settle matters as to take equal shares of all business, and so as that two of them shall serve at every meeting, viz. one to take the minutes, and one to read all letters and papers that may be communicated to the Society. It is also the business of the two Secretaries of each particular meeting, to copy into the minute-book the proceedings of that meeting, in order to produce the same fair to the next meeting. They are further to copy into the proper books all such letters, papers and essays, as the Society may think fit to preserve on record, and to have the same ready to be laid before the next meeting.

The other two Secretaries are, in the mean while, to give notice to new members of their election, and agreeable to the directions of the Society, to write or answer letters; and, in general, to *manage all matters of correspondence.*

The Secretaries may, for their own ease, change places; so that the two who have served as *corresponding Secretaries,* for one month or limited time, shall take their turn to serve for the like time as *fitting or attending Secretaries.*

VIII. *Of*

VIII. *Of the Curators.*

The bufinefs of the *Curators* fhall be to take charge of, and preferve, all *Specimens of natural Productions*, whether of the *Animal, Vegetable* or *Fossil* kingdom ; all models of machines and inftruments, and all other matters and things belonging to the Society, which fhall be committed to them ; to clafs and arrange them in their proper order, and keep an exact lift of them, with the names of the refpective donors, in a book provided for that purpofe; which book fhall be laid before the Society, as often as called for.

The Curators, on entering upon their office, fhall give fuch a receipt for every thing that is committed to their charge, as the Society fhall think proper; and, at the end of their term, fhall deliver up the fame to their fucceffors. For the faithful performance of their duty, and of the truft repofed in them, they fhall give bond to the Prefidents and Vice-Prefidents, in fuch a fum as they, or any three of them, fhall require.

IX. *Of the Meetings of the Society.*

The ordinary meetings of the Society fhall be on the firft and third Fridays of every month, from October to May, both inclufive, at fix o'clock in the evening, and on the third Friday in each of the other four months at feven o'clock.

No meeting fhall be continued after ten o'clock, nor any new matter be introduced by motion, or otherwife, after nine o'clock.

X. *Of the Difpofition of Money, and making new Laws.*

No part of the Society's ftock fhall be difpofed of in *Premiums*, or otherwife, nor fhall any new laws be made,

b   until

until the fame have been propofed at one meeting, and are agreed to by two-thirds of twenty or more Members prefent at a fubfequent meeting.

XI. *Of other Proceedings of the Society.*

No queftion fhall be put on a *motion*, unlefs the motion be *feconded ;* and the determination of any queftion fhall be by *ballot*, inftead of open fuffrage, if defired by any four Members. In cafe of an equality of votes on any queftion, the fame fhall be deferred to another meeting.

When any Member fpeaks he fhall ftand up, and addrefs himfelf to the chair, and the reft fhall remain filent in their feats. When two or more offer to fpeak at the fame time, the prefiding Member, in that, as in other matters of order, fhall regulate and determine who fhall fpeak firft.

XII. *Of Committees.*

The Members of this Society fhall be claffed into one or more of the following *Committees.*

1. Geography, Mathematics, Natural Philofophy and Aftronomy.
2. Medicine and Anatomy.
3. Natural Hiftory and Chemiftry.
4. Trade and Commerce.
5. Mechanics and Architecture.
6. Hufbandry and American Improvements.

Thefe *Committees* fhall meet on their own adjournments, and at fuch other times as the Society fhall appoint, for the confideration of any matters referred to them, and fhall have power to chufe their own chairman. But no Committee, as fuch, fhall take up any new bufinefs of the Society, but fhall confine themfelves only to the fubjects for which they are appointed, and to matters referred to them by the Society.

An *ACT for Incorporating the American Philofophical Society, held at Philadelphia, for Promoting ufeful Knowledge.*

WHEREAS the cultivation of ufeful knowledge, and the advancement of the liberal arts and fciences in any country, have the moft direct tendency towards the improvement of agriculture, the enlargement of trade, the eafe and comfort of life, the ornament of fociety, and the increafe and happinefs of mankind. *And whereas* this country of North-America, which the goodnefs of Providence hath given us to inherit, from the vaftnefs of its extent, the variety of its climate, the fertility of its foil, the yet unexplored treafures of its bowels, the multitude of its rivers, lakes, bays, inlets, and other conveniencies of navigation, offers to thefe United States one of the richeft fubjects of cultivation, ever prefented to any people upon earth. *And whereas* the experience of ages fhews that improvements of a public nature, are beft carried on by focieties of liberal and ingenious men, uniting their labours, without regard to nation, fect or party, in one grand purfuit, alike interefting to all, whereby mutual prejudices are worn off, a humane and philofophical fpirit is cherifhed, and youth are ftimulated to a laudable diligence and emulation in the purfuit of wifdom. *And whereas,* upon thefe principles, divers public fpirited gentlemen in Pennfylvania, and other American ftates, did heretofore unite themfelves, under certain regulations, into one voluntary fociety, by the name of " *The Ameri-* " *can Philofophical Society, held at Philadelphia for pro-* " *moting ufeful Knowledge,*" and by their fuccefsful la-

bours

bours and inveftigations, to the great credit of America, have extended their reputation fo far, that men of the firft eminence in the republic of letters in the moft civilized nations in Europe, have done honour to their publications, and defired to be enrolled among their members. *And whereas* the Society, after having been long interrupted in their laudable purfuits by the calamities of war, and the diftreffes of our country, have found means to revive their defign, in hopes of being able to profecute the fame with their former fuccefs, and being further encouraged therein by the public, for which purpofe they have prayed us, *The Reprefentatives of the Freemen of the Commonwealth of Pennfylvania,* that they may be created one body politic and corporate forever, with fuch powers, privileges, and immunities, as may be neceffary for anfwering the valuable purpofes which the faid Society had originally in view.

Wherefore, in order to encourage the faid Society in the profecution and advancement of all ufeful branches of knowledge, for the benefit of their country, and of mankind ; *Be it enacted, and it is hereby enacted, by the Reprefentatives of the Freemen of the Commonwealth of Pennfylvania in General Affembly met, and by the authority of the fame,* That the members of the faid American Philofophical Society heretofore voluntarily affociated for promoting ufeful knowledge, and fuch other perfons as have been duly elected members and officers of the fame agreeably to the fundamental laws and regulations of the faid Society, comprifed in twelve fections, prefixed to their volume of Tranfactions, publifhed in Philadelphia by *William* and *Thomas Bradford,* in the year of our Lord one thoufand feven hundred and feventy-one ; and who fhall in all refpects conform themfelves to the faid laws and regulations, and fuch other laws, regulations and ordinances, as fhall hereafter be duly made and enacted by the faid Society, according to the tenor hereof, be, and for-
ever

ever hereafter fhall be one body corporate and politic in
deed, by the name and ftyle of *The American Philofophical Society, held at Philadelphia, for promoting ufeful
knowledge,* and by the fame name they are hereby con-
ftituted and confirmed one body corporate and politic, to
have perpetual fucceffion, and by the fame name they and
their fucceffors are hereby declared and made able and capable in law, to have, hold, receive, and enjoy lands, tenements, rents, franchifes, hereditaments, gifts and bequefts of what nature foever, in fee-fimple, or for term
of life, lives, years, or otherwife, and alfo to give, grant,
let, fell, alien, or affign the fame lands, tenements, hereditaments, goods, chattels, and premifes, according to the
nature of the refpective gifts, grants and bequefts, made
to them the faid Society, and of their eftate therein.

Provided, That the amount of the clear yearly value
of fuch real eftate do not exceed the value of ten thoufand
bufhels of good merchantable wheat.

And be it further enacted by the authority aforefaid,
That the faid Society be, and fhall be for-ever hereafter
able and capable in law to fue, and be fued, plead and be
impleaded, anfwer and be anfwered unto, defend and be
defended, in all or any of the courts or other places,
and before any judges, juftices, and other perfon and perfons, in all manner of actions, fuits, complaints, pleas,
caufes and matters, of what nature or kind foever, within this commonwealth; and that it fhall and may be lawful to and for the faid Society, for-ever hereafter to have
and ufe one common feal in their affairs, and the fame at
their will and pleafure to break, change, alter and renew.

And be it further enacted by the authority aforefaid,
That for the well governing the faid Society, and ordering their affairs, they fhall have the following officers,
that is to fay, one Patron, who fhall be his Excellency
the Prefident of the Supreme Executive Council of this
commonwealth, for the time being, and likewife one Prefident,

fident, three Vice-Prefidents, four Secretaries, three Curators, one Treafurer, together with a Council of twelve
Members ; and that on the firft Friday of January next,
between the hours of two and five in the afternoon, as
many of the members of the faid Society as fhall have paid
up their arrears due to the Society, and fhall declare their
willingnefs to conform to the laws, regulations and ordinances of the Society, then duly in force, according to
the tenor hereof, by fubfcribing the fame, and who fhall
attend in the hall, or place of meeting of the faid Society,
within the time aforefaid, fhall choofe by ballot, agreeably
to the fundamental laws and regulations herein before referred to, one Prefident, four Secretaries, three Curators,
and one Treafurer, and at the fame time and place, the
Members met and qualified as aforefaid, fhall in like manner choofe four Members for the Council, to hold their
offices for one year, four more Members for the Council
to hold their offices for two years, and four more Members for the Council to hold their offices for three years.
And on the firft Friday in January, which fhall be in the
year of our Lord one thoufand feven hundred and eighty-
two, and fo likewife on the firft Friday of January, yearly
and every year thereafter, between the hours of two and
five in the afternoon, the Members of the faid Society met
and qualified as aforefaid, fhall choofe one Prefident, three
Vice-Prefidents, four Secretaries, three Curators and one
Treafurer, to hold their refpective offices for one year ;
and four Councilmen, to hold their offices for three years.
Provided, That no perfon refiding within the United
States fhall be capable of being Prefident, Vice-Prefident,
Secretary, Treafurer, or Member of the Council, or of
electing to any of the faid offices, who is not capable of
electing and being elected to civil offices within the ftate
in which he refides. *Provided alfo,* That nothing herein contained, fhall be confidered as intended to exclude
any of the faid officers or counfellors, whofe times fhall
be

expired, from being re-elected, according to the pleasure
of the said Society ; and of the day, hours, and place of
all such elections, due notice shall be given by the Secretaries, or some one of them, in one or more of the public news-papers of this state, agreeably to the said fundamental laws and regulations before referred to.

And be it further enacted by the authority aforesaid,
That the officers and council of the said Society shall be
capable of exercising such power for the well governing
and ordering the affairs of the Society, and of holding
such occasional meetings for that purpose, as shall be described, fixed, and determined by the statutes, laws, regulations and ordinances of the said Society, hereafter to be
made. *Provided always,* That no statute, law, regulation or ordinance shall ever be made or passed by the said
Society, or be binding upon the Members thereof, or any
of them, unless the same hath been duly proposed, and
fairly drawn up in writing, at one stated meeting of the
Society, and enacted or passed at a subsequent meeting at
least the space of fourteen days after the former meeting,
and upon due notice in some of the public news-papers,
that the enacting of statutes and laws, or the making and
passing ordinances and regulations, will be part of the business of such meeting ; nor shall any statute, law, regulation or ordinance be then or at any time enacted or passed, unless thirteen Members of the said Society or such
greater number of Members as may be afterwards fixed
by the rules of the Society be present, besides such quo-
rum of the officers and council as the laws of the Society
for the time being may require, and unless the same be
voted by two-thirds of the whole body then present ; all
which statutes, laws, ordinances and regulations so as
aforesaid duly made, enacted and passed, shall be binding
upon every Member of the said Society, and be from time
to time inviolably observed, according to the tenor and
effect thereof ; provided they be not repugnant or contrary

trary to the laws of this commonwealth, for the time being in force and effect.

And whereas nations truly civilized (however unhappily at variance on other accounts) will never wage war with the arts and fciences and the common interefts of humanity.

Be it further enacted by the authority aforefaid, That it fhall and may be lawful for the faid Society, by their proper officers, at all times, whether in peace or war, to correfpond with learned focieties, as well as individual learned men, of any nation or country, upon matters merely belonging to the bufinefs of the faid Society; fuch as the mutual communication of their difcoveries and proceedings in philofophy and fcience; the procuring books, apparatus, natural curiofities, and fuch other articles and intelligence as are ufually exchanged between learned bodies for furthering their common purfuits. *Provided always*, That fuch correfpondence of the faid Society be at all times open to the infpection of the Supreme Executive Council of this commonwealth.

(Signed)   JOHN BAYARD, *Speaker*.

Enacted into a Law at Philadelphia, on
   Wednefday the fifteenth day of March,
   Anno Domini one thoufand feven hundred and eighty.

(Signed)   THOMAS PAINE, *Clerk*
                of the General Affembly.

(Copy)

A Law to encrease the annual Subscriptions of the Members
of the American Philosophical Society held at Philadel-
phia for promoting useful knowledge, and also to encrease
the Deposites of newly elected Members on their admission
into the said Society.

WHEREAS the cuſtomary annual payment of *Ten Shillings* from each Member of the American Philoſophical Society, and alſo the cuſtomary depoſite of *Ten Shillings* by each newly elected Member, on his ad- miſſion into the ſaid Society, hath been found inadequate to the neceſſary and occaſional expenditures of the Society.

Be it therefore enacted, and it is hereby enacted by the American Philoſophical Society, held at Philadelphia for promoting uſeful knowledge, by virtue of the chartered rights to the ſaid Society granted, and by authority of the ſame, That for the future, that is to ſay, from and after the firſt of March next, the payments to be made by every Member of the ſaid Society ſhall be *Four Dollars* annual- ly, and the depoſite to be made by every newly elected Member, from and after the ſaid firſt of March, ſhall be *Ten Dollars.* And no Member who ſhall be in arrear for his annual ſubſcription or depoſite, ſhall be eligible to any office in the ſaid Society, or be permitted to vote at elec- tions, or at the ordinary meetings of the Society, until he ſhall have fully paid up his ſaid arrears.

And be it further enacted, That no newly elected Mem- ber ſhall receive a certificate of his election, or be admit- ted as a Member of the ſaid Society, until he ſhall have paid into the treaſury the ſaid depoſite of *Ten Dollars* and alſo his arrearages of *Four Dollars* per annum, if any ſuch ſhall have accrued from the time of his election.

c   Provided

Provided always, That honorary Members in foreign parts, fhall not be fubject to this law, nor fhall their certificates of election be with-held on account of their not paying the depofite or annual fubfcription aforefaid. Neverthelefs, if any fuch foreign Member fhould happen to come to the city of Philadelphia with a view of fettlement or refidence, then fuch Member fhall pay the depofite money as before directed, and fhall thenceforth be liable for the annual fubfcription in common with other refident Members.

And be it further enacted, That all former laws, ordinances or cuftoms inconfiftent with or contradictory to this act, be, and the fame are hereby repealed.

Enacted into a law at a meeting of the American Philofophical Society, according to Charter, this fixth day of January, Anno Domini, one thoufand feven hundred and eighty-fix.

Ex-

Extracts from the Minutes of the American Philosophical Society, respecting a Donation proposed by Mr. J. H. de MAGELLAN, *of London.*

January 1786,

MR. J. H. de Magellan of London, having in a letter, dated the 17th of September last, and communicated to the society by Mr. Vaughan, one of the Vice-Presidents, made an offer to the society of *two hundred guineas*, to be vested in a permanent fund, that the interest arising therefrom may be disposed of in annual premiums, to the authors of the best discoveries or most useful improvements relating to navigation, or to natural philosophy, mere natural history only excepted: And the society having most thankfully accepted the generous offer, appointed a committee to frame rules and conditions for the disposition of the proposed premiums, agreeable to the intention of the donor, expressed in his letter, but more precise in the terms; which being done, and approved of by the society, were immediately transmitted in a letter to Mr. Magellan, for his confirmation or amendment. They are as follow, viz.

1. The candidate shall send his discovery, invention or improvement, addressed to the President or a Vice-President of the Society, free of postage or other charges; and shall distinguish his performance by some motto, device or signature, at his pleasure. Together with his discovery, invention or improvement, he shall also send a sealed letter, containing the same motto, device or signature, and subscribed with the real name and place of residence of the author.

2. Persons

2. Perfons of any nation, fect, or denomination whatever, fhall be admitted as candidates for this premium.

3. No difcovery, invention or improvement fhall be entitled to this premium, which hath been already publifhed, or for which the author hath been publicly rewarded elfewhere.

4. The candidate fhall communicate his difcovery, invention or improvement either in the Englifh, French, German, or Latin language.

5. All fuch communications fhall be publicly read or exhibited to the Society, at fome ftated meeting, not lefs than one month previous to the day of adjudication; and fhall at all times be open to the infpection of fuch members as fhall defire it. But no member fhall carry home with him the communication, defcription or model, except the officer to whom it fhall be entrufted: nor fhall fuch officer part with the fame out of his cuftody, to any but the judges, who may demand it for confideration.

6. The twelve counfellors, together with the other officers annually elected according to the charter and laws of the Society, fhall be judges of the merits of the feveral communications, and award the premium. Which adjudication fhall be determined by a majority of judges met; provided that fuch majority be not lefs than feven concurring votes.

7. And for this purpofe the counfellors and other officers, or at leaft feven of them, fhall meet on the fecond Monday in December, in every year, to form their judgment and award the premium. After due confideration had, a vote fhall firft be taken on this queftion, viz. " Whe-
" ther any of the communications then under infpection,
" are worthy of the propofed premium ?" If this fhall be determined in the *negative*, the whole bufinefs fhall be deferred till another year: But if in the *affirmative*, the judges fhall then proceed to determine, by vote, the difcovery, invention or improvement moft ufeful and worthy.

And

And that difcovery, invention or improvement which fhall
be found to have the greateft number of concurring votes.
(being not lefs than feven) in its favour, fhall be fuccefsful. Whereupon a certificate in writing fhall be forthwith
drawn of this adjudication, and figned by thofe who voted
for the crowned fubject: And then, *and not till then*, the
fealed letter accompanying the crowned performance, fhall
be opened and the name of the author announced; which
certificate fhall be prefented to the Society at their next
ftated meeting, and delivered to the Secretary to be entered on record, in a bound book provided for this purpofe.

8. A full account of the crowned fubject fhall be publifhed by the Society as foon as may be, after the adjudication, either in a feparate publication, or in the next fucceeding volume of their Tranfactions, or in both.

9. The unfuccefsful performances fhall lie over for confideration, and remain, as candidates for the premium, for
five fucceeding years next after their prefentment; unlefs
the author or authors fhall think fit to withdraw them or
any of them: And the Society fhall publifh annually an
abftract of the titles, object or fubject matter of the communications fo under confideration, fuch only excepted as
the counfellors and other officers fhall, by vote as aforefaid,
have determined not worthy of public notice.

10. No counfellor or officer who is a candidate fhall fit
in judgment, or give his vote.

11. The letters containing the names of authors whofe
performances fhall be rejected, or fhall be found unfuccefsful after a trial of five years, fhall be burnt without
breaking the feals.

12. In cafe there fhould be a failure, in any year, of
any communication worthy of the propofed premium,
there will then be two premiums awarded in the next
year. But no accumulation of premiums fhall entitle an
author to more than one premium for any one difcovery,
invention or improvement.

13. The

13. The premium ſhall conſiſt of an oval plate of ſolid ſtandard gold, of the value of *Ten Guineas*. On one ſide thereof ſhall be neatly engraved the following motto, ————————— together with theſe words, *The donation of* —— *of London, eſtabliſhed in the year* 1786. And on the other ſide of the plate ſhall be engraved theſe words, *Awarded by the A. P. S. to* —— —— *for his diſcovery of* —— —— *A. D.* 17——. —— —— *Preſident.* And the ſeal of the Society ſhall be annexed to the ſaid golden plate, by a ribbon paſſing through a ſmall hole near the lower edge thereof.

LIST

LIST of the OFFICERS

OF THE

AMERICAN PHILOSOPHICAL SOCIETY,

Held at PHILADELPHIA, for promoting uſeful Knowledge,

For the Year 1786.

PATRON. His Ex^{cy} the Preſident of the Supreme Executive Council of the Commonwealth, for the time being.

PRESIDENT. His Excellency Dr. Benjamin Franklin, Eſquire, L. L. D F. R. S. &c. &c.

VICE-PRESIDENTS.
{ Rev. Dr. John Ewing, Provoſt of the Univerſity of Pennſylvania,.
Rev. Dr. William White.
Samuel Vaughan, Eſq.

SECRETARIES.
{ Dr. James Hutchinſon.
Mr. Robert Patterſon, Profeſſor of Mathematics in the Univerſity of Pennſylvania.
Rev. Dr. Samuel Magaw, Vice-Provoſt of the Univerſity of. Pennſylvania..
Dr. John Foulk.

CURATORS.
{ Dr. Samuel Duffield.
Dr. Barnabas Binney.
William Bradford, Eſq. Attorney General of Pennſylvania.

TREASURER.
{ The Honorable Francis Hopkinſon, Eſq. Judge of the Admiralty in Pennſylvania.

COUN-

COUNSELLORS.
{
The Hon. Thomas M'Kean, Efquire, L. L. D. Chief Juftice of the Supreme Court of Pennfylvania.

The Hon. George Bryan, Efquire, a Juftice of the Supreme Court of Pennfylvania.

Sieur Barbé de Marbois.

Mr. Samuel Caldwell.

Jared Ingerfoll, Efq.

Jonathan Bayard Smith, Efq.

Rev. Mr. Robert Blackwell.

David Rittenhoufe, Efq.

Dr. Benjamin Rufh, Profeffor of Chemiftry in the Univerfity of Pennfylvania.

Dr. John Jones.

Dr. Adam Kuhn, Profeffor of Materia Medica in the Univerfity of Pennfylvania.

Rev. Mr. George Duffield.
}

LIST of MEMBERS of the AMERICAN PHILOSOPHICAL SOCIETY, elected fince the Publication of the Firft Volume of Tranfactions, viz. fince the 18th of January, 1771.

A

JOSEPH Aftolinge, Efq. of Georgia.

B

Mr. Gerard Banker.

Dr. William Bryant, of New-Jerfey. *

Mr. James Bringhurft.

Honorable Thomas Bee, Efq. of South-Carolina.

John Beale Boardley, Efq. of Maryland.

Rev. Jeremy Belknap, of New-Hampfhire.

Dr. Barnabas Binney.

Rev. Mr. Robert Blackwell.

William

Note, Thofe Members whofe places of refidence are not fpecified, are of Philadelphia; and thofe marked with an * are deceafed.

William Bradford, Esq. Attorney-General of Pennsylvania.

C

Dr. John Carson.
Rev. Manasseh Cutler, of Ipswich, Massachusetts.

D

Sharp Delany, Esq.
Rev. Dr. Robert Davidson, of Carlisle.
Mr. John Dunlap.

E

Dr. Jonathan Elmer, of New-Jersey.
Joseph Ellicott, Esq. Bucks county. *
Andrew Ellicott, Esq. of Maryland.

F

Mr. George Fox.
Dr. John Foulk.

G

Mr. George Gauld, of Pensacola.
Isaac Gray, Esq.
George Gray, Esq.
Mr. Archibald Gamble, Professor of English and Oratory, University, Philadelphia. *
Dr. Samuel Powell Griffitts.

H

Dr. James Hutchinson.
Thomas Hutchins, Esq. Geographer to the United States.
Ebenezer Hazard, Esq. Postmaster-General.
Samuel Huntington, Esq. of Connecticut. *
Rev. Dr. Just. Hen. Christ. Helmuth, Prof. of the Germ. and Oriental Languages, University, Philadelphia.
Thomas Hayward, jun. Esq. of South-Carolina.

I

Dr. Walter Jones, of Virginia.
Dr. John Jones, of Maryland.
Jared Ingersoll, Esq.
His Excellency Thomas Jefferson, Esq. of Virginia, Minister Plenipotentiary to the Court of France.

K

Rev. Dr. John C. Kunze, of New-York.

L

Mr. Jesse Lukens. *
Henry Laurens, Esq. of South-Carolina.
Rev. Mr. William Ludlam, of Leicester.

Dr. James

Dr. James Lloyd, of Boſton.

M

Mr. Archibald M'Clean, of York county. *

Capt. John Matreſon, of New-York.

Timothy Matlack, Eſq.

Dr. George Millegan, of South-Carolina.

James M'Clurg, M. D. Williamſburgh, Virginia.

Mr. Benjamin Morgan.

Rev. Dr. Samuel Magaw, Vice-Provoſt of Univer. Phila.

Hon. Dr. James M'Henry, Eſq. of Baltimore.

Rev. Dr. James Madiſon, Preſident of the College of William and Mary, Virginia.

Rev. Mr. Henry Muhlenberg, of Lancaſter.

P

Dr. John Perkins, of Boſton, Maſſachuſetts.

Dr. Thomas Park.

Mr. Robert Patterſon, Prof. Math. Univer. Philadelphia.

Hon. Mann Page, Eſq. of Frederickſburgh, Virginia.

Thomas Paine, Eſq. of Bordentown.

Charles Pettit, Eſq.

R

Mr. Bernard Romans, of Penſacola.

S

Dr. Hugh Shiell. *

Jonathan Bayard Smith, Eſq.

Jonathan Dickinſon Sergeant, Eſq.

Rev. Dr. Samuel Smith, Vice-Preſident of the College in New-Jerſey.

T

Dr. James Tilton, of Dover.

Mr. John Ternant.

V

Samuel Vaughan, Eſq.

Mr. John Vaughan.

W

His Excellency General Waſhington, Virginia.

Rev. Samuel Williams, L. L. D. Hol. Prof. Mor. and Nat. Philoſ. College of Cambridge, Maſſachuſetts.

Dr. Nicholas Way, of Wilmington.

George Wall, jun. Eſq. of Bucks county.

Hon. Anthony Wayne, Eſq. Gen. in the Armies of the United States.

Mr. Benjamin Workman, Teacher of Math. Univerſity, Philadelphia.

FOREIGN

FOREIGN MEMBERS.

A

Monſieur le Marquis d'Angeville, of Paris.

Dr. Adams, of Barbadoes.

Lieut. Stephen Adye, of the Royal Artillery.

B

Dr. Forbern Bergman, Prof. Math. Stockholm.

Major Frederick F. S. de Brahm, Triers.

His Excellency M. J. Peter Van Berckel, Miniſter Plenipotentiary from the United Provinces of the Netherlands.

Frederick Eugene Francis Baron de Beelen Bertholf, Imperial Councellor of Commerce to the United States, Bruſſels.

C

Le Chevalier de Chaſtellux, Marſhal of the Field in the Armies of France, Chevalier of the Royal Military Order of St. Louis, and one of the forty members of the French Academy.

Count de Campomanes, Fiſcal of the Council of Caſtile.

Dr. Adair Crawford, Phyſician to St. Thomas's Hoſpital, London.

Dr. Coſte.

Rev. Thomas Coombe, Ireland.

Daniel Coxe, Eſq. England.

D

Mr. Peter Dollond, of London.

Dr. Andrew Duncan, of Edinburgh.

Monſieur Daubenton, of the Royal Academy of Sciences at Paris.

Monſieur Dubourg, of Paris. *

Chev. Danmours, Conſul of France for the Southern Department.

E

Hon. John Ellis, Eſq. of Jamaica. *

Hon. Bryan Edwards, Eſq. of Jamaica.

F

Le Marquis de la Fayette, Major General in the Armies of the United States of America.

Abbé Fontana, Director of the Great Duke's Cabinet of Natural Hiſtory.

G

Rev. Thomas Gibbons, D. D. of London.

Count de Guichen, Lieut. Gen. in the French Army.

H

Hon. Samuel Guſtavus Baron Hermelin, of Stockholm.

William

William Herfchell, Efq. F. R. S. of Bath, England.

I

Dr. Hugh James, of Jamaica.

K

Timothy Baron de Kleingftedt, Councellor of State to the Emprefs of Ruffia.

Brigadier-General Thadeus Kofcuzko.

L

Le Chev. de la Luzerne.

Monfieur Lavoifier, of the Academy of Sciences in Paris.

M

Monfieur Barbé de Marbois, Intendant of St. Domingo.

Lord Mahone.

Monfieur Macquer, of Paris. *

Samuel Moore, Efq. of London.

Dr. Benjamin Mofley, of Jamaica.

Mr. John Hyacinth de Magellan, F. R. S. and Member of feveral Academies, London.

Chrift. Fred. Michaelis, M. D. of Gottenburgh.

Mr. John Mandrillon, Merchant, Amfterdam.

P

Rev. Jofeph Prieftley, L. L. D. F. R. S. of Birmingham, England.

Rev. Richard Price, D. D. F. R. S. of London.

Dr. Robert Percival, Prof. Chym. Trinity College, Dublin.

Mr. William Parker, of London.

R

Monfieur le Roy, Vice-Director of the Academy of Sciences in Paris.

Monfieur le Roux.

Abbé Raynal.

Abbé Rofier, of the Academy of Sciences in Lyons.

S

Monfieur Süe, Profeffor Royal of Anatomy, &c. at Paris.

Monfieur Jean Baptifte Süe, Prof. Surgery in Paris.

Right Hon. Earl of Stanhope. *

Mr. Alexander Small, of London.

Mr. James Six, of Canterbury. England.

V

Monfieur le Count de Vergennes, Minifter of State for Foreign Affairs, France.

W

Fortunatus de Warris, Efq.

William Wright, M. D. F. R. S. in the Parifh of Trelawney, Jamaica.

(xxix)

CONTENTS

OF

VOLUME II.

XII. Ac-

XXV. *An*

CONTENTS. xxxi

TRANS-

TRANSACTIONS

OF THE

American PHILOSOPHICAL SOCIETY, *&c.*

N° I.

A Letter from Dr. B. FRANKLIN *to Dr.* INGENHAUSZ, *Phyſician to the Emperor, at Vienna.*

Dear Friend,   At ſea, Auguſt 28th, 1785.

Read 21ſt
Oct. 1785.
IN one of your letters, a little before I left France, you deſire me to give you in writing my thoughts upon the conſtruction and uſe of chimneys, a ſubject you had ſometimes heard me touch upon in converſation. I embrace willingly this leiſure afforded by my preſent ſituation to comply with your requeſt, as it will not only ſhow my regard to the deſires of a friend, but may at the ſame time be of ſome utility to others; the doctrine of chimneys appearing not to be as yet generally well underſtood, and miſtakes reſpecting them being attended with conſtant inconvenience, if not remedied; and with fruitleſs expence, if the true remedies are miſtaken.

Thoſe who would be acquainted with this ſubject ſhould begin by conſidering on what principle ſmoke aſcends in any chimney. At firſt many are apt to think that ſmoke

is

is in its nature and of itself specifically lighter than air, and rises in it for the same reason that cork rises in water. These see no cause why smoke should not rise in the chimney, though the room be ever so close. Others think there is a power in chimneys to *draw* up the smoke, and that there are different forms of chimneys which afford more or less of this power. These amuse themselves with searching for the best form. The equal dimensions of a funnel in its whole length is not thought artificial enough, and it is made, for fancied reasons, sometimes tapering and narrowing from below upwards, and sometimes the contrary, &c. &c. A simple experiment or two may serve to give more correct ideas. Having lit a pipe of tobacco, plunge the stem to the bottom of a decanter half filled with cold water; then putting a rag over the bowl, blow through it and make the smoke descend in the stem of the pipe, from the end of which it will rise in bubbles through the water; and being thus cooled, will not afterwards rise to go out through the neck of the decanter, but remain spreading itself and resting on the surface of the water. This shows that smoke is really heavier than air, and that it is carried upwards only when attached to, or acted upon, by air that is heated, and thereby rarefied and rendered specifically lighter than the air in its neighbourhood.

Smoke being rarely seen but in company with heated air, and its upward motion being visible, though that of the rarefied air that drives it is not so, has naturally given rise to the error.

I need not explain to you, my learned friend, what is meant by rarefied air; but if you make the public use you propose of this letter, it may fall into the hands of some who are unacquainted with the term and with the thing. These then may be told, that air is a fluid which has weight as well as others, though about eight hundred times lighter than water. That heat makes the particles of air

recede

recede from each other and take up more fpace, fo that the fame weight of air heated will have more bulk, than equal weights of cold air which may furround it, and in that cafe muft rife, being forced upwards by fuch colder and heavier air, which preffes to get under it and take its place. That air is fo rarefied or expanded by heat, may be proved to their comprehenfion by a lank blown bladder, which laid before a fire will foon fwell, grow tight and burft.

Another experiment may be to take a glafs tube about an inch in diameter, and twelve inches long, open at both ends and fixed upright on legs fo that it need not be handled, for the hands might warm it. At the end of a quill faften five or fix inches of the fineft light filament of filk, fo that it may be held either above the upper end of the tube or under the lower end, your warm hand being at a diftance by the length of the quill. If there were Plate I. Figure 1. any motion of air through the tube, it would manifeft itfelf by its effect on the filk; but if the tube and the air in it are of the fame temperature with the furrounding air, there will be no fuch motion, whatever may be the form of the tube, whether crooked or ftrait, narrow below and widening upwards, or the contrary; the air in it will be quiefcent. Warm the tube, and you will find as long as it continues warm, a conftant current of air entering below and paffing up through it, till difcharged at the top; becaufe the warmth of the tube being communicated to the air it contains, rarefies that air and makes it lighter than the air without, which therefore preffes in below, forces it upwards, follows and takes its place, and is rarefied in its turn. And, without warming the tube, if you hold under it a knob of hot iron, the air thereby heated will rife and fill the tube, going out at its top, and this motion in the tube will continue as long as the knob remains hot, becaufe the air entering the tube below is heated and rarefied by paffing near and over that knob. That

That this motion is produced merely by the difference of specific gravity between the fluid within and that without the tube, and not by any fancied form of the tube itself, may appear by plunging it into water contained in a glass jar a foot deep, through which such motion might be seen. The water within and without the tube being of the same specific gravity, balance each other, and both remain at rest. But take out the tube, stop its bottom with a finger and fill it with olive oil, which is lighter than water, then stopping the top, place it as before, its lower end under water, its top a very little above. As long as you keep the bottom stopt, the fluids remain at rest, but the moment it is unstopt, the heavier enters below, forces up the lighter, and takes its place. And the motion then ceases, merely because the new fluid cannot be successively made lighter, as air may be by a warm tube.

In fact, no form of the funnel of a chimney has any share in its operation or effect respecting smoke, except its height. The longer the funnel, if erect, the greater its force when filled with heated and rarefied air, to *draw* in below and drive up the smoke, if one may, in compliance with custom, use the expression *draw*, when in fact it is the superior weight of the surrounding atmosphere that *presses* to enter the funnel below, and so *drives up* before it the smoke and warm air it meets with in its passage.

I have been the more particular in explaining these first principles, because, for want of clear ideas respecting them, much fruitless expence has been occasioned; not only single chimneys, but in some instances, within my know-ledge, whole stacks having been pulled down and rebuilt with funnels of different forms, imagined more powerful in *drawing* smoke; but having still the same height and the same opening below, have performed no better than their predecessors.

What is it then which makes a *smoky chimney*, that is, a chimney which instead of conveying up all the smoke, discharges

difcharges a part of it into the room, offending the eyes and damaging the furniture ?

The caufes of this effect, which have fallen under my obfervation, amount to *nine*, differing from each other, and therefore requiring different remedies.

1. *Smoky chimneys in a new houfe, are fuch, frequently from mere want of air.* The workmanfhip of the rooms being all good, and juft out of the workman's hand, the joints of the boards of the flooring, and of the pannels of wainfcotting are all true and tight, the more fo as the walls, perhaps not yet thoroughly dry, preferve a damp-nefs in the air of the room which keeps the wood-work fwelled and clofe. The doors and the fafhes too, being worked with truth, fhut with exactnefs, fo that the room is as tight as a fnuff-box, no paffage being left open for air to enter, except the key-hole, and even that is fome-times covered by a little dropping fhutter. Now if fmoke cannot rife but as connected with rarefied air, and a column of fuch air, fuppofe it filling the funnel, cannot rife, unlefs other air be admitted to fupply its place; and if, therefore, no current of air enter the opening of the chimney, there is nothing to prevent the fmoke coming out into the room. If the motion upwards of the air in a chimney that is freely fupplied, be obferved by the rifing of the fmoke or a feather in it, and it be confidered that in the time fuch feather takes in rifing from the fire to the top of the chimney, a column of air equal to the content of the fun-nel muft be difcharged, and an equal quantity fupplied from the room below, it will appear abfolutely impoffible that this operation fhould go on if the tight room is kept fhut; for were there any force capable of drawing con-ftantly fo much air out of it, it muft foon be exhaufted like the receiver of an air pump, and no animal could live in it. Thofe therefore who ftop every crevice in a room to prevent the admiffion of frefh air, and yet would have their chimney carry up the fmoke, require inconfiftencies,

and

and expect impoffibilities. Yet under this fituation, I have feen the owner of a new houfe, in defpair, and ready to fell it for much lefs than it coft, conceiving it uninhabitable, becaufe not a chimney in any one of its rooms would carry off the fmoke, unlefs a door or window were left open. Much expence has alfo been made, to alter and amend new chimneys which had really no fault; in one houfe particularly that I knew, of a nobleman in Weftminfter, that expence amounted to no lefs than three hundred pounds, *after* his houfe had been, as he thought, finifhed and all charges paid. And after all, feveral of the alterations were ineffectual, for want of underftanding the true principles.

Remedies. When you find on trial, that opening the door or a window, enables the chimney to carry up all the fmoke, you may be fure that want of air *from without*, was the caufe of its fmoking. I fay *from without*, to guard you againft a common miftake of thofe who may tell you, the room is large, contains abundance of air, fufficient to fupply any chimney, and therefore it cannot be that the chimney wants air. Thefe reafoners are ignorant, that the largenefs of a room, if tight, is in this cafe of fmall importance, fince it cannot part with a chimney full of its air without occafioning fo much vacuum; which it requires a great force to effect, and could not be borne if effected.

It appearing plainly, then, that fome of the outward air muft be admitted, the queftion will be, how much is *abfolutely neceffary*; for you would avoid admitting more, as being contrary to one of your intentions in having a fire, viz. that of warming your room. To difcover this quantity, fhut the door gradually while a middling fire is burning, till you find that, before it is quite fhut, the fmoke begins to come out into the room, then open it a little till you perceive the fmoke comes out no longer. There hold the door, and obferve the width of the open crevice between

tween the edge of the door and the rabbit it fhould fhut into. Suppofe the diftance to be half an inch, and the door eight feet high, you find thence that your room requires an entrance for air equal in area to ninety fix half inches, or forty eight fquare inches, or a paffage of fix inches by eight. This however is a large fuppofition, there being few chimneys, that, having a moderate opening and a tolerable height of funnel, will not be fatisfied with fuch a crevice of a quarter of an inch; and I have found a fquare of fix by fix, or thirty fix fquare inches, to be a pretty good medium, that will ferve for moft chimneys. High funnels with fmall and low openings, may indeed be fupplied through a lefs fpace, becaufe, for reafons that will appear hereafter, the *force of levity*, if one may fo fpeak, being greater in fuch funnels, the cool air enters the room with greater velocity, and confequently more enters in the fame time. This however has its limits, for experience fhows that no increafed velocity fo occafioned, has made the admiffion of air through the key-hole equal in quantity to that through an open door; though through the door the current moves flowly, and through the key-hole with great rapidity.

It remains then to be confidered how and where this neceffary quantity of air from without is to be admitted fo as to be leaft inconvenient. For, if at the door, left fo much open, the air thence proceeds directly to the chimney, and in its way comes cold to your back and heels as you fit before your fire. If you keep the door fhut, and raife a little the fafh of your window, you feel the fame inconvenience. Various have been the contrivances to avoid this, fuch as bringing in frefh air through pipes in the jams of the chimney, which pointing upwards fhould blow the fmoke up the funnel; opening paffages into the funnel above, to let in air for the fame purpofe. But thefe produce an effect contrary to that intended: For as it is the conftant current of air paffing from the room *through*

the

the opening of the chimney into the funnel which prevents
the fmoke coming out into the room, if you fupply the
funnel by other means or in other ways with the air it
wants, and efpecially if that air be cold, you diminifh the
force of that current, and the fmoke in its efforts to enter
the room finds lefs refiftance.

The wanted air muft then *indifpenfably* be admitted into
the room, to fupply what goes off through the opening
of the chimney.   M. Gauger, a very ingenious and intelligent French writer on the fubject, propofes with
judgment to admit it *above* the opening of the chimney ;
and to prevent inconvenience from its coldnefs, he directs
its being made to pafs in its entrance through winding
cavities made behind the iron back and fides of the fire-
place, and under the iron hearth-plate ; in which cavities
it will be warmed, and even heated, fo as to contribute
much, inftead of cooling, to the warming of the room.
This invention is excellent in itfelf, and may be ufed with
advantage in building new houfes ; becaufe the chimneys
may then be fo difpofed, as to admit conveniently the cold
air to enter fuch paffages : But in houfes built without
fuch views, the chimneys are often fo fituated, as not to
afford that convenience, without great and expenfive alterations.   Eafy and cheap methods, though not quite fo
perfect in themfelves, are of more general utility ; and
fuch are the following.

In all rooms where there is a fire, the body of air warmed and rarefied before the chimney is continually changing
place, and making room for other air that is to be warmed in its turn.   Part of it enters and goes up the chimney,
and the reft rifes and takes place near the ceiling.   If the
room be lofty, that warm air remains above our heads as
long as it continues warm, and we are little benefited by
it, becaufe it does not defcend till it is cooler.   Few can
imagine the difference of climate between the upper and
lower parts of fuch a room, who have not tried it by the
thermometer,

thermometer, or by going up a ladder till their heads are
near the ceiling. It is then among this warm air that the
wanted quantity of outward air is beſt admitted, with
which being mixed, its coldneſs is abated, and its inconvenience diminiſhed ſo as to become ſcarce obſervable.
This may be eaſily done, by drawing down about an inch
the upper faſh of a window ; or, if not moveable, by cutting ſuch a crevice through its frame ; in both which caſes,
it will be well to place a thin ſhelf of the length, to conceal the opening, and ſloping upwards to direct the entering air horizontally along and under the ceiling. In ſome
houſes the air may be admitted by ſuch a crevice made in
the wainſcot, corniſh or plaſtering, near the ceiling and
over the opening of the chimney. This, if practicable,
is to be choſen, becauſe the entering cold air will there
meet with the warmeſt riſing air from before the fire, and
be ſooneſt tempered by the mixture. The ſame kind of
ſhelf ſhould alſo be placed here. Another way, and not
a very difficult one, is to take out an upper pane of glaſs
in one of your faſhes, ſet it in a tin frame, giving
it two ſpringing angular ſides, and then replacing Plate I.
it, with hinges below on which it may be turned Figure 2.
to open more or leſs above. It will then have the appearance of an internal ſky light. By drawing this pane
in, more or leſs, you may admit what air you find neceſſary. Its poſition will naturally throw that air up and
along the ceiling. This is what is called in France a *Was
iſt das ?* As this is a German queſtion, the invention is
probably of that nation, and takes its name from the frequent aſking of that queſtion when it firſt appeared. In
England, ſome have of late years cut a round hole about
five inches diameter in a pane of the faſh and placed againſt
it a circular plate of tin hung on an axis, and cut into
vanes, which being ſeparately bent a little obliquely, are
acted upon by the entering air, ſo as to force the plate continually round like the vanes of a windmill. This ad-

B   mits

mits the outward air, and by the continual whirling of
the vanes, does in fome degree difperfe it. The noife
only, is a little inconvenient.

2. A fecond caufe of the fmoking of chimneys is, *their·
openings in the room being too large ;* that is, too wide, too
high or both.   Architects in general have no other ideas
of proportion in the opening of a chimney, than what
relate to fymmetry and beauty, refpecting the dimenfions
of the room* ; while its true proportion, refpecting its
function and utility depends on quite other principles ;
and they might as properly proportion the ftep in a ftaircafe to the height of the ftory, inftead of the natural ele-
vation of men's legs in mounting.   The proportion then
to be regarded, is what relates to the height of the funnel.
For as the funnels in the different ftories of a houfe are
neceffarily of different heights or lengths, that from the
loweft floor being the higheft or longeft, and thofe of the
other floors fhorter and fhorter, till we come to thofe in
the garrets, which are of courfe the fhorteft ; and the force
of draft being, as already faid, in proportion to the height
of funnel filled with rarefied air ; and a current of air from
the room into the chimney, fufficient to fill the opening,
being neceffary to oppofe and prevent the fmoke coming
out into the room ; it follows that the openings of the
longeft funnels may be larger, and that thofe of the fhorter
funnels fhould be fmaller.   For if there be a large opening to a chimney that does not draw ftrongly, the funnel
may happen to be furnifhed with the air it demands by a
partial current entering on one fide of the opening, and
leaving the other fide free of any oppofing current, may
permit the fmoke to iffue there into the room.   Much too
of the force of draft in a funnel depends on the degree of
rarefaction in the air it contains, and that depends on the
nearnefs to the fire of its paffage in entering the funnel.
If it can enter far from the fire on each fide, or far above
the fire, in a wide or high opening, it receives little heat

in

* See Appendix, N° I.

in paffing by the fire, and the contents of the funnel is by that means lefs different in levity from the furrounding atmofphere, and its force in drawing confequently weaker. Hence if too large an opening be given to chimneys in upper rooms, thofe rooms will be fmoky: On the other hand, if too fmall openings be given to chimneys in the lower rooms, the entering air operating too directly and violently on the fire, and afterwards ftrengthening the draft as it afcends the funnel, will confume the fuel too rapidly.

Remedy. As different circumftances frequently mix themfelves in thefe matters, it is difficult to give precife dimenfions for the openings of all chimneys. Our fathers made them generally much too large; we have leffened them; but they are often ftill of greater dimenfion than they fhould be, the human eye not being eafily reconciled to fudden and great changes. If you fufpect that your chimney fmokes from the too great dimenfion of its opening, contract it by placing moveable boards fo as to lower and narrow it gradually, till you find the fmoke no longer iffues into the room. The proportion fo found will be that which is proper for that chimney, and you may employ the bricklayer or mafon to reduce it accordingly. However, as, in building new houfes, fomething muft be fometimes hazarded, I would make the openings in my lower rooms about thirty inches fquare and eighteen deep, and thofe in the upper, only eighteen inches fquare and not quite fo deep; the intermediate ones diminifhing in proportion as the height of funnel diminifhed. In the larger openings, billets of two feet long, or half the common length of cord-wood, may be burnt conveniently; and for the fmaller, fuch wood may be fawed into thirds. Where coals are the fuel, the grates will be proportioned to the openings. The fame depth is nearly neceffary to all, the funnels being all made of a fize proper to admit a chimney-fweeper. If in large and elegant rooms cuftom or fancy fhould re-

B 2　　　　　　　　quire

quire the appearance of a larger chimney, it may be formed of expenfive marginal decorations, in marble, &c. In
time perhaps that which is fitteft in the nature of things,
may come to be thought handfomeft. But at prefent when
men and women in different countries fhow themfelves
diffatisfied with the forms God has given to their heads,
waifts and feet, and pretend to fhape them more perfectly, it is hardly to be expected that they will be content
always with the beft form of a chimney. And there are
fome I know fo bigotted to the fancy of a large noble
opening, that rather than change it, they would fubmit
to have damaged furniture, fore eyes and fkins almoft
fmoked to bacon.

3. Another caufe of fmoky chimneys is, *too fhort a funnel.* This happens neceffarily in fome cafes, as where
a chimney is required in a low building; for, if the funnel be raifed high above the roof, in order to ftrengthen
its draft, it is then in danger of being blown down, and
crufhing the roof in its fall.

Remedies. Contract the opening of the chimney, fo as
to oblige all the entering air to pafs through or very near
the fire; whereby it will be more heated and rarefied, the
funnel itfelf be more warmed, and its contents have more
of what may be called the force of levity, fo as to rife
ftrongly and maintain a good draft at the opening.

Or you may in fome cafes, to advantage, build additional ftories over the low building, which will fupport a
high funnel.

If the low building be ufed as a kitchen, and a contraction of the opening therefore inconvenient, a large one being neceffary, at leaft when there are great dinners, for the
free management of fo many cooking utenfils; in fuch
cafe I would advife the building of two more funnels joining to the firft, and having three moderate openings, one
to each funnel, inftead of one large one. When there is
occafion to ufe but one, the other two may be kept fhut
by

b, fliding plates, hereafter to be defcribed*; and two or all of them may be ufed together when wanted. This will indeed be an expence, but not an ufelefs one, fince your cooks will work with more comfort, fee better than in a fmoky kitchen what they are about, your victuals will be cleaner dreffed and not tafte of fmoke, as is often the cafe; and to render the effect more certain, a ftack of three funnels may be fafely built higher above the roof than a fingle funnel.

The cafe of too fhort a funnel is more general than would be imagined, and often found where one would not expect it. For it is not uncommon, in ill-contrived buildings, inftead of having a funnel for each room or fireplace, to bend and turn the funnel of an upper room fo as to make it enter the fide of another funnel that comes from below. By this means the upper room funnel is made fhort of courfe, fince its length can only be reckoned from the place where it enters the lower room funnel; and that funnel is alfo fhortened by all the diftance between the entrance of the fecond funnel and the top of the ftack: For all that part being readily fupplied with air through the fecond funnel, adds no ftrength to the draft, efpecially as that air is cold when there is no fire in the fecond chimney. The only eafy remedy here is, to keep the opening fhut of that funnel in which there is no fire.

4. Another very common caufe of the fmoking of chimneys, is, *their overpowering one another.* For inftance, if there be two chimneys in one large room, and you make fires in both of them, the doors and windows clofe fhut, you will find that the greater and ftronger fire fhall overpower the weaker, and draw air down its funnel to fupply its own demand; which air defcending in the weaker funnel will drive down its fmoke, and force it into the room. If, inftead of being in one room, the two chimneys are in two different rooms, communicating by a door, the cafe is the fame whenever that door is open. In a very

tight

tight houfe, I have known a kitchen chimney on the loweft floor, when it had a great fire in it, overpower any
other chimney in the houfe, and draw air and fmoke into
its room, as often as the door was opened communicating
with the ftaircafe.

Remedy. Take care that every room have the means
of fupplying itfelf from without, with the air its chimney
may require, fo that no one of them may be obliged to
borrow from another, nor under the neceffity of lending.
A variety of thefe means have been already defcribed.

5. Another caufe of fmoking is, *when the tops of chim-*
neys are commanded by higher buildings, or by a hill, fo that
the wind blowing over fuch eminences falls like water over
a dam, fometimes almoft perpendicularly on the tops of
the chimneys that lie in its way, and beats down the fmoke
contained in them.

Remedy. That commonly applied to this cafe, is a
turncap made of tin or plate iron, covering the chimney
above and on three fides, open on one fide, turning on a
fpindle, and which being guided or governed by a vane,
always prefents its back to the current. This I believe may
be generally effectual, though not certain, as there may be
cafes in which it will not fucceed. Raifing your funnels
if practicable, fo as their tops may be higher, or at leaft
equal with the commanding eminence, is more to be depended on. But the turning cap, being eafier and cheaper,
fhould firft be tried. If obliged to build in fuch a fituation,
I would chufe to place my doors on the fide next the hill,
and the backs of my chimneys on the furtheft fide; for
then the column of air falling over the eminence, and of
courfe preffing on that below and forcing it to enter the
doors, or *Was-ift-das*es on that fide, would tend to balance
the preffure down the chimneys, and leave the funnels
more free in the exercife of their functions.

6. There is another cafe of command, the reverfe of
that laft mentioned. It is where the commanding eminence

nence is farther from the wind than the chimney commanded. To explain this a figure may be neceffary.
Suppofe then a building whofe fide A, happens to be expofed to the wind, and forms a kind of dam againft its
progrefs. The air obftructed by this dam will like Plate I.
                                                    Figure 3.
water prefs and fearch for paffages through it; and
finding the top of the chimney B, below the top of the
dam, it will force itfelf down that funnel, in order to get
through by fome door or window open on the other fide
of the building. And if there be a fire in fuch chimney,
its fmoke is of courfe beat down, and fills the room.

Remedy. I know of but one, which is to raife fuch
funnel higher than the roof, fupporting it, if neceffary, by
iron bars. For a turn-cap in this cafe has no effect, the
dammed up air preffing down through it in whatever pofition the wind may have placed its opening.

I know a city in which many houfes are rendered fmoky
by this operation. For their kitchens being built behind,
and connected by a paffage with the houfes, and the tops
of the kitchen chimneys lower than the top of the houfes,
the whole fide of a ftreet when the wind blows againft its
back, forms fuch a dam as above defcribed; and the wind
fo obftructed forces down thofe kitchen chimneys, (efpecially when they have but weak fires in them) to pafs
through the paffage and houfe, into the ftreet. Kitchen
chimneys fo formed and fituated, have another inconvenience. In fummer, if you open your upper room wind-
dows for air, a light breeze blowing over your kitchen
chimney towards the houfe, though not ftrong enough to
force down its fmoke as aforefaid, is fufficient to waft it
into your windows, and fill the rooms with it; which, befides the difagreeablenefs, damages your furniture.

7. Chimneys, otherwife drawing well, are fometimes
made to fmoke by *the improper and inconvenient fituation
of a door*. When the door and chimney are on the fame
fide of the room as in the figure, if the door A, being in
the

Plate I.
Figure 4.

the corner is made to open againſt the wall, which is common, as being there, when open, more out of the way, it follows, that when the door is only opened in part, a current of air ruſhing in paſſes along the wall into and acroſs the opening of the chimney B, and flirts ſome of the ſmoke out into the room. This happens more certainly when the door is ſhutting, for then the force of the current is augmented, and becomes very inconvenient to thoſe who, warming themſelves by the fire, happen to ſit in its way.

The *Remedies* are obvious and eaſy. Either put an intervening ſkreen from the wall round great part of the fireplace ; or, which is perhaps preferable, ſhift the hinges of your door, ſo as it may open the other way, and when open throw the air along the other wall.

8. A room that has no fire in its chimney, is ſometimes filled with *ſmoke which is received at the top of its funnel and deſcends into the room.* In a former paper * I have already explained the deſcending currents of air in cold funnels; it may not be amiſs however to repeat here, that funnels without fires have an effect according to their degree of coldneſs or warmth, on the air that happens to be contained in them. The ſurrounding atmoſphere is frequently changing its temperature ; but ſtacks of funnels covered from winds and ſun by the houſe that contains them, retain a more equal temperature. If, after a warm ſeaſon, the outward air ſuddenly grows cold, the empty warm funnels begin to draw ſtrongly upward; that is, they rarefy the air contained in them, which of courſe riſes, cooler air enters below to ſupply its place, is rarefied in its turn and riſes ; and this operation continues, till the funnel grows cooler, or the outward air warmer, or both, when the motion ceaſes. On the other hand, if after a cold ſeaſon, the outward air ſuddenly grows warm and of courſe lighter, the air contained in the cool funnels, being heavier, deſcends into the room ; and the

warmer

* See Appendix, N° II.

warmer air which enters their tops being cooled in its turn, and made heavier, continues to defcend; and this operation goes on, till the funnels are warmed by the paffing of warm air through them, or the air itfelf grows cooler. When the temperature of the air and of the funnels is nearly equal, the difference of warmth in the air between day and night is fufficient to produce thefe currents, the air will begin to afcend the funnels as the cool of the evening comes on, and this current will continue till perhaps nine or ten o'clock the next morning, when it begins to hefitate; and as the heat of the day approaches, it fets downwards, and continues fo till towards evening, when it again hefitates for fome time, and then goes upwards conftantly during the night, as before mentioned. Now when fmoke iffuing from the tops of neighbouring funnels paffes over the tops of funnels which are at the time drawing downwards, as they often are in the middle part of the day, fuch fmoke is of neceffity drawn into thefe funnels, and defcends with the air into the chamber.

The *Remedy* is to have a fliding plate, hereafter defcribed*, that will fhut perfectly the offending funnel.

9. Chimneys which generally draw well, do neverthelefs fometimes give fmoke into the rooms, *it being driven down by ftrong winds paffing over the tops of their funnels*, though not defcending from any commanding eminence. This cafe is moft frequent where the funnel is fhort, and the opening turned from the wind. It is the more grievous, when it happens to be a cold wind that produces the effect, becaufe when you moft want your fire, you are fometimes obliged to extinguifh it. To underftand this, it may be confidered that the rifing light air, to obtain a free iffue from the funnel, muft pufh out of its way or oblige the air that is over it to rife. In a time of calm or of little wind this is done vifibly, for we fee the fmoke that is brought up by that air rife in a column above the chimney. But when a violent current of air, that is, a

C   ftrong

* See Appendix, Nº II.

ftrong wind, paffes over the top of a chimney, its particles
have received fo much force, which keeps them in a horizontal direction and follow each other fo rapidly, that the
rifing light air has not ftrength fufficient to oblige them
to quit that direction and move upwards to permit its iffue.
Add to this, that fome of the current paffing over that fide
of the funnel which it firft meets with, viz. at A,
having been compreffed by the refiftance of the
funnel, may expand itfelf over the flue, and ftrike
the interior oppofite fide at B, from whence it may be reflected downwards and from fide to fide in the direction of
the pricked lines c c c.

Plate I.
Figure 5.

Remedies. In fome places, particularly in Venice, where
they have not ftacks of chimneys but fingle flues, the cuftom is, to open or widen the top of the flue rounding in the true form of a funnel; which fome think
may prevent the effect juft mentioned, for that the
wind blowing over one of the edges into the funnel may
be flanted out again on the other fide by its form. I have
had no experience of this; but I have lived in a windy
country, where the contrary is practifed, the tops of the
flues being *narrowed* inwards, fo as to form a flit for the
iffue of the fmoke, long as the breadth of the funnel, and
only four inches wide. This feems to have been contrived
on a fuppofition that the entry of the wind would thereby
be obftructed, and perhaps it might have been imagined,
that the whole force of the rifing warm air being condenfed, as it were, in the narrow opening, would thereby
be ftrengthened, fo as to overcome the refiftance of the
wind. This however did not always fucceed; for when
the wind was at north-eaft and blew frefh, the fmoke was
forced down by fits into the room I commonly fat in, fo as
to oblige me to fhift the fire into another. The pofition
of the flit of this funnel was indeed north-eaft and fouth-
weft. Perhaps if it had lain acrofs the wind, the effect
might have been different. But on this I can give no certainty.

Plate I.
Figure 6.

tainty. It feems a matter proper to be referred to experiment. Poffibly a turn-cap might have been ferviceable,
but it was not tried.

Chimneys have not been long in ufe in England. I formerly faw a book printed in the time of queen Elizabeth,
which remarked the then modern improvements of living,
and mentioned among others the convenience of chimneys.
" Our forefathers," faid the author, " had no chimneys.
" There was in each dwelling houfe only one place for a
" fire, and the fmoke went out through a hole in the
" roof; but now there is fcarce a gentleman's houfe in
" England that has not at leaft one chimney in it."—
When there was but one chimney, its top might then be
opened as a funnel, and perhaps, borrowing the form from
the Venetians, it was then the flue of a chimney got that
name. Such is now the growth of luxury, that in both
England and France we muft have a chimney for every
room, and in fome houfes every poffeffor of a chamber,
and almoft every fervant, will have a fire; fo that the flues
being neceffarily built in ftacks, the opening of each as a
funnel is impracticable. This change of manners foon
confumed the firewood of England, and will foon render
fuel extremely fcarce and dear in France, if the ufe of
coals be not introduced in the latter, kingdom as it has been
in the former, where it at firft met with oppofition; for
there is extant in the records of one of queen Elizabeth's
parliaments, a motion made by a member, reciting, " that
" many dyers, brewers, fmiths, and other artificers of Lon-
" don, had of late taken to the ufe of pitcoal for their fires,
" inftead of wood, which filled the air with noxious va-
" pours and fmoke, very prejudicial to the health, parti-
" cularly of perfons coming out of the country; and there-
" fore moving that a law might pafs to prohibit the ufe
" of fuch fuel (at leaft during the feffion of parliament)
" by thofe artificers."—It feems it was not then commonly ufed in private houfes. Its fuppofed unwholefomenefs

was an objection. Luckily the inhabitants of London
have got over that objection, and now think it rather contributes to render their air falubrious, as they have had no
general peftilential diforder fince the general ufe of coals,
when, before it, fuch were frequent. Paris ftill burns wood
at an enormous expence continually augmenting, the inhabitants having ftill that prejudice to overcome. In Germany you are happy in the ufe of ftoves, which fave fuel
wonderfully: Your people are very ingenious in the management of fire; but they may ftill learn fomething in
that art from the Chinefe*, whofe country being greatly
populous and fully cultivated, has little room left for the
growth of wood, and having not much other fuel that is
good, have been forced upon many inventions during a
courfe of ages, for making a little fire go as far as poffible.

I have thus gone through all the common caufes of the
fmoking of chimneys that I can at prefent recollect as having fallen under my obfervation; communicating the remedies that I have known fuccefsfully ufed for the different cafes, together with the principles on which both the
difeafe and the remedy depend, and confeffing my ignorance wherever I have been fenfible of it. You will do
well, if you publifh, as you propofe, this letter, to add in
notes, or as you pleafe, fuch obfervations as may have occurred to your attentive mind; and if other philofophers
will do the fame, this part of fcience, though humble, yet
of great utility, may in time be perfected. For many years
paft, I have rarely met with a cafe of a fmoky chimney,
which has not been folvable on thefe principles, and cured
by thefe remedies, where people have been willing to apply them; which is indeed not always the cafe; for many
have prejudices in favour of the noftrums of pretending
chimney-doctors and fumifts, and fome have conceits and
fancies of their own, which they rather chufe to try, than
to lengthen a funnel, alter the fize of an opening, or admit air into a room, however neceffary; for fome are as
                                                much

* See Appendix, N° III.

much afraid of fresh air as persons in the hydrophobia are
of fresh water. I myself had formerly this prejudice, this
aerophobia, as I now account it, and dreading the supposed
dangerous effects of cool air, I considered it as an enemy,
and closed with extreme care every crevice in the rooms I
inhabited. Experience has convinced me of my error. I
now look upon fresh air as a friend: I even sleep with an
open window. I am persuaded that no common air from
without, is so unwholesome as the air within a close room
that has been often breathed and not changed. Moist air
too, which formerly I thought pernicious, gives me now
no apprehensions: For considering that no dampness of
air applied to the outside of my skin, can be equal to what
is applied to and touches it within, my whole body being
full of moisture, and finding that I can lie two hours in
a bath twice a week, covered with water, which certainly
is much damper than any air can be, and this for years
together, without catching cold, or being in any other manner disordered by it, I no longer dread mere moisture, either
in air or in sheets or shirts: And I find it of importance to
the happiness of life, the being freed from vain terrors,
especially of objects that we are every day exposed in-
evitably to meet with. You physicians have of late happily discovered, after a contrary opinion had prevailed
some ages, that fresh and cool air does good to persons in
the small pox and other fevers. It is to be hoped that in
another century or two we may all find out, that it is not
bad even for people in health. And as to moist air, here
I am at this present writing in a ship with above forty
persons, who have had no other but moist air to breathe
for six weeks past; every thing we touch is damp, and
nothing dries, yet we are all as healthy as we should be
on the mountains of Switzerland, whose inhabitants are
not more so than those of Bermuda or St. Helena, islands
on whose rocks the waves are dashed into millions of particles, which fill the air with damp, but produce no dif-
eases

eafes, the moifture being pure, unmixed with the poifon-
ous vapours arifing from putrid marfhes and ftagnant
pools, in which many infects die and corrupt the water.
Thefe places only, in my opinion, (which however I fubmit to yours) afford unwholefome air ; and that it is not
the mere water contained in damp air, but the volatile
particles of corrupted animal matter mixed with that water, which renders fuch air pernicious to thofe who breathe
it.   And I imagine it a caufe of the fame kind that renders the air in clofe rooms, where the perfpirable matter
is breathed over and over again by a number of affembled
people, fo hurtful to health.   After being in fuch a fituation, many find themfelves affected by that *febricula*,
which the Englifh alone call *a cold*, and, perhaps from the
name, imagine that they caught the malady by *going out*
of the room, when it was in fact by being in it.

You begin to think that I wander from my fubject, and
go out of my depth.   So I return again to my chimneys.

We have of late many lecturers in experimental philofophy.   I have wifhed that fome of them would ftudy this
branch of that fcience, and give experiments in it as a part
of their lectures.   The addition to their prefent apparatus
need not be very expenfive.   A number of little reprefen-
tations of rooms compofed each of five panes of fafh glafs,
framed in wood at the corners, with proportionable doors,
and moveable glafs chimneys, with openings of different
fizes, and different lengths of funnel, and fome of the
rooms fo contrived as to communicate on occafion with
others, fo as to form different combinations, and exem-
plify different cafes ; with quantities of green wax taper
cut into pieces of an inch and ha'f, fixteen of which ftuck
together in a fquare, and lit, would make a ftrong fire for
a little glafs chimney, and blown out would continue to
burn and give fmoke as long as defired.   With fuch an
apparatus all the operations of fmoke and rarefied air in
rooms and chimneys might be feen through their tranfparent

rent fides; and the effect of winds on chimneys, commanded or otherwife, might be fhown by letting the entering air blow upon them through an opened window of
the lecturer's chamber, where it would be conftant while
he kept a good fire in his chimney. By the help of fuch
lectures our fumifts would become better inftructed. At
prefent they have generally but one remedy, which perhaps they have known effectual in fome one cafe of fmoky
chimneys, and they apply that indifcriminately to all the
other cafes, without fuccefs,—but not without expence to
their employers.

With all the fcience, however, that a man fhall fuppofe
himfelf poffeffed of in this article, he may fometimes meet
with cafes that fhall puzzle him. I once lodged in a houfe
at London, which, in a little room, had a fingle chimney
and funnel. The opening was very fmall, yet it did not
keep in the fmoke, and all attempts to have a fire in this
room were fruitlefs. I could not imagine the reafon, till
at length obferving that the chamber over it, which had
no fire-place in it, was always filled with fmoke when a
fire was kindled below, and that the fmoke came through
the cracks and crevices of the wainfcot; I had the wainfcot
taken down, and difcovered that the funnel which went up
behind it, had a crack many feet in length, and wide
enough to admit my arm, a breach very dangerous with
regard to fire, and occafioned probably by an apparent irregular fettling of one fide of the houfe. The air entering this breach freely, deftroyed the drawing force of the
funnel. The remedy would have been, filling up the
breach or rather rebuilding the funnel :. But the landlord
rather chofe to ftop up the chimney.

Another puzzling cafe I met with at a friend's country
houfe near London. His beft room had a chimney in
which, he told me, he never could have a fire, for all the
fmoke came out into the room. I flattered myfelf I could
eafily find the caufe, and prefcribe the cure.. I had a fire
made

made there, and found it as he faid. I opened the door, and perceived it was not want of air. , I made a temporary contraction of the opening of the chimney, and found that it was not its being too large that caufed the fmoke to iffue. I went out and looked up at the top of the chimney : Its funnel was joined in the fame ftack with others, fome of them fhorter, that drew very well, and I faw nothing to prevent its doing the fame. In fine, after every other examination I could think of, I was obliged to own the infufficiency of my fkill. But my friend, who made no pretenfion to fuch kind of knowledge, afterwards difcovered the caufe himfelf. He got to the top of the funnel by a ladder, and looking down, found it filled with twiggs and ftraw cemented by earth, and lined with feathers. It feems the houfe, after being built, had ftood empty fome years before he occupied it ; and he concluded that fome large birds had taken the advantage of its retired fituation to make their neft there. The rubbifh, confiderable in quantity, being removed, and the funnel cleared, the chimney drew well, and gave fatisfaction.

In general, fmoke is a very tractable thing, eafily governed and directed when one knows the principles, and is well informed of the circumftances. You know I made it *defcend* in my Pennfylvania ftove. I formerly had a more fimple conftruction, in which the fame effect was produced, but vifible to the eye. It was compof-
Plate I. ed of two plates A B and C D, placed as in the
Figure 7. figure. The lower plate A B refted with its edge in the angle made by the hearth with the back of the chimney. The upper plate was fixed to the breaft, and lapt over the lower about fix inches, leaving a fpace of four inches wide and the length of the plates (near two feet) between them. Every other paffage of air into the funnel was well ftopped. When therefore a fire was made at E, for the firft time with charcoal, till the air in the funnel was a little heated through the plates, and then

wood

wood laid on, the fmoke would rife to A, turn over the
edge of that plate, defcend to D, then turn under the edge
of the upper plate, and go up the chimney. It was pretty
to fee, but of no great ufe. Placing therefore the under
plate in a higher fituation, I removed the upper
plate C D, and placed it perpendicularly, fo that Plate 1.
the upper edge of the lower plate A B came with- Figure 8.
in about three inches of it, and might be pufhed farther
from it, or fuffered to come nearer to it by a moveable
wedge between them. The flame then afcending from
the fire at E, was carried to ftrike the upper plate, made
it very hot, and its heat rofe and fpread with the rarefied
air into the room.

I believe you have feen in ufe with me, the contrivance
of a fliding-plate over the fire, feemingly placed to oppofe
the rifing of the fmoke, leaving but a fmall paffage for it,
between the edge of the plate and the back of the chimney.
It is particularly defcribed, and its ufes explained, in my
former printed letter, and I mention it here only as another inftance of the tractability of fmoke*.

What is called the Staffordfhire chimney, affords an example of the fame kind. The opening of the chimney is
bricked up, even with the fore-edge of its jams, leaving
open only a paffage over the grate of the fame width, and
perhaps eight inches high. The grate confifts of femicircular bars, their upper bar of the greateft diameter, the
others under it fmaller and fmaller, fo that it has the appearance of half a round bafket. It is, with the coals it
contains, wholly without the wall that fhuts up the chimney, yet the fmoke bends and enters the paffage above it,
the draft being ftrong, becaufe no air can enter that is not
obliged to pafs near or through the fire, fo that all that
the funnel is filled with is much heated, and of courfe
much rarefied.

D   Much

* See Appendix, N⁰ II.

STAFFORDSHIRE FIRE-PLACE.

SIDE VIEW.   FRONT VIEW.

Much more of the profperity of a winter country depends on the plenty and cheapnefs of fuel, than is generally imagined. In travelling I have obferved, that in
thofe parts where the inhabitants can have neither wood
nor coal nor turff but at exceffive prices, the working people live in miferable hovels, are ragged, and have nothing
comfortable about them.   But where fuel is cheap, (or
where they have the art of managing it to advantage) they
are well furnifhed with neceffaries, and have decent habi-
tations.   The obvious reafon is, that the working hours
of fuch people are the profitable hours, and they who cannot afford fufficient fuel have fewer fuch hours in the
twenty four, than thofe who have it cheap and plenty :
For much of the domeftic work of poor women, fuch as
                                                spinning,

spinning, fewing, knitting ; and of the men in thofe ma-
nufactures that require little bodily exercife, cannot well
be performed where the fingers are numbed with cold :
Thofe people, therefore, in cold weather, are induced to go
to bed fooner, and lie longer in a morning, than they
would do if they could have good fires or warm ftoves to
fit by ; and their hours of work are not fufficient to produce the means of comfortable fubfiftence. Thofe public works, therefore, fuch as roads, canals, &c. by which
fuel may be brought cheap into fuch countries from diftant
places, are of great utility ; and thofe who promote them
may be reckoned among the benefactors of mankind.

I have great pleafure in having thus complied with your
requeft, and in the reflection that the friendfhip you honour me with, and in which I have ever been fo happy,
has continued fo many years without the fmalleft interruption. Our diftance from each other is now augmented, and nature muft foon put an end to the poffibility of
my continuing our correfpondence : But if confcioufnefs
and memory remain in a future ftate, my efteem and refpect for you, my dear friend, will be everlafting.

B. F.

APPENDIX.

APPENDIX.

NOTES for the LETTER upon CHIMNEYS.

N° I.

THE lateſt work on architecture that I have ſeen, is that entitled NUTSHELLS, which appears to be written by a very ingenious man, and contains a table of the proportions of the openings of chimneys; but they relate ſolely to the proportions he gives his rooms, without the ſmalleſt regard to the funnels. And he remarks, reſpecting thoſe proportions, that they are ſimilar to the harmonic diviſions of a monochord*. He does not indeed lay much ſtreſs on this; but it ſhows that we like the appearance of principles; and where we have not true ones, we have ſome ſatisfaction in producing ſuch as are imaginary.

N° II.

THE deſcription of the ſliding plates here promiſed, and which hath been ſince brought into uſe under various names, with ſome immaterial changes, is contained in a former letter to J. B. Eſq. as follows:

To J. B. *Eſq. at Boſton, in New-England.*

Dear Sir, London, Dec. 2, 1758.

I HAVE executed here an eaſy ſimple contrivance, that I have long ſince had in ſpeculation, for keeping rooms
warmer

---

* " It may be juſt remarked here, that upon comparing theſe proportions with thoſe ariſing " from the common diviſions of the monochord, it happens that the firſt anſwers to uniſon, " and although the ſecond is a diſcord, the third anſwers to the third minor, the fourth to the " third major, the fifth to the fourth, the ſixth to the fifth, and the ſeventh to the octave." NUTSHELLS, page 85.

warmer in cold weather than they generally are, and with
lefs fire. It is this. The opening of the chimney is contracted, by brick-work faced with marble flabs, to about
two feet between the jams, and the breaft brought down
to within about three feet of the hearth.—An iron frame is
placed juft under the breaft, and extending quite to the
back of the chimney, fo that a plate of the fame metal
may flide horizontally backwards and forwards in the
grooves on each fide of the frame. This plate is juft fo
large as to fill the whole fpace, and fhut the chimney entirely when thruft quite in, which is convenient when there
is no fire. Drawing it out, fo as to leave a fpace between its
further edge and the back, of about two inches; this fpace
is fufficient for the fmoke to pafs; and fo large a part of
the funnel being ftopt by the reft of the plate, the paffage
of warm air out of the room, up the chimney, is obftructed and retarded, and by that means much cold air is prevented from coming in through crevices, to fupply its
place. This effect is made manifeft three ways. Firft,
when the fire burns brifkly in cold weather, the howling
or whiftling noife made by the wind, as it enters the room
through the crevices, when the chimney is open as ufual,
ceafes as foon as the plate is flid in to its proper diftance.
Secondly, opening the door of the room about half an inch,
and holding your hand againft the opening, near the top
of the door, you feel the cold air coming in againft your
hand, but weakly, if the plate be in. Let another perfon
fuddenly draw it out, fo as to let the air of the room go up
the chimney, with its ufual freedom where chimneys are
open, and you immediately feel the cold air rufhing in
ftrongly. Thirdly, if fomething be fet againft the door,
juft fufficient, when the plate is in, to keep the door nearly
fhut, by refifting the preffure of the air that would force
it open: Then, when the plate is drawn out, the door will
be forced open by the increafed preffure of the outward
cold air endeavouring to get in to fupply the place of the
warm

warm air, that now paſſes out of the room to go up the chimney. In our common open chimneys, half the fuel is waſted, and its effect loſt; the air it has warmed being immediately drawn off. Several of my acquaintance having ſeen this ſimple machine in my room, have imitated it at their own houſes, and it ſeems likely to become pretty common. I deſcribe it thus particularly to you, becauſe I think it would be uſeful in *Boſton*, where firing is often dear.

Mentioning chimneys puts me in mind of a property I formerly had occaſion to obſerve in them, which I have not found taken notice of by others; it is, that in the ſummer time, when no fire is made in the chimneys, there is, neverthelefs, a regular draft of air through them; continually paſſing upwards, from about five or ſix o'clock in the afternoon, till eight or nine o'clock the next morning, when the current begins to ſlacken and heſitate a little, for about half an hour, and then ſets as ſtrongly down again, which it continues to do till towards five in the afternoon, then ſlackens and heſitates as before, going ſometimes a little up, then a little down, till in about a half an hour it gets into a ſteady upward current for the night, which continues till eight or nine the next day; the hours varying a little as the days lengthen and ſhorten, and ſometimes varying from ſudden changes in the weather; as if, after being long warm, it ſhould begin to grow cool about noon, while the air was coming down the chimney, the current will then change earlier than the uſual hour, *&c.*

This property in chimneys I imagine we might turn to ſome account, and render improper, for the future, the old ſaying, *as uſeleſs as a chimney in ſummer.* If the opening of the chimney, from the breaſt down to the hearth, be cloſed by a ſlight moveable frame or two, in the manner of doors, covered with canvas, that will let the air through, but keep out the flies; and another little frame ſet within upon the hearth, with hooks on which to hang joints of meat, fowls, *&c.* wrapt well in wet linen cloths, three or

four

four fold, I am confident that if the linen is kept wet, by
fprinkling it once a day, the meat would be fo cooled by the
evaporation, carried on continually by means of the paffing
air, that it would keep a week or more in the hotteft weather.   Butter and milk might likewife be kept cool, in veffels or bottles covered with wet cloths.   A fhallow tray, or
keeler, fhould be under the frame to receive any water that
might drip from the wetted cloths.   I think, too, that this
property of chimneys might, by means of fmoke-jack vanes,
be applied to fome mechanical purpofes, where a fmall but
pretty conftant power only is wanted.

If you would have my opinion of the caufe of this changing current of air in chimneys, it is, in fhort, as follows.
In fummer time there is generally a great difference in the
warmth of the air at mid-day and midnight, and, of courfe,
a difference of fpecific gravity in the air, as the more it is
warmed the more it is rarefied.   The funnel of a chimney
being for the moft part furrounded by the houfe, is pro-
tected, in a great meafure, from the direct action of the
fun's rays, and alfo from the coldnefs of the night air.   It
thence preferves a middle temperature between the heat of
the day, and the coldnefs of the night.   This middle temperature it communicates to the air contained in it.   If
the ftate of the outward air be cooler than that in the funnel of the chimney, it will, by being heavier, force it to
rife, and go out at the top.   What fupplies its place from
below, being warmed, in its turn, by the warmer funnel,
is likewife forced up by the colder and weightier air below,
and fo the current is continued till the next day, when the
fun gradually changes the ftate of the outward air, makes
it firft as warm as the funnel of the chimney can make it,
(when the current begins to hefitate) and afterwards warmer.   Then the funnel being cooler than the air that comes
into it, cools that air, makes it heavier than the outward
air, of courfe it defcends; and what fucceeds it from a-
bove, being cooled in its turn, the defcending current continues

tinues till towards evening, when it again hefitates and
changes its courfe, from the change of warmth in the
outward air, and the nearly remaining fame middle temperature in the funnel.

Upon this principle, if a houfe were built behind *Beacon-
hill*, an adit carried from one of the doors into the hill horizontally, till it met with a perpendicular fhaft funk from
its top, it feems probable to me, that thofe who lived in the
houfe, would conftantly, in the heat even of the calmeft
day, have as much cool air paffing through the houfe, as
they fhould chufe; and the fame, though reverfed in its
current, during the ftilleft night.

I think, too, this property might be made of ufe to mi-
ners; as where feveral fhafts or pits are funk perpendicularly into the earth, communicating at bottom by horizontal paffages, which is a common cafe, if a chimney of thirty
or forty feet high were built over one of the fhafts, or fo
near the fhaft, that the chimney might communicate with
the top of the fhaft, all air being excluded but what fhould
pafs up or down by the fhaft, a conftant change of air
would, by this means, be produced in the paffages below,
tending to fecure the workmen from thofe damps which
fo frequently incommode them. For the frefh air would
be almoft always going down the open fhaft, to go up the
chimney, or down the chimney to go up the fhaft. Let
me add one obfervation more, which is, that if that part
of the funnel of a chimney, which appears above the
roof of a houfe, be pretty long, and have three of its fides
expofed to the heat of the fun fucceffively, viz. when he is
in the eaft, in the fouth, and in the weft, while the north
fide is fheltered by the building from the cool northerly
winds; fuch a chimney will often be fo heated by the
fun, as to continue the draft ftrongly upwards, through the
whole twenty four hours, and often for many days together. If the outfide of fuch a chimney be painted black,
the effect will be ftill greater, and the current ftronger.

N° III.

N° III.

I T is faid the northern Chinefe have a method of warming their ground floors, which is ingenious.   Thofe
floors are made of tile a foot fquare and two inches thick;
their corners being fupported by bricks fet on end, that
are a foot long and four inches fquare, the tiles, too, join
into each other, by ridges and hollows along their fides.
This forms a hollow under the whole floor, which on one
fide of the houfe has an opening into the air, where a fire
is made, and it has a funnel rifing from the other fide to
carry off the fmoke.   The fuel is a fulphurous pitcoal,
the fmell of which in the room is thus avoided, while the
floor and of courfe the room is well warmed.   But as the
underfide of the floor muft grow foul with foot, and a thick
coat of foot prevents much of the direct application of the
hot air to the tiles, I conceive that burning the fmoke by
obliging it to defcend through red coals, would in this
conftruction be very advantageous, as more heat would be
given by the flame than by the fmoke, and the floor being thereby kept free from foot would be more heated
with lefs fire.   For this purpofe I would propofe erecting
the funnel clofe to the grate, fo as to have only an iron
plate between the fire and the funnel, through which plate
the air in the funnel being heated, it will be fure to draw
well, and force the fmoke to defcend, as in the figure
Plate I. where A is the funnel or chimney, B the grate on
Figure 9.
which the fire is placed, C one of the apertures
through which the defcending fmoke is drawn into the channel D of figure 10, along which channel it is conveyed by a
circuitous rout, as defignated by the arrows, until it arrives at the fmall aperture E, figure 10, through which it
enters the funnel F.   G in both figures is the iron plate
againft which the fire is made, which being heated thereby, will rarefy the air in that part of the funnel, and caufe
the fmoke to afcend rapidly.   The flame thus dividing
E   from

from the grate to the right and left, and turning in paſſages diſpoſed, as in figure 13, ſo as that every part of the
floor may be viſited by it before it enters the funnel F, by
the two paſſages E E, very little of the heat will be loſt,
and a winter room thus rendered very comfortable.

N° IV.

PAGE 8. *Few can imagine,* &c. It is ſaid the Ice-
landers have very little fuel, chiefly drift wood that
comes upon their coaſt. To receive more advantage from
its heat, they make their doors low, and have a ſtage round
the room above the door, like a gallery, wherein the women can ſit and work, the men read or write, &c. The
roof being tight, the warm air is confined by it and kept
from riſing higher and eſcaping; and the cold air which
enters the houſe when the door is opened, cannot riſe
above the level of the top of the door, becauſe it is heavier than the warm air above the door, and ſo thoſe in the
gallery are not incommoded by it. Some of our too lofty
rooms might have a ſtage ſo conſtructed as to make a temporary gallery above, for the winter, to be taken away in
ſummer. Sedentary people would find much comfort
there in cold weather.

N° V.

PAGE 26. *Where they have the art of managing it,* &c.
In ſome houſes of the lower people among the northern
nations of Europe, and among the poorer ſort of Germans
in Pennſylvania, I have obſerved this conſtruction, which
appears very advantageous. A is the kitchen with its chimney; B an iron ſtove in the ſtove-room. In a corner
of the chimney is a hole through the back into the
ſtove, to put in fuel, and another hole above it to let
the ſmoke of the ſtove come back into the chimney. As ſoon
as the cooking is over, the brands in the kitchen chimney are

Plate I.
Figure 11.

put

put through the hole to fupply the ftove, fo that there is
feldom more than one fire burning at a time. In the floor
over the ftove-room, is a fmall trap door, to let the warm
air rife occafionally into the chamber. Thus the whole
houfe is warmed at little expence of wood, and the ftove-
room kept conftantly warm ; fo that in the coldeft winter
nights, they can work late, and find the room ftill comfortable when they rife to work early. An Englifh farmer in America who makes great fires in large open chimneys, needs the conftant employment of one man to cut
and haul wood for fupplying them ; and the draft of cold
air to them is fo ftrong, that the heels of his family are
frozen while they are fcorching their faces, and the room
is never warm, fo that little fedentary work can be done
by them in winter. The difference in this article alone
of œconomy, fhall, in a courfe of years, enable the German to buy out the Englifhman, and take poffeffion of
his plantation.

MISCELLANEOUS OBSERVATIONS.

CHIMNEYS whofe funnels go up in the north wall of
a houfe and are expofed to the north winds, are not fo
apt to draw well as thofe in a fouth wall ; becaufe when
rendered cold by thofe winds, they draw downwards.

Chimneys enclofed in the body of a houfe are better than
thofe whofe funnels are expofed in cold walls.

Chimneys in ftacks are apt to draw better than feparate
funnels, becaufe the funnels that have conftant fires in
them, warm the others in fome degree that have none.

One of the funnels in a houfe I once occupied, had a particular funnel joined to the fouth fide of the ftack, fo that three
of its fides were expofed to the fun in the courfe of the day,
viz. the eaft fide E during the morning, the fouth fide
Plate I. S in the middle part of the day, and the weft fide W
Figure 12. during the afternoon, while its north fide was fhelter-

ed

ed by the ftack from the cold winds. This funnel, which came from the ground floor, and had a confiderable height above the roof, was conftantly in a ftrong drawing ftate day and night, winter and fummer.

Blacking of funnels expofed to the fun, would probably make them draw ftill ftronger.

In Paris I faw a fire-place fo ingenioufly contrived as to ferve conveniently two rooms, a bedchamber and a ftudy. The funnel over the fire was round. The fire-place was of caft iron, having an upright back A, and two ho-

Plate I.
Figure 13.

rizontal femicircular plates B C, the whole fo order-ed as to turn on the pivots D E. The plate B al-ways ftopped that part of the round funnel that was next to the room without fire, while the other half of the fun-nel over the fire was always open. By this means a fervant in the morning could make a fire on the hearth C, then in the ftudy, without difturbing the mafter by going into his chamber ; and the mafter when he rofe, could with a touch of his foot turn the chimney on its pivots, and bring the fire into his chamber, keep it there as long as he wanted it, and turn it again when he went out into his ftudy. The room which had no fire in it, was alfo warmed by the heat coming through the back plate, and fpreading in the room as it could not go up the chimney.

Explanation

N° II.

Explanation of an Optical Deception.

BY D. RITTENHOUSE.

Read March 3, 1780. SOME experiments were long ago communicated to the Royal Society of London, shewing, that through the double microscope, the surfaces of bodies sometimes appear to be reversed, that is, those parts which are elevated seem depressed, and the contrary. But the cause of this appearance, for any thing I know, remains still to be explained.

In order to produce this effect, no other apparatus is necessary than two convex lenses placed in a tube, at a distance from each other nearly equal to the sum of their focal distances.. Through these glasses, objects that appear distinctly, always appear inverted ; for they are not seen directly, but by means of an image formed either between the two glasses, or between both of them and the eye.

If we look through such glasses at cornishes, picture frames and other mouldings in carpenters work, and some sorts of carved work, those parts which are raised generally appear depressed, and those parts which are depressed appear raised. But a very ready object, and which succeeds as well as any thing I know of, is a brick pavement ; whether it be a chimney-hearth, or pavement out of doors. Viewed through the tube above described, every little cavity in the bricks, and the chinks between them, almost always appear to be so many elevations above the surface of the bricks.

When I considered this odd appearance, the first probable cause that offered was, that those parts of the object which are sunk, and farthest from the eye, might have their correspondent parts of the image formed by the glasses nearest to the eye, and therefore would appear raised.

But

But this is not the cafe; for thofe parts which are fartheft from the eye in the object, will always be fartheft from the eye in the image, and often in a much greater propor-tion. After fome time I concluded it to be a neceffary confequence of the apparent inverfion of the object; and many things tended to confirm me in this opinion, before I made the experiments which feem perfectly decifive.

It has often been matter of furprize to me, when view-ing the moon through a good telefcope, in company with perfons not accuftomed to fuch obfervations, that whilft the cavities and eminences of the moon's furface appeared to me marked out with the utmoft certainty by their light and fhades, my companions generally conceived it to be a plain furface of various degrees of brightnefs. The rea-fon I fuppofe to be this; the aftronomer knows from the moon's fituation with refpect to the fun, and even from the figure of its enlightened part, precifely in what direc-tion the light falls on its furface, and therefore judges rightly of its hills and vallies, from their different degrees of light, according to thofe rules which are imperceptibly formed in the mind, and confirmed by long experience. But a perfon unacquainted with aftronomy knows nothing of the direction of the fun's light on the moon, nor does he attend to the moon's globular figure, and is befides, perhaps, poffeffed with a notion of its being felf-luminous; no wonder then that the fame object has a very different effect on his imagination. It feems to be thofe rules of judging, which we begin to form in our earlieft infancy, which we fet afide, re-eftablifh, alter, correct and confirm, and at length rely on with the utmoft confidence, even without knowing that we do fo, or that we have any fuch rules: It is thefe rules, of fuch infinite general ufe to us, that fometimes miflead us on new and extraordinary oc-cafions, and particularly in the cafe now before us. A perfon entering into a room perceives, at a fingle glance, whence the light comes which illuminates the objects be-

fore

fore him ; and that without remaining confcious for a moment that he has attended to this circumftance : But the
effect remains, and will influence his judgment.   If on
looking at a brick hearth he perceives that thofe lines which
divide the bricks have a dark fhade on that fide oppofite
to the light, and a bright ftreak on the contrary fide next
to the light, he muft at the fame time perceive that they
have the property which he has conftantly obferved in,
ridges, not in furrows.   And fince the appearance of the
hearth will be fuch, through the glaffes, in confequence of
their inverting the fituation of its feveral parts, with refpect
to the light, the obferver will inftantly pronounce the chinks
between the bricks, and every little cavity in them, to be
fo many perfect elevations above the common furface, nor
can any effort of the mind correct the imagination or alter
the appearance.

Though I was well fatisfied of the truth of this explanation, I refolved neverthelefs to bring it to the teft of experiment, which I did in the following manner.

In order to give my experiment fair play, I fhut all the
windows of my chamber excepting one directly oppofite
to the chimney.   I then took the tube, with two convex
glaffes, and looking through it at the hearth, all the bricks
appeared depreffed and the clefts between them elevated,
as ufual.   I then placed a looking-glafs againft the chimney back, fo that it reflected the light from the window
upon the hearth, and fet up a fmall board before the hearth
to intercept the direct light of the window from it.   Then
looking at the hearth through the glaffes, I was much
pleafed to find it appear in its natural ftate, with the bricks
elevated.   I then fat down on a chair at the edge of the
hearth, and looking through the tube which I held to my
eye with one hand, whilft with the other I moved the
board fo as to make it fometimes intercept the direct light
of the window, and at other times the reflected light of
the looking-glafs, I conftantly found that when the hearth
was.

was illuminated by reflected light, it appeared in its natural ſtate, and when illuminated by the direct light, in its unnatural ſtate ; for ſo I call it when the bricks appear depreſſed and the chinks between them elevated.

I then conſidered that ſince the hearth appeared in its natural ſtate by reflected light, and in its unnatural ſtate by direct light, only in conſequence of the inverting property of the glaſſes, the appearance ought to be directly the contrary when it was viewed with the naked eye. And accordingly I found, upon taking out both of the glaſſes, and looking through the open tube, that the hearth appeared as perfectly, and as conſtantly in its unnatural ſtate by reflected light, and in its natural ſtate by direct light, as it had before done the reverſe through the glaſſes. But it muſt be obſerved that ſomething like a tube is neceſſary to confine the ſight from other adjoining objects, which not being in the ſame circumſtances would otherwiſe correct the imagination.

If we look through ſuch a tube and glaſſes at the hearth or other object, ſuppoſe a piece of chocolate, the furrows in it appear ſo many ridges, on removing the tube they ſink into furrows, on applying it they again riſe into ridges, and the illuſion might perhaps be repeated a thouſand times, without the mind being at all able to conceive the object to appear through the tube like what it really is. But if whilſt you are looking through the tube, and the object appears in its unnatural ſtate, that is, when its furrows appear ridges, you apply your finger and feel that they really are furrows, the deception vaniſhes in a moment and the object appears in its natural ſtate. This I at firſt ſuppoſed to ariſe from the ſuperior confidence which we have in the ſenſe of touching, as knowing by experience that this ſenſe more perfectly repreſents the figure of bodies than the ſight does. But I was, at leaſt in part, miſtaken. For if whilſt you ſee the object in its unnatural ſtate, another perſon puts his finger to the part you are

looking

looking at, the deception vanifhes as well as in the former cafe. The application of a writing pen or pencil will produce the fame effect. And, which is very remarkable, after the mind has been undeceived by thefe means once or twice, it does not readily admit of the impofition again: Though, as I obferved before, if it be done by removing the glaffes, the deception will return again as often as you pleafe. The truth feems to be, that the mind chufes the leaft difficulty; and though in confequence of the judgment it has formed concerning the direction of the light, it will fubmit to fuch a fmall impofition as to fuppofe one piece of chocolate may have ridges where others ufually have furrows, when indeed it has not, yet it will not readily endure fuch a grofs one, as to fuppofe it to have cavities of the figure and colour of a finger or a writing pen. Or perhaps the vifible motion attending fuch application produces the principal effect in convincing the mind that thofe bodies are really elevated*, and then their fhades and modifications of the light, fhew in what direction it falls on them; and the miftake of the mind in that particular being rectified, the whole object muft affume its natural appearance.

The explanation I have given of this phænomenon will account for an odd circumftance mentioned (I think) by Mr. Short; which once appeared fo whimfical to me as neither to merit credit or attention. Mr. Short carefully examined the Caffegrain telefcope, and in all probability fet it by the fide of one of the Gregorian form, in order to determine its comparative merits: He gives the preference to the Gregorian, and mentions as a principal defect of the Caffegrain telefcope, that it reprefents the mountains in the moon as vallies, and the contrary. I doubt not but this,

F   otherwife

---

* Whilft I was making thefe experiments, I thought of a carved filver fhoe buckle, as a very proper object to prevent a deception of this fort from taking place. But placing it on a brick pavement, and looking at it through the glaffes, it neverthelefs appeared perfectly depreffed. Precifely as if you had taken a buckle and ftrewing on it a white fhining powder, had preffed it into the brick whilft foft, and then removing the buckle, the glittering powder had remained in the impreffion.

otherwife unaccountable appearance, was occafioned intire-ly by its inverting the object, for the reafons above given. If it be afked, why then do not the common long refractors, which generally invert, produce the fame deception? I anfwer, very probably they would do fo if fet befide a Gregorian reflector and the eye applied alternately to the one and to the other*.

N° III.

Defcription of the White Mountains in New-Hampfhire.

BY THE REV. JEREMY BELKNAP OF NEW-HAMPSHIRE.

Read Oct. 15, 1784.

THE white mountains in the northern part of New-Hampfhire have, from the earlieft fettlement of the country, attracted the attention of all forts of perfons. They are undoubtedly the higheft lands in New-England, and are difcovered in clear weather by veffels coming on the eaftern coaft, before any other land; but by reafon of their bright appearance are frequently miftaken for clouds. They are feen on fhore at the diftance of fixty or eighty miles on the fouth and fouth-eaft fides, and are faid to be plainly vifible in the neighbourhood of Quebec. The Indians had a fuperftitious veneration for them as the habitation of invifible beings, and for this reafon never ventured to afcend their fummits, and always endeavoured to difcourage every perfon who attempted it. From them, and the captives whom they formerly led to Canada through the pafs of thefe mountains, many fictions have been propagated through the country which have in time fwelled to marvellous and incredible ftories; particularly,

* The above was written in 1774, when I had no achromatic aftronomical telefcope in my poffeffion.

larly, it has been reported that carbuncles have been seen at immense heights, and inaccessible spots which give a lustre in the night.

Those who have attempted to give an account of these mountains, have ascribed their brightness to shining rocks or white moss, and the highest summit has been represented as inaccessible by reason of the extreme cold which threatens to freeze the traveller in the midst of summer. They have also differed so widely from each other, and their accounts have been embellished with so many marvellous circumstances, and on the whole have been so unsatisfactory, that I have long wished for an opportunity to visit these mountains in company with some gentlemen of a philosophical turn, furnished with proper instruments and materials for a full exploration of the phenomena that might occur. This pleasure I have in part enjoyed the present summer; and though the roughness of the way which prevented the use of convenient carriages, proved fatal to some of our instruments, and the almost continual cloudiness of the weather while we were in that region hindered us from making some observations which we intended; yet till a better account can be obtained, I flatter myself that what follows will prove more satisfactory than any which has yet been published or reported.

The white mountains are the highest part of a ridge which extends north-east and south-west to an unknown length. The area of their base is an irregular figure somewhat resembling an isoceles triangle, whose longest extremity is toward the south, and whose whole circuit cannot be less than fifty miles. The number of summits within this area cannot be ascertained at present, the country round them being a thick wilderness. On the north-west side seven summits are in plain view, and this is the greatest number that can be seen at once from any station that is cleared of woods. Of these, four at least are bald. The highest of them is on the eastern side of the cluster,

on

on which fide we afcended, having firft gained the height
of land between the waters of Saco and Amarifcogin rivers,
to which there is a gradual afcent for twelve miles from
the plains of Pigwacket. At this height of land there is
a meadow which was formerly a beaver-pond with a dam
at each end. The water iffues out of a mountain on its
eaftern fide in the form of fprings, and meandering through
the channels of the meadow appears ftagnant in the middle but dividing its courfe, at the fouth end of the meadow
it runs into Ellis river, a branch of Saco ; and at the north
end into Peabody river, a branch of Amarifcogin. From
this meadow there is an uninterrupted afcent on a ridge
between two deep gullies to the higheft fummit.

The fides of the mountains are covered with fpruce trees ;
the furface is compofed of loofe rocks covered with very
long green mofs, which reaches from rock to rock, and
is in many places fo thick and ftrong as to fupport a man's
weight. This immenfe bed of mofs, fpread over the furface of thefe mountains ferves, as a fpunge to retain the
moifture brought by the clouds and vapors which are continually rifing and gathering round the mountains ; the
thick growth of fpruce prevents the fun's rays from penetrating to exhale it ; fo that there is a conftant fupply of
water to the numberlefs fprings with which this region
abounds, and an unceafing circulation of fluid, the procefs
of which is highly entertaining to the fpectator ; for no
fooner has a fhower defcended from the clouds, but the
vapor rifes from the leaves of the foreft in innumerable
little columns, which, having gained a certain height in
the atmofphere, collect and converge toward the mountains, where they either fall again in fhowers or are imbibed by the mofs and depofited in the crevices of the rocks,
feeking their way to the hard ftratum or pan which is
impenetrable, and which guides them till they find vent
in fprings. The fame liquid tribute is daily exhaled from
the rivers, ponds and low grounds, and attracted to the
mountains,

mountains, which by thefe means are always replenifhed with water in every part.

The rocks, of which thefe mountains are compofed, are in fome parts flate, in others flint, but toward the top a dark grey ftone, which, when broken, fhows fpecks of ifing-glafs. On the bald parts of the mountains the ftones are covered with a fhort grey mofs, and at the very fummit the mofs is of a yellowifh colour and adheres firmly to the rock.

Eight of our company afcended the higheft mountain on the 24th of July, and were fix hours and fifty one minutes in gaining the fummit, deducting one hour and thirty eight minutes for the neceffary ftops. The fpruce and firs, as you afcend, grow fhorter till they degenerate to fhrubs and bufhes, then you meet with low vines bearing a red and a blue berry, and laftly a fort of grafs called winter grafs mixed with the mofs.

Having afcended the fteepeft precipice, you come to what is called the plain, where the afcent becomes gentle and eafy. This plain is compofed of rocks, covered with winter grafs and mofs, and looks like the furface of a dry pafture or common. In fome openings between the rocks you meet with water, in others dry gravel. The plain is an irregular figure, its area uncertain, but from its eaftern edge to the foot of the fugar-loaf, is upwards of a mile; on the weftern fide it extends farther. The fugar-loaf is a pyramidal heap of loofe grey rocks, not lefs than three hundred feet in perpendicular height, but the afcent is not fo difficult as the precipice below the plain. From this fummit in clear weather is a noble view, extending to the ocean on the fouth-eaft; to the highlands on the weft and northweft, which feparate the waters of Connecticut river from thofe of lake Champlain and St. Laurence; on the fouth it extends to Winipifeogee lake, and the highlands fouthward of Pemigewaffet river.

It

It happened unfortunately for our company, that a thick cloud covered the mountain almoſt the whole time that they were on it, ſo that ſome of the inſtruments which, with much labor they had carried up, were uſeleſs. In the barometer the mercury ranged at 22.6 inches, in 44 degrees of heat by Fahrenheit's thermometer. It was our intention to have placed one of each of theſe inſtruments at the foot of the mountain, at the ſame time that others were carried to the top; but they were unhappily broken in the courſe of our journey, and the barometer which was carried to the ſummit, had ſuffered ſo much agitation that an allowance was neceſſary to be made in calculating the height of the mountain, which our ingenious companion, the Rev. Mr. Cutler, of Ipſwich, eſtimates in round numbers at 5500 feet above the meadow, the meadow being 3500 feet above the level of the ſea, and this ſeems to be as low an eſtimation as can be admitted. We intended to have made a geometrical menſuration of the altitude, but in one place where we attempted it, we could not obtain a baſe of ſufficient length, and in another, where this convenience was removed, we were prevented by the almoſt continual obſcurations of the mountains by clouds.

On every ſide of theſe mountains are many long winding gullies, beginning at the precipice below the plain and deepening in the deſcent; they are from one hundred to one thouſand feet deep, and perhaps more. In winter, the ſnow driving with the north-weſt winds over the tops of the mountains, is lodged in theſe gullies, and forms a compact body which is not eaſily diſſolved by the vernal ſun. It is obſerved to lie longer on the ſouth, than on the northweſt ſides; which is the caſe with moſt other hills in this part of the country. In 1774 ſome men who were at work on a road under the eaſtern ſide of the mountain, aſcended to the ſummit on the 6th of June, and upon the ſouth ſide found a body of ſnow thirteen feet deep, and ſo hard as to

bear

bear them.   The man from whom I had this account, and
who had the direction of the work, afcended the mountain
on the 19th of June, with fome of the fame party, and in
the fame fpot the fnow was five feet deep.   On the 22d
of July this year, we were affured by perfons who live
within plain view of the mountains, on the fouth fide, at
the diftance of fixteen miles, that the fnow had not been
gone more than ten days.   We were alfo credibly informed that two men, who attempted to afcend the mountain
the firft week of September laft year, found the bald top
fo covered with fnow and ice, then newly made, that they
could not gain the fummit; but this does not happen every
year fo foon, for the mountain has been afcended fo late as
the firft week in October, when no fnow was upon it; and
fometimes the firft fnows that come diffolve before the
winter fets in; but generally the mountains begin to be
covered with fnow and ice, either in the latter part of September, or the beginning of October, and it never wholly
leaves them till July.   During this period of nine or ten
months, they exhibit more or lefs of that bright appearance,
from which they are denominated *white*.   In the fpring
when the fnow is partly diffolved, they appear of a pale
blue ftreaked with white; and after it is wholly gone, at the
diftance of forty or fixty miles, they are altogether of a
pale blue inclining to the colour of the fky; while viewed
at the diftance of only ten miles, they are of the grey colour of the rock inclining to brown.   Thefe changes are
obferved by people who live within conftant view of them,
and from thefe facts and obfervations it may juftly be concluded that the whitenefs of them is to be afcribed wholly
to the fnow and ice and not to any other white fubftance,
for in reality there is none.   There are indeed in the fummer months fome ftreaks which appear brighter than other
parts, but thefe, when viewed through a telefcope, I have
plainly difcerned to be the enlightened edges or fides of
the long deep gullies, and the dark parts the fhaded fides
of

of them; and in the courfe of a day thefe fpots may be feen
to vary according to the pofition of the fun.

It may not be amifs to query here, if fo great a quantity of fnow is accumulated and remains on thefe mountains, may it not be fuppofed to add a keennefs to the
winds which blow over them? And how many more mountains may there be toward the north and weft, whofe hoary
fummits contain the like or greater bodies of fnow and ice,
fome of which, at the remoteft regions, may remain un-
diffolved through the year? May we not then afcribe the
piercing cold of our north-weft winds to the infinite ranges
of frozen mountains, rather than to the lakes and forefts?

Thefe immenfe heights which I have been defcribing,
being copioufly replenifhed with water, exhibit a variety
of beautiful cafcades, fome of which fall in a perpendicular fheet or fpout, others are winding and narrow, others
fpread on the level furface of fome wide rock and then
gufh in cataracts over its edge. A romantic imagination
may find full gratification amidft thefe rugged fcenes, if
its ardor be not checked by the fatigue of the approach.
Three of the largeft rivers in New-England receive a great
part of their waters from this region. Amonoofuck and
Ifrael rivers, two principal branches of Connecticut, fall
from the weftern fide of the mountains, Peabody river and
another branch of Amarifcogin from the north-eaftern fide,
and almoft the whole of Saco defcends from the fouthern
fide. The declivities being very fteep caufe this latter
river to rife very fuddenly in a time of rain, and as fuddenly to fubfide.

On the weftern part of thefe mountains is a pafs which
in the narroweft place meafures but twenty two feet between two perpendicular rocks. Here a road is conftructing with great labor and expence, which is the fhorteft
rout to the upper Cohofs on Connecticut river, and to that
part of Canada which borders on the river St. Francis. At
the height of this narrow pafs the river Saco takes its rife.

A brook

A brook defcends from the mountain, and meanders through a meadow which was formerly a beaver-pond, and is furrounded by fteep, and on one fide, perpendicular rocks—a ftrikingly picturefque fcene! the rivulet glides along the weftern fide of the defile, (the eaftern being formed into a road) and tributary ftreams augment its waters, one of which is called the Flume, from the near refemblance it bears to the flume of a mill. The pafs between the mountains widens as you defcend; but for eight or ten miles they are fo near as only to leave room for the river and its intervals. In the courfe of this defcent you fee at immenfe heights, and in fpots perfectly inacceffible, feveral rocks, fome of a whitifh and fome of a reddifh hue, whofe faces are polifhed by the continual trickling of water over them. Thefe, when incrufted with ice, being open to the fouth and weft, are capable in the night of reflecting the moon and ftar-beams to the wondering traveller, buried in the dark valley below; and thefe are fufficient, by the help of imagination, to give rife to the fiction of carbuncles.

We found no ftones of any higher quality than flint[*]; no limeftone, though we tried the moft likely with aqua fortis. It is faid there is a part of the mountain where the magnetic needle refufes to traverfe; this may contain rock ore, but our guide could not find the place. It is alfo faid that a mineral, fuppofed to be lead ore, has been difcovered on the eaftern fide. One of the fprings which we met with in our afcent on that fide afforded a thick frothy fcum and a faponaceous tafte. All fearches for fubterranean treafures in thefe mountains have as yet proved fruitlefs. The moft certain riches which they yield are the frefhets which bring down the foil to the intervals below, and form a fine mould, producing corn, grain and herbage in the moft luxuriant plenty.

G   *Defcription*

---

[*] Some fpecimens of rock-chryftal have been found lately by other perfons, but we did not hear of it till after our return.

N° IV.

Defcription of a remarkable ROCK *and* CASCADE, *near the
weftern fide of the Youghiogeny river, a quarter of a
mile from Crawford's ferry, and about twelve miles from
Union-Town, in Fayette county, in the ftate of Pennfylvania.*

BY THO. HUTCHINS.

Read Janua-
ry 28, 1786.

THIS cafcade is occafioned by a rock of a femicircular form, the chord of which, from
one extreme end of the arch to the other, is nearly one
hundred yards; the arch or circular part is extenfive, and
upwards of twenty feet in height, exhibiting a grand and
romantic appearance. This very curious production is
compofed of ftone of variegated colours, and a fpecies of
marble beautifully chequered with veins running in different directions, prefenting on a clofe infpection a faint
refemblance of a variety of mathematical figures of different angles and magnitudes. The operations of nature
in this ftructure feems to be exceedingly uniform and ma-
jeftic; the layers or rows of ftone of which it is compofed
are of various lengths and thickneffes, more refembling the
effects of art than nature. A flat thin ftone from eight to
ten inches thick, about twenty feet wide, forms the upper
part of this amphitheatre, over which the ftream precipi-
tates. The whole front of this rock is made up from top
to bottom, as well as from one extremity of the arch to
the other, of a regular fucceffion, principally, of limeftone,
ftrata over ftrata, and each ftratum or row, projecting in
an horizontal direction a little further out than its bafe, until it terminates into one entire flat, thin, extenfive piece,
as already mentioned; and which jets out at right angles

or

or in a parallel line with the bottom, over which it impends fifteen or twenty feet, and that without columns or even a fingle pillar for its fupport. This circumftance, together with the grand circular walk between the front of the rock and the fheet of water falling from the fummit, exhibits fo noble and fingular an appearance, that a fpeĉtator cannot behold it without admiration and delight.

N° V.

Letter to Mr. NAIRNE, *of London.*

Paſſy, near Paris, Nov. 13th, 1780.

SIR,

Read January 28, 1786. THE qualities hitherto fought in a hygrometer, or inftrument to difcover the degrees of moifture and drynefs in the air, feem to have been, an aptitude to receive humidity readily from a moift air, and to part with it as readily to a dry air. Different fubftances have been found to poffefs more or lefs of this quality; but when we fhall have found the fubftance that has it in the greateft perfeĉtion, there will ftill remain fome uncertainty in the conclufions to be drawn from the degree fhown by the inftrument, arifing from the aĉtual ftate of the inftrument itfelf as to heat and cold. Thus, if two bottles or veffels of glafs or metal being filled, the one with cold and the other with hot water, are brought into a room, the moifture of the air in the room will attach itfelf in quantities to the furface of the cold veffel, while if you aĉtually wet the furface of the hot veffel, the moifture will immediately quit it, and be abforbed by the fame air. And thus in a fudden change of the air from cold to warm, the inftrument remaining longer cold may condenfe and abforb more moifture, and mark the air as having become

G 2 more

more humid than it is in reality, and the contrary in a change from warm to cold.

But if such a suddenly changing instrument could be freed from these imperfections, yet when the design is to discover the different degrees of humidity in the air of different countries, I apprehend the quick sensibility of the instrument to be rather a disadvantage; since, to draw the desired conclusions from it, a constant and frequent observation day and night in each country will be necessary for a year or years, and the mean of each different set of observations is to be found and determined. After all which some uncertainty will remain respecting the different degrees of exactitude with which different persons may have made and taken notes of their observations.

For these reasons, I apprehend that a substance which, though capable of being distended by moisture and contracted by dryness, is so slow in receiving and parting with its humidity that the frequent changes in the atmosphere have not time to affect it sensibly, and which therefore should gradually take nearly the medium of all those changes and preserve it constantly, would be the most proper substance of which to make such an hygrometer.

Such an instrument, you, my dear sir, though without intending it, have made for me; and I, without desiring or expecting it, have received from you. It is therefore with propriety that I address to you the following account of it; and the more, as you have both a head to contrive and a hand to execute the means of perfecting it. And I do this with greater pleasure, as it affords me the opportunity of renewing that antient correspondence and acquaintance with you, which to me was always so pleasing and so instructive.

You may possibly remember, that in or about the year 1758, you made for me a set of artificial magnets, six in number, each five and a half inches long, half an inch broad, and one eighth of an inch thick. These, with two

pieces

pieces of foft iron, which together equalled one of the magnets, were inclofed in a little box of mahogany wood, the grain of which ran with, and not acrofs, the length of the box; and the box was clofed by a little fhutter of the fame wood, the grain of which ran acrofs the box; and the ends of this fhutting piece were bevelled fo as to fit and flide in a kind of dovetail groove when the box was to be fhut or opened.

I had been of opinion that good mahogany wood was not affected by moifture fo as to change its dimenfions, and that it was always to be found as the tools of the workman left it. Indeed the difference at different times in the fame country, is fo fmall as to be fcarcely in a common way obfervable. Hence the box which was made fo as to allow fufficient room for the magnets to flide out and in freely, and, when in, afforded them fo much play that by fhaking the box one could make them ftrike the oppofite fides alternately, continued in the fame ftate all the time I remained in England, which was four years, without any apparent alteration. I left England in Auguft 1762, and arrived at Philadelphia in October the fame year. In a few weeks after my arrival, being defirous of fhowing your magnets to a philofophical friend, I found them fo tight in the box, that it was with difficulty I got them out; and conftantly during the two years I remained there, viz. till November 1764, this difficulty of getting them out and in continued. The little fhutter too, as wood does not fhrink length ways of the grain, was found too long to enter its grooves, and not being ufed, was miflaid and loft; and I afterwards had another made that fitted.

In December 1764 I returned to England, and after fome time I obferved that my box was become full big enough for my magnets, and too wide for my new fhutter; which was fo much too fhort for its grooves, that it was apt to fall

fall out; and to make it keep in, I lengthened it by adding to each end a little coat of fealing-wax.

I continued in England more than ten years, and during all that time after the firſt change, I perceived no alteration. The magnets had the ſame freedom in their box, and the little ſhutter continued with the added fealing-wax to fit its grooves, till ſome weeks after my ſecond return to A-merica.

As I could not imagine any other cauſe for this change of dimenſions in the box, when in the different countries, I concluded, firſt generally that the air of England was moiſter than that of America. And this I ſuppoſed an ef-fect of its being an iſland, where every wind that blew muſt neceſſarily paſs over ſome ſea before it arrived, and of courſe lick up ſome vapour. I afterwards indeed doubt-ed whether it might be juſt only ſo far as related to the city of London, where I reſided; becauſe there are many cauſes of moiſture in the city air, which do not exiſt to the ſame degree in the country; ſuch as the brewers and dyers boiling caldrons, and the great number of pots and teaket-tles continually on the fire, ſending fourth abundance of vapour; and alſo the number of animals who by their breath continually increaſe it; to which may be added, that even the vaſt quantity of ſea coals burnt there, do in kindling diſcharge a great deal of moiſture.

When I was in England, the laſt time, you alſo made for me a little achromatic pocket teleſcope, the body was braſs, and it had a round caſe, (I think of thin wood) covered with ſhagrin. All the while I remained in England, though poſſibly there might be ſome ſmall changes in the dimenſions of this caſe, I neither perceived nor ſuſpected any. There was always comfortable room for the tele-ſcope to ſlip in and out. But ſoon after I arrived in Ame-rica, which was in May 1775, the caſe became too ſmall for the inſtrument, it was with much difficulty and vari-ous contrivances that I got it out, and I could never after

get

get it in again, during my ſtay there, which was eighteen
months. I brought it with me to Europe, but left the caſe
as uſeleſs, imagining that I ſhould find the continental air
of France as dry as that of Pennſylvania, where my magnet box had alſo returned a ſecond time to its narrowneſs,
and pinched the pieces, as heretofore, obliging me too, to
ſcrape the ſealing-wax off the ends of the ſhutter.

I had not been long in France, before I was ſurpriſed to
find, that my box was become as large as it had always been
in England, the magnets entered and came out with the ſame
freedom, and, when in, I could rattle them againſt its ſides;
this has continued to be the caſe without ſenſible variation. My habitation is out of Paris diſtant almoſt a league,
ſo that the moiſt air of the city cannot be ſuppoſed to have
much effect upon the box. I am on a high dry hill in a
free air as likely to be dry as any air in France. Whence
it ſeems probable that the air of England in general may
as well as that of London, be moiſter than the air of America, ſince that of France is ſo, and in a part ſo diſtant from
the ſea.

The greater dryneſs of the air in America appears from
ſome other obſervations. The cabinet work formerly ſent
us from London, which conſiſted in thin plates of fine
wood glued upon fir, never would ſtand with us, the van-
eering, as thoſe plates are called, would get looſe and come
off; both woods ſhrinking, and their grains often croſſing,
they were forever cracking and flying. And in my electrical experiments there, it was remarkable, that a mahogany table on which my jars ſtood under the prime conductor to be charged, would often be ſo dry, particularly
when the wind had been ſome time at north-weſt which
with us is a very drying wind, as to iſolate the jars, and
prevent their being charged till I had formed a communication between their coatings and the earth. I had a like
table in London which I uſed for the ſame purpoſe all the
time I reſided there; but it was never ſo dry as to refuſe
conducting the electricity. Now

Now what I would beg leave to recommend to you, is, that you would recollect, if you can, the species of mahogany of which you made my box, for you know there is a good deal of difference in woods that go under that name; or if that cannot be, that you would take a number of pieces of the closest and finest grained mahogany that you can meet with, plane them to the thinness of about a line, and the width of about two inches across the grain, and fix each of the pieces in some instrument that you can contrive, which will permit them to contract and dilate, and will show, in sensible degrees, by a moveable hand upon a marked scale, the otherwise less sensible quantities of such contraction and dilatation. If these instruments are all kept in the same place while making, and are graduated together while subject to the same degrees of moisture or dryness, I apprehend you will have so many comparable hygrometers, which being sent into different countries, and continued there for some time, will find and show there the mean of the different dryness and moisture of the air of those countries, and that with much less trouble than by any hygrometer hitherto in use.

With great esteem,

I am, dear sir,

Your most obedient,

And most humble servant,

B. FRANKLIN.

Description

N° VI.

Description of a new STOVE *for burning of Pitcoal, and consuming all its Smoke.*

BY DR. B. FRANKLIN.

Read January 28, 1786. TOWARDS the end of the laſt century an ingenious French philoſopher, whoſe name I am ſorry I cannot recollect, exhibited an experiment to ſhow that very offenſive things might be burnt in the middle of a chamber, ſuch as woollen rags, feathers, &c. without creating the leaſt ſmoke or ſmell. The machine in which the experiment was made, if I Plate II. remember right, was of this form, made of plate Figure 1. iron. Some clear burning charcoals were put into the opening of the ſhort tube A, and ſupported there by the grate B. The air as ſoon as the tubes grew warm would aſcend in the longer leg C and go out at D, conſequently air muſt enter at A deſcending to B. In this courſe it muſt be heated by the burning coals through which it paſſed, and riſe more forcibly in the longer tube in proportion to its degree of heat or rarefaction, and length of that tube. For ſuch a machine is a kind of inverted ſyphon ; and as the greater weight of water in the longer leg of a common ſyphon in deſcending is accompanied by an aſcent of the ſame fluid in the ſhorter ; ſo, in this inverted ſyphon, the greater quantity of levity of air in the longer leg, in riſing is accompanied by the deſcent of air in the ſhorter. The things to be burned being laid on the hot coals at A, the ſmoke muſt deſcend through thoſe coals, be converted into flame, which, after deſtroying the offenſive ſmell, came out at the end of the longer tube as mere heated air.

H　　　　　　　　　　　　Whoever

Whoever would repeat this experiment with fuccefs, muft take care that the partA , B, of the fhort tube be quite full of burning coals, fo that no part of the fmoke may defcend and pafs by them without going through them, and being converted into flame ; and that the longer tube be fo heated as that the current of afcending hot air is eftablifhed in it before the things to be burnt are laid on the coals ; otherwife there will be a difappointment.

It does not appear either in the Memoirs of the Academy of Sciences, or Philofophical Tranfactions of the Englifh Royal Society, that any improvement was ever made of this ingenious experiment, by applying it to ufeful pur-pofes.. But there is a German book, entitled *Vulcanus Famulans*, by Joh. George Leutmann, P. D. printed at Wir-temberg in 1723, which defcribes, among a great variety of other ftoves for warming rooms, one which feems to have been formed on the fame principle, and probably from the hint thereby given, though the French experi-ment is not mentioned. This book being fcarce, I have tranflated the chapter defcribing the ftove, viz.

" Vulcanus Famulans, by John George Leutmann, P. D.
" Wirtemberg, 1723.

" C H A P.   VII.

" On a ftove, which draws downwards.

" Here follows the defcription of a fort of ftove, which
" can eafily be removed and again replaced at pleafure.
" This drives the fire down under itfelf, and gives no
" fmoke, but however a very unwholefome vapour.

" In the figure, A is an iron veffel like a fun-
Plate II. " nel, in diameter at the top about twelve inches,
Figure 20.
" at the bottom near the grate about five inches ;
" its height twelve inches. This is fet on the barrel C,
" which is ten inches diameter and two feet long, clofed
" at

" at each end E E. From one end rifes a pipe or flue
" about four inches diameter, on which other pieces of pipe
" are fet, which are gradually contracted to D, where the
" opening is but about two inches. Thofe pipes muft to-
" gether be at leaft four feet high. B is an iron grate.
" F F are iron handles guarded with wood, by which the
" ftove is to be lifted and moved. It ftands on three legs.
" Care muft be taken to ftop well all the joints, that no
" fmoke may leak through.

    " When this ftove is to be ufed, it muft firft be carried
" into the kitchen and placed in the chimney near the fire.
" There burning wood muft be laid and left upon its grate
" till the barrel C is warm, and the fmoke no longer rifes
" at A, but defcends towards C. Then it is to be carried
" into the room which it is to warm. When once the
" barrel C is warm, frefh wood may be thrown into the
" veffel A as often as one pleafes, the flame defcends and
" without fmoke, which is fo confumed that only a va-
" pour paffes out at D.

    " As this vapour is unwholefome, and affects the head,
" one may be freed from it, by fixing in the wall of the
" room an inverted funnel, fuch as people ufe to hang over
" lamps, through which their fmoke goes out as through
" a chimney. This funnel carries out all the vapour cle-
" verly, fo that one finds no inconvenience from it, even
" though the opening D be placed a fpan below the mouth
" of the faid funnel G. The neck of the funnel is better
" when made gradually bending, than if turned in a right
" angle.

    " The caufe of the draft downwards in the ftove is the
" preffure of the outward air, which falling into the veffel
" A in a column of twelve inches diameter, finds only
" a refifting paffage at the grate B, of five inches, and
" one at D, of two inches, which are much too weak
" to drive it back again ; befides, A ftands much higher
" than B, and fo the preffure on it is greater and more

" forcible,

" forcible, and beats down the flame to that part where
" it finds the leaft refiftance. Carrying the machine firft
" to the kitchen fire for preparation, is on this account,
" that in the beginning the fire and fmoke naturally afcend,
" till the air in the clofe barrel C is made thinner by the
" warmth. When that veffel is heated, the air in it is
" rarefied, and then all the fmoke and fire defcends
" under it.

" The wood fhould be throughly dry, and cut into
" pieces five or fix inches long, to fit it for being thrown
" into the funnel A." Thus far the German book.

It appears to me by Mr. Leutmann's explanation of
the operation of this machine, that he did not underftand
the principles of it, whence I conclude he was not the inventor of it; and by the defcription of it, wherein the
opening at A is made fo large, and the pipe E, D, fo fhort,
I am perfuaded he never made nor faw the experiment, for
the firft ought to be much fmaller and the laft much higher,
or it hardly will fucceed. The carrying it in the kitchen,
too, every time the fire fhould happen to be out, muft be fo
troublefome, that it is not likely ever to have been in practice, and probably has never been fhown but as a philofophical experiment. The funnel for conveying the vapour out of the room, would befides have been uncertain
in its operation, as a wind blowing againft its mouth would
drive the vapour back.

The ftove I am about to defcribe, was alfo formed on
the idea given by the French experiment, and completely
carried into execution before I had any knowledge of the
German invention; which I wonder fhould remain fo many
years in a country where men are fo ingenious in the management of fire, without receiving long fince the improvements I have given it.

DESCRIPTION

DESCRIPTION of the PARTS.

A, the bottom plate which lies flat upon the hearth, with its partitions 1, 2, 3, 4, 5, 6, that Plate II. Figure 2. are caft with it, and a groove Z Z, in which are to flide, the bottom edges of the fmall plates Y, Y, figure 12; which plates meeting at X clofe the front.

B 1, figure 3, is the cover plate fhowing its under fide, with the grooves 1, 2, 3, 4, 5, 6, to receive the top edges of the partitions that are fixed to the bottom plate. It fhows alfo the grate W W, the bars of which are caft in the plate, and a groove V V, which comes right over the groove Z Z, figure 2, receiving the upper edges of the fmall fliding plates Y Y, figure 12.

B 2, figure 4, fhows the upper fide of the fame plate, with a fquare impreffion or groove for receiving the bottom mouldings T T T T of the three fided box C, figure 5, which is caft in one piece.

D, figure 6, its cover, fhowing its under fide with grooves to receive the upper edges S S S of the fides of C, figure 5, alfo a groove R, R, which when the cover is put on comes right over another Q Q in C, figure 5, between which it is to flide.

E, figure 7, the front plate of the box.

P, a hole three inches diameter through the cover D, figure 6, over which hole ftands the vafe F, figure 8, which has a correfponding hole two inches diameter through its bottom.

The top of the vafe opens at O, O, O, figure 8, and turns back upon a hinge behind when coals are to be put in; the vafe has a grate within at N N of caft iron H, figure 9, and a hole in the top one and a half inches diameter to admit air, and to receive the ornamental brafs guilt flame M, figure 10, which ftands in that hole and, being itfelf hollow and open, fuffers air to pafs through it to the fire.

G, figure 11, is a drawer of plate iron, that flips in between in the partitions 2 and 3, figure 2, to receive the falling

falling afhes. It is concealed when the fmall fliding plates
Y Y, figure 12, are fhut together.

   I, I, I, I, figure 8, is a niche built of brick in the chimney and plaftered. It clofes the chimney over the vafe, but
leaves two funnels one in each corner communicating with
the bottom box K K, figure 2.

DIMENSIONS of the PARTS.

	Feet.	In.
Front of the bottom box, - -	2	0
Height of its partitions, - -	0	$4\frac{1}{4}$
Length of N° 1, 2, 3 and 4, each, -	1	3
Length of N° 5 and 6, each - -	0	$8\frac{1}{4}$
Breadth of the paffage between N° 2 and 3,	0	6
Breadth of the other paffages each, -	0	$3\frac{1}{4}$
Breadth of the grate, - -	0	$6\frac{1}{4}$
Length of ditto, - - -	0	8
Bottom moulding of box C, fquare, -	1	0
Height of the fides of ditto, - -	0	4
Length of the back fide, - -	0	10
Length of the right and left fides, each, -	0	$9\frac{1}{4}$
Length of the front plate E, where longeft,	0	11
The cover D, fquare, - -	0	12
Hole in ditto, diameter, - -	0	3
Sliding plates Y Y their length, each, -	1	0
————————their breadth, each, -	0	$4\frac{1}{4}$
Drawer G, its length, - - -	1	0
————————breadth, - - -	0	$5\frac{3}{4}$
————————depth, - - -	0	4
————————depth of its further end, only,	0	1
Grate H in the vafe, its diameter to the extre-		
mity of its knobs, - - -	0	$5\frac{3}{4}$
Thicknefs of the bars at top, - -	0	$0\frac{1}{4}$
————————————at bottom, lefs, -	0	0
Depth of the bars at the top, - -	0	$0\frac{3}{4}$
Height of the vafe, - - -	1	6
Diameter of the opening O, O, in the clear,	0	8

Diameter

	Feet.	In.
Diameter of the air-hole at top, - -	o	1½
———of the flame hole at bottom, -	o	2

To fix this Machine.

Spread mortar on the hearth to bed the bottom plate A, then lay that plate, level, equally diſtant from each jamb, and projecting out as far as you think proper. Then puting ſome Windſor loam in the grooves of the cover B, lay that on: Trying the ſliding plates Y Y, to ſee if they move freely in the groves Z Z, V V, deſigned for them.

Then begin to build the niche, obſerving to leave the ſquare corners of the chimney unfilled; for they are to be funnels. And obſerve alſo to leave a free open communication between the paſſages at K K, and the bottom of thoſe funnels, and mind to cloſe the chimney above the top of the niche, that no air may paſs up that way. The concave back of the niche will reſt on the circular iron partition 1 A 4, figure 2, then with a little loam put on the box C over the grate, the open ſide of the box in front.

Then, with loam in three of its grooves, the groove R R being left clean, and brought directly over the groove Q Q in the box, put on the cover D, trying the front plate E, to ſee if it ſlides freely in thoſe grooves.

Laſtly, ſet on the vaſe, which has ſmall holes in the moulding of its bottom to receive two iron pins that riſe out of the plate D at I I, for the better keeping it ſteady.

Then putting in the grate H, which reſts on its three knobs H H H againſt the inſide of the vaſe, and ſlipping the drawer into its place; the machine is fit for uſe.

To uſe it.

Let the firſt fire be made after eight in the evening or before eight in the morning, for at thoſe times and between thoſe hours all night, there is uſually a draft up a chimney, though it has long been without fire; but between thoſe hours in the day there is often in a cold chimney

ney a draft downwards, when if you attempt to kindle a fire, the fmoke will come into the room.

But to be certain of your proper time, hold a flame over the air-hole at the top. If the flame is drawn ftrongly down for a continuance, without whiffling, you may begin to kindle a fire.

Firft put in a few charcoals on the grate H.

Lay fome fmall fticks on the charcoals,

Lay fome pieces of paper on the fticks,

Kindle the paper with a candle,

Then fhut down the top, and the air will pafs down through the air-hole, blow the flame of the paper down through the fticks, kindle them, and their flame paffing lower, kindles the charcoal.

When the charcoal is well kindled, lay on it the feacoals, obferving not to choak the fire by putting on too much at firft.

The flame defcending through the hole in the bottom of the vafe, and that in plate D into the box C paffes down farther through the grate W W in plate B 1, then paffes horizontally towards the back of the chimney; there dividing, and turning to the right and left, one part of it paffes round the far end of the partition 2, then coming forward it turns round the near end of partition 1, then moving backward it arrives at the opening into the bottom of one of the upright corner funnels behind the niche, through which it afcends into the chimney, thus heating that half of the box and that fide of the niche. The other part of the divided flame paffes round the far end of partition 3, round the near end of partition 4, and fo into and up the other corner funnel, thus heating the other half of the box, and the other fide of the niche. The vafe itfelf, and the box C will alfo be very hot, and the air furrounding them being heated, and rifing, as it cannot get into the chimney, it fpreads in the room, colder air
fucceeding

ſucceeding is warmed in its turn, riſes and ſpreads, till by the continual circulation the whole is warmed.

If you ſhould have occaſion to make your firſt fire at hours not ſo convenient as thoſe above mentioned, and when the chimney does not draw, do not begin it in the vaſe, but in one or more of the paſſages of the lower plate, firſt covering the mouth of the vaſe. After the chimney has drawn a while with the fire thus low, and begins to be a little warm, you may cloſe thoſe paſſages and kindle another fire in the box C, leaving its ſliding ſhutter a little open; and when you find after ſome time that the chimney being warmed draws forcibly, you may ſhut that paſſage, open your vaſe, and kindle your fire there, as above directed. The chimney well warmed by the firſt day's fire will continue to draw conſtantly all winter, if fires are made daily.

You will, in the management of your fire, have need of the following implements:

A pair of ſmall light tongs, twelve or fifteen inches long, plate II, figure 13.

A light poker about the ſame length with a flat broad point, figure 14.

A rake to draw aſhes out of the paſſages of the lower plate, where the lighter kind eſcaping the aſh-box will gather by degrees, and perhaps once in a week or ten days require being removed, figure 15.

And a fork with its prongs wide enough to ſlip on the neck of the vaſe cover, in order to raiſe and open it when hot, to put in freſh coals, figure 16.

In the management of this ſtove there are certain precautions to be obſerved, at firſt with attention, till they become habitual. To avoid the inconvenience of ſmoke, ſee that the grate H be clear before you begin to light a freſh fire. If you find it clogged with cinders and aſhes, turn it up with your tongs and let them fall upon the grate below; the aſhes will go through it, and the cinders may

I   be

be raked off and returned into the vafe when you would burn them. Then fee that all the fliding plates are in their places and clofe fhut, that no air may enter the ftove but through the round opening at the top of the vafe. And to avoid the inconvenience of duft from the afhes, let the afh-drawer be taken out of the room to be emptied ; and when you rake the paffages, do it when the draft of the air is ftrong inwards, and put the afhes carefully into the afh-box, that remaining in its place.

If being about to go abroad, you would prevent your fire burning in your abfence, you may do it by taking the brafs flame from the top of the vafe, and covering the paffage with a round tin plate, which will prevent the entry of more air than barely fufficient to keep a few of the coals alive. When you return, though fome hours abfent, by taking off the tin plate and admitting the air, your fire will foon be recovered.

The effect of this machine, well managed, is to burn not only the coals, but all the fmoke of the coals, fo that while the fire is burning, if you go out and obferve the top of your chimney, you will fee no fmoke iffuing, nor any thing but clear warm air, which as ufual makes the bodies feen through it appear waving.

But let none imagine from this, that it may be a cure for bad or fmoky chimneys, much lefs, that as it burns the fmoke it may be ufed in a room that has no chimney. 'Tis by the help of a good chimney, the higher the better, that it produces its effect; and though a flue of plate iron fufficiently high might be raifed in a very lofty room, the management to prevent all difagreeable vapour would be too nice for common practice, and fmall errors would have unpleafing confequences.

It is certain that clean iron yields no offenfive fmell when heated. Whatever of that kind you perceive, where there are iron ftoves, proceeds therefore from fome foulnefs burning or fuming on their furface. They fhould
therefore

therefore never be fpit upon, or greafed, nor fhould any duft be fuffered to lie upon them. But as the greateft care will not always prevent thefe things, it is well once a week to wafh the ftove with foap lees and a brufh, rinfing it with clean water.

The Advantages of this Stove.

1. The chimney does not grow foul, nor ever need fweeping; for as no fmoke enters it, no foot can form in it.

2. The air heated over common fires inftantly quits the room and goes up the chimney with the fmoke; but in the ftove, it is obliged to defcend in flame and pafs through the long winding horizontal paffages, communicating its heat to a body of iron plate, which having thus time to receive the heat, communicates the fame to the air of the room, and thereby warms it to a greater degree.

3. The whole of the fuel is confume d by Leingturned into flame, and you have the benefit of its heat, whereas in common chimneys a great part goes away in fmoke which you fee as it rifes, but it affords you no rays of warmth. One may obtain fome notion of the quantity of fuel thus wafted in fmoke, by reflecting on the quantity of foot that a few weeks firing will lodge againft the fides of the chimney, and yet this is formed only of thofe particles of the column of fmoke that happen to touch the fides in its afcent. How much more muft have paffed off in the air? And we know that this foot is ftill fuel; for it will burn and flame as fuch, and when hard caked together is indeed very like and almoft as folid as the coal it proceeds from. The deftruction of your fuel goes on nearly in the fame quantity whether in fmoke or in flame: but there is no comparifon in the difference of heat given. Obferve when frefh coals are firft put on your fire, what a body of fmoke arifes. This fmoke is for a long time too cold to take flame. If you then plunge a burning candle into it, the candle inftead of inflaming the fmoke will in-

I 2   ftantly

ſtantly be itſelf extinguiſhed. Smoke muſt have a certain
degree of heat to be inflammable. As ſoon as it has acquired that degree, the approach of a candle will inflame
the whole body, and you will be very ſenſible of the difference of the heat it gives. A ſtill eaſier experiment may
be made with the candle itſelf. Hold your hand near the
ſide of its flame, and obſerve the heat it gives ; then blow
it out, the hand remaining in the ſame place, and obſerve
what heat may be given by the ſmoke that riſes from the
ſtill burning ſnuff. You will find it very little. And yet
that ſmoke has in it the ſubſtance of ſo much flame, and
will inſtantly produce it, if you hold another candle above
it ſo as to kindle it. Now the ſmoke from the freſh coals
laid on this ſtove, inſtead of aſcending and leaving the fire
while too cold to burn, being obliged to deſcend through
the burning coals, receives among them that degree of
heat which converts it into flame, and the heat of that
flame is communicated to the air of the room, as above
explained.

4. The flame from the freſh coals laid on in this ſtove,
deſcending through the coals already ignited, preſerves
them long from conſuming, and continues them in the
ſtate of red coals as long as the flame continues that ſur-
rounds them, by which means the fires made in this ſtove
are of much longer duration than in any other, and fewer
coals are therefore neceſſary for a day. This is a very
material advantage indeed. That flame ſhould be a kind
of pickle, to preſerve burning coals from conſuming, may
ſeem a paradox to many, and very unlikely to be true, as
it appeared to me the firſt time I obſerved the fact. I muſt
therefore relate the circumſtances, and ſhall mention an
eaſy experiment, by which my reader may be in poſſeſſion
of every thing neceſſary to the underſtanding of it. In
the firſt trial I made of this kind of ſtove, which was conſtructed of thin plate iron, I had inſtead of the vaſe a kind
of inverted pyramid like a mill-hopper ; and fearing at

firſt that the ſmall grate contained in it might be clogged by cynders, and the paſſage of the flame ſometimes obſtructed, I ordered a little door near the grate, by means of which I might on occaſion clear it. Though after the ſtove was made, and before I tried it, I began to think this precaution ſuperfluous, from an imagination, that the flame being contracted in the narrow part where the grate was placed, would be more powerful in conſuming what it ſhould there meet with, and that any cynders between or near the bars would be preſently deſtroyed and the paſſage opened. After the ſtove was fixed and in action, I had a pleaſure now and then in opening that door a little, to ſee through the crevice how the flame deſcended among the red coals, and obſerving once a ſingle coal lodged on the bars in the middle of the focus, a fancy took me to obſerve by my watch in how ſhort a time it would be conſumed. I looked at it long without perceiving it to be at all diminiſhed, which ſurpriſed me greatly. At length it occurred to me, that I and many others had ſeen the ſame thing thouſands of times, in the conſervation of the red coal formed in the ſnuff of a burning candle, which while envelloped in flame, and thereby prevented from the contact of paſſing air, is long continued and augments inſtead of diminiſhing, ſo that we are often obliged to remove it by the ſnuffers, or bend it out of the flame into the air, where it conſumes preſently to aſhes. I then ſuppoſed that to conſume a body by fire, paſſing air was neceſſary to receive and carry off the ſeparated particles of the body; and that the air paſſing in the flame of my ſtove, and in the flame of a candle, being already ſaturated with ſuch particles, could not receive more, and therefore left the coal undiminiſhed as long as the outward air was prevented from coming to it by the ſurrounding flame, which kept it in a ſituation ſomewhat like that of charcoal in a well luted crucible, which, though long kept in a ſtrong fire, comes out unconſumed.

An

An eafy experiment will fatisfy any one of this con-
ferving power of flame envelloping red coal. Take a fmall
ftick of deal or other wood the fize of a goofe quill, and
hold it horizontally and fteadily in the flame of the candle above the wick, without touching it, but in the body
of the flame. The wood will firft be inflamed, and burn
beyond the edge of the flame of the candle, perhaps a
quarter of an inch. When the flame of the wood goes out,
it will leave a red coal at the end of the ftick, part of which
will be in the flame of the candle and part out in the air.
In a minute or two you will perceive the coal in the air
diminifh gradually, fo as to form a neck; while the part
in the flame continues of its firft fize, and at length the
neck being quite confumed it drops off; and by rolling it
between your fingers when extinguifhed you will find it
ftill a folid coal.

However, as one cannot be always putting on frefh fuel
in this ftove to furnifh a continual flame as is done in a
candle, the air in the intervals of time gets at the red coals
and confumes them. Yet the confervation while it lafted,
fo much delayed the confumption of the coals, that two
fires, one made in the morning, and the other in the afternoon, each made by only a hatfull of coals, were fufficient to keep my writing room, about fixteen feet fquare and
ten high, warm a whole day. The fire kindled at feven in
the morning would burn till noon ; and all the iron of
the machine with the walls of the niche being thereby
heated, the room kept warm till evening, when another
fmaller fire kindled kept it warm till midnight.

Inftead of the fliding plate E, which fhuts the front of the
box C, I fometimes ufed another which had a pane of glafs,
or, which is better, of Mufcovy talc, that the flame might be
feen defcending from the bottom of the vafe and paffing in a
column through the box C, into the cavities of the bottom
plate, like water falling from a funnel, admirable to fuch
as are not acquainted with the nature of the machine, and
in itfelf a pleafing fpectacle.   Every

Every utenſil, however properly contrived to ſerve its purpoſe, requires ſome practice before it can be uſed adroitly. Put into the hands of a man for the firſt time, a gimblet or a hammer, (very ſimple inſtruments) and tell him the uſe of them, he ſhall neither bore a hole or drive a nail with the dexterity or ſucceſs of another who has been a little accuſtomed to handle them. The beginner therefore in the uſe of this machine, will do well not to be diſcouraged with little accidents that may ariſe at firſt from his want of experience. Being ſomewhat complex, it requires as already ſaid a variety of attentions; habit will render them unneceſſary. And the ſtudious man who is much in his chamber, and has a pleaſure in managing his own fire, will ſoon find this a machine moſt comfortable and delightful. To others who leave their fires to the care of ignorant ſervants, I do not recommend it. They will with difficulty acquire the knowledge neceſſary, and will make frequent blunders that will fill your room with ſmoke. It is therefore by no means fit for common uſe in families. It may be adviſeable to begin with the flaming kind of ſtone coal, which is large, and, not caking together, is not ſo apt to clog the grate. After ſome experience, any kind of coal may be uſed, and with this advantage, that no ſmell, even from the moſt ſulphurous kind can come into your room, the current of air being conſtantly into the vaſe, where too that ſmell is all conſumed.

The vaſe form was choſen as being elegant in itſelf, and very proper for burning of coals: Where wood is the uſual fuel, and muſt be burnt in pieces of ſome length, a long ſquare cheſt may be ſubſtituted, in which A is the cover opening by a hinge behind, B the grate, C the Plate 2. Figure 17. hearth box with its diviſions as in the other, D the plan of the cheſt, E the long narrow grate. This I have not tried, but the vaſe machine was compleated in 1771, and uſed by me in London three winters, and one afterwards in America, much to my ſatisfaction; and I have not yet thought

thought of any improvement it may be capable of, though
fuch may occur to others.   For common ufe, while in
France, I have contrived another grate for coals, which has
in part the fame property of burning the fmoke and preferving the red coals longer by the flame, though not fo
completely, as in the vafe, yet fufficiently to be very
ufeful, which I fhall now defcribe as follows.

A, is a round grate, one foot (French) in dia-   Plate 2.
meter, and eight inches deep between the bars and   Figure 18.
the back; the fides and back of plate iron; the fides having holes of half an inch diameter diftant 3 or 4 inches from
each other, to let in air for enlivening the fire.   The back
without holes.   The fides do not meet at top nor at bottom by eight inches: that fquare is filled by grates of fmall
bars croffing front to back to let in air below, and let out
the fmoke or flame above.   The three middle bars of the
front grate are fixed, the upper and lower may be taken
out and put in at pleafure, when hot, with a pair of pincers.
This round grate turns upon an axis, fupported by the
crotchet B, the ftem of which is an inverted conical tube
five inches deep, which comes on as many inches upon a
pin that fits it, and which is fixed upright in a caft iron
plate D, that lies upon the hearth; in the middle of the top
and bottom grates are fixed fmall upright pieces E E about
an inch high, which as the whole is turned on its axis ftop
it when the grate is perpendicular.   Figure 19 is another
view of the fame machine.

In making the firft fire in a morning with this grate,
there is nothing particular to be obferved.   It is made as
in other grates, the coals being put in above, after taking
out the upper bar, and replacing it when they are in.   The
round figure of the fire when thoroughly kindled is agreeable, it reprefents the great giver of warmth to our fyftem.
As it burns down and leaves a vacancy above, which you
would fill with frefh coals, the upper bar is to be taken
out, and afterwards replaced.   The frefh coals while the

grate

grate continues in the same position, will throw up as usual a body of thick smoke. But every one accustomed to coal fires in common grates, must have observed that pieces of fresh coal stuck in below among the red coals have their smoke so heated as that it becomes flame as fast as it is produced, which flame rises among the coals and enlivens the appearance of the fire. Here then is the use of this swivel grate. By a push with your tongs or poker, you turn it on its pin till it faces the back of the chimney, then turn it over on its axis gently till it again faces the room, whereby all the fresh coals will be found under the live coals, and the greater part of the smoke arising from the fresh coals will in its passage through the live ones be heated so as to be converted into flame : Whence you have much more heat from them, and your red coals are longer preserved from consuming. I conceive this construction, though not so complete a consumer of all the smoke as the vase, yet to be fitter for common use, and very advantageous. It gives too a full sight of the fire, always a pleasing object, which we have not in the other. It may with a touch be turned more or less from any one of the company that desires to have less of its heat, or presented full to one just come out of the cold. And supported in a horizontal position, a tea-kettle may be boiled on it.

The author's description of his Pennsylvania fire-place, first published in 1744, having fallen into the hands of workmen in Europe, who did not, it seems, well comprehend the principles of that machine, it was much disfigured in their imitations of it; and one of its main intentions, that of admitting a sufficient quantity of fresh air warmed in entering through the air-box, nearly defeated, by a pretended improvement, in lessening its passages to make more room for coals in a grate. On pretence of such improvements, they obtained patents for the invention, and for a while made great profit by the sale, till the public became sensible of that defect, in the ex-

K   pected

pected operation. If the fame thing fhould be attempted
with this vafe ftove, it will be well for the buyer to examine thoroughly fuch pretended improvements, left, being the mere productions of ignorance, they diminifh or
defeat the advantages of the machine, and produce inconvenience and difappointment.

The method of burning fmoke, by obliging it to defcend
through hot coals, may be of great ufe in heating the
walls of a hot-houfe. In the common way, the horizontal paffages or flues that are made to go and return in thofe
walls, lofe a great deal of their effect when they come to
be foul with foot; for a thick blanket-like lining of foot
prevents much of the hot air from touching and heating
the brick work in its paffage, fo that more fire muft be
made as the flue grows fouler: But by burning the fmoke
they are kept always clean. The fame method may alfo
be of great advantage to thofe bufineffes in which large
coppers or caldrons are to be heated..

Written at Sea, 1785.

N° VII.

A Theory of Lightening and Thunder Storms, by ANDREW
OLIVER, *Efq. of Salem in the State of Maffachufetts.*

Read Janu-
ary, 1774.
IT has been generally, and, confidering the phenomena themfelves, very naturally fuppofed,
that the electric charges which are exhibited in repeated
flafhes of lightening during a thunder ftorm, are previoufly
accumulated in the vapors which conftitute the cloud; and
that thefe vapors, when by any means they become either
over-charged with electric matter, or are deprived of their
natural

natural quantities of it*, difcharge their furplufage to, or receive the neceffary fupplies from, either the earth or the neighbouring clouds, in fucceffive explofions, till an equilibrium is reftored between them. But I fhall endeavour in the following pages to prove, that thefe charges refide, not in the cloud or vapors of which it confifts, but in the air which fuftains them ; and that, previous to the formation of the cloud, or even the afcent of the vapors of which it is formed. But, in order to convey my ideas upon this fubject with perfpicuity, I find it neceffary to introduce them with a quotation from doctor *Franklin*'s letters on electricity, in which the doctor compares water, whether in its natural ftate, or rarefied into vapors, to a fponge ; and the electric fluid, in connection with it, to water applied to the fponge.

" When a fponge (fays he) is fomewhat condenfed by " being fqueezed between the fingers, it will not receive " and retain fo much water as when it is in its more loofe " and open ftate. If more fqueezed and condenfed, fome " of the water will come out of its inner parts, and flow " on the furface. If the preffure of the fingers be intire- " ly removed, the fponge will not only refume what was " lately forced out, but attract an additional quantity. As " the fponge in its rarer ftate will *naturally* attract and " abforb *more* water ; and in its denfer ftate will *naturally* " attract and abforb *lefs* water ; we may call the quantity " it abforbs in either ftate, its *natural quantity*, the ftate " being confidered."

The doctor then fuppofes, " that what the fponge is to " water, the fame is water to the electric fluid ;—that " when a portion of water is in its common denfe ftate, " it can hold no more electric fluid than it has ; if any be " added it fpreads upon the furface." He adds, " when " the fame portion of water is rarefied into vapor and forms

K 2 " a cloud,

---

* A body is faid to be electrically charged, whenever it has either *more* or *lefs* than its natural quantity of electric matter.

" a cloud, it is then capable of receiving and abforbing a
" much greater quantity, as there is room for each parti-
" cle to have an electric atmofphere.   Thus water in its
" rarefied ftate, or in the form of a cloud, will be in a
" negative ftate of electricity ; it will have lefs than its
" *natural quantity*, that is, lefs than it is naturally .capable
" of attracting and abforbing in that ftate*."

The foregoing paffages I have copied *verbatim* from
that celebrated electrician, as I purpofe in the courfe of this
effay to avail myfelf of his idea of the fponge, in order to
illuftrate a different theory of thunder clouds, which I now
beg leave, though with diffidence of my own judgment,
and with all due deference to that of fo great a man, to
fubftitute in the room of the foregoing ; which I muft confefs at firft fight carries great appearance of probability
with it, and is highly corroborated by the curious and
beautiful experiment the doctor made with the filver cann,
brafs chain, and lock of cotton†.

But in reading doctor *Prieftley*'s hiftory of electricity,
fome thoughts of fignior *Beccaria* occurred, which fatisfied me that this hypothefis, however ingenious and plau-
fible, was infufficient for the purpofe of accounting for the
rife and phenomena of thunder ftorms, the frequent extent and violence of which feem to require a more general
caufe than that hinted above, to fupply them with fufficient
quantities of electric matter.

" Confidering the vaft quantity of electric fire that ap-
" pears in the moft fimple thunder ftorms (fays doctor
" Prieftly‡) fignior *Beccaria* thinks it impoffible that any
" cloud, or number of clouds, fhould ever contain it all,
" fo as either to difcharge or receive it.   Befides, during
" the progrefs and increafe of the ftorm, though the light-
" ening frequently ftruck to the earth, the fame clouds
" were

---

* Franklin's Letters, page 119.
† Page 121.
‡ Prieftley's Hiftory of Electricity, page 325.

" were the next moment ready to make a ftill greater dif-
" charge, and his apparatus continued to be as much af-
" fected as ever. The clouds muft confequently have *re-*
" *ceived* at one place the moment that a *difcharge* was
" made from them in another."

Signior *Beccaria* accounts for this vaft exhibition of
electric fire from a thunder cloud, by fuppofing that fome
parts of the earth may become more highly charged with
the electric fluid than others, and that great quantities of
it do fometimes rufh out of particular parts, and rife through
the air into the higher regions of the atmofphere; other
parts of the earth becoming cafually deftitute of their natural quantity of the fluid at the fame time, and ready to
receive it: That a chain of clouds nearly contiguous, or
a fingle cloud extending from one of thefe regions to another, in an oppofite ftate, might ferve as a conductor or
conductors to reftore the electric equilibrium between them,
which would equally caufe thunder and lightening in both
regions, and throughout the intermediate clouds*. Here
doctor *Prieftley* juftly obferves, that " the greateft difficul-
" ty attending this theory of the origin of thunder ftorms
" relates to the *collection* and *infulation* of electric matter
" within the body of the earth." With regard to the *collection*, the doctor obferves that his author " has nothing
" particularly to fay:" Nor indeed without a previous *infulation* of thofe parts of the earth which may be concerned in the production of the phenomena, can any fuch *collection* take place. Now if we confider that in order to
have two regions of the earth thus infulated, and of fufficient dimenfions, one to fupply, and the other to receive
the quantities of electric fire difcharged during one thunder ftorm of any extent and continuance, the parts infulated muft be not fuperficial regions, but muft reach to a
confiderable depth; and we muft fuppofe, with doctor
Prieftley, " that the electric matter which forms and ani-
" mates the thunder cloud, iffues from places far below
" the

* Ibid.

" the furface of the earth, and that it buries itfelf there*." But, with deference to the judgment of that unwearied friend to fcience, I apprehend that fuch an infulation is hardly confiftent with that diftribution of conductors, efpecially of water, which provident nature has made through all parts of our globe; the higheft mountains being furnifhed with *internal* fprings and fountains, and watered *externally* by rivulets, which derive their origin from condenfing mifts or melting fnows upon their fummits : While the furface of the earth in general, not excepting the moft fandy deferts, affords fupplies of water to thofe who will be at the pains of digging for it.   If then the vapors which conftitute the cloud are, of themfelves, incapable of furnifhing fuch quantities of electric matter as are neceffary for the repeated difcharges in a fevere thunder ftorm, as fignior *Beccaria* thinks they are, and as feems to me indubitable ; and if the infulations of large portions of the furface or exterior parts of the earth, which are abfolutely neceffary to fupport *Beccaria*'s hypothefis, cannot take place ; which, how they can in our terraqueous mafs, is difficult to conceive, confiftently with the *hitherto* difcovered properties of the electric fluid : We muft feek for fome other fubftance in nature which may be capable of affording thofe reiterated fupplies, of that powerful element which are ufually exhibited in a thunder ftorm.   This I prefume, we fhall find in the atmofphere over our heads; not in the *vapors* which float therein, but in the *air* itfelf which fuftains them.

Air is by electricians juftly claffed with *electric* fubftances, as it poffeffes the fame general properties in common with others of that denomination, particular inftances of which may occur in the following pages ; wherein I fhall endeavour to prove,

I. That the *electric capacity* of air is leffened by condenfation.

II. That *this* capacity is increafed by heat.

Premifing

* Prieftley, page 335.

Premifing that by *air* I here intend *that* fluid in its common compreffed ftate with us near the furface of the earth; and by its *electric capacity*, that ftate of it which difpofes it, under any circumftances whatever, " to attract, abforb and retain," what doctor *Franklin* calls its *natural quantity*, or the quantity which is *natural* to it in that ftate.

I. I fhall endeavour to prove that the *electric capacity* of air is leffened by condenfation.

That a change of denfity in air produces alfo a change in its electric capacity (as above defined), follows from fome experiments of monfieur de *Faye* and doctor *Prieftley*, the former of whom found, upon repeated trials, that no electricity could be excited by the friction of a glafs tube in which the air was condenfed*. The doctor, repeating the experiments with fome variation, found, that when one additional atmofphere was forced into the tube, the electricity excited by rubbing it was fcarcely difcernable. Now, though the effect was a fufpenfion of the operation of the excited tube *without*, the caufe was evidently the condenfed ftate of the air *within;* which may be accounted for if we confider, that although it is certain from many experiments that glafs is abfolutely impermeable to the electric fluid, infomuch that it cannot force its way through a pane of glafs, or the fides of a phial, without breaking the glafs, as was the cafe in thofe fpontaneous difcharges of feveral of the jars in the electrical battery mentioned by doctor *Prieftley†;* yet it is as certain, that this impermeability of the glafs to the fluid itfelf, is no obftruction to the operation of that repellent power upon which the vifible effects of this element feem principally to depend; which power undeniably acts from one fide of the glafs, through the very fubftance of it, upon the fame fluid on the other fide, provided there be any other fubftance on that fide capable of receiving it when thus repelled.

This is the cafe in the *Leyden* experiment in every form in which it can be made; the charge given to one fide of the

* Page 50.　† Page 487.

the glaſs, repelling and throwing off an equal quantity of
the electric fluid from the oppoſite ſurface, through the
non-electric coating in contact with it; nor can any charge
be given to either ſide without a proportional diſcharge
from the other. In like manner, when an uncoated tube
is excited by friction, a quantity of the fluid, equal to that
which is excited and condenſed upon the outer ſurface, is
thrown out from the inner, provided there is any ſubſtance within in a capacity to receive and abſorb it, without which no excitation can take place. " A glaſs tube,
" out of which the air is exhauſted, diſcovers no ſigns of
" electricity outwards*," there being no ſubſtance within
capable of receiving and abſorbing the fluid from the inner ſurface, which though repelled from it inwards during the operation, yet returns to it again inſtantly upon a
ceſſation of the action of the rubber without. But upon
a readmiſſion of air the excitation is eaſy, and is attended
with the uſual effects. Air then, which is the only ſubſtance admitted (excepting perhaps a few ſtraggling vapors which float in it) receives and abſorbs a ſufficient
quantity of the electric fluid from the inner ſurface to permit an excitation of the tube which contains it. But as
we have ſeen that air, when condenſed within, prevents
the viſible effects of an excitation, equally with a total va-
cuity, we may adopt the idea of doctor *Franklin, mutatis
mutandis,* and conlcude that " what the ſponge is to water
" the ſame is *air* to the electric fluid:" At leaſt that this capacity of air if leſſened by condenſation in a manner, not
indeed perfectly ſimilar, but, ſomewhat analogous to that in
which the capacity of a ſponge to receive and retain water
is leſſened by compreſſion. Agreeably to which idea, the
condenſed air within the tube, having its electric capacity
filled and even crowded with the electric matter, will receive none from the inner ſurface, which, on the contrary,
is thereby prevented from being forced out of it, without
which

---

* Prieſtley's hiſtory of electricity, page 55c.

which none can be forced into or condenfed upon the outer furface, fo as to exhibit any figns of electricity; as obferved before,

II. I fhall endeavour to prove that the electric capacity
of air is increafed by heat.

This alfo appears probable, at leaft, from the above cited
experiments of doctor *Prieftley* ; for after the air in his
tube had had this capacity fo far diminifhed by condenfation as not to permit an excitation without, that capacity,
together with the confequent excitability of the tube, was
reftored by the action of heat upon the included air. " Re-
" peating my attempts (fays he) to excite the tube above
" mentioned, I found that, after very hard rubbing, it be-
" gan to act a little, and that its virtue increafed with the
" labour. Thinking it might be the warmth which pro-
" duced this effect, I held the tube to the fire and found
" that when it was pretty hot, it would act almoft as well
" as when it contained no more than its ufual quantity
" of air*."

In page 553, doctor *Prieftley* tells us that fome of his
electrical friends were of opinion, " that the reafon why
" a tube with condenfed air in it cannot be excited is, that
" the denfe air within prevents the electric fluid from be-
" ing forced out of the infide of the tube, without which
" none can be forced into the outfide; and that heating
" the tube makes the air within lefs electrical." That is,
as I conceive their meaning, puts it in a capacity to receive and abforb more of the electric fluid than it could
otherwife do in that condenfed ftate. The doctor indeed
queries by way of objection to the foregoing folution,—
" How upon this principle can a folid ftick of glafs be ex-
" cited ?" To which I would anfwer, that poffibly, when
a folid ftick of glafs is excited, as much of the electric fluid
may be drawn out of one fide of it as is thrown into, or condenfed upon the other; if fo, although it may fhew equal
figns of electricity on both fides, yet one fide will be in a

                            L   pofitive

* Page 551.

positive, the other in a negative state; when it will exactly resemble the curious stone called the *tourmalin*, by
some *lapis electricus*, which doctor *Priestley* says * " has
" always, *at the same time*, a positive and a negative elec-
" tricity; one of its sides being in one state, and the other
" in the opposite;" which does not depend upon the external form " of the stone." But the truth of this solution must be determined by future experiments.

That the electrical state of the air is liable to be affected
by heat, is further evident from a course of experiments
which were made by the abbé *Mazeas*, with an apparatus
that was constructed solely with a view of determining the
electricity of the atmosphere, anno 1753 †. With this apparatus the abbé observed, that from the 17th of June, when
he began his experiments, the electricity of the air was
sensibly felt every day, *from sun rise till seven or eight
o'clock in the evening*, when the weather was *dry*; but
that in the driest *nights* of that summer he could discover
no signs of electricity in the air, nor till the morning,
when the sun began to appear above the horizon, and
that " they vanished again in the evening, about half an
" hour after sun set;" and further, " that the *strongest*
" common electricity of the atmosphere, during the sum-
" mer, was perceived in the month of *July* on a *very dry*
" day, the heavens being very clear, and the sun *extreme-*
" *ly hot.*"

Now, as this electricity of the air was sensible only during *day light*, no electricity being discoverable therein even
in the *driest nights*, and as the air exhibited the *strongest*
signs of electricity when the sun shone *extremely hot*; is
not the conclusion unavoidable, that heat somehow affects
the electric capacity of air, either enlarging it, and thereby disposing the air to attract, receive and absorb greater
quantities of electric matter than it is capable of absorbing
in its natural state; or superadding to its *natural quantity*
more than it can absorb, and thereby disposing it to throw
off

* Page 299.   † Page 342.

off the redundancy upon any objects which may be in a fituation to receive it ? One or the other feems neceffarily to follow, but the former is moft agreeable to doctor *Prieftley*'s experiment of the condenfed air in the tube above mentioned, and is perfectly confonant with the obfervations of doctor *Franklin*, Mr. *Kinnerfley* and others, that thunder clouds are generally in the *negative* ftate of electricity*. But more upon this head hereafter. I would however obferve here, that many, and perhaps all other electric fubftances, even the moft firm and folid, as well as air, are liable to have their electric capacities thus diverfified by heat, more particularly the tourmalin above mentioned. But as, in treating of the properties of this ftone, doctor *Prieftley* has thought it deferving of a diftinct fection in his electric hiftory, to that I fhall refer the reader for a particular account of them †; wherein he will find a difcovery made by Meffrs *Canton* and *Wilfon*, that thefe properties are not peculiar to the tourmalin, but that many gems have a natural difpofition to afford the fame appearances ; from whence we may conclude as above, by analogy, that all electric fubftances are, more or lefs, affected in like manner, by the fame caufe. But to return to the fubject.

If from the foregoing confiderations the reader fhould be fatisfied, that the *electric capacity* of air, in its condenfed ftate in the lower regions of the atmofphere, is liable to be diminifhed by a further condenfation, and that, *cæteris paribus*, it is increafed by heat *et vice verfa ;* the folution of the phenomena of thunder and lightening, to his fatisfaction, upon electrical principles, will perhaps be no difficult tafk.

For let us conceive a region of the atmofphere, extending over a large tract of country, to be rarefied and heat-

ed

---

* Epitome of Phil. Tranf. Gent. Mag. Sept. 1773, page 447. Mr. Henley thinks cold electrifies the atmofphere pofitively, and thence conjectures that heat electrifies it negatively. His conclufions are founded upon a courfe of experiments.
† Page 297.

ed during a hot fummer's day, not only by the paffage of the fun's direct rays through it, and by the reflectinoof thofe rays from the furface of the earth into it; but chiefly, by the communication of the heat acquired by that furface to it : The *electric capacity* of that region of air would be increafed, both on account of the heat it undergoes, and of the rarefaction confequent upon that heat : It will then have lefs than its *natural quantity*, or the quantity it is *naturally* difpofed to receive and abforb in that ftate; it will confequently be, in the language of electricians, *negatively* electrified, or in a craving ftate, requiring and forcing fupplies from all fubftances capable of affording them, provided it be itfelf in a condition to receive them. But, however craving, it cannot receive thofe fupplies from the neighbouring regions of the atmofphere, while thofe regions feverally remain in the ftate of pure air, even fuppofing the latter to poffefs more than their *natural quantities*, and thereby as much difpofed to impart, as the former is to receive them, without the intervention of non-electric conductors; and that, owing to the impermeability of air, as fuch, to the electric fluid. This I fhall endeavour, 1. To illuftrate by experiments made with glafs. 2. To prove by experiments made upon air itfelf.

1. If a pane of glafs be coated on both fides, by the application of plates of tin to them, the glafs may be charged in the fame manner as the *Leyden* phial ; when, after the removal of the plates, no difcharge having previoufly taken place, both fides of the glafs will remain charged, one pofitively, the other negatively; the former having more than its *natural quantity*, the latter being proportionably deficient, and in a craving ftate. Thefe ftates both furfaces will obftinately maintain for a long time : Nor do I know of any method of reftoring the electric equilibrium between them, but, either to immerfe the pane in water or fome other non-electric fluid, which will do it inftantly, and filently; or to reapply the metalline coatings to both

fides

fides as they were placed at firft, with a good conductor
introduced between them, which will anfwer the fame purpofe, and be attended with an explofion, or fmart fpark
and fnap ; or laftly, to place it in a fituation where it may
be expofed to air replete with moift vapors, where, after
fome time, the vapors will, by condenfing upon each fide,
furnifh it with a moifture equivalent to a non-electric coating, while the vapors which remain in the furrounding
air will, by continually impinging upon and receding from
the two furfaces, at length reftore both to their natural
ftate.

It is evident from the foregoing experiment, *Firft*, That
the charges refide in the glafs itfelf, as they remain after
the coatings are removed. *Secondly*, That the oppofite fides
have a very ftrong propenfity, one to give, the other to receive the fluid, and thereby to reftore the electric equilibrium between themfelves; which is done with violence,
as obferved above, when they are put in a condition of doing it by the reapplication of the metalline coatings, with
a conductor between them, and *Laftly*, That notwithftanding the violent propenfity in the fides of the glafs, to reftore themfelves and each other to their natural electric
ftates, and the fmall diftance between them, they can never effect it, without the intervention of non-electric conductors.

2. I fhall now fhew by other experiments, that different
regions or ftrata of air *may* become charged, both pofitively and negatively, in the fame manner as the fides of
the pane of glafs were in the foregoing; and that the
effects of fuch charges are precifely the fame.

Meffrs *Wilkie* and *Æpinus* at *Berlin*, having the hint
naturally fuggefted to them by a previous courfe of experiments, endeavoured to give the electrical fhock by means
of *air*, in the fame manner in which it may be given by
glafs; " in which after making feveral attempts (fays doc-
" tor Prieftley*) they at length fucceeded, by fufpending
" large

* Page 242.

" large boards of wood covered with tin, with the flat fides
" towards one another, and at fome inches afunder. For
" they found, that upon electrifying one of the boards
" pofitively, the other was always negative. But the dif-
" covery was made complete and indifputable by a perfon's
" touching one of the plates with one hand, and bringing
" his other hand to the other plate; for he then received
" a fhock through his body exactly like that of the *Ley-*
" *den* experiment. With this plate of air, as we may call
" it, they made a variety of experiments. The two me-
" tal plates, being in oppofite ftates, ftrongly attracted one
" another, and would have rufhed together if they had
" not been kept afunder by the ftrings. Sometimes the
" electricity of both would be difcharged by a ftrong fpark
" between them, as when a pane of glafs burfts with too
" great a charge. A finger put between them promoted
" the difcharge, and felt the fhock. If an eminence was
" made on either of the plates the felf-difcharge would al-
" ways be made through it, and a pointed body fixed up-
" on either of them prevented their being charged at all."

To the foregoing relation of the experiments themfelves,
I fhall fubjoin the conclufions drawn from them by the curious electricians who made them, in the words of doctor
Prieftley, viz. " The ftate of thefe two plates, they " (*Wil-*
kie and *Æpinus*) " excellently obferve, juftly reprefents the
" ftate of the clouds and the earth" (and perhaps of different clouds at various heights one over another) " dur-
" ing a thunder ftorm; the clouds being always in one
" ftate, and the earth in the oppofite; while the body of
" air between them anfwers the fame purpofe as the fmall
" plate of air between the boards, or the plate of glafs be-
" tween the two metal coatings in the *Leyden* experiment.
" The phenomenon of lightening is the burfting of the
" plate of air by a fpontaneous difcharge, which is always
" made through eminencies, and the bodies through which
" the difcharge is made are violently fhocked."

As

As in the former experiment made with the pane of glaſs, the charges, both poſitive and negative, reſide in the glaſs itſelf, and not in the coatings, thoſe remaining after theſe are removed; ſo in the latter, which is completely analogous to it, the charges are accumulated and reſide in the air ſituated between the boards, and not in their tin linings, which ſerve only as conductors, to diſtribute the fluid equally over, or to convey it equally from, the whole ſurface of air which is limited by, and in contact with them, on either ſide; whereby the whole of each ſurface may be equally charged at the ſame time, or diſcharged by the ſame exploſion.

If two or more regions of the atmoſphere, when free from vapors, become thus differently electrical in their ſtate and capacities, which, that they may, from the heat and conſequent rarefaction in a ſummer's day, we have already ſeen, and perhaps from a variety of other cauſes to us unknown; and if from the contrary currents of air which frequently take place at different heights, they ſhould perchance become ſituated one over or adjacent to another, like ſtrata of minerals within the bowels of the earth; what the metalline coating is to the pane of glaſs, or the tinned boards to the plate of air in the laſt experiment, the ſame would clouds, formed and floating therein, be to theſe regions of air; the electric equilibrium between which might be reſtored through their intervention, either by ſpontaneous diſcharges through the pure air between them in ſevere flaſhes of lightening or through the falling drops of rain, which in their ſucceſſive deſcent form a chain of natural conductors between one region of the air and another, and betwixt each of them and the earth; the paſſage of the electric fluid through which would alſo be attended with lightening and thunder, but not ſo ſevere as when the diſcharge is made through the pure air; the moſt fatal lightening uſually preceding the fall of the rain.

It

It is not uncommon, during the rife and progrefs of a
thunder ftorm, to fee different fets of clouds, at various
heights in the atmofphere, moving promifcuoufly in all
directions, as though they were impelled hither and thither by contending winds; when probably the whole phenomenon arifes from the different electrical ftates of the
regions of the air in which they float; as they approach
one or other of which, they are attracted or repelled, and
move accordingly, communicating, receiving, or tranfmitting the electric fluid, to or from them refpectively, as they
may be either deficient of their natural quantity, or poffefs
a redundancy of this fluid.   And as in the experiment of
Meffrs *Wilkie* and *Æpinus* mentioned above, the two tin
plates with the boards they covered, would have rufhed
together had they not been kept afunder by the ftrings, fo
thefe clouds floating freely in air, and being at liberty
to act upon every impulfe, gradually coalefce, reftoring
the electric equilibrium to the neighbouring atmofphere
by repeated difcharges as they unite*; till at length they
form one denfe mafs of humid vapors, which precipitating
in a heavy fhower of rain, refrefh the thirfty foil, leaving
the atmofphere above in a homogenous electric ftate, calm
and ferene.

How thefe clouds are generated, formed, and adapted
to thofe grand purpofes in the œconomy of nature, is next
to be confidered: In profecution of which inquiries I fhall
fubmit the following obfervations to the candor of the
reader.

Whatever the immediate caufe of evaporation may be,
it is certain that the fuperficial moifture of all bodies is
perpetually exhaling in vapors, which afcend into the
higher regions of the atmofphere, where they gather and
are formed into clouds, and at length recondenfe, defcending

---

* It is certain that in moft thunder ftorms the flafhes of lightening are chiefly difcharged
from cloud to cloud, very few, and frequently none at all taking place between the cloud and
the earth.

ing in dew, mift or rain upon the furface of the earth from whence they fprang.

Thefe vapors are either detached in ftreams from the humid ground by the influence of the fun, or thrown off by the perfpirations of thofe infinite multitudes of animals and plants which cover the face of the earth*, or fupplied by evaporation, from the ocean, or other grand collections of water.

Ignorant as we are of the nature of thefe operations, and of the manner in which they are performed, it is natural to fuppofe, that the vapors themfelves afcend in the fame electric ftate, whether pofitive, neutral or negative, with the fubftances from which they arife. Accordingly fignior *Beccaria*, in making fome of his experiments, obferved, that " fteam rifing from an electrified eolipile diffufes it-" felf with the fame uniformity with which thunder clouds " fpread themfelves and fwell into arches, extending itfelf " towards any conducting fubftance†." This ftream then was electrified as well as the eolipile from whence it proceeded. The fea muft neceffarily be fuppofed, in common with the whole terraqueous mafs, to contain juft its natural quantity of the electric fluid, and no more: We may therefore conclude that both the vapors which arife immediately from it, and the air which fuftains them, and from its fituation enjoys a more equable temperature, than that over the land, are in the fame electrical ftate with the fea itfelf, containing neither *more* nor *lefs* than their *natural quantity*.

Confidering the vaft extent of the ocean, and the comparatively fmall degree of moifture of which the dry land is fufceptible, we may conclude, that a very fmall proportion of the clouds which are formed in the atmofphere are exhaled from the latter, and that the ocean is the grand fource from whence they principally derive their origin.

M   Our

---

* See *Hales's* vegetable ftatics, and Chambers's *cyclopes*, under the word, Perfpiration.
† Prieftley's Hiftory, page 327.

Our fenfes accordingly convince us that the fea-air is always replete with moift vapors, even when its natural
tranfparency is not in the leaft interrupted by them.
Hence in a hot fummer's day, when the wind fuddenly
fhifts from weft to eaft, we immediately perceive a chill
from the fea-breeze; and fometimes long before the thermometer indicates a change in the temperature of the
atmofphere. Thefe vapors, when they firft arife from the
fea, are generally fo nearly of the fame denfity with the
furrounding and contiguous air, that the rays of light in
paffing through them, undergo no fenfible change in their
refraction; they are therefore at firft generally invifible,
but when the weather is extreamly cold, and the air of
confequence uncommonly denfe, they are always vifible,
and appear like a fteam arifing from boiling water*. Not
that vapors afcend moft copioufly in the coldeft feafons,
which feems contrary both to reafon and experience; but
that the different denfities of the air next the furface of the
water, and of the vapors which afcend in it, render the
latter vifible, by the irregular refractions of the rays of
light in paffing through them. For the fame reafon our
breath is vifible in the winter, but not in warm weather.

Let us now fuppofe the atmofphere, on a fummer's
morning, to be all around in a homogenous ftate, as indicated by a cloudlefs fky and a dead calm. As the fun
rifes on the eaftern coafts of America, and warms and rarefies the atmofphere eaftward, the rarefied air naturally
afcends, and a current of air as naturally flows thither from
the oppofite quarter, which is but juft emerging from the
cool fhades of night, to fupply its place. The confequence
of which is a light wefterly breeze. As the fun afcends
higher, the air over the land becomes heated and rarefied,
both by the paffage of the fun's direct and reflected rays
through it, and by the reverberation of the heat acquired
from

---

* This is always the appearance in a clear, ftill morning, when the mercury in Farenheit's
thermometer is at o, or below it.

from them by the furface of the earth; till at length that whole region of the atmofphere has its electrical capacity enlarged, thereby becoming negatively electrifed, or in a craving ftate, as obferved before. On the contrary the fun's rays which fall upon the furface of the fea, efpecially when ruffled by wind, chiefly enter that tranfparent medium, in which they are refracted and irrecoverably abforbed; very few, comparatively, being reflected; whence very little heat can be reverberated from that element to warm the incumbent air, which is fenfibly affected only by the paffage of the fun's direct rays through it, unlefs the weather be calm and the furface very fmooth*. Befides, it is colder at fea than afhore in the fummer feafon, when, and when only thunder fhowers are frequent, and indeed warmer in the winter, for the following reafon, viz. as the fea is every moment changing its furface, neither heat nor cold can affect it fo foon as they do the furface of the earth, which continues the fame.

The air over the land, when thoroughly heated and rarefied, naturally afcends into the higher regions, while the denfer air from the fea neceffarily flows in and takes its place. Hence, probably, the eafterly winds which ufually fpring up near the middle of the day, after a fultry morning.

This body of warm air afcends till it arrives at that region of the atmofphere in which thunder clouds are formed; while the vapors which are wafted to the continent by the eaftern current, being attracted by this now fuperior air which demands a fupply of the electric fluid, con-

M 2 tinually

---

* In a perfect calm the furface of the fea acts like a mirror upon the fun's rays, ftrongly reverberating them back into the atmofphere, when the heat is as fenfible upon water as upon the dry land. But whenever that furface becomes agitated and broken by the force of wind acting upon it, thofe rays, by perpetually impinging upon an infinite variety of new formed, fluctuating furfaces undergo innumerable refractions, in all directions, whereby they are abforbed and loft within the fluid mafs in fome proportion to the violence of the agitation. Accordingly when the weather is ferene and calm, the furface like a looking-glafs reflects the phenomena of the fky over head; upon the firft fpringing up of a breeze it changes to a light blue, which deepens to a fine fky-blue as the wind rifes, to a deeper fea-green in a brifk gale, and to a fullen blacknefs in a ftorm, excepting where the waves are interfperfed with white heads of foam, which, by contraft, only render the fcene more gloomy.

tinually afcend till they arrive at it, leaving the denfer air, with which they were firft connected, behind. As thefe vapors move freely through and mix with air, they eafily infinuate themfelves between the particles of that fluid, and unite with it, whereby every particle of air which, from the caufes aforefaid, is become in any degree deftitute of the quantity of electric matter which is natural to it in its prefent ftate, may and will attract and attach to itfelf one or more particles of this vapor, and thereby furnifh itfelf with a non-electric coating, and thus become qualified to receive from any neighbouring object fuch a fupply of the electric fluid as its ftate may demand.

Thus provided, this body of air, together with the vapors which are more or lefs attached to every particle of it, will conftitute a denfe cloud ; and as the air itfelf was before (by fuppofition) in a craving or negative ftate of electricity ; and as the vapors are prefumed to have arifen from the ocean in their natural or neutral ftate, the whole body of a cloud formed by them will ftill be in a negative ftate, and thereby conftitute a complete thunder cloud ; which when formed, if uniform in denfity and contexture, fhould it be attracted within the *ftriking diftance* from any object ftanding upon the earth, would have its electric equilibrium reftored at once by a flafh of lightening darting from the earth : Or fhould it pafs near another cloud in a different ftate, the flafh would reftore an equilibrium between the two clouds.

That a body of air, either in a pofitive or negative ftate of electricity, while pure, fhould be incapable of communicating its furplufage of the electric element to, or receiving fupplies from the neighbouring regions, though in a contrary ftate ; and that the fame air, when replete with watery vapors, may be reftored to an equilibrium throughout its whole extent by an inftantaneous difcharge, may yet require fome further evidence before it be admitted.

But,

But, as the particles both of air and vapor are feverally too minute to fall under our notice, I fhall endeavour to illuftrate by analogy what cannot be directly demonftrated by experiment. In order to this, I fhall firft give a general defcription of, and then fubjoin fome obfervations upon doctor *Prieftley's* electrical battery.

This battery confifted of fixty four cylindrical glafs jars fixed in a fquare box; the jars were coated within and without with tin foil, and the floor of the box was covered with the fame, whereby the outfides of all the jars formed but one continued electrical furface. In like manner, by means of fmall brafs bars extending over the mouths of the jars in their feveral ranges, and by wires which connected the feveral bars, together with others which defcended from them, communicating with the inner coating of each jar, their interior furfaces were fo connected as to form, in the fame fenfe, but one furface. Thus conftructed, the whole battery is capable of being equally charged in every part at the fame time, and of being difcharged throughout by the fame explofion.

Here I would obferve, that if, inftead of the metalline coatings, the jars were filled with water to the fame height with them, and were immerfed in the fame order in a fquare veffel of water to an equal depth, the bars and wire remaining as before, the fuccefs of all the experiments made with them would be the fame as above. Let then a battery be conftructed and charged in this form; after which let the bars and wires aforefaid be removed, and the water contained in the jars be decanted off by glafs fyphons, and let the water be drawn off from the veffel in which they ftand. It is evident from the experiment of the charged pane of glafs already mentioned, and other experiments recited in doctor Franklin's letters, that thefe jars will remain *feverally* charged, as they were *jointly* before. They may now, when dry, be taken out and handled at pleafure with fafety; nor can they be eafily reftored.

ftored to their natural ftates, but either by immerfing them fingly under water, or by replacing the whole apparatus and filling both the jars, and the box which contains them, with water as at firft, and introducing a metalline conductor betwixt the water without the jars and any one of the wires which connect their infides ; then the whole will be inftantly difcharged with an explofion*.

To apply thefe obfervations to the prefent fubject, we may regard every particle of a body of pure†, but incidentally electrified air, in the fame light with one of the jars in the battery aforefaid, which, after having been charged, is deprived of its adventitious coatings : Each particle, like one of thofe jars, will retain the ftate it may happen to be in, fo long as it remains deftitute of a conducting appendage. But when, and by what means foever, a fufficiency of moift vapors fhall become interfperfed amongft thefe particles of air to furnifh them feverally with non-electric coatings, and by the nearnefs or contiguity of thefe vapors to form a communication from one to another throughout the whole, they will then be in the fame connected ftate with the jars in the battery, when complete in every part, and charged; and like thofe jars be the particles ever fo numerous, they will be in a capacity of jointly receiving or communicating the electric fire. And as, by the addition of jars in the conftruction of the battery, the explofion at the difcharge may be increafed indefinitely, fo will the violence of the explofion from a thunder cloud be increafed in proportion to its extent, and to the multitude of aerial particles together with their appendant vapors of which it confifts, and which are fo connected as to be capable of uniting in the fame difcharge. But as a thunder cloud is not ufually formed at once, but by degrees, fmaller clouds generally forming themfelves

in

---

* Thefe experiments I never faw particularly made, but the conclufions neceffarily follow from fome which I have feen, as well as from thofe pointed out above.

† Pure as to the purpofes of electricity, or free from conducting vapors; perhaps pure elementary air is not to be found in our atmofphere.

in feparate parties before they join the main body ; and as
the electrical ftates of thefe clouds may be very different
from each other, from the different electrical ftates of
thofe parts of the atmofphere in which they gather ; the
general equilibrium of the atmofphere over a country cannot be reftored by a fingle difcharge, but fucceffive flafhes
will dart from cloud to cloud, and betwixt thefe and the
earth, till at length the whole collected mafs of vapor is
fpent and diffolved in rain.

Here a common obfervation naturally occurs, viz. that
frequently after a flafh of lightening a fudden fhower defcends in large drops. The mutual attraction between the
vapors and the air, when in this electrical ftate, is fufficient to fuftain the former, notwithftanding that they are by
this attraction greatly condenfed, being as it were forced
into a phyfical contact, both with the particles of air, and
with each other*. But as foon as the air is reftored to its
natural electric ftate by a flafh of lightening, this attraction
ceafes, and the vapors precipitate by their own fpecific
gravity in a heavy fhower.

Long and extenfive calms, in certain latitudes and feafons, take place upon the ocean, during the continuance
of which, the heat is fcarcely tolerable. (See note, page 91.)
Where thefe take place the air will naturally undergo the
fame changes, in its denfity and electric capacity, as the
air over the land does in the fummer feafon, and, when
                                                    fufficiently

---

* A gentleman of my acquaintance, who is both intelligent and curious, informed me fome
years fince, that he was once upon the top of a mountain in Spain, upon which a thunder cloud
gathered ; that as foon as the cloud became infulated from the mountain it difcharged a violent tempeft of thunder and lightening upon the plains below ; that he never was fo thoroughly foaked in the moft violent fhower as when in the body of this cloud, though without a drop
of rain, feeling as if he had been immerfed in a river. This idea is further juftified by the folid appearance of the clouds that rife in the weft on a hot fummer's day, compared with thofe
which float in the atmofphere at other feafons ; which fhews a manifeft difference in their denfity and contexture : And when we obferve attentively the feveral parts of a thunder cloud, tho
diftinctnefs of their borders and their fwelling furbeloes ; how ftrongly they reflect the rays of
the fun, thereby exhibiting the moft vivid lights and deep contrafting fhades ; and on the other
hand obferve the beautiful effects of their refractive power in the intenfe golden fkirts which
adorn the rifing cloud with a fetting fun behind it ; we muft neceffarily conclude, that, although the vapors of which fuch clouds confift are collected and condenfed in higher regions of
the atmofphere than are thofe which ufually form clouds at other feafons, yet their denfity and
fpecific gravity is much greater ; and they derive their fupport from the electric principle.

fufficiently heated and rarefied, will in like manner afcend, its place being fupplied by the denfer air from all quarters without the limits of the calm. This heated and confequently (granting the principles of the prefent theory) electrical air, when raifed to a certain height in the atmofphere, may become as well adapted to the formation of a thunder cloud, from the vapors which are perpetually exhaling from the fea, as the air over the land under the like circumftances. Wherefore, in fome latitudes in all feafons, and perhaps in all latitudes in different feafons of the year, thunder ftorms may as well happen at fea, even at remote diftances from land, as afhore.

I now proceed to confider an objection which may be raifed againft the foregoing theory, which I fhall firft ftate in its full force, and then endeavour to give a fatisfactory anfwer to it.

Objection. If the electrification of that body of air in which a thunder cloud is formed depends upon the *heat* it has previoufly acquired, whence is it that thunder ftorms are frequently attended with fhowers of hail, which hail is fometimes fo large as to indicate its defcent from the coldeft regions of the atmofphere?

Anfwer. Sir *Ifaac Newton* afferts from experiments of his own, that " the denfity of the air in the atmofphere of " the earth is as the weight of the whole *incumbent* air." Confequently the air gradually decreafes in denfity from the furface of the earth to the top of the atmofphere. The body of air which is fuppofed in this *theory* to be qualified by the action of heat upon it, to become a proper *fubftratum* for the formation and fupport of a thunder cloud, is thereby expanded and rarefied; and thence becomes fpecifically higher than it was before: It therefore afcends till it arrives at that height in the atmofphere at which the air is naturally, from its fituation, of the fame rarety with itfelf; and there it refts in equilibrio. This region is extreamly cold at all feafons, as appears from the teftimonies

of

of travellers who have visited the tops of very high mountains, even under the line. The greater the heat which this body of air acquires below, the greater degree of rarefaction it undergoes, and the higher, of consequence, it ascends in the atmosphere, where the cold is proportionably more severe than is usual near the surface of the earth. But though it was the heat which it acquired below that first rarefied and expanded it, it will by no means be proportionably recondensed by the cold which it meets with in its ascent; for as the heat which occasioned its rarefaction decreases upon that account, the pressure of the incumbent atmosphere upon it decreases as it rises, whereby its density may, upon the whole, remain nearly the same; if so, may we not suppose its electrical state also, previous to the formation of the cloud, to continue nearly the same? For should this warm air ascend all together as in a body, without intermixing with the denser surrounding air through which it rises, as a bubble of air does in any other fluid, and as *this* air probably would in a calm season, the denser parts of the atmosphere easily giving way to it, till it arrives at that region the density of which is equal to its own, where it would be at rest; should this, I say, be the case, it would not, even in that cold region, cool so suddenly as to undergo any immediate change in its electrical state, from the natural coldness of the region; neither would it be from condensation, its density remaining nearly the same, as observed above.

But when the cloud is formed, or rather when a number of clouds are forming in the neighbourhood of each other, and joining their forces preparatory to the tempest, a general confusion takes place in the atmosphere; various and even contrary currents of air flowing promiscuously hither and thither, as is evident from the visible irregular motions of detached parts of the clouds. In this general effort of nature to restore an equilibrium, some of these aerial currents will probably introduce air, which having been

N   till

till now at a diſtance from the ſcene of action, has ſuffered
no material change in its *natural* electric ſtate*; and is on
the contrary fraught with all the cold which is natural to
the region of the atmoſphere from whence it came.   In
falling through this adventitious current of air, the drops
of rain, precipitating from the body of clouds above, are
congealed into ice, and deſcend in hail, which as it falls
collects other ſnowy or icy particles round it ; a hail-ſtone
when it comes to the ground reſembling denſe ſnow with
a nucleus or kernel of ſolid ice in the middle.

That the air which this hail-ſtone falls through is colder than the region from whence it deſcends, may be thus
proved, viz. If the freezing took place where, and as ſoon
as the vapors were firſt ſet at liberty by a flaſh of lightening, it would be impoſſible for them ever to unite into
drops, but they muſt deſcend in the fineſt chryſtals, an
aſſemblage of which conſtitutes a flake of ſnow ; the nucleus, or proper hail-ſtone then muſt have been firſt a fluid
drop, and afterwards congealed in its fall through a colder
region than that in which it was formed.

It may be further objected, that a thunder cloud, in the
eaſtern parts of America, always makes its firſt appearance
in the weſt, over the land, its progreſs being *towards* the
ſea; which ſeems to contradict the ſuppoſition in the theory, that the vapors of which it conſiſts are chiefly ſuppli-
ed *from* the ſea.

To which I anſwer, 1. That a thunder cloud is with us
very rarely, indeed ſcarcely ever formed in the weſt, without a ſea-breeze ſpringing up previouſly from the eaſt,.
2. That the ſea air, as obſerved before, always abounds
with vapors, although from the cauſes already aſſigned,
they are uſually, at their firſt riſing, inviſible. 3. That the
firſt appearance of a cloud will always be where the vapors
are

* This ſuppoſition will be juſtified by conſidering, that ſuch is frequently the ſtate of the
atmoſphere, that the thunder clouds which are formed in it are but of ſmall extent; notwithſtanding which, the change in the ſtate of the air occaſioned by them is perceived to the distance of many leagues round.

are firſt collected into a body and condenſed, and thereby rendered viſible, which in a thunder cloud will be in the weſt, notwithſtanding the vapors of which it conſiſts may chiefly have ariſen from the ſea. 4. That when a thunder cloud is once formed it will be in a ſtate of attraction with the earth in general, and more eſpecially ſo with all ſubſtances which are natural conductors of the electric fluid, ſuch as the water contained in rivers, bays, arms of the ſea, &c. and by theſe the courſe of a thunder cloud is known to be very ſenſibly affected.

But the ocean is the grand object towards which its courſe will be directed; accordingly the progreſs of the clouds is from the weſtern horizon, eaſtward, be the weather below what it may, not excepting the moſt violent eaſterly ſtorms, which are ſometimes, though but rarely, accompanied with thunder and lightening.

To the foregoing obſervations I would add, 5. That when an extenſive thunder cloud is forming in the atmoſphere by means of the mutual attraction of the condenſing vapors, and the body of electrified air which ſuſtains and condenſes them, the increaſing denſity of the whole compound maſs of air and vapor will, by degrees, occaſion its redeſcent towards the earth, from the law of gravity; it will alſo be attracted by, and move towards the ocean, upon the principles of electricity; the cloud will then deſcend obliquely, in a diagonal between the directions of theſe two powers; and both, continually acting upon it, will jointly accelerate its motion. Such a cloud, if denſe and large, would end in a perfect tornado, either upon the land or water, as thunder ſhowers frequently do; ſmaller clouds being alſo, uſually, accompanied with guſts or flurries of wind.

I ſhall here add one obſervation more which I have frequently made, and which may tend to confirm the foregoing theory, viz. That as the general courſe of the eaſtern coaſt of north America is from north-eaſt to ſouth-weſt;

the

the courfe of a thunder cloud is ufually from the north-
weft, with the wind at fouth-eaft, perpendicular to the direction of the coaft, and contrary to each other.

Inland feas and great lakes, fuch as are thofe in North-
America, may anfwer the fame purpofes in the interior
parts of the country, as the ocean does near the limits of
the continent; both by affording the neceffary fupplies of
vapors for the formation of the clouds, and by their attrac-
tive influence upon thofe clouds when formed.

I now conclude with a few hints, which I fhall throw
into the form of queries.

1. Whatever the primary caufe of evaporation may be,
does not the formation of vapors into diftinct clouds depend upon the electrical ftate of the atmofphere?

2. Were the atmofphere always uniformly electrical
could we have any rain*; in that cafe, if evaporation be
performed independent of electricity, fhould we not be
invelloped in everlafting fogs?

3. Mr. *Canton* fuppofes that the *aurora borealis* may be
" the flafhing of electric fire from pofitive towards nega-
" tive clouds, throughout the upper part of the atmof-
" phere." But as the air is ufually charged more or lefs
with vapors, even when perfectly pellucid; and as the
moft remarkable *aurora* frequently appear without a cloud
in the hemifphere, may not this phenomenon be rather
occafioned by the " flafhing of electric fire," from one
region or body of air to another in a different ftate of electricity, through the intervening vapors?

4. May not the reafon of its ufual appearance in the north
and of its flafhing fouthward be, that, in every northern
latitude, the air to the fouthward is at all feafons of the
year, *cæteris paribus*, more affected by the heat of the fun
than the air northward of the fame latitude; and does not
this occafion an electrical current to flow from north to
south,

---

* Signior *Beccaria* concludes from experiments, that gentle rains are the effects of a moderate,
as thunder fhowers are of a more plentiful, electricity.

fouth, fo often as the above mentioned circumftances con-
cur, though with fome interruption from the irregular difpofition of the conducting vapors; and may not this occafion thofe gleams and ftreams with which this phenomenon
is ufually attended?

N° VIII.

Theory of Water Spouts, by ANDREW OLIVER, *Efquire,
of Salem in the State of Maffachufetts.*

IN my laft I took the liberty to communicate to the Philofophical Society a Theory of *Lightening* and *Thunder
Storms*, which was fuggefted to my mind upon the peru-
fal of doctor *Prieftley's hiftory of electricity*. In the in-
veftigation of which theory, while I was endeavouring to
account for the exhibitions of thofe phenomena upon the
ocean, at great diftances from the land, fome thoughts naturally occurred relative to the *water fpout;* a phenomenon as curious perhaps as any one in nature, and which
can rarely take place but at fea.

WATER SPOUTS have by fome been fuppofed to be merely electrical in their origin; particularly by fignior *Beccaria,
(Prieftley's* hift. of elect. p. 355, 356) who feems to have
fupported his hypothefis by fome experiments. But as
feveral fucceffive phenomena are neceffary to conftitute a
complete water fpout, (fome of which undoubtedly depend upon the electric principle) if we attend to the moft
authentic defcriptions of thefe fpouts, through their various ftages, from their firft exhibition to their total diffipa-
tion, we fhall be obliged to have recourfe to fome other
principle, in order to obtain a complete folution. I fhall
therefore, *firft,* defcribe thefe phenomena according to the
beft obfervations I have met with; and *then,* endeavour to

give·

give a general philofophical folution of them. But I muft
here obferve, that the following defcriptions are all taken
from the accounts of mariners, who are indeed the only
perfons that have opportunities of viewing them; but, unfortunately for the caufe of philofophy, do not ufually obferve them with that circumftantial accuracy, refpecting
the previous and fubfequent ftates of the atmofphere, which
may be neceffary to found a complete phyfical folution
upon; nor with any view to that end, as it is foreign to
their main bufinefs, trade and commerce. But as fuch accounts are the beft I have met with even in the Tranfactions of the Royal Society down to 1744, lower than which
I have not feen them; from fuch I fhall endeavour to draw
the beft conclufion which the nature of the evidence will
juftify.

. The moft intelligent and beautiful account of a water
fpout that I ever met with, is in the abridgment of the
Phil. Tranf. vol. viii, by *Martin*, pa. 655, as it was obferved by Mr. *Jofeph Harris*, May 21, 1732, about fun-
fet, lat. 32° 30' N. long. 9° E. from cape Florida; which
I fhall here tranfcribe.

" When firft we faw the fpout (fays he) it was whole
" and entire, and much of the fhape and proportion of a
" fpeaking trumpet; the fmall end being downwards, and
" reaching to the fea, and the big end terminated in a black
" thick cloud. The fpout itfelf was very black, and the
" more fo the higher up. It feemed to be exactly perpen-
" dicular to the horizon, and its fides perfectly fmooth,
" without the leaft ruggednefs. Where it fell the fpray
" of the fea rofe to a confiderable height, which made
" fomewhat the appearance of a great fmoke. From the
" firft time we faw it, it continued whole about a minute,
" and till it was quite diffipated about three minutes. It
" began to wafte from below, and fo gradually up, while
" the upper part remained entire, without any vifible al-
" teration, till at laft it ended in the black cloud above.
" Upon

" Upon which there feemed to fall a very heavy rain in
" that neighbourhood.   There was but little wind, and
" the fky elfewhere was pretty ferene——"

In other accounts contained in the Philofophical Tranfactions, thefe phenomena are defcribed as having the appearance of a fword pointing downwards, fometimes perpendicularly fometimes obliquely towards a column of water or froth, which feems to rife out of the fea to meet it,
attended with a violent ebullition or perturbation at the furface. Again in others the appearance is compared to fmoke
afcending vifibly as through the funnel of a chimney, either
directly, or with a fpiral motion, which according to the
fancies of fome refembles the afcent of water in the fcrew
of *Archimedes*; by fuppofing fomething fimilar to which
in the atmofphere, they have endeavoured to account for
the rife of the water from the fea in a water-fpout. To
which I would add, that, from the relations of fome perfons who ufe the fea, with whom I have converfed upon
the fubject, I find that it is no uncommon thing, during
a calm below, and a ferene fky above, to obferve at the
diftance of two or three leagues a fmall cloud hovering in
the air, from whence the commencing fpout feems to dart
downward to the fea, upon which the ufual phenomena
take place in their order. I have alfo been informed (and
to information I muft truft, having never been at fea) that
it is common during thefe appearances for fhips to fail,
even within hail of each other, with different winds; and
within the limits of the fame vifible horizon, with contrary
winds: And laftly, that the rife and progrefs of this phenomenon is fometimes fo rapid, that, even in a ferene fky, a
few minutes will be fufficient to generate a cloud from one
of thefe fpouts, and to difcharge from thence a heavy fhower of rain.

Before I proceed to attempt a philofophical folution of
thefe curious productions of nature, in which the two
principal fluids of our globe, air and water, are largely
concerned;

concerned; it may be neceffary to make fome obfervations upon the nature and properties of fluids in general, as fuch.

1. No fluid can be at reft unlefs every part of it refpectively be acted upon by an equal force or preffure in every direction, till when its feveral parts will neceffarily recede from the greater preffure towards the leffer, nor can an equilibrium take place.

2. If two or more fluids of different natures and denfities come together, fuch as quickfilver, water, oil and air, which will not mix; they will take their places according to their fpecific gravities, the denfeft remaining at the bottom.

3. If a veffel be filled with either of thefe fluids, and a denfer be admitted into it, the latter will expel, and take place of the former.

4. If an empty cylindrical fpace be furrounded on all fides by a fluid, which is excluded by fome refifting furface terminating that fpace, the fluid will neceffarily, upon the fudden removal of the obftacle, immediately flow in from every fide towards the center of the void; and as it flows inwards the parts next furrounding this fpace will thereby be crowded together, and force each other upwards, till at length when clofed, the fluid will by its afcent have formed a column directly over the middle of the fpace, to a height proportionable to the united force of the converging currents. This muft be the cafe with every fluid thus flowing into a vacuum; and in a leffer degree when a denfer fluid in a fimilar fituation fupplants a rarer: And the greater the difference of the denfities of the two fluids might be, the more confpicuous would be the effect.

This reafoning may be illuftrated, and the conclufions exemplified by facts which muft have occurred to the obfervation of every one. Do we not obferve when a fhower of hail, or rain in large drops, falls upon the furface of ftagnant water, that the water rifes wherever they fall, like fo many little inverted icicles, which again instantly

inftantly fubfide ? The caufe of which undoubtedly is, that thefe drops, or hail-ftones, defcending from a great height in the atmofphere, acquire feverally fuch a momentum in their fall as to plunge through the furface to a proportional depth, driving the fuperficial water back on every fide, and leaving a momentary vacuum behind them; not indeed a pure vacuum, but fuch, relative to the furrounding fluid, which immediately returns'to fill up the chafm, and, as it clofes, gathers and rifes in the little columns above defcribed. When a large round ftone, or any other heavy body plunges, the effect is proportionably greater.

5. Let us, for argument's fake, fuppofe the atmofphere over any certain circular tract of ocean of fome miles in diameter, to be for a moment annihilated, the fpace it occupied before being reduced to a pure vacuum : The furrounding atmofphere, when at liberty, would rufh in from every quarter towards the centre, where the converging currents would immenfely croud each other, and force up a vaft quantity of air through a very narrow funnel, contracted below by the united preffure of thofe currents from all fides, into the higher regions; which funnel, as the denfity of the air leffens according to its height, and the furrounding preffure which contracts it muft decreafe nearly in the fame proportion, would more and more diverge and expand the higher it rofe above the furface of the fea. This would be attended with a moft furious blaft of wind up to, and far above the top of the atmofphere. In like manner,

6. If inftead of a pure vacuum, or a total annihilation of fuch part of the atmofphere, we fuppofe the fame to become, by any means whatever, fpecifically lihgter than the furrounding regions, the effect would be the fame as above, in kind, though not in degree; the denfer air flowing in, but with lefs rapidity, from all quarters without, expelling the lighter and fupplying its place, as in article four; upon which alfo a large quantity of this confluent air, for the

O   fame

fame reafon, would be driven up with violence through a
like narrow vent, yet not with the fame impetuofity, nor
to the fame height as if forced through this funnel into a
pure vacuum.

That the atmofphere over large tracts of fea or land may
thus become fpecifically lighter than that over the furrounding regions, will be evident, if we confider, 1. That
heat has a natural tendency to rarefy and expand the air
upon which it acts.   2. That the atmofphere over our heads
does not confift of mere elementary air, but is an univerfal receptacle of all the heterogeneous vapors and effluvia
that are perpetually exhaling from every fubftance that
exifts upon the face of the earth, whether animal, vegetable or mineral.   3. That, by the cafual difpofition of
thefe vapors and effluvia in the atmofphere, the air, which
is, of itfelf, naturally enough difpofed to acquire heat from
the paffage of the fun's rays through it, may become more
difpofed to imbibe and retain that heat, in one region, than
in another in its neighbourhood; which, from the intervention of clouds, or from its purity and freedom from
thofe fteams and vapors with which the former is charged,
may, in a great degree, retain its natural coolnefs and
denfity, while the other becomes heated, rarefied and expanded, and is thereby rendered fpecifically lighter.

That thefe different affections of the atmofphere *actually* take place, and difpofe the air, at one time and in one
place, even in the fame feafons of the year, to imbibe and
retain the heat excited by the fun's rays, more than at
another, is not a matter of mere conjecture; but, whatever the caufe may be, is notorious to all perfons of obfervation.

Thefe things being premifed, I beg leave to obferve further, that fome parts of the ocean are liable to long and
extenfive calms, during the continuance of which the heat
is fcarcely tolerable.   Where thefe take place the air muft
neceffarily undergo proportional changes in its denfity and

electric

electric capacity*; and when heated and rarefied to some certain degree will give way, as obferved above, to the denfer air, now proportionably difpofed to flow in from all quarters without the limits of the calm.

When once this ftagnated air, efpecially if of any great extent, becomes fpecifically lighter than the furrounding air, and fufficiently rare to be fupplanted by it ; the latter will, of courfe, fet it from every fide in horizontal currents; which will flow, either directly, or obliquely, towards one point, in or near the centre of the becalmed region aforefaid ; the obliquities of which currents will depend upon the directions and velocities of the winds, or currents of air which might previoufly have taken place in the furrounding regions.   When thefe currents arrive at the centre of their mutual convergency, all the ftagnated and rarefied air which was before incumbent upon the calm furface of the fea, will have been expelled and forced higher up into the atmofphere; upon which thefe currents, by their mutual concourfe in one place, will exceffively croud each other, as obferved above, wherever it happens, driving the central air upwards with a violent blaft ; which, fhould the currents fet in obliquely, and fo converge with a fpiral motion towards the centre of their mutual concourfe, would afcend as through the fcrew of Archimedes, or the worm of a cork-fcrew, to both of which navigators have likened thefe fpouts : Otherwife it would rife through a ftrait, narrow funnel, as in articles five and fix above; which if filled with any opaque matter would become vifible, and at a diftance would refemble a fpeaking trumpet with the fmall end downwards, in which form the water fpout frequently appears.   In the former cafe a whirlwind round about the centre would undoubtedly be the confequence ; and in either, a water fpout would probably be produced†.

O 2   For

---

* See Theory of Lightening, &c. page 81.

† We fhall in the fequel fee abundant reafon to conclude with doctor *Franklin* and others, that water fpouts at fea and whirlwinds on the land (fome fpecies of them at leaft) are produced by the fame caufes.

For the preffure of the atmofphere is taken off from that
part of the furface of the fea, which is directly under the
funnel through which the air is driven up; whereas the
furrounding furface is at the fame time uncommonly preffed, from the confluence of the currents from all quarters*,
whereby the water muft neceffarily be forced up to a certain height, proportional to the furrounding preffure,
through the fame funnel with the air itfelf, nor is this all,
for in their afcent the air and water become confufedly
mixed together, whereby the latter is broken and attenu-
ated into the fineft globules and particles, as when one
forcibly blows water out of his mouth; and from this
mixture of the two fluids doubtlefs arifes that opacity
which renders the fpout vifible.

This opaque column of air and water, together with the
paffage through which it afcends, will expand as it rifes,
in proportion as the compreffure diminifhes; and, to fpec-
tators at too great a diftance to difcern the narrow ftem
next the water, will refemble a fword, or acute cone
pointing downwards from a fmall cloud; to which they
are frequently likened. But that they do at the fame time
communicate with the fea is evident from the perturbation of the water directly under them, which fometimes
boils and foams at a great rate. This is ufually the firft
appearance of one of thefe fpouts, the duration of which
is either longer or fhorter, and the fubfequent phenomena more or lefs confiderable, according to the extent of the
caufe, and the mode of its operation.

The water being thus raifed from the fea, and forced
irrefiftably upwards in the fineft globules by the protrud-
ing air, arrives at length at the warm electrical air † lately
expelled,

---

* In the abridgment of Philofophical Tranfactions, vol. II. (by Eames and Martin) page 61,
at the bottom, it appears, that the meeting of two contrary currents of air or contrary winds, raifes the mercury in the barometer near the place where it happens, which indicates an increafe of
the preffure of the atmofphere upon the furface of the earth or fea. How much more then muft
that preffure be increafed, from a general confluence of the air from all quarters towards one
fpot ?

† See Theory of Lightening, &c. page 90.

expelled, which was previoufly incumbent upon the calm
furface beneath; the electric attraction of which probably
affifts the further afcent of thefe particles after the firft fury
of the blaft is fpent. There it undergoes another operation being converted into vapor, whereby it is wholly difcharged of the marine falts it carried up with it*; which
are now left to fhift for themfelves, together with innumerable other heterogeneous corpufcles which fuceffively
float in the atmofphere, and which in due time, become
feverally fubfervient to many wife purpofes in the œconomy of nature. Thefe vapors will then be greedily attached by the craving particles of this air, now deficient of its
natural quantity of electric matter†, and form a denfe
cloud, in like manner as thunder clouds are formed over
the land; but with much greater expedition, as the fupply
of vapors is more fudden. This cloud will then be ready
in a fhort time to difcharge a fhower of frefh water upon
the fea from whence it rofe, and may be attended with
thunder and lightening, or not, as the air in which the
cloud was formed was more or lefs electrical, or the cloud
extenfive.

A previous calm may not be *neceffary* to the production
of thefe phenomena, and indeed they frequently happen
without one: But, upon the fame principle, if it be calm-
er where they are produced, or the ftate of the atmofphere
there be fuch as to difpofe it to acquire and retain the heat
acquired from the fun's rays, more than in the furrounding regions, which, as we have feen above, may be the
cafe, the effects may be the fame in kind, though perhaps
not in degree; the moft perfect water fpouts probably rifing from whence there has previoufly been a dead calm,
or nearly fuch, for the foregoing reafons.

If

---

* The water carried up in one of thefe fpouts is undoubtedly falt when it firft rifes from the
fea, as it afcends in great quantities, and in a very denfe column; but it is always frefh when it
defcends again in a fhower: It muft therefore in the mean time have gone through a compleat
natural diftillation.
† Theory of Lightening, &c. page 92.

If there be any wind at the time of the phenomenon, the aerial funnel through which the water afcends, inftead of being perpendicular to the horizon, as it would be in a calm, might incline more or lefs to it, in proportion to the ftrength or weaknefs of the prevailing current of air: Or, inftead of continuing in one fpot, it might have a progref-five motion over the furface of the fea, in the direction of the general current; both of which circumftances frequently take place.   In either cafe it is natural to fuppofe, that both air and water would afcend fpirally, as through the worm of a fcrew, every current which fets in towards the centre receiving an oblique bias from the prevailing current.

It fometimes happens, that after the fubfiding of a fpout, it is fucceeded by a fecond, and that by a third, either in the fame place, or at no great diftance from it.   But this alfo is analogous to what we obferve upon the plunging of heavy bodies out of air into water.   For, after the firft fubfiding of the fmall column of water which is occafion-ed by it, and is above refembled to an icicle, the water again rifes and fubfides as at firft, though not in the fame degree, as may be concluded from thofe fainter concentric circles which expand from the fame centre after the fub-fidence of the firft column.   The fame thing which here takes place in water, may alfo take place in air, under fimilar circumftances.

Since writing the foregoing, while I was endeavouring to contrive fome experiment to illuftrate the fubject, a very fimple one was fuggefted to my mind, the fuccefs of which I think demonftrates the truth of the hypothefis introduced above to account for the firft afcent of the water in the fpout; the event being precifely the fame as was expected before hand, and as ought to have taken place upon the principles above advanced.

EXPERIMENT.

In a ftiff paper card I made a hole juft big enough to infert a goofe quill fo as that it might be fixed perpendicularly

cularly to the plane of the card : After cutting the quill
off fquare at both ends and fixing it, I laid the card upon
the mouth of a wine glafs, filled with water to within one
fifth or fixth part of an inch from the lower orifice of the
quill ; then applying my mouth to the upper part, I drew
out the air in the quill by a ftrong fuction, and in one
draught of my breath drew in about a fpoonful of the water ; this by ftronger fuctions I was able to repeat again
and again, the quill remaining as before. The water, as
I expected, did not afcend to the mouth in a ftream, as it
would have done had the quill reached below the furface ;
but broken and confufedly mixed with the air which afcended with it ; as is above fuppofed to be the cafe in the afcent
of water in a fpout at fea.

In this experiment the fuction occafioned a vacuum, or
at leaft a great rarefaction of the air, within and directly
under the quill; the furrounding air of courfe flowed in
from every quarter to fupply it, rufhing up into the quill,
and through it to the mouth ; the preffure of the atmofphere being thereby taken off from the furface of the water immediately under the orifice, while the preffure upon
the furrounding furface remained, and was probably increafed, the water was forced up together with the air as
above notwithftanding the quill had no manner of communication with the water. If the fuction be made very
ftrong, and the quill be fixed at the diftance of a quarter
of an inch or more from the water, a confiderable agitation
and ebullition takes place in the water under it, fimilar to
that obferved in moft natural water fpouts, and the paffage
of the water from the furface to the quill becomes very
vifible.

It was hinted in a preceding note, that water fpouts at
fea and whirlwinds at land, fome fpecies of them at leaft,
arife from the fame caufe, how different foever their apparent effects may be. This I think is made fufficiently
evident from the obfervations of a couple of land fpouts at
Hatfield.

Hatfield in *Yorkſhire*, by Mr. *Abr. de la Pryme**, whoſe accounts of them I ſhall here tranſcribe, as the Tranſactions of the Royal Society are in the hands of but few among us, and as the facts related by him tend ſtrongly to confirm the preſent theory, however his concluſions from them may differ from it.

" On the 15th of Auguſt, 1687, (ſays he) appeared a
" ſpout in the air at *Hatfield* in *Yorkſhire* ; it was about a
" mile off coming directly to the place where I was ; I
" took my proſpective glaſſes to obſerve it as well as I
" could.

" The ſeaſon was very dry, the weather *extreme hot*,
" and the air very cloudy ; the wind aloft, and pretty
" ſtrong, and (which is remarkable) blowing out of ſeve-
" ral quarters at the ſame time, and filling the air here-
" abouts with mighty thick and black clouds, layer upon
" layer ; the wind thus blowing ſoon created a great *vor-*
" *tex, gyration* and *whirling* among the clouds ; the cen-
" tre of which every now and then dropt down in the
" ſhape of a thick, long, black pipe, commonly called a
" ſpout ; in which I could diſtinctly view a motion like
" that of a ſcrew, continually drawing upwards, and ſcrew-
" ing up (as it were) whatever it touched. In its progreſs
" it moved ſlowly over a hedge-row and grove of young
" trees which it made to bend like hazle wands, in a cir-
" cular motion ; then going forward to a great barn it
" twitched off in a minute all the thatch, and filled the
" whole air therewith. Coming to a very great oak tree,
" it made it bend like the foregoing trees, and broke off
" one of the greateſt and ſtrongeſt branches that would
" not yield to its fury, and twiſting it about, flung it to a
" very conſiderable diſtance off ; then coming to the place
" where I ſtood, within three hundred yards of me, I be-
" held this odd phenomenon, and found that it proceeded
" from nothing but a *gyration of the clouds by contrary*
winds

---

* Abridgment of Philoſophical Tranſactions, vol. IV. by Jones, page 106, 107.

" *winds meeting in a point or centre ;* and where the great-
" eſt condenſation and gravitation was, falling down into
" a pipe or great tube (ſomething like the *cochlea Archi-*
" *medis)* and that in its working or whirling motion, ei-
" ther ſucks up water, or deſtroys ſhips, &c. Having tra-
" velled about a quarter of a mile farther, it diſſolved by
" the prevalency of the wind that came out of the eaſt."

The account of the other is as follows, viz. " 1 have
" ſeen another ſpout in the ſame place, which very much
" conﬁrms me in my notion of the origin and nature of
" them.—The 21ſt of June, 1702, was *pretty warm ;* on
" the afternoon of which day, about two of the clock, *no*
" *wind ſtirring below* though it was ſomewhat great in the
" air, the clouds began to be mightily agitated and driven
" together ; whereupon they became very black, and were
" (moſt viſibly) *hurried round,* from whence proceeded a
" moſt audible whirling noiſe, like that commonly heard
" in a mill. After a while, a long tube or ſpout came
" down from the centre of the congregated clouds, in
" which was a ſwift *ſpiral motion* like that of a ſcrew, or
" the *cochlea Archimedis* when it is in motion, by which
" ſpiral nature and ſwift turning, water aſcends up into
" the one as well as into the other. It travelled ſlowly
" from weſt to north-eaſt, broke down a great oak tree or
" two, frighted ſome out of the fields, and made others
" lie down flat upon their bellies, to ſave being whirled
" about and killed by it, as they ſaw many jackdaws to
" be, that were ſuddenly caught up, carried out of ſight,
" and then caſt a great way amongſt the corn ; at laſt it
" paſſed over the town of *Hatfield,* to the great terror of
" the inhabitants, filling the whole air with the thatch that
" it plucked oﬀ from ſome of the houſes ; then touching
" upon a corner of the church, it tore up ſeverál ſheets of
" lead, and rolled them ſtrangely together ; ſoon after
" which it diſſolved and vaniſhed without doing any fur-
" ther miſchief.

P " By

" By all the obfervations that I could make of this, and
" the former, I found that had they been at fea and joined
" to the furface thereof, they would have carried a vaft
" quantity of water up into the clouds, and the tubes would
" then have become much more ftrong and opaque than
" they were, and have continued much longer.

" It is commonly faid that at fea the water collects and
" bubbles up a foot or two high under thefe fpouts before
" that they be joined : But the miftake lies in the pellu-
" cidity and finenefs of thofe pipes, which do moft certain-
" ly touch the furface of the fea before that any confider-
" able motion be made in it, and that, when the pipe be-
" gins to fill with water, it then becomes opaque and
" vifible."

I fhall here make a remark or two upon the above cited
author's mode of expreffion in the foregoing accounts,
which is evidently adapted to a preconceived idea of the
cochlea Archimedis, by fuppofing fomething fimilar to
which, as taking place in our atmofphere, he is not alone
in endeavouring to account for thefe phenomena. In con-
formity to this idea he fpeaks of the fpout as *drawing upwards*, and *fcrewing up* whatever it touched ; and fuppofes that by its *fpiral motion* and *fwift turning*, water
afcends in it as in the *fcrew of Archimedes*. But this hypothefis, however fpecious, has been long fince exploded
as unphilofophical.

Mr. *de la Pryme* mentions the appearance of a long black
pipe which now and then dropped down from the centre
of the gyrating clouds ; in which pipe he diftinctly viewed a motion like that of a fcrew ; and as fuch he feems to
have fuppofed it acted, viz. either in the manner of a cork-
fcrew upon folids, or as the *cochlea Archimedis* upon fluids,
drawing them up into the atmofphere. But as he himfelf
afterwards, when applying his obfervations to a fpout at
fea, very juftly concludes that the pellucidity and finenefs
of thefe pipes over the water render them invifible below,
" notwithftanding

" notwithſtanding (as he conceives) that the pipes do moſt
" certainly touch the ſurface of the ſea before any conſider-
" able motion be made in it, and that they are then rendered
" opaque and viſible when they begin to fill with water ;"
might he not with equal reaſon have ſuppoſed that thoſe
aerial pipes which he obſerved over the land were alſo continued from the clouds down to the ſurface of the earth, as
from their effects below, one would naturally conclude
they were, and that they were pellucid and inviſible ſo
long as they contained nothing but air ; but that " every
" now and then," when they met with any ſubſtances
which might perchance paſs within the compaſs of their
gyration, or which they could eaſily carry up ; ſuch as
detached parts of the broken clouds ; water from ſtagnant
ponds, brooks and rivers, hay, ſtubble, thatch, duſt, &c.
they then become opaque and viſible, and that they appeared to dart downwards by a kind of optical deception ?
For upon the foregoing principles theſe pipes of air muſt
neceſſarily be broadeſt above, as we have already ſeen, and
terminate in a narrow ſtem below, the broadeſt part being,
at a diſtance, firſt viſible, and the ſhank ſeemingly tapering downwards to a point. It is however certain from the
effects of the above mentioned ſpouts, that, whatever the
appearances were *aloft*, they were all occaſioned by the
ruſhing of the air upwards through a narrow paſſage, that
was contracted *below*, by the concourſe and preſſure of the
oppoſite currents of that fluid, and dilated above from the
diminution of that preſſure.

I have reſerved for this place an account of a curious
ſpout which made its appearance *anno* 1694, not at ſea,
but in the harbour of *Topſham**, and at low water ; which
paſſed with a ſlow progreſſive motion over both land and
water; acting as a complete water ſpout over the latter, and
as a whirlwind upon the former : For when it paſſed over
the channel of the river, it threw up the water in a denſe

ſtream,

* Lowthorp's Abridgm. Phil. Tranſ. vol. II. page 104.

stream, as if it had been impelled through the hose of a
fire engine, and the stream accordingly ended in a thick
mist, resembling a dark smoke; the surface of the water,
round about the spot from whence it rose, being greatly
agitated, as is usual in those phenomena. In its course it
met with the hull of a new ship of about one hundred tons,
which was much shaken by it, but received no hurt. In
passing over the flats it took hold of a boat which was
fastened to an anchor, whirled both boat and anchor to
some height in the air, and rent the boat " from the *head*
" to the *keel*." When it reached the shore it lifted up another boat about six feet from the ground, letting it fall
again upsidedown; and had a strange effect upon a parcel
of planks, some of which were raised up perpendicularly,
and stood upon their ends while it passed along; and in
its further progress it was attended with the usual effects
of a whirlwind, such as stripping off, not only thatch, but
sheets of lead from the tops of houses, and tearing off the
limbs of trees. This account may tend to confirm the
theory here offered, as it proves to a demonstration, that
the water spout therein described, was occasioned by a previous whirlwind in the atmosphere; which whirlwind was
also occasioned by the rushing of a large quantity of air,
upwards, from all quarters near the surface of the earth,
through a very contracted aerial passage, towards the top
of the atmosphere; the narrowness of which passage, as
determinable from the effects observed in its progress, shews
it to have been compressed upon all sides by a general con-
flux of opposite currents of air; as the rushing of the air
through it with such violence from beneath, does, that the
density of the fluid and the compressive force of the currents were greatest there. The ascending air carried up
the water with it through the same passage; not by any
mechanical operation upon it, like the action of a screw of
any kind; but, merely, by taking off the pressure of the
atmosphere from the surface of the water directly under

it;

it; whence the water muft neceffarily afcend, as in any common hydraulic machine; and that with a force proportional to the preffure of the atmofphere upon the furrounding furface, now greatly increafed by the confluence of thofe currents.

Before I clofe this fubject, I fhall juft mention, without making any remarks, the effects which a whirlwind had amongft a number of fhocks of corn at *Warrington* in *Northamptonfhire*, Auguft 1ft, 1694; out of which from eighty to a hundred fhocks were carried up into the air, a great part of them out of fight; thefe when the fury of the blaft was fpent, fell down again at the diftance of fome miles from their own field. The account of this whirlwind immediately precedes the article laft quoted from the *Philofophical Tranfactions*. Should the foregoing theory be adjudged tenable, it will render very credible thofe ftrange accounts which we have fometimes had, of its raining tadpoles and frogs, which have been found upon the tops of houfes after a fhower; and even fmall fifhes, a fhower of which fell at *Cranftead* near *Wrotham* in *Kent*, *anno* 1696, on the Wednefday before Eafter (Lowthorp's abridgement of Philofophical Tranfactions, vol. II. page 144.) For fhould one of thofe aerial pipes pafs over a frog pond, or the fhallow parts of a fifh pond, the fame natural caufe which in a fpout at fea, would carry up the water from the ocean, would alfo carry up the water from the ponds aforefaid, together with the contents; whether tadpoles, frogs or fifhes: Thefe muft defcend again fomewhere; and wherever they fell, a fhower of fifhes, frogs or tadpoles, would be the confequence.

Experiments

N° IX.

Experiments on Evaporation, and Meteorological Observations made at Bradford in New-England, in 1772, by the Rev. SAMUEL WILLIAMS, A. M.

IN making experiments on the quantity of water that evaporated in the year 1771, the method I ufed, was to fill the veffel the beginning of every month: In the courfe of thefe experiments, I obferved that in the beginning of the month when the tube was newly filled, it exhaufted much fafter than towards the latter end, when one or two inches of the water was evaporated; and that the quantity of evaporation meafured this way, came out lefs than the quantity of rain that fell in the courfe of the year. The beginning of the year 1772, I attempted to examine this matter more carefully. With this view I made the following experiments.

EXPERIMENT I.

I procured two cylindrical veffels of three inches diameter, and fix deep, as much alike as they could be made: One, I filled with water as I had done in 1771, once a month; the other, with the fame kind of water, once a week; and placed them about fix inches apart, in fuch a manner as to be expofed to the wind, and fun, but covered from the rain. The refult was, that which was filled once a week, exhaufted about one third more than the other. In *January* and *February*, the difference was a little lefs; in *March* and *April*, it was a little more. In *May*, the laft month in which I compared them, the evaporation from the former was 6.35 inches; from the other 4.10. By this

experiment

experiment I was convinced that it never could be known with much accuracy by either of thefe methods, what quantity of water does really evaporate from the furface of feas, lakes and rivers.   For in the one cafe, after about an inch is exhaufted the furface of the water is too much fheltered from the wind, which greatly retards the evaporation.   In the other, as the water has all the advantage of the wind, and is heated by the fun, and atmofphere, to a confiderable greater degree than the water in feas, lakes and rivers, the quantity of evaporation comes out too much.   And therefore nothing certain as to the real quantity of evaporation from watery fluids, can be determined by fuch experiments, however carefully they may be made.

EXPERIMENT II.

To meafure with more certainty the real quantity of evaporation, I attempted in the next place to examine what it was in fact from the furface of a river.   This experiment was made in the following manner: I filled one of the veffels with river water, and placed it as before. The other I fixed in the centre of a circular board of three feet diameter.   This inftrument, by means of a line faftened to a tree on a fmall ifland, was placed fo as to float near the middle of *Menimack* river.   To defend the tube againft the dews and rain, a circular piece of glafs, fifteen inches diameter, was fupported by wires fixed to the board, eight inches above the tube; and the whole was fo balanced by weights as to leave half an inch of the tube above the furface of the water.   When thus afloat I filled the tube with water, propofing to let it remain in this fituation a week, to fee how much would evaporate in that fpace of time.   After repeated difappointments by the rain, wind and waves, for three months, I at laft fucceeded in trying the experiment from *Auguft* 26th, to *September* 2d.   During that time there was little wind,

ftill

ftill water, no rain, nor any thing to difturb the experiment. The event was, that at the end of the feventh day,
the tube was exhaufted 1.15 inch. And that no water
had got into the tube in that time, I was certain from this
circumftance; all that part of the furface of the board
which was within half a foot of the tube was dry every
morning and evening. In the other tube, the evaporation
in the fame time was 1.50 inch; which gives 35 decimal
parts of an inch difference between the real evaporation
from the furface of the river, and that of the water when
fufpended in the air, as in the other veffel. All the eva-
porations therefore meafured the latter of thefe ways,
ought to be diminifhed in this proportion, to have the true
quantity fuch as it is in nature.

EXPERIMENT III.

Thefe experiments on watery fluids put me upon en-
quiring what the evaporation was from the furface of the
earth. To determine this, *Sept.* 14, two days after there
had been any rain, I funk one of the veffels into the earth
in a light foil, fo as to take up all the earth contained in
a fpace equal to the contents of the veffel. Having carefully weighed the veffel with the earth it contained, I fixed it in the ground in a plain open field, where it was expofed to the fun and wind, but defended from the dew and
rain, as in the former experiment. At the end of *feven
days* I took it up, and weighing it again found it had loft
783 grains, *troy.* The diameter of the veffel being three
inches, its furface expreffed in whole numbers was equal
to nine fquare inches. Dividing the number of grains that
evaporated, 783, by the number of fquare inches contained in the furface of the veffel, 9, we fhall have 87 grains
for the evaporation from one fquare inch; and this, (affuming 254 grains as the weight of a cubic inch of water)
will give $\frac{1.34}{1000}$ parts of an inch, as the depth of water that
paffed off by evaporation. In the other veffel filled with
water,

water, and placed as before, the evaporation in the fame time was exactly one inch.   If this experiment may be fuppofed to reprefent the operations of nature, the conclufion will be, that the evaporation from the furface of the earth, is but little more than *one third* of what the evaporation is from the furface of water.

EXPERIMENT IV.

Another thing I had in view was to know what the evaporation was from plants and trees.   In order to make an eftimate of this, *Auguft* 20, I took up four different forts of plants, with as much of the earth adjoining to each as wholly covered their roots.   Each plant, with the earth thus about it, being fix inches fquare, I put into a wooden box of the fame form and fize.   The boxes were covered with thin lead, well cemented at the joints, that nothing might evaporate that way; and had two apertures at the top; one, to admit the ftem of the plant, the other, that the plant might be fupplied with water, but which was kept ftopped when not in ufe.   Having taken the weight of each, I placed them in the ground that they might have the fame degree of heat as before; leaving as much of the plant above the furface of the earth, as when it was in its natural ftate.   In this fituation I added known quantities of water, aiming to put in from time to time as much as I thought they would throw off.   At the end of *thirty days* I took them up, taking an account of their weight as before, and alfo that of each plant.   The refult is expreffed in the following particulars:

The feveral forts of plants.	*Weight of the plants.*	*Water evaporated in 30 days.*
	Grains.	Grains.
Apple tree, - - -	23	- - - - 1271
Alder tree, - - -	30	- - - - 2593
Spear mint, - - -	22	- - - - 5186
Clover, - - - -	43	- - - - 1894

Q

In

In this experiment, the evaporation from thefe four very fmall plants was 10944 grains; amounting to about 43 cubic inches of water, in thirty days. The evaporation in the fame time from the veffel fufpended in the air, was 4.25 inches in depth: The quantity therefore thrown off by the plants, was more than what the evaporation would have been from a watery furface, of ten inches fquare. If this way of reafoning may be applied to fields covered with trees, grafs, and other vegetables, the inference will be, that the evaporation for feveral months is greater from them, than it is from equal areas of the furface of water.

METEOROLOGICAL OBSERVATIONS made at BRADFORD in 1772.

THE inftruments ufed in the following obfervations, the times at which they were taken, and the method in which they are fet down, were defcribed in the paper fent to the Society laft year. With regard to thofe of the prefent year the following things are to be obferved: The *barometrical* obfervations till Nov. 6, muft be viewed as imperfect, being taken with a barometer of too fmall a bore. From the 6th of November to the end of the year, they are very exact; being taken by a very good barometer made by *Nairne*. In meafuring the quantity of evaporation, I ufed a tube three inches diameter and fix deep; which was filled once a week. The rain was meafured by a tube of the fame form and fize. In all other refpects, the fame method was obferved as in the meteorological obfervations of 1771.

The obfervations taken by the *barometer* and *thermometer* are fet down in three columns; the firft column contains the obfervations taken ufually about 6^h A. M. the fecond at noon, and the third at 9^h P. M. The other columns give the general ftate of the winds and weather of the day.

JANU-

JANUARY, 1772.

Days.	Barometer.			Thermometer.			Winds.	Weather.
1	30,0½	30,1	30,1	18½	25	26½	W. to S. W. little.	Fair day; ſnow in the night.
2	30,1½	30,1½	30,1	27	32	30	W. little.	Fine pleaſant weather.
3	29,7½	29,5	29,4½	18	23	33	S.	Cloudy day; rain in the night.
4	29,4	29,6	29,7½	37½	40	41	S. W.	Fine pleaſant weather.
5	29,7¼	29,7½	29,8	26	24	18	N. W. ſtrong.	Clear bright day.
6	29,9½	29,9½	30,0½	13	15½	20	N. W.	Ditto. *Aurora Borealis* in the evening.
7	30,1	30,1	30,1	15½	18½	22½	W. to S.	Cloudy, dull weather.
8	30,1	30,1	30,1½	23	30	29½	W. little.	Fine pleaſant day.
9	30,1½	30,1	30,1	27	31½	34	Ditto.	Ditto.
10	30,1½	30,1	30,1¼	28½	30	26½	Ditto.	Ditto.
11	30,1¼	30,1	30,0½	21	25	26	Ditto.	Ditto.
12	29,8	29,6½	29,4¼	26	27	32	E. freſh.	Cloudy day; ſnow in the night.
13	29,6	29,6	29,6	35	40½	34½	S. W. to W.	Flying clouds with bright intervals.
14	29,7½	29,7½	29,8	28	31½	30	W. little.	Mild pleaſant day.
15	29,8	29,7¼	29,6	23	25	25	Ditto.	Ditto.
16	29,2	29,2	29,0½	23	27	28	S. E. to W.	Snow A. M. clear P. M.
17	29,4½	29,5	29,5	21	21	20	W.	Clear bright day.
18	29,3¼	29,2	29,2	10	14	18	N.	Cloudy, with ſome ſnow.
19	29,1½	29,1	29,1	18	21	27	N. to S. W.	Cloudy dull weather.
20	29,0	28,8½	28,6½	27½	26½	20	N. to N. W.	Storm of ſnow, all day; bright evening.
21	28,9	29,1½	29,2	11½	20	19	N. W.	Fair weather.
22	29,2	29,1½	29,1	18	29½	28½	S. E.	Cloudy dull day.
23	29,0	29,0	29,0	28½	34	36½	S. little.	Cloudy, with bright intervals.
24	29,0½	29,0¼	29,0½	37	39½	40	Ditto.	Dull miſling day.
25	29,3¼	29,3	29,3	38	35	30	W. little.	Fine pleaſant day.
26	29,6	29,6	29,6¼	23	26	21½	N. W.	Ditto.
27	29,7	29,5½	29,5	9	12	10½	N.	Cloudy dull weather.
28	29,2	29,2	29,1½	7	11	17	Ditto.	Ditto, with rain.
29	29,3	29,3	29,3½	16½	23	26	W. little.	Fair and clear.
30	29,0	28,7½	28,6	20	32	32	N. E. freſh.	Cloudy day; ſtorm of ſnow in the night.
31	28,7	28,9	28,9	26	37	34	N. E. to S.	Cloudy dull weather.

Quantity of rain in January, 2,00 }
Quantity of water evaporated, 1,55 } Inches.

FEBRU-

FEBRUARY, 1772.

Days.	Barometer.			Thermometer.			Winds.	Weather.
1	29,0½	29,1	29,1½	31	37	35	S.	Fair A. M; cloudy P. M.
2	29,3½	29,4	29,6⅓	29	35	32	W. little.	Fine bright day.
3	29,2	29,1¼	29,0	20	23	26½	E. fresh.	Clo. day; hea. stor. of sn. & hail in the nig.
4	28,9	29,2½	29,4½	26	32	31½	S. to N. W. fresh.	Dull cloudy day.
5	29,7½	29,7½	29,9¼	21½	23½	21½	N. W. fresh.	Flying clouds, with bright intervals.
6	30,1	30,1¼	30,1¼	14½	20½	14	N. W. little.	Fine bright day. *Aur. Bor.* in the night.
7	30,0⅙	29,9⅔	30,0¼	23	31	32½	S. W. to W.	Fine pleasant weather.
8	30,2¼	30,2½	30,0	23	25	31½	N. to E. S. E.	Cloudy dull day.
9	29,4¼	29,1	29,2⅔	37	40	38	S. to W. fresh.	Rainy A. M; cloudy P. M. bright even.
10	29,7½	29,9	30,0	22	25½	26	N. W. fresh.	Fair and clear.
11	30,0	29,6½	29,7	25	30	34½	S. W. to W. fresh.	Ditto.
12	30,2⅔	30,2	30,3¼	20	19½	14	N. W.	Fair day.
13	30,4	30,4	30,4	3	11	11	N. W. to N. E.	Fair day; cloudy evening.
14	30,2	29,9	29,9½	11½	12½	15	N. to W.	Snow A. M; clear P. M.
15	30,1¼	30,1	29,2	7½	14	32	W. to E.	Clo. A. M; sn. with ra. P. M. & in the nig.
16	29,2¼	29,1	29,1¼	27	32	29½	S. W. little.	Fair pleasant day.
17	29,6	29,6	29,6	16½	26	24	W. to S. W. fresh.	Flying clouds, with bright intervals.
18	29,6	29,6	29,6	25	34	39	S. W. little.	Fine pleasant day.
19	29,6½	29,6½	29,6⅓	36½	39	41½	S. W.	Ditto.
20	29,6¼	29,6½	29,6½	40½	44½	49½	Ditto.	Cloudy day; rain in the night.
21	29,2¼	29,4	29,6	49½	51	48	W. S. W.	Fine pleasant day.
22	29,5⅔	29,2⅓	29,5	44	47½	49	Ditto. fresh.	Ditto.
23	29,6	29,6	29,8	42	43	42½	W.	Ditto.
24	29,8½	29,8½	29,8½	38	40	39½	S. W. to E.	Ditto.
25	29,5½	29,0	28,4½	35	34	35	N. E. to S. strong.	Heavy storm of snow and rain all day.
26	28,6	28,6½	29,1	31	32	28½	W. to N. strong.	Flying clouds, with bright intervals.
27	29 3½	29,3½	29 3½	25	33	35	W.	Fine pleasant day. *Aur. Bor.* in the nig.
28	29,3½	29,4	29,2½	31	37	40	S. W. little.	Ditto.
29	29,2	29,2	29,3½	37	39	32	Ditto. fresh.	Ditto.

Quantity of rain in February, 2,40 } Inches.
Quantity of water evaporated, 1,65 }

MARCH,

MARCH, 1772.

Days.	Barometer.			Thermometer.			Winds.	Weather.
1	29,0½	29,5	29,4½	28	31	30	N. W. to S.	Fair weather.
2	29,0	29,3½	29,4	29	36½	31	S. W. little.	Fine bright day.
3	29,0	29,9	29,9½	27	31	33	N. E.	Cloudy dull weather.
4	30,0½	30,0	30,0	30	34	32	N. to W. little.	Fine pleaſant day.
5	29,8	29,4	28,8	27½	33	33	N. E. ſtrong.	Heavy ſtorm of ſnow.
6	28,8	29,1	29,4	31	34	27	W. freſh.	Clear pleaſant weather.
7	29,8	29,8	29,8	16	25	25	W. little.	Ditto.
8	29,9	29,9	29,9½	23	37	34	Ditto.	Ditto.
9	30,2	30,1½	30,0½	26	23½	20½	N. freſh.	Cloudy with ſome ſnow.
10	30,0	30,0	30,0	17½	31	25	E. little.	Fine pleaſant day.
11	29,7½	29,5	28,8	17	27½	31	N. N. E.	Clo. A. M; heavy ſtorm of ſnow P. M.
12	28,7	29,2½	29,8	30	32	25	W. freſh.	Cloudy morning; clear bright day.
13	29,8	29,8	29,8	16	28	26	N.	Cloudy with ſome ſnow.
14	29,8	29,8	30,0½	22	27	20	W.	Clear bright day.
15	30,2	30,2	30,2	12	23	20	Ditto.	Ditto.
16	30,2	30,1	29,6½	10½	25	29½	W. to S. freſh.	Dull cloudy weather.
17	29,6	29,7	29,8½	28	31	28	W. to S. freſh.	Clear bright day.
18	30,0	30,0	29,6½	20	35	36½	W. to S.	Clear A. M; cloudy P. M.
19	29,6	29,4	29,4½	33	49½	39½	S. W. to S. E.	Ditto Ditto.
20	29,4½	29,2½	29,1	34	32½	31½	N. E. to N.	Clo. mor. ſtor. of ſn. P. M. & in the even.
21	28,9	28,9	29,0½	33	38	38	W. S. W. freſh.	Cloudy weather.
22	29,3	29,3½	29,5½	37	40	42	Ditto.	Flying clouds, with bright intervals.
23	29,6	29,6½	29,6	40½	47	46	S. little.	Fine pleaſant day.
24	29,6	29,6	29,6	39	45	42	S. to S. E.	Cloudy weather.
25	29,6	29,6	29,6	39	46½	42½	S. to E. little.	Fine pleaſant day.
26	29,6	29,6	29,6	36	39	39½	N. to S. E. little.	Dull miſling weather.
27	29,6	29,6	29,6	38	47½	42	S. to E. little.	Fine pleaſant weather.
28	29,7½	29,7½	29,7½	36	40	37½	E. to N. E. freſh.	Cloudy day; rainy evening and night.
29	29,3	29,2½	29,2	36	39	36	E. freſh	Heavy ſtorm of ſnow & rain, all day.
30	29,3	29,4	29,5½	36	36½	35½	N. N. E.	Rainy weather.
31	29,8	29,9	29,8½	36	44	39½	N. to E. little.	Fine pleaſant day.

Quantity of rain in March, 4,93 } Inches.
Quantity of water evaporated, 1,45 }

R APRIL,

APRIL, 1772.

Days.	Barometer.			Thermometer.			Winds.	Weather.
1	29,8	29,8	29,8	35	46½	47	S. little.	Fine pleaſant weather.
2	29,7¼	29,7½	29,6	37	38½	35	N. E. freſh.	Cloudy dull day.
3	29,3½	29,3½	29,4	32½	35	36	N. ſtrong.	Ditto, with ſome ſnow.
4	29,6	29,6	29,7	33	39½	39½	N. to W. little.	Cloudy A. M.—fair and pleaſant P. M.
5	29,8	29,8	29,8	33½	44	45	W. to S. W. little.	Fine pleaſant weather.
6	29,5	29,4	29,4	41½	50½	45	E. little.	Ditto.
7	29,5½	29,5½	29,5½	39	54	48	S. E. little.	Ditto.
8	29,5½	29,4	29,4	41½	50	48	E.	Clear A. M. clou. P. M. and in the night.
9	29,2¼	29,0	29,1	42	39½	38	N.E. to N. ſtrong.	Storm of rain all day.
10	29,2¼	29,2½	29,2½	40	50	51	N. W. to S. W.	Fine pleaſant day. [night.
11	29,2½	29,2½	29,1½	46	57	54½	S. W. to S. little.	Fair day; clo. evening; ſmall ſhowers in the
12	29,0	29,0	29,1½	47	48	46	S. W. to W. freſh.	Fair weather. *Aur. Bor.* in the night.
13	29,2	29,2	29,2	41	46	41½	Variable.	Cloudy dull day.
14	29,2	29,2	29,3½	40	48½	47½	S. W. freſh.	Flying clouds, with bright intervals.
15	29,6	29,6	29,8½	41½	49	43	W. by S.	Fine bright day; rain in the night.
16	29,8	29,5	29,5½	44	47	53	S. to S. E.	Rainy all day.
17	29,4	29,5½	29,8	48½	52	50½	S. E. to W. little.	Fair pleaſant weather.
18	29,9½	30,0	30,0½	43	53	49	W. little.	Ditto.
19	30,1	30,1	30,0½	42	48	44	N. E.	Fair A. M. cloudy P. M.
20	29,8	29,1½	29,2	36	38	39½	NE to N W ſtrong.	Storm of rain 'till 4 P. M. clou. evening.
21	29,4½	29,5	29,6¼	38½	44	47	N. W. freſh.	Fair A. M. ſhowers P. M. & in the even.
22	29,7	29,7	29,4½	43½	53½	55	S. W.	Fine pleaſant day.
23	29,3	29,1	29,1½	51	58	53	S. to W. freſh.	Fair A. M. ſhowers P. M. and in the even.
24	29,2	29,2	29,4	45	49	47	Variable.	Dull cloudy day.
25	29,5	29,5	29,6	41	48½	45½	N. E. to W.	Ditto.
26	29,6½	29,6	29,6	39½	55	53	W. to S. S. E.	Fine pleaſant day.
27	29,7½	29,7½	29,5¼	50	64	64½	S. little.	Ditto.
28	29,6	29,6	29,6	57½	59½	62	Ditto.	Ditto.
29	29,8	29,8½	29,3	54	60	58½	E. freſh.	Ditto.
30	29,8	29,6	29,5½	53	65½	69	S. W.	Ditto.

Quantity of rain in April, 2,90 } Inches.
Quantity of water evaporated, 3,45 }

MAY,

MAY, 1772.

Days.	Barometer.			Thermometer.			Winds.	Weather.
1	29,6	29,5½	29,3	64	75½	77½	S. W.	Fair weather.
2	29,3	29,3	29,3	71	77	75	Ditto freſh.	Do. Lightg. in the night, with thund.
3	29,8	29,9	30,0	58½	55	54	N. W.	Cloudy, with bright intervals.
4	30,2	30,2	30,1¾	42½	57	59	E.	Clear A.M. clou. P.M. & in the evening.
5	30,1½	30,1½	29,9½	46	48	51	S. E.	Dull cloudy weather.
6	29,9½	29,8½	29,9½	49	55	50½	Variable.	Fine pleaſant day.
7	30,0	30,0	30,0	47½	58½	55	E.	Ditto.
8	30,0	29,9	29,5	49	51	52	N. E. to N. N. W.	Cloudy A.M. rainy P.M. & in the night.
9	29,1	29,1	29,2	51	57	55	S. W. freſh.	Fair A. M. ſmall ſhowers P. M.
10	29,4½	29,4½	29,7	49	52½	49½	N. W. freſh.	Fair and pleaſant.
11	29,8¼	29,8¾	29,8½	43	52½	53	W.	Ditto.
12	29,8	29,7	29,6½	50	59½	62	Variable.	Cloudy A. M. rainy P. M.
13	29,7½	29,7½	29,8	52	58	56	W.	Clear and pleaſant.
14	29,8½	29,8	29,7½	49	60½	56	Ditto.	Ditto.
15	29,6¾	29,5¾	29,4	52½	63	63	S. W. little.	Ditto.
16	29,3½	29,3½	29,3½	52½	67	64	Ditto.	Ditto.
17	29,3	29,3	29,3	52	60	56	Variable.	Ditto.
18	29,5	29,5	29,4¾	54	59	53½	E.	Cloudy A. M. rainy P. M.
19	29,4¾	29,5	29,5	53	60	57	N. E.	Fair day ; cloudy evening.
20	29,3½	29,3½	29,4½	54	59½	57	S. W. to N. W.	Small ſhowers A. M. cloudy P. M.
21	29,5	29,6½	29,6½	49½	59½	59½	N. W.	Fine pleaſant day.
22	29,5	29,5	29,6	56	70½	65	S. W. freſh.	Ditto.
23	29,7	29,5	29,4	57	72	71	Ditto.	Ditto.
24	29,3½	29,2	29,3½	65	77½	64	S. W. to N. E.	Fair till 3 P. M. cloudy evening & night.
25	29,3½	29,5	29,8	53	57	56	N. to N. E.	Dull cloudy day.
26							Ditto.	Ditto. } Small ſhowers.
27							Ditto.	Ditto. }
28							N. E. to S. W.	Ditto. }
29	29,7	29,7	29,7½	55	59	56½	S. W. to N.	Ditto. }
30	29,7	29,6½	29,6½	55	61	66	N. W. to S.	Fair and pleaſant.
31	29,5½	29,4	29,3	63	70	75	S. W. freſh.	Ditto.

Quantity of rain in May, 1,00 } Inches.
Quantity of water evaporated, 6,35 }

JUNE,

JUNE, 1772.

Days	Barometer		Thermometer			Winds	Weather
1	29,4	29,4	65	77	70½	S. W. fresh.	Fair day; thun. & lighten. in the night.
2	29,5	29,6	64	60	60	N. E.	Dull cloudy weather.
3	29,8	29,9	55	59½	54	Ditto.	Fine pleasant day.
4	30,0	30,0	51	73	61	N. W.	Ditto.
5	30,1	30,0	55½	78	67	W. to S. S. W.	Ditto.
6	30,0	29,6	61	72½	72½	S. W.	Ditto.
7	29,6	29,6	63½	71½	65	S. W. to N. N. E.	Ditto.
8	29,5	29,6	62	62	64	S. S. W.	Ditto.
9	29,5	29,8	55½	62	54	W.	Fair A. M; cloudy P. M.
10	29,8	29,8	55	58	57	W. to N. E.	Cloudy day; showers in the night.
11	29,7	29,6	55	64	58	N. E. to S. S. E.	Fine bright day.
12	29,3	29,6	57	67	62	W. fresh.	Ditto. lightening in the evening.
13	29,6	29,6	54½	67	67	Ditto.	Ditto.
14	29,6	29,4	65	77	77	S. W.	Cloudy A. M; rainy P. M.
15	29,5	29,5	73	83	75½	S. W. fresh.	Cloudy dull day.
16	29,3	29,5	69½	73	69	S. W. to W. fresh.	Rainy day.
17	29,5	29,5	62	66	64	N.	Ditto.
18	29,4	29,5	60	61½	60½	Ditto.	Ditto. Fair evening.
19	29,4	29,4	58½	63½	60½	Ditto.	Cloudy dull day.
20	29,3	29,3	57	67½	64	N. to E.	Cloudy, with showers.
21	29,4	29,4	59	67½	60	N. E.	Fair evening.
22	29,4	29,3	56	56½	54	N. E.	Cloudy dull day.
23	29,3	29,4	53	61	65	N. to W.	Flying clouds with bright intervals.
24	29,4	29,4	64	70	69	Ditto.	Ditto.
25	29,4	29,4	66½	74	71	Ditto.	Cloudy, with rain.
26	29,3	29,3	62½	61½	59	N. W. to E.	Flying clouds, with bright intervals.
27	29,4	29,4	63	71	67	N. W. fresh.	Fine pleasant weather.
28	29,7	29,8	70	76	73	W,	Ditto.
29	29,8	29,7	66½	82	76	S. W.	Ditto.
30	29,8	29,6	70	83½	79	Ditto.	Ditto.

Quantity of rain in June, 1,25 } Inches.
Quantity of water evaporated, 5,45 }

JULY,

JULY, 1772.

Days.	Barometer.			Thermometer.			Winds.	Weather.
1	29,4	29,4	29,4	74	78	77½	S. W.	Small ſhowers A. M. fair & pleaſ. P. M.
2	29,4	29,4	29,4	71	77	75	Ditto.	Cloudy, with ſmall ſhowers.
3	29,4½	29,4½	29,3	74	77	73	N. to E.	Ditto, lightening in the evening.
4	29,3½	29,3½	29,2½	71	78½	79	S. W. to W.	Ditto.
5	29,6	29,6½	29,6	73½	80½	75	W.	Fine pleaſ. day. *Aur. Bor.* in the evening.
6	29,6	29,6	29,6	71½	81	73	S. W.	Fair A. M; cloudy P. M.
7	29,8	29,7½	29,5½	72	79	80	S. W. ſtrong.	Fair till 2 P. M. clou. with th. & ra. nig.
8	29,5¼	29,2	29,4½	77	86	76	S. W. to N. W.	Fair day. *Aur. Bor.* in the night.
9	29,6	29,6	29,6	77	81	72	W.	Fine pleaſant day.
10	29,6	29,6	30,0	66	77	67	Ditto.	Fair A. M. ſhower of rain and hail P. M.
11	30,1	30,1	30,1	62	74	68½	Ditto.	Fine pleaſant day.
12	30,0½	30,0	30,0	78	78	74	Ditto.	Ditto.
13	29,9	29,9½	29,9½	70	75	73	W. to S. little.	Ditto.
14	29,9	29,9	29,9½	70	78	77½	S. W.	Ditto.
15	29,6	29,6½	29,6½	73	77½	73	Ditto.	Fair A. M. a ſmall ſhower P. M.
16	29,6	29,6½	29,6	71	80	76	Ditto.	Cloudy, dull weather.
17	29,6½	29,6½	29,6	74	78	70	Ditto.	Cloudy, with bright intervals.
18	29,8	29,9	29,9	65	77½	72	Ditto.	Fine pleaſant weather.
19	29,9½	30,0	29,9½	72	81	71	Ditto.	Fair A. M. cloudy P. M.
20	30,1½	30,1½	30,1	72	79	70	Ditto.	Fine pleaſant day.
21	30,1	30,0½	29,9	68	75	70	Ditto.	Fair A.M. cloudy P.M. rain in the night.
22	30,0½	29,7	29,7	66	73	72	Ditto.	Cloudy A. M. clear P. M.
23	29,5	29,5	29,6	65	75	71	N. E. to W.	Ditto, ditto.
24	29,6	29,6	29,6½	68	79	72	Variable.	Cloudy, with thunder and rain.
25	29,8½	29,9	30,0	73	82½	76	W. to N.	Pleaſant day. Rem. *Aur. Bor.* in the nig.
26	30,0½	30,0	29,7	74	84½	80½	S. W.	Fair pleaſant weather.
27	29,8½	29,8	29,6½	76	86½	79	S. to S. W.	Ditto. Lightening in the evening.
28	29,8	29,6	29,4	78	95¼	87	Ditto.	Ditto.
29	29,5	29,3	29,3	81½	*96½	81	Ditto.	Ditto.
30	29,4	29,3	29,3	78	85	78	Ditto.	Fair A. M. thunder and rain P. M.
31	29,8	28,9	28,7	72½	72	71½	Variable.	Dull rainy day.

Quantity of rain in July, 2,95 } Inches.
Quantity of water evaporated, 4,60 }

* This obſervation was taken at 1½ P. M. The thermometer being hung in a ſhade in the open air.

S AUGUST,

AUGUST, 1772.

Days.	Barometer.			Thermometer.			Winds.	Weather.
1	29,5	29,5	29,6	65	70	64½	N. W.	Flying clouds, with bright intervals.
2	29,9½	30,0½	30,1	66	73½	69½	W.	Fine pleaſant weather.
3	30,3¼	30,3½	30,3	65	79	69	Ditto, little.	Ditto.
4	30,2	30,2	30,2	64	78	71½	S.	Ditto.
5	30,1¼	29,6	29,2½	67	70	70	N.	Heavy ſhowers; clears up in the night.
6	29,7	29,7	29,6½	71	82	77	S. W.	Fair weather.
7	29,7	29,7	29,7	75	83	77½	Ditto.	Ditto.
8	29,7	29,5	29,3	76	86	80	Ditto.	Fair day; terr. thun. & lightg. in the nig.
9	29,4	29,4	29,5	78	75	70	Variable.	Cloudy A. M; fair P. M.
10	29,6	29,6	29,6	65	67	66	N. E. little.	Cloudy day; ſmall ſhowers in the even.
11	29,5	29,2	28,6½	67	81	75	Variable.	Unſettled weather.
12	28,9	28,9	28,9½	62	79	74	S. W.	Fair and pleaſant.
13	29,2	29,2	29,1½	70	80	80	Ditto.	Ditto.
14	29,5	29,5	29,5	74	80½	76	Ditto.	Ditto.
15	29,5	29,4	29,2½	75	84½	78½	S.	Fair A. M. ſhowers P. M.
16	29,4½	29 4	29,5	70	72	68	N. E.	Dull cloudy day.
17	29,5	29,5	29,5½	65	66	63½	Ditto.	Cloudy day; rain in the night.
18	29,5	29,4	29,6½	60½	60½	59	Ditto.	Dull rainy weather.
19	29,6	29,6	29,7½	59½	68	64½	S. to N. E.	Unſettled weather.
20	29,8	29,5½	29,6¼	62½	63½	65½	Variable.	Ditto.
21	29,9	29,9½	30,0	63	70	67½	W.	Fine pleaſant weather.
22	29,9	29,8	29,6⅔	62½	76	71	S. W.	Ditto.
23	29,5	29,3½	29,2	67	80	74	Ditto.	Fair A. M. ſmall ſhowers P. M.
24	29,8½	29,9½	30,0½	66	67½	62½	N. E. to E. little.	Fine pleaſant day.
25	29,9¼	29,9	28,4½	58	69	67	E.	Cloudy day; heavy ſhowers in the night.
26	28,3½	28,2⅔	28,6½	65	72	75½	S. ſtrong.	Flying clouds, with bright intervals.
27	29,2½	29,2	29,2½	72	78	75	Ditto, little.	Fine pleaſant day.
28	29,6½	29,7	28,8¼	73	78½	71	W.	Ditto.
29	29,9½	30,0	30,0½	62	72	69	Ditto.	Ditto.
30	30,1	30,3	30,2½	62	74	67½	Ditto.	Ditto.
31	30,1	29,9	29,6½	64	76	76	S. W. little.	Ditto.

Quantity of rain in Auguſt, 3,15 } Inches.
Quantity of water evaporated, 4,35 }

SEP-

SEPTEMBER, 1772.

Days	Barometer		Thermometer			Winds.	Weather.
1	29,6	29,6½	71	75	73	E. little.	Fair pleasant weather.
2	29,7	29,9	67	69	67	N. to N. E.	Cloudy day; storm of rain in the night.
3	29,2½	29,2	67½	68	70	N. fresh.	Rainy till 4 P. M. clears up in the night.
4	29,8	30,0½	68½	81½	73	W.	Fine pleasant day.
5	30,1	30,1	67	70	62½	Ditto.	Ditto.
6	30,1	30,1	53	61	62½	Ditto.	Ditto.
7	30,1	29,8½	57	67½	65½	W. to S.	Fair A. M. cloudy P. M.
8	29,8	29,8	62	64	67	S. to W.	Cloudy day; fair evening.
9	29,6	29,7½	65	73	75	S.	Cloudy dull weather.
10	29,4	29,4	58½	57½	55	N.	Rainy day; fair evening.
11	29,2	29,1	52	56	53	N. strong.	Storm of rain all day.
12	29,1½	29,2	50	51	52	N. to W.	Rainy A. M. cloudy P. M. fair evening.
13	29,8½	30,3	51½	58	59	W. little.	Fine pleasant day.
14	30,0	30,0½	58	68	63	W. to S. W. little.	Ditto.
15	30,0	29,9	51	60½	56	W.	Ditto.
16	29,9	29,8	55	57	55	W. to N.	Fair A. M. cloudy P. M. rain in the night.
17	29,4½	29,7½	58	57	61	S. to W.	Rainy day; fair evening.
18	29,5	29,8½	55	65	62	W. little.	Fair day.
19	29,3	29,7	54	66½	65½	Ditto.	Ditto.
20	29,8	29,7	59	64	66½	S. little.	Ditto.
21	29,8	29,8	62½	63	63	Ditto.	Ditto.
22	29,8	29,9	55	62½	59	S. to E.	Ditto.
23	29,4½	29,4	62	64½	63	S.	Rainy day.
24	29,6½	29,6½	59½	58	57	N.	Cloudy dull weather.
25	29,8	29,8	57	61	55	Ditto.	Flying clouds, with bright intervals.
26	29,8	29,9	49	52	62	Ditto.	Fair weather.
27	29,9	29,9½	52	59	65	N. to E.	Ditto.
28	29,9	29,8	59	65	65	S. to S. W.	Fine bright day.
29	29,7	29,7	59	60	57	E.	Dull misling day.
30	29,7	29,7	57	59	56	Ditto.	Ditto.

Quantity of rain in September, 2,95 } Inches.
Quantity of water evaporated, 4,50 }

OCTO-

OCTOBER, 1772.

Days.	Barometer.			Thermometer.			Winds.	Weather.
1	29,7	29,7	29,7⅓	56	65	58½	N.	Dull cloudy day.
2	29,7⅓	29,6½	29,6½	56½	64	63	W.	Fine plea. day. *Aur. Bor.* in the night.
3	29,8½	29,8½	29,9	52	55	51	Ditto.	Ditto.
4	29,9½	30,0	30,0	43	54	53	Ditto.	Ditto.
5	30,0	29,9½	29,9	47½	56	57	S. little.	Fair weather.
6	29,9¼	29,9	29,8½	53	58	59	N. E.	Dull cloudy day.
7	29,7½	29,6½	29,5½	57½	56½	55	N.	Storm of rain all day.
8	28,8	28,6	28,5½	53	54	54½	Ditto.	Ditto.
9	28,6	28,8	28,9½	54	56	57	Ditto.	Dull misling day.
10	29,2	29,2	29,6½	54½	57	57½	Ditto.	Ditto.
11	29,6¼	29,6¼	29,7½	54	57	60	W. little.	Fair pleasant weather.
12	29,8½	29,8½	29,9½	54	62	60	S. W. little.	Ditto.
13	30,0	30,0	30,0	53½	57	53	W. N. W.	Ditto.
14	30,0½	30,0	30,1	46	55	55	Ditto.	Ditto.
15	30,0½	30,0	30,1	50	55½	59	Ditto.	Ditto.
16	30,2	30,2	30,2½	54	62	59	E. to N. W.	Ditto.
17	30,0½	30,0	29,9	55	62	60	W. to S. E.	Ditto.
18	29,7½	29,7½	29,7½	56½	57½	59	Variable.	Cloudy dull day,
19	29,7	29,6½	29,5	60	65	61½	S. W. little.	Fine pleasant day.
20	29,2	29,2	29,2	57	61	59	N. E. little.	Cloudy A.M. misling P.M. & in the nig.
21	29,3	29,2½	29,2	56½	56	52	N.	Cloudy A. M; rainy P. M.
22	29,2	29,2	29,2	48½	50	48	W. fresh.	Fair weather.
23	29,4	29,4	29,4	42½	50	49	W.	Fine pleasant day.
24	29,4½	29,4	29,3½	42	54	53½	W. to S. W.	Ditto.
25	29,4	29,3	29,3	53	60½	58½	S. W. fresh.	Cloudy A. M; fair P. M.
26	29,3	29,3	29,5½	52½	50½	57½	S. W.	Fine pleasant day.
27	29,6	29,4½	29,2	50	50	48	N. E. fresh.	Clo. day: sto. of ra. P. M. & in the nig.
28	29,2	29,2	29,2	49	49	50	N. E.	Cloudy with some rain.
29	29,2½	29,2	29,2½	48½	53	52	S. W.	Dull cloudy weather.
30	29,1	29,1	29,1½	47½	51	52	S. E. fresh.	Cloudy A. M; rain P. M. & in the nig.
31	29,4	29,5½	29,6	50	52½	52	N. W. fresh.	Flying clouds with bright intervals.

Quantity of rain in October, 6,70 } Inches.
Quantity of water evaporated, 3,75 }

NOVEM-

NOVEMBER, 1772.

Days.	Barometer.			Thermometer.			Winds.	Weather.
1	29,6	29,6	29,7	48	53	53	S. W. little.	Fine pleafant day.
2	29,7½	29,7	29,6½	47½	55	53	S. E.	Fair A. M; clo. P. M. fho. in the nig.
3	29,7	29,7	29,7	50	51	49	N. W. frefh.	Fair and pleafant.
4	29,6	29,6	29,5½	42	52	46	S.	Ditto.
5	29,6	29,6	29,6	42	42	36	N. W. frefh.	Ditto.
6	29,9	29,9½	30,0½	35	39	41½	Ditto.	Ditto.
7	30,0½	30,0⅔	30,0⅔	37½	46	45	S. little.	Ditto.
8	30,1½	30,3	30,3½	40	48	47	W. little.	Ditto.
9	30,4⅔	30,5	30,4¼	40	47	53	S. E. little.	Ditto.
10	30,2⅓	30,0	29,8	45	49	53	S. frefh.	Cloudy dull weather.
11	29,8½	29,8⅔	30,0¼	47	48	46	N. W. frefh.	Fair weather.
12	30,0⅓	30,0½	30,0	38	42	42	Ditto.	Fine pleafant day.
13	29,9	29,6⅔	29,1	35	38	49	S. E. to E. frefh.	Rainy day.
14	29,5⅔	29,6½	29,8	41½	43	41	N. W.	Fair pleafant weather.
15	29,9½	30,0	30,1½	36½	39	38	S. W. to W.	Ditto.
16	30,3	30,4	30,5	31	35	32	W.	Ditto.
17	30,5⅓	30,5⅔	30,5	27	32	32	Ditto.	Ditto.
18	30,3½	30,2⅓	30,3¼	28	34	37½	S. W. to W.	Ditto.
19	30,4	30,4	30,4	33½	40	39	Ditto.	Ditto.
20	30,3¾	30,3½	30,3½	33	43	40	W.	Ditto.
21	30,4⅓	30,4⅔	30,4⅔	37	40	43	N.	Dull cloudy day.
22	30,3⅓	30,3½	30,3	42	43	45	Variable.	Ditto.
23	30,3	30,4	30,4	42	44	42	W.	Fair pleafant weather.
24	30,4	30,4	30,3	37	38	40½	Variable.	Cloudy dull day.
25	30,2½	30,0	29,9	43	49	48½	S. E.	Dull rainy weather.
26	29,8⅓	29,7½	29,6	48	51	46	S. E. to E.	Ditto.
27	29,4⅓	29,4⅔	29,6⅓	43	45	44	N. E. to N. W.	Cloudy day; fair evening.
28	29,7½	29,8½	30,0	38	41	41	W. little.	Fine pleafant day.
29	30,0½	30,0	29,7½	42	43	50	E. frefh	Cloudy with rain; ftormy night.
30	29,7	29,6	29,6	50	50½	48	Variable.	Cloudy day; fair evening.

Quantity of rain in November, 3,90 }
Quantity of water evaporated, 2,45 } Inches.

DECEM-

DECEMBER, 1772.

Days.	Barometer.			Thermometer.			Winds.	Weather.
1	29,8	29,8⅔	29,8½	43	45	45	Variable.	Fair day; rainy evening.
2	29,8	29,8	29,7	47	47½	47	S. E.	Rainy weather.
3	29,6	29,6	29,7¼	43	43	40½	N. W. fresh.	Cloudy A. M; fair P. M.
4	29,8	29,8⅓	29,8½	38	39½	35	W. little.	Fine pleasant day.
5	29,9	29,9	29,9	34	36	36	Ditto.	Ditto.
6	30,0	30,0	30,1	29½	34	32	N. W. to N. E.	Cloudy unpleasant weather.
7	30,1	30,0½	30,0	25	28	26½	N. W.	Fair day.
8	29,9	29,9	29,9	26	31	30	Ditto.	Flying clouds, with bright intervals.
9	29,9½	29,9	29,8¼	29	32	32	W. to S.	Fair A. M. clo. with small showers P. M.
10	29,8	29,8	29,9	32	35	33	S. fresh.	Fine pleasant day.
11	29,9	29,9½	30,0	32	30	25	N. W. fresh.	Fair and clear.
12	30,0½	30,1¼	30,1¼	25	30	28	N. W. little.	Ditto.
13	29,9	29,7½	29,7¼	29	33	39	S. fresh.	Cloudy day; fair evening.
14	29,8½	29,8¾	30,0½	36	39½	39	W. little.	Fine pleas. day. *Aur. Bor.* in the night.
15	30,3	30,3⅔	30,4¼	34½	36	36	E.	Fair A. M. cloudy P. M.
16	30,4	30,2¼	30,0	33½	36½	41	N. E. fresh.	Cloudy A. M; rainy P. M.
17	30,0	30,0½	30,1	38	40	40	S. W.	Cloudy unsettled weather.
18	30,2	30,2½	30,2½	39	38½	40½	Ditto.	Ditto.
19	30,1⅔	30,2	30,2½	39	40½	41½	Ditto.	Fine pleasant day.
20	30,2	30,2	29,9	25½	38½	41½	N. E.	Cloudy A. M; rainy P. M.
21	29,8½	29,9	30,0½	40½	42	41½	W. little.	Fine pleasant day.
22	30,1	30,0½	29,8⅔	38	40½	44	S. little.	Ditto.
23	29,8	29,9	29,9½	42	44	43	W.	Ditto.
24	30,0	29,9	29,8½	40	40	38	N.	Cloudy day; snow in the evening.
25	29,7½	29,9	30,0½	36	37½	35	W.	Fine pleasant day.
26	30,1	30,1	29,9½	28	32	38	S. W. to E.	Cloudy day; rain in the night.
27	29,5½	29,4½	29,2	42	42	41	Variable.	Dull misling day.
28	29,4	29,6	29,7	41	41	39½	N. W.	Fine pleasant weather.
29	29,8½	29,8⅔	29,6½	38	43	45	Why S. little.	Ditto.
30	29,6	29,6⅔	29,9	43	44	35	N. W.	Ditto.
31	29,9⅔	29,9	29,9	33½	34	35	S.	Cloudy, dull weather.

Quantity of rain in December, 2,15 } Inches.
Quantity of water evaporated, 3,10 }

The

The greateſt height of the barometer this year, was on the 17th of November: The mercury was then at 30.5 ÷ inches. The leaſt height was 28.2 ÷ inches on Auguſt the 26th. The thermometer on the 29th of July, roſe to 96° ÷; on February the 13th, it ſtood at 3°: The former was the greateſt, the latter its leaſt height. The quantity of rain that fell in the year was 36.30 inches. The quantity of evaporation, meaſured by filling the veſſel once a week, came out 42.65 inches.

It is however to be obſerved that different methods of meaſuring the evaporation, will lead to different concluſions. It was becauſe the tube was of too ſmall a diameter, and not filled often enough, that the quantity of evaporation came out ſo ſmall in 1771. The method of making the experiments being altered, the evaporation turns out very different in 1772. If the experiments could be made on the ſurface of a watery fluid the reſult would determine the quantity of evaporation, with much greater certainty and accuracy, than can ever be done by means of a veſſel ſuſpended in the air.

OBSERVATIONS IN 1773.

The quantity of rain which fell in

January, was	1,95
February,	0,95
March,	1,75
April,	1,90
May,	2,10
June,	1,70
July,	1,00
Auguſt,	4,15
September,	1,05
October,	4,10
November,	1,90
December,	4,00

To

To meafure the quantity of *rain*, I fixed a tube about three inches diameter, in fuch a manner as to receive the rain as it fell; which I meafured as foon as it was over, and added up the whole of each month together. In this account the *fnow* and *hail* are included: Thefe were meafured by taking up in the tube all the fnow or hail that fell on a fpace equal to its furface, and then melting it. The method of meafuring the quantity of *evaporation* by a tube fufpended in the air being uncertain and inaccurate, thofe obfervations are omitted.

The greateft height of the barometer this year, was on the 22d and 23d of February: The mercury at 12^h on each of thefe days, was at 30.6 inches. The leaft height was $28.6\frac{1}{2}$ inches, on December 26th at 12^h. The thermometer on the 8th of July, at $12^h\frac{1}{2}$, rofe to $96°\frac{1}{4}$: On February the 22d, at $8\frac{1}{4}$ A. M. it ftood at $9°\frac{1}{4}$ below o. At both thefe times the thermometer was hung in the open air, in a fhade: The former was the greateft, the latter its leaft height. The quantity of rain this year amounted to 26,55 inches.

On the 17th of July there was an *Aurora*, uncommon in this refpect, that there were feveral appearances of it in the *fouth*: The firft of thefe was about 9^h. It began about $20°$ above the horizon and inftantly fpread itfelf in a horizontal direction to the diftance of $30°$ each way from the meridian. For the fpace of one quarter of an hour there were five fuch appearances, all in the fouth as before; their duration was not more than half a minute, and their colour a pale light, exactly like that of the Aurora in the north.

There was alfo a remarkable HURRICANE this year, the effects of which were principally felt at *Salisbury*, *Amesbury*, and *Haverhill*. Thefe towns lie on Merrimack river, on the north fide; Salifbury being the place where the river empties itfelf into the ocean.

The

The hurricane came on *August* 14th, 1773. Its *rise* was very fudden, and without any previous uncommon appearance in the fky, or other fymptom of its approach. In the morning there was a light breeze of wind at the eaft, attended with plentiful fhowers. At 7ʰ ¼ the wind veered about to fouth-eaft, where it became a brifk gale. In about two minutes, it got into the fouth-weft, and became on a fudden very violent. From thence in about two minutes more, it fhifted to weft-north-weft, and then fuddenly died away to a moderate breeze. While the wind was thus changing, it feemed to blow in every direction ; the gufts became very violent, and formed many little whirlwinds all around, attended with a very heavy fhower of rain, and an uncommon darknefs.

At the place where *Salisbury* and *Amesbury* join, the *violence* of the hurricane was very great. Its firft appearance was on Merrimack river. At the time when the wind was veering to the fouth-eaft, its waters feemed to be inftantly thrown into a violent agitation ; and came rolling from the eaft as if they would have overflowed the banks. The hurricane immediately ftruck the fhore at Salifbury-Point and Amefbury, levelling before it feveral well built houfes almoft new, unroofing, twifting, and wrecking others ; and thus tearing down, or fhattering moft of the buildings that were in its way. Several buildings were fhattered to pieces, and others removed in an inftant. A fail-maker's loft in which a man was fitting, was carried away and difperfed in a moment ; the unhappy man being found fenfelefs at the diftance of 94 feet from the place where the loft ftood. A large oak poft 14 feet in length and 11 inches in diameter, was taken up and carried by the wind 138 feet. Two new veffels of 90 tons burthen, were lifted up from the blocks and carried to the diftance of 22 feet. And a large bundle of fhingles was taken up from the earth and thrown near 330 feet, in a direction contrary to that of the poft and veffels. The trees around were

were torn up, the fences were thrown down, fcattered or carried off, and the various kinds of lumber that lay difperfed on the fhore, were whirled about in different directions, and to different diftances.　Some houfes and veffels that feemed the moft expofed to the wind, fuffered nothing at all; and others that feemed to be the leaft expofed, were much damaged or carried off.　The number of buildings that fuffered was about 120: And though many perfons were carried to fome diftance, and others much hurt, being covered in the ruins or in the cellars of their houfes, no lives were loft.　At the place where this deftruction was done, the buildings were pretty thick, amounting to about 150.　The general *direction* of the hurricane was from caft-fouth-eaft to weft-north-weft.　Its *extent*, in width, was about a quarter of a mile; in length, about a mile and three quarters: And its *duration*, not more than four minutes from the time it firft began till all became ftill and quiet again.

At the fame time confiderable damage was done at *Haverhill*, ten miles higher up the river.　There the hurricane came on from the fouth-weft.　Its firft effect was the deftruction of a large new barn.　The barn containing a large quantity of hay and grain, was crufhed down in an inftant.　The hay, boards and fhingles were fcattered round to all points of the compafs, to the diftance of four or five rods from the place where the barn ftood; and fome of them were carried to the diftance of three miles north-eaft.　A large dwelling houfe at eight or ten rods diftance, was much damaged; every board and rib was torn from the roof, and the chimney wrecked to the foundation.　Five barns were almoft wholly deftroyed, and a number of houfes and other buildings were much damaged.　In fome, the windows and doors were drove in; in others, the boards and fhingles were ripped off and fcattered in all directions.　The ftone walls in fome places were almoft levelled with the ground; and the trees to the
number

number of five hundred were fwept off in the fpace of a mile. The general *direction* of the hurricane was different here from what it was in Salifbury, being from fouth-weft to north-eaft. Its *extent* was about three miles in length, and half a mile in width: Its *duration* not more than four minutes. The *violence* of the hurricane was probably as great at Haverhill, as it was at Salifbury: But as it paffed half a mile above or north-weft of the centre of the town, where the buildings were not very thick, the damage done by it was much lefs.

To what *extent* the difturbance in the atmofphere reached, cannot be exactly determined. Though it did not form whirlwinds of fuch force as to produce any remarkable effects at any other places but thofe mentioned above, it evidently extended to all the towns on Merrimack river, from the mouth to fome miles above Haverhill. In all the adjacent towns, the fudden change and different directions of the wind, with their effects in twifting the trees, corn, &c. were obferved to the diftance of fix or eight miles on each fide of the river. And yet there did not feem to be any very great alterations in the *weight* or *temperature* of the atmofphere, at any confiderable diftance from the place where the winds were fo violent. At *Bradford* oppofite to Haverhill, and not more than a mile from the place where the damage was done, the *barometer* at 7^h A. M. ftood at 29,8$\frac{1}{2}$ inches. At the time of the hurricane it fuddenly fell to 29,6$\frac{1}{4}$; and juft after to 29,5$\frac{3}{4}$, which was its leaft height that day. By noon it rofe to 29,7$\frac{1}{4}$, and at 9^h P. M. it got up to 29,8$\frac{1}{4}$; alterations very common in this part of America. *Farenheit's thermometer* in the morning was at 74°; at noon and 9^h P. M. it was one degree lower: The wind continuing very moderate between weft and north-weft from 8^h A. M. till night.

From thefe phenomena we may form fome probable conjectures as to the *caufe* and *origin* of the hurricane. What occafioned fuch a violent irregular commotion in the air,

air, was probably the great *rarefaction* of it. The weather, for a week before, had been uncommonly hot, and
the wind conftantly at fouth or fouth-weft. The air next
to the furface of the earth muft therefore have been greatly heated and rarefied; and probably was become fpecifically lighter than the air in the higher regions. The confequence would be that the lighter rarefied air would afcend, while the heavier condenfed air would defcend; and
in this way the *equilibrium* of the air would be deftroyed:
To the place where the equilibrium of the air was thus broken, the adjacent air would inftantly flow on every fide as to
a common centre; forming eddies and whirlpools, and thus
affuming a *circular motion*. And this it is probable gave rife
to thofe fudden changes, different directions, and violent
gufts of the wind. The place where this circular motion
began, feems to have been in the upper region of the air,
at fome diftance from the furface of the earth; for feveral
of the effects of the hurricane bear the marks of a *defcent*.
At the place where it firft ftruck Merrimack river, it hove
up the waters, as if fome great force had been impreffed
upon its furface: And at Haverhill, where it was firft felt
it crufhed a barn to pieces as if fome immenfe weight had
fallen upon it. When the defcending air and whirl came
to the earth, being ftopped in its defcent it feems to have
inftantly fpread itfelf in to a larger circle or compafs, blowing every way from the centre. And hence the pieces of
the barn that was crufhed down by it, became fcattered
to the diftance of four or five rods all around. A defcent
of the air in one place would be immediately fucceeded
with an *afcent* of it in another. And thus the whirlwind,
where the air was defcending crufhed down the buildings
before it: But where the air was afcending, lifted up, un-
roofed, or carried them away; fhattering and throwing off
the materials thus carried up, as they came to the extremity of the whirl, in tangent lines, to different diftances and in all directions. Befides this circular, the whirlwinds

winds had alſo a *progreſſive* motion. Had the different winds by which the whirlwinds were formed been of equal violence, the whirlwinds would have been ſtationary conſiſting only of a circular motion ; but being of unequal violence, the whirlwinds had a progreſſive motion, proceeding in different directions at different places, according to the direction of the ſtrongeſt wind.

The *ſummer* preceding this hurricane had been in ſome reſpects different from what is common in this part of the country. There had been an uncommon drought for two months before, which was no where more ſevere than in the towns upon the river ; and in no ſummer for ſeveral years, have we had ſo much hot weather. This circumſtance is agreeable to the preſumption of theory ; for, if whirlwinds and hurricanes are derived from the great rarefaction of ſome part of the atmoſphere, it might be expected that the times in which they would happen, would be in the moſt calm, or hot weather.

N° X.

A Letter from J. MADISON, *Eſquire, to* D. RITTENHOUSE, *Eſquire.*

DEAR SIR,

William and Mary College, Virginia, November, 1779.

AGREEABLY to promiſe, I now tranſmit you a ſeries of obſervations upon our climate. They comprehend an entire year, and part of the ſucceeding. I thought once of ſending you only a mean of the obſervations for each month, but as it was a part of our natural hiſtory, which has never yet been made public, I have therefore ſent a copy of the journal. Some ſingular cir-

U   cumſtances

cumftances too attending the barometer I thought deferved to be particularly noted, which could not have been done had the firft idea been adopted. For the obfervations upon the barometer not only fhew us the different ftates of the atmofphere, but, perhaps, may throw farther light upon the true caufe of the Aurora Borealis. The fact is, that a fall of the barometer always fucceeds that phenomenon. The frequency of its appearance lately, gave me an opportunity of obferving this effect at different times. It has for fome time been fuppofed (after Dr. Franklin had firft given rife to the opinion) to be an electrical appearance; and I think, the levity of the atmofphere, as proved by the barometer, adds great weight to that fuppofition: fince it is well known to every electrician, that a rarefaction of the air, in our experiments, will always produce fimilar appearances. One circumftance indeed was obfervable, that a change of weather, to wet, generally fucceeded; but as this effect was not fo conftant, it was not much attended to. But the barometer by fhewing that the atmofphere is actually lighter, and of confequence more rarefied at the time of fuch appearances than at others, evinces at leaft, that it is in a ftate the moft likely to exhibit them; it is to be obferved alfo, that the greateft fall of the barometer is not prior to, but always fucceeds this appearance; fhewing that the rarefaction firft begins in the upper parts of the atmofphere.

It is remarkable that the range of the barometer was not more than one inch and a tenth throughout the whole year, nor do I remember ever to have feen a greater difference at any time not included in the journal; whilft we fee in other countries, the atmofphere undergoing changes fo great as to effect a difference of three or four inches. Whence is it then that we are expofed to more violent ftorms of wind and rain? Perhaps indeed the changes here, though not fo great, may be more fudden, of which fome remarkable inftances may be feen in the journal.

Our

Our coldeſt winds, as well as the moſt violent, are the
north-weſt. The ſouth and ſouth-weſt winds are the hotteſt, though the ſenſations of heat to which we are expoſed, do not correſpond to the different degrees marked by
the thermometer, as they depend much upon a current of
air with which we are generally favoured about the hotteſt
time of the day, and copious ſweating. I do not recollect
ever to have ſeen the thermometer here at more than 95,
though Dr. Franklin mentions that in June 1750, it ſtood
at 100 in the ſhade at Philadelphia, when he obſerves,
" I expected that the natural heat of the body, 96, added
" to the heat of the air, 100, ſhould jointly have created
" or produced a much greater degree of heat in the body;
" but the fact was, that my body never grew ſo hot as the
" air that ſurrounded it, or the inanimate bodies immerſ-
" ed in the ſame. For I remember well, that the deſk,
" when I laid my arm upon it, a chair when I ſat down
" in it, all felt exceeding warm to me, as if they had been
" warmed before the fire. And I ſuppoſe a dead body
" would have acquired the temperature of the air, though
" a living one, by continual ſweating, and by the eva-
" poration of that ſweat was kept cold." I have been
the more particular in tranſcribing this paſſage from
the works of this philoſopher, as it certainly ſhews to
whom the merit of certain late diſcoveries, which have
made ſo much noiſe in the philoſophical world, moſt juſtly
belongs; I mean, that power which the human as well
as all animate bodies have, of counteracting the heat of
an atmoſphere in which they are placed. For what do all
the experiments upon heated rooms evince, farther than
had before been publiſhed by the doctor? It is thus that
Franklin ſetting in his chair, like Newton reaſoning upon
the figure of the earth, could ſhew what muſt coſt others
infinite labour and fatigue. But, though the effect was
obſerved and attributed to evaporation, yet I do not remember that it is any where ſhewn in what manner eva-

U 2   poration

poration produces cold. Hamilton, in his excellent effay upon the afcent of vapors, fpeaking of the natures of
folution and evaporation, has thefe words, " how cold is
" produced in either cafe, I cannot pretend to fay." The
doctor has given the moft probable explanation of the
manner in which it is produced by folution, and I think
the following, which is collected from his general doctrine
may be applied to evaporation. It is admitted that there
is a ftronger attraction between heat and water, or fuch like
fluid, than between heat and any other body, for on this
account it is that bodies are cooled when plunged into water. When ever therefore, water for inftance, is put upon
any part of the human body, its natural heat is more attracted in that part by the water, than by the flefh, and
therefore, the water in going off in the form of vapour
carries with it part of the heat, and confequently leaves
that place in a negative ftate, or with lefs than its natural
quantity. It is the fame with the thermometer. Hence
it is, that we are much hotter frequently when the thermometer fcarcely exceeds 82 or 83, there being no current
of air to carry off the moifture from the furface of the body,
than when it even ftands as high as 90 or 95.

I am, with the greateft refpect,

Your fervant and friend,

J. MADISON.

JULY,

JULY, 1777.

The Observations upon the Thermometer were made at eight, twelve and four o'clock, in the summer. In the winter, the last at three, the other observations at eight o'clock.

Days	Winds	Weather	Barometer	Thermometer 8 H.	12 H.	4 H.	Observations
3	N by E	Clear	30 1 3		73	73½	
4	N b E	Clear	30 1 0	69¼	73	74	
5	N b E	Clear	30 0 0	70¼	74	76,5	
6	N E	Rain	29 1 0	74	77		
7	E b N	Cloudy & rain	30 0 0	73	73	73,5	
8	E b N	Cloudy & rain	30 1 5	72	74	76	
9	S b W	Clear	30 0 8	75	78	79	
10	E b N	Clear	30 0 0	78	83	84	
11	S	Clear	30 0 2	77	82	83	
12	S W	Clear	30 8 4	80	83	85	
13	N b E	Rainy	29 7 2	79	80	81	
14	E b s	Cloudy	29 9 0	75	78	76	
15	E b N	Cloudy	29 9 0	75	78	80	
16	S E	Clear	29 9 8	79	81		
21	S W	Clear	29 9 4	77	81	82	
22	S W	Cloudy	29 8 7	79	82	82	
23	N W	Clear	30 0 2	74	75	75	
24	N b W	Clear	30 0 5	73	73	74	
25	N b E	Cloudy	30 0 5	74	75	74	
26	S W	Clear	29 9 9	74	77		
27	N b E	Clear	29 9 0	77	80	80	
28	S W	Clear	29 9 0	80	80	82	
29	W	Clear	29 3 0	80	81	82	
30	N b W	Clear	30 0 0	78	79	80	
31	N E	Clear	30 1 3	77	78	79	

Note, That the height of the mercury in the barometer is determined by a scale divided into inches and tenths with a nonius; so that 30.1.3 will be read 30 inches, 1 tenth, and 3 tenths of a tenth.

AUGUST,

AUGUST, 1777.

Days.	Winds.	Weather.	Barometer.	Thermometer. 8 H.	12 H.	4 H.	Observations.
1	S W	Clear	30 1 3	77	80	83	
2	S W	Clear	30 1 4	79	83	84	
3	S W	Clear	30 2 8	83	85	88	
4	S W	Clear	30 1 8	83	86	86	Much lightening in the evening.
5	S W	Clear	30 0 5	81	86	87	* Rain with lightening. The barometer was observed to rise before the rain to 30 1 0.
6	S W	Rainy	30 0 5	82	83	82	
7	S W	Cloudy	30 0 9	80	82	80	
8	S W	Clear	30 2 2	80	82		
9	S W	Clear	30 2 2	80	84		
10	S W	Clear	30 1 7	83	86	86	It was hotter according to the sensation of the human body this evening than had been observed this summer. There was no wind.
11	S W	Clear	30 1 7	83	87	88	
12	S W	Clear	30 1 8	84	86½	88	
13	S W	Clear	30 1 8	84	86	88	
14	S W	Clear	30 1 8	84	86	89	
15	S W	Clear	30 0 0	86	88	91	
16	S W	Clear	30 1 1	86	88	87	Much rain and lightening. The point was driven off the Capitol rod, considerably fused.
17	W	Clear	30 1 4	82	84		
18	E	Clear	30 1 4	83	85		
19	W	Cloudy	30 1 4		82		
20	W	Clear	30 1 4	79	82	83	Frequent rain.
21	W	Clear	30 1 2	82	82	85	
22	S W	Clear	30 1 2	85	85	86	Rain with lightening.
23	S W	Clear	30 2 6	83	86	83	
24	S W	Clear	30 0 6	80	85	83	
25	N W	Cloudy	30 0 5	82	84		Rain.
26	N E	Cloudy	30 2 1	76	79	72	
27	N E	Clear	30 1 0	73	76	76	
28	N E	Clear	30 1 0	73	75	75	
29	S W	Clear	30 2 0	74	74		

S E P-

SEPTEMBER, 1777.

Days	Winds	Weather	Barometer	Thermometer 8 H.	12 H.	4 H.	Observations.
1	S E	Clear	30 1 8	73	76	77	
2	N E	Clear	30 1 8	75	78	78	
3	N E	Cloudy	30 3 0	72	73	72	
4	N E	Cloudy	30 3 3	69	71		
5	S E	Clear	30 2 5	73	75	74	
6	S W	Clear	30 1 9	72	78		
7	S	Clear	30 1 0	78	82	80	Rain.
8	N E	Clear	30 1 7	76	76	75	
9	E	Clear	30 3 0	75	79	79	
10	S W	Cloudy	30 1 7	74	81		
11	S E	Clear	29 0 1	81	82	80	Rain.
12	S E	Clear	29 9 4	76	73		
13	N E	Clear	30 2 1	73	74	72	
14	S E	Clear	30 2 6	72	71	73	
15	N E	Cloudy	30 2 6	72	69	70	
16	E	Rain	29 9 0	69	68	68	Rain.
17	N W	Cloudy	29 9 0	68	67½	67	Showery.
18	N E	Cloudy	30 0 6	69	70	70	
19	E	Clear	30 0 6	69	77	77	
20	S W	Clear	30 0 8	73	79		
21	E	Clear	30 0 8	67	69	71	
22	N E	Clear	30 0 5	67	69	70	
23	N E	Clear	30 0 0	69	72		
24	S W	Clear	30 1 5	69	74	71	Rain.
25	S W	Cloudy	30 2 0	60	63	63	
26	N W	Clear	30 1 9	61	60	62	
27	N E	Cloudy	30 1 6	59	60	60	
28	N E	Clear	30 9 6	58	61	61	
29	N E	Cloudy	30 2		60	60	
30							

OCTO-

OCTOBER, 1777.

Days.	Winds.	Weather.	Barometer.	Thermometer. 8 H.	12 H.	4 H.	Observations.
1	N E	Clear	30 0	58	61	62	
2	W	Clear	30 3	61	64	65	
3	S W	Clear	30 3	62	65	66	
4	S	Clear	30 6	67			
5		Clear	30 2	70	44	75	
6	S E	Clear	30 7	70	74	75	
7	N E	Cloudy	30 1	72	72	72	
8	N E	Clear	30 1	66	68	68	
9	S	Rain	30 4	67	67	71	
10	N E	Clear	30 5	64	65	65	
11	N E	Cloudy	30 .3 0	62	62	62	
12	N E	Cloudy	30 3	62	63	63	
13	S W	Cloudy	30 1	61	63	64	
14	N E	Clear	30 2	62	64	65	
15	N E	Clear	30 3	61	61	62	
16	N W	Cloudy	30 9	58	60	62	
17	N E	Cloudy	30 9	59	61	63	
18	N E	Clear	30 0	61			
19	S W	Clear	30 1	66			
28	N by E	Rain	29 6 8*	56	57	65	Much rain. * The lowest.
29	S W	Cloudy	29 7 0	48	59		
30	W b S	Clear	30 0 0	49	60		
31	W	Clear	30 2 0	50			

N O V E M-

NOVEMBER, 1777.

Days.	Winds.	Weather.	Barometer.	Thermometer. 8 H.	12 H.	3 H.	Observations.
1	N E	Clear	30 5 8	56	53	52	The ground frozen.
2	N E	Cloudy	30 4		58		
10	W	Clear	30 1 3	42	49	50	Frost.
11	S W	Clear	29 7 0	42	52	55	Wind high and cold.
12	W	Clear	29 0 0	47	55	58	* Remarkable Aurora Borealis at 7 o'clock
13	W b N	Clear	30 0 8	41	45	49	this evening. It was terminated towards the
15	N	Cloudy	30 0 8	43	47	49	eaſt by the two ſtars β and θ in Auriga,
16	N	Cloudy	30 0 9	44	45	47	and its greateſt altitude reached nearly Capel-
17	N	Clear	30 3 7	41	52	54	la. The ſtars in the tail of the Great Bear ter-
18	N	Clear	30 2 9	37	42	45	minated it to the weſt. It is obſervable that
19	N W	Clear	30 2 9	53	39	50	the barometer was falling from the 18th and
20	S W	Clear	30 4 0	37	48	57	was never obſerved ſo low but once, little after
21	W b S	Clear	30 1 7	39	55	61	the vernal equinox, throughout the whole year,
22	S W	Clear	30 0 5	54	59	64	as it was ſo ſoon after the Aurora. Its ſudden
23	S W	Clear	30 0 3	55	59	63	riſe was alſo remarkable. It became cloudy
24	W	Clear	30 0 2	57	59	59	about one o'clock.
25	N W	Clear	30 0 4	55	56	60	† Snow fell 7¼ inches in 24 hours.
26	W	Clear	30 8 9	36	59	48	
27	E b S	Cloudy	29 3	42	42	41	
28	N W	Snow	29 4	41	39	37	
30	N W	Rain		39	39	40	

V   DECEM-

DECEMBER, 1777.

Days	Winds	Weather	Barometer	8 H.	12 H.	3 H.	Observations
1	W	Clear	29 7	35	45	47	
2	W	Clear	30 4	37	51	50	
3	W b S	Clear	30 4	37	48	55	
4	W b N	Clear	29 6	44	53		
5	N	Clear	30 1	40			
6	N	Clear	30 3	41			
7	S W	Clear	30 2	43	49	51	
8	S W	Clear	30 4	54	58	60	
9	N	Rain	29 8	52	62	67	
10	N b W	Cloudy	30 1	41	47	47	
11	N W	Clear	30 8	36	45	46	
12	S W	Clear	30 2	36	47	50	
13	S W	Clear	30 2	40	57	60	
14	N W	Cloudy	30 1	45	50	57	
15	N W	Clear	30 1	46	58	66	Snow in the evening.
16	W	Cloudy	30 0	46	59	62	
17	S W	Clear	29 9	49	51	59	
18	N E	Cloudy	29 8	47	51	56	
19	N b W	Clear	29 9	48	50	56	
20	N	Clear	30 1	46	49	51	
21	S W	Clear	30 0	36	45	49	
22	N E	Clear	30 0	43	47	55	
23	N E	Snow	30 0	40	44	45	
24	N W	Cloudy	30 4	35	41	43	
25	S W	Cloudy	30 0	41	46	48	
26	S W	Cloudy	30 0	50	49	52	
27	N E	Rain	29 9	41	56	59	An Aurora. Cloudy evening.
28	N W	Clear	30 1	41	44	46	
29	N W	Clear	30 6	35	37	39	
30	N	Clear	30 4	25	27	28	
31	E by N	Clear	30 3	27	32	38	

JANUARY,

JANUARY, 1778.

Days.	Winds.	Weather.	Barometer.	Thermometer. 8 H.	12 H.	3 H.	Observations.
1	N E	Clear	30 9	30	39	40	
2	S W	Cloudy	30 3	40	47	49	
3	S W	Cloudy	30 1	50	55	58	
4	W b N	Clear	30 0	41	57	59	
5	S W	Clear	30 0	50	60	63	
6	S W	Clear	30 2	55	62	66	
7	N b W	Clear	30 3	50	56	57	
8	W	Rain	30 6	45	54		
9	W	Clear	29 7	48	58		
10	S W	Clear	29 3	47	47	61	
11	N W	Rain	30 1	48	47	47	
12	N	Clear	30 4	43	47		
13	W	Clear	30 1	37	50	50	
14	N	Clear	30 8	47			
15	N	Clear	30 9	30	37	39	
16	N	Clear	30 5	27	40	43	
18	W	Clear	29 7	41	45	47	
19	W	Clear	30 0	41	43	46	
20	S W	Cloudy	29 8	40	51	56	
21	N W	Cloudy	29 8	40	52	55	
22	N E	Clear	29 9	41	37	40	
23		Cloudy		34			
24				37			
25	S W	Cloudy	29 8	47	50	57	
26	N W	Clear	30 1	38	42	44	
27	N W	Clear	30 3	32	40	43	
28	S W	Cloudy	30 3	38	52	57	
29	S W	Rain	29 9	61	62	63	
30	N W	Clear	30 3	47	55	57	
31	S W	Rain	30 2	48	54	56	

FEBRU-

FEBRUARY, 1778.

Days.	Winds.	Weather.	Barometer.	Thermometer. 8 H.	12 H.	3 H.	Observations.
1	S W	Clear	30 0 0	54	52	49	
2	W	Cloudy	30 4 3	43	48	57	
3	W by S	Clear	30 4 3	40	53	61	
4	S W	Clear	30 3 3	56	60	62	
5	S E	Clear	30 3 0	52	61	57	
6	S E	Clear	30 3 0	57	57	55	
7	N W	Clear	30 3 8	49	44	44	
8	N E	Clear	30 2 7	45	44	41	
9	N W	Clear	30 2 3	31	40		
10	S E	Cloudy	30 1 3	35			
11	W	Rainy	30 1 4	42	43	43	Much rain in the evening.
12	N W	Clear	30 0 7	42	47	47	
13	W b N	Clear	30 0 9	40	47	48	
14	W	Clear	30 1 6	40	45	46	
15	E	Rainy	30 1 0	40	42	43	
16	W	Cloudy	30 1 3	41			
17	N W	Clear	30 3 0	31	40	42	
18	N W	Clear	30 3 3	32	41	42	
19	S W	Cloudy	30 8 3	39			
20	S W	Rain	29 8 0	45	46	46	
21	N W	Clear	30 1 5	38	45	37	
22	F b S	Cloudy	30 0 7	36	37	47	
23	W	Clear	30 7 2	39	49		
24	W b N	Clear	30 0 2	39	54		Wind W at 8.
25	S W	Cloudy	30 0 6	47	38	60	
26	S W	Cloudy	29 9 0	60	70	70	
27	W	Rain	29 6 6	64	60	59	
28	W b S	Clear	29 9 0	42	51		

MARCH,

MARCH, 1778.

Days.	Winds.	Weather.	Barometer.	Thermometer. 8 H.	12 H.	3 H.	Observations.
1	W	Clear	29 9	36	47	48	
2	N W	Clear	30 6	35	41	44	Snows very fast.
3	E b N	Cloudy	27 6	36	32	31	
4	N W	Clear	30 0	24¾	35	39	
5	S W	Clear	30 0	23	42	45	
6	W	Clear	30 7	42	49	53	
7	s W	Clear	30 2	47	57	60	
8	E	Clear	30 8	45	46		
9	E	Cloudy	30 9	45	48	49	
10	N	Cloudy	30 5	47	47	57	
11	s W	Cloudy	30 4	59	52	64	Peach trees in blossom.
12	s W	Clear	30 0	68	69	70	
13	s W	Clear	30 0	69	71	76	
14	s W	Cloudy	30 1	65	72	79	
15	s W	Cloudy	30 8	63	66	65	The wind at N W for part of the day.
16	s W	Clear	29 6	67	74	76	
17	s W	Clear	30 2	51	67	65	
18	N	Cloudy	30 9	47	51	58	
19	s	Clear	29 9	50	54	55	
20	N W	Clear	29 2	49	50	60	
21	N W	Cloudy	30 1	39	51	59	
22	N b E	Clear	30 0	44	45	54	
23	E	Rain	29 6	45	51	56	
24	E	Clear	29 5	48	51	53	
25	s E	Clear	29 7	46	47	48	
26	N W	Rainy	29 8	47	57		
27	N W	Clear	29 3	50	56	57	Winds very high.
28	S E	Rainy	29 5	45	54	49	Ditto.
29	N W	Cloudy	29 9	47	48	54	
30	N W	Clear			49		

W   APRIL,

APRIL, 1778.

Days	Winds	Weather	Barometer	Thermometer 8 H.	12 H.	3 H.	Observations
1	N	Clear	29 9 0	48	54	55	
2	S E	Clear	29 7 3	54	57	59	
3	W	Clear	29 7 8	45	54	55	
5	W	Clear	29 7 7	44	57	60	
6	W	Clear	29 8 0	47	58	58	
7	N W	Cloudy	29 8 0	52	56	61	
8	N W	Clear	30 0 0	52	60	61	
9	E W	Clear	30 2 0	51	60	64	
10	S W	Clear	30 2 8	51	63	61	
11	S E	Rainy	30 1 0	59	60	60	
12	E b S	Rainy	30 1 3	58	60	70	
13	S W	Clear	30 1 0	59	63	71	
14	S W	Rainy	30 0 5	61	73	69	
15	N W	Rainy	30 0 0	66	67	65	
16	N W	Rainy	29 9 0	59	62		
17		Clear	29 7 7	58			
18							
26	W	Clear	29 8 6	56	65	61	
27	E	Rainy	29 9 3	58	56	56	
28	E b N	Rainy	29 7 1	57	58	57	
29	E b N	Rainy	29 5 7	57	57	57	
30	N b W	Clear	29 6 5	56	59	59	Lightening and thunder.

MAY,

MAY, 1778.

Days.	Winds.	Weather.	Barometer.	Thermometer. 8 H.	12 H.	3 H.	Observations.
1	N W	Clear	29 8	54	58	59	
2	N E	Clear	29 6	55	57	58	
3	N E	Clear	29 6	55			
4	N W	Clear	29 7	56	62	63	
5	N W	Clear	29 8	61	68	71	
6	S W	Clear	29 8	62	72	77	
7	S E	Clear	29 8	67	76	79	
8	S	Clear	29 0	65	66	79	
9	N	Clear	29 8	59	60	66	
10	W	Clear	30 0	65			
11	S	Clear	29 8	68	75	77	Rain.
12	S	Clear	30 0	69	76	78	
15	S W	Clear	30 1	69	75	77	
16	S W	Clear	30 1	75	80	83	
17	S W	Clear	30 1	78	80	79	Rain.
18	S W	Clear	30 0	78	82	83	Rain.
19	S W	Clear	30 0	75	84	85	
20	S W	Clear	30 0	71	80	85	
21	N E	Rain	30 1	70	74	71	
22	N by E	Clear	30 0	65	74	-75	
23	E	Clear	29 9	64	72	80	
24	S W	Clear	29 9	75	81	85	Rain.
25	N	Clear	29 8	74	81	82	
26	N	Clear	29 9	75	72	73	
27	W	Clear	29 1	70	63	65	
28	N W	Clear	30 3	60	62	63	
29	W	Clear	30 2	60	66	70	
30	E by S	Cloudy	30 9	60			

JUNE,

JUNE, 1778.

Days.	Winds.	Weather.	Barometer.	Thermometer. 8 H.	12 H.	3 H.	Observations.
1	S E	Rainy	30 0	65	69	72	
2	N W	Cloudy	30 1	70	75	76	
3	N b E	Cloudy	30 0	70	74	75	
4	E	Clear	30 2	64	70	71	
5	S E	Cloudy	30 2	64	70	78	
6	E	Cloudy	30 0	65	75	73	
7	E	Cloudy	29 8		74	75	
8	N	Clear	29 8	65	74	75	
9	N	Clear	30 6		75	76	
11	W b S	Clear	29 9	70	80	84	
12	N E	Cloudy	29 8	70	73	74	
13	N E	Clear	29 9	68	73	74	
14	N E	Clear	29 6	64	65	69	
15	N E	Cloudy	30 3	68	70	72	
16	W	Clear	30 0	67	75	78	Rain.
17	S W	Clear	30 0	70	80	84	
18	S W	Clear	29 5	78	87	86	
19	E	Rainy	29 3	78	79	79	
20	E	Rainy	29 7	79	79	78	
21	S E	Cloudy	29 5	75	83	86	
22	S W	Clear	29 2	76	83	87	
23	S b E	Cloudy	29 7	75	77	77	Rain.
24	S b E	Cloudy	29 0	75	80	81	Much Rain.
25	S W	Clear	30 0	78	84	86	
26	S W	Clear	30 0	78	85	87	
27	S W	Clear	29 5	80		86	
28	S W	Clear	29 9	80	87	86	
29	S W	Clear	29 0	75	86	88	
30	S W	Clear	30 0	80	86	89	

JULY,

JULY, 1778.

Days.	Winds.	Weather.	Barometer.	Thermometer 8 H.	12 H.	4 H.	Observations.
1	S W	Clear	29 9	80	86	89	
2	W	Clear	29 9	70	84	80	
3	W	Clear	29 5	77	83	81	Rain.
4	N W	Cloudy	29 8	73	75	76	
5	E. N E.	Clear	30 0	73	76	79	
6	W	Clear	30 6	75	77	81	
7	W	Clear	30 7	76	78	88	
8	S W	Clear	30 3	78	85	86	Rain.
9	S W	Clear	30 0	80	86	88	
10	S W	Clear	30 0	80	88	90	
11	S W	Clear	29 9	80	87	88	Rain.
12	S W	Clear	29 9	77	80	81	
13	E N E	Cloudy	30 7	70	73	75	
14	N W	Cloudy	30 0	71	75	77	
15	N E	Clear	30 5	73	75	78	
16	N E	Clear	30 2	73	76	77	
17	E	Cloudy					
21	N E	Cloudy	30 0	77	77	78	Rain.
22	E	Rain	29 8	75	76	76	Rain.
23	N E	Cloudy	29 9	69	73	75	
24	E	Clear	29 9	72	77	77	Rain.
25	E	Cloudy	30 1	73	75	77	Rain.
26	N E	Rain	30 6	73	78	78	Rain.
27	N E	Cloudy	30 7	75	82	85	Rain.
28	S W	Clear	30 0	75	83	86	
29	S W	Clear	30 0	78	85	87	
30	S W	Clear	30 0	78	85	87	
31	S W	Clear	30 0				

X   AUGUST,

AUGUST, 1778.

Days.	Winds.	Weather.	Barometer.	Thermometer. 8 H.	12 H.	4 H.	Observations.
1	S W	Clear	30 00	79	86	90	
2	S W	Clear	30 00	80	81	89	
3	S W	Clear	29 99	78	84	86	
4	S W	Cloudy	29 96	75	77	79	
5	S W	Cloudy	30 01	75	75	81	
6	S W	Clear	30 10	76	79	82	
7	S W	Clear	30 00		80	83	
8	E	Clear	30 02	76		85	
9	S	Cloudy	30 07	77	78	81	
10	E	Clear	30 03	77	77		
11	N W	Rain	29 78	72		72	Much rain.
12		Cloudy	29 70	67		76	Rain.
13	S E	Cloudy	29 70	66	67	68	
14	S	Cloudy	29 90	68	67	67	
15	S	Cloudy	29 90	75	72	75	
16	S W	Cloudy	30 02	75	80	82	
17							

Description

N.° XI.

Defcription of a Machine for Meafuring a Ship's Way through the Sea, by F. HOPKINSON, *Efquire.*

Read July 11, 1783. THE errors and uncertainties incident to the mariner's log, in common ufe, are too obvious not to be univerfally acknowledged. Were it not for the obfervations navigators are accuftomed to make of a fhip's progrefs, by the apparent paffage of the water along fide, and the figns that ufually prefent on approaching the land, the log, alone, would be a very unfafe dependence.

Several attempts have, therefore, been made to improve the log, and render its indications more accurate, but without fuccefs. All the machines of this kind, that I have heard of, were compofed of a number of wheels, which were to be put in motion by the twifting of a line let out aftern, having a drag at the end fo conftructed as to whirl round, fafter or flower, according to the motion of the fhip.

The objections to a machine, fo conftructed, are, *Firft*, If the line is not very long the drag will be confiderably affected by the fhip's wake; and, if it is very long, the twiftings will be irregular, and the line liable to kink. *Secondly*, If the drag is fo heavy as to fink below the bottoms of the waves, when the fhip fails faft, it will be too heavy, and fink too deep when fhe hath but a flow progreffive motion : Or, otherwife, if the drag is of a proper weight when fhe makes but little way, it will fkip from wave to wave through the air when fhe fails with a brifk gale, and fo be of no ufe. And, *Thirdly*, It will be liable to moft of the other irregularities to which the log in common ufe is expofed.

The

The machine now propofed will, it is hoped, be free from, at leaft, fome of thefe objections. And, although it may not be able to afcertain a fhip's way through the fea to a mathematical precifion, yet if it fhould be found to anfwer the purpofe better than any inftrument hitherto contrived, it may be admitted as an acquifition to the art of navigation.

This machine, in its moft fimple form, is reprefented by *Fig.* 1, *Plate* 3. Wherein AB is a ftrong rod of iron moveable on the fulcrum C. D is a thin circular plate of brafs rivetted to the lower extremity of the rod. E an horizontal arm connected at one end with the top of the rod AB by a moveable joint F, and at the other end with the bottom of the index H by a like moveable joint G. H is the index turning on its centre I and travelling over the graduated arch K; and L is a ftrong fpring bearing againft the rod AB and conftantly counteracting the preffure upon the palate D. The rod AB fhould be applied clofe to one fide of the cut water or ftem, and fhould be of fuch a length that the palate D may be no higher above the keel than is neceffary to fecure it from injury when the veffel is aground or fails in fhoal water. As the bow of the fhip curves inward towards the keel M, the palate D will be thrown to a diftance from the bottom of the veffel, although the perpendicular rod, to which it is annexed, lies clofe to the bow above; and, therefore, the palate will be more fairly acted upon. The arm E fhould enter the bow fomewhere near the hawfer hole, and lead to any convenient place in the forecaftle, where a fmooth board or plate may be fixed, having the index H and graduated arch K upon it.

It is evident from the figure, that as the fhip is urged forward by the wind, the palate D will be preffed upon by the refifting medium, with a greater or lefs force according to the progreffive motion of the fhip: and this will operate upon the levers fo as to immediately affect the index; making the leaft encreafe or diminution of the fhip's

way

way vifible on the graduated arch.   The fpring L always counteracting the preffure upon the palate, and bringing back the index on any relaxation of the force impreffed.

A fhip going through the fea opens a paffage for herfelf, making a hole in the water equal to her immerged bulk.   As fhe paffes on, this vacancy is filled up by the tumbling in of the waters from each fide, and from underneath, at the ftern, with great violence.   So that there is a fair current of water from her bow to her ftern, paffing under the bottom and along fide; the force of which current is in direct proportion to the velocity of the fhip's progreffive motion.   This machine is, therefore, advantageoufly placed at the bow of the fhip, where the current firft begins, and acts fairly upon the palate; in preference to the ftern, where the tumultuous clofing of the waters caufes a wake, vifible to a great diftance.   The palate D is funk nearly as low as the keel, that it may not be influenced by the heaping up of the water, and the dafhing of the waves at and near the water-line.   The arch K is to afcertain how many knots or miles fhe would run in one hour, at her then rate of failing.   But the graduations on this arch muft be unequal; becaufe the refiftance of the fpring L will encreafe as it becomes more bent; fo that the index will travel over a greater fpace from one to five miles (which I fuppofe to be a medium) than from five to twelve.   Laftly, the palate, rod, fpring and all the metallic parts of the inftrument fhould be covered with a ftrong varnifh, to prevent ruft from the corrofive quality of the falt water and fea air.

IMPROVEMENT of this MACHINE.

Let the rod or fpear AB *Fig.* 1, be a round rod of iron or fteel; and inftead of moving on the fulcrum or joint as at C, let it pafs through and turn freely in a focket, to which focket the moveable joint muft be annexed as, reprefented

prefented in *Fig.* 2. The rod muft have a fhoulder to bear on the upper edge of the focket, to prevent its flipping quite down. The rod muft alfo pafs through a like focket at F, *Fig.* 1. The joint of the lower focket muft be fixed to the bow of the fhip, and the upper joint or focket muft be connected with the horizontal arm E. On the top of the uppermoft focket, let there be a fmall circular plate, bearing the 32 points of the mariner's compafs ; and let the top of the rod AB come through the centre of this plate, fo as to carry a fmall index upon it, as is reprefented in *Fig.* 3. This fmall index muft be fixed to the top of the rod on a fquare ; fo, that by turning the index round the plate, the rod may alfo turn in the fockets, and of courfe carry the palate D round with it. The little index always pointing in a direction with the face of the palate. The fmall compafs plate fhould not be faftened to the top of the focket, but only fitted tightly on, that it may be moveable at pleafure. Suppofe, then, the intended port to bear fouth-weft from the place of departure ; the palate muft be turned on the focket till the fouth-weft point thereon looks directly to the fhip's bow ; fo that the fouth-weft and north-eaft line on the compafs plate may be precifely parallel with the fhip's keel ; and in this pofition the plate muft remain during the whole voyage. Suppofe then the fhip to be failing in the direct courfe of her intended voyage, with her bowfprit pointing fouth-weft, let the little index be brought to the fouth-weft point on the compafs plate, and the palate D will neceffarily prefent its broad face toward the port of deftination ; and this it muft always be made to do, be the fhip's failing courfe what it may. If, on account of unfavourable winds, the fhip is obliged to deviate from her intended courfe, the little index muft be moved fo many points from the fouth-weft line of the compafs plate, as the compafs in the binnacle fhall fhew that fhe deviates from her true courfe. So that, in whatever direction the fhip fhall fail, the palate D will

always

always look full to the fouth-weft point of the horizon,. or towards the port of deftination ; and, confequently, will prefent only an oblique furface to the refifting medium— more or lefs oblique as the fhip deviates more or lefs from the true courfe of her voyage. As, therefore, the refiftance of the water will operate lefs upon the palate in an oblique than in a direct pofition, in exact proportion to its obliquity, the Index H will not fhew how many knots the veffel runs in her then courfe, but will (it is expected) indicate how many fhe gains in the direct line of her intended voyage. Thus, in *Fig.* 5, if the fhip's courfe lies in the direction of the line AB, but fhe can fail by the wind no nearer than AC; fuppofe then, her progreffive motion fuch as to perform AC, equal to five knots or miles in one hour; yet the index H will only point to four knots on the graduated arch, becaufe fhe gains no more than at that rate on the true line of her voyage, viz. from A to B. Thus will the difference between her real motion and that pointed out by the index be always in proportion to her deviation from the intended port, until fhe fails in a line at right angles therewith, as AD; in which cafe the palate would prefent only a thin fharp edge to the refifting medium; the preffure of which fhould not be fufficient to overcome the friction of the machine, and the bearing of the fpring L. So that at whatever rate the fhip may fail on that line yet the index will not be affected: Shewing that fhe gains nothing on her true courfe. In this cafe, and alfo when the veffel is not under way, the action of the fpring L fhould caufe the index to point at o; as reprefented by the dotted lines in figure 1 and 4.

As the truth of this inftrument muft depend on the equal preffure of the refifting medium upon the palate D according to the fhip's velocity, and the proportionable action of the fpring L, there fhould be a pin or fcrew at the joints C and F, fo that the rod may be readily unfhipped and taken in, in order to clean the palate from any

foulnefs

foulnefs it may contract; which would greatly increafe its operation on the index H, and thereby render the gradu-ated arch, falfe and uncertain.

Further, the fpring L may be expofed too much to in-jury from the falt water, if fixed on the outfide of the fhip's bow. To remedy this it may be brought under cover by conftructing the machine as reprefented by figure 4. Where, A B is the rod, C the fulcrum or centre of its mo-tion; D the palate; E the horizontal arm leading through a fmall hole into the forecaftle: M is a ftrong chain, faft-ened at one end to the arm E and at the other to a rim or barrel on the wheel G, which by means of its teeth gives motion to the femicircle I and index H.   The fpring L is fpiral and enclofed in a box or barrel, like the main fpring of a watch: A fmall chain is fixed to and paffing round the barrel is faftened by the other end to the fuzee W. This fuzee is connected by its teeth with the wheel G, and counteracts the motion of the palate D.   NN are the two fockets through which the rod A B paffes, and in which it is turned round by means of the little index R.   S is the fmall compafs plate, moveable on the top of the upper focket N.   The plate S hath an upright rim round its edge cut into teeth or notches; fo that when the index R is a little raifed up, in order to bring it round to any intended point, it may fall into one of thefe notches and be detained there: Otherwife the preffure of the water will force the palate D from its oblique pofition, and turn the rod and index round to the direction in which the fhip fhall be then failing.   Should it be apprehended that the palate D, being placed fo far forward, may affect the fhip's fteerage or obftruct her failing, it fhould be confidered that a very fmall plate will be fufficient to work the machine.   I fhould fuppofe that one of three or four inches in diameter would fully anfwer the purpofe: And yet not be large enough to have any fenfible operation on the helm or fhip's way.

The

The greateſt difficulty, perhaps, will be in graduating the arch K; (if the machine is conſtructed as in *figure* 1.) the unequal diviſions of which can only be aſcertained by actual experiment on board of each ſhip reſpectively; in as much as the accuracy of theſe graduations will depend on three circumſtances, viz. The poſition of the fulcrum C with reſpect to the length of the rod, the ſize of the palate D and the ſtrength or bearing of the ſpring L. When theſe graduations, however, are once aſcertained for the machine on board of any one veſſel, they will not want any future alterations; provided the palate D be kept clean, and the ſpring L retains its elaſticity.

But the unequal diviſions of the graduated arch will be unneceſſary, if the machine is conſtructed as in *figure* 4. For as the chain goes round the barrel L, and then winds through the ſpiral channel of the fuzee W, the force of the main-ſpring muſt operate equally, or nearly ſo, in all poſitions of the index; and conſequently, the diviſions of the arch K may, in ſuch caſe, be equal.

After all, it is not expected that a ſhip's longitude can be determined to a mathematical certainty by this inſtrument. The irregular motions and impulſes to which a ſhip is continually expoſed, make ſuch an accuracy unattainable perhaps by any machinery : But if it ſhould be found, as I flatter myſelf it will on fair experiment, that it anſwers the purpoſe much better than the common log, it may be conſidered as an acquiſition to the art of navigation.

It ſhould be obſerved that in aſcertaining a ſhip's longitude by a time-piece, this great inconvenience occurs, that a ſmall and trifling miſtake in the time, makes a very great and dangerous error in the diſtance run : Whereas the errors of this machine will operate no farther than their real amount; which can never be great or dangerous, if corrected by the uſual obſervations made by mariners for correcting the common log.

A like machine made in its ſimple form, (as at fig. 1.) ſo conſtructed as to ſhip and unſhip, might occaſionally

Y   be

be applied along fide about midfhips in order to afcertain the lee-way; which, if rightly fhewn will give the fhip's precife longitude. As to fea-currents, this and all other machines hitherto invented, muft be fubject to their influence; and proper allowances muft be made, according to the fkill and knowledge of the navigator.

Laftly, fome difcretion will be neceffary in taking obfervations from the machine to be entered on the log-book. I mean, that the moft favourable and equitable moment fhould be chofen for the obfervation. Not whilft the fhip is rapidly defcending the declivity of a wave; or is fuddenly checked by a ftroke of the fea; or is in the very act of plunging. In all cafes, I fuppofe, periods may be found in which a fhip proceeds with a true average velocity; to difcover which a little experience and attention will lead the fkilful mariner*.

N° XII.

Account of an Electrical Eel, or the Torpedo of Surinam, by WILLIAM BRYANT, Efquire.

SURINAM a colony of South America belonging to the ftates of Holland, abounds with as many natural curiofities as any country in the world. But that which I look upon to be as furprifing as any in it, and which I believe has not yet been accurately defcribed, is a fifh of the fpecies of eel, and is caught there in nets among other fifh; generally in muddy rivers, and I believe is found in moft of the neighbouring provinces. In fize and colour

---

* An ingenious mechanic would probably conftruct this machine to better advantage in many refpects. The author only meant to fuggeft the principle; experiment alone can point out the beft method of applying it. He is fenfible of at leaft one deficiency, viz. That the little index R, figure 4, will not be ftrong enough to retain the palate D in an oblique pofition when the fhip is failing by the wind; more efpecially as the compafs plate S, in whofe notched rim the index R is to fall, is not fixed to, but only fitted tight on the focket N. Many means however might be contrived to remedy this incouvenience.

colour it is not unlike a common eel of Europe or America, and in ſhape reſembles it more, except that it is thicker in proportion to its length, and the head is more flat and not ſo pointed; but differs from them in this reſpect, that it comes to the ſurface to breathe in the air. It is called by the Dutch *Beave Aal*, and by the Engliſh inhabitants the Numbing Eel. As to the other qualities, of which I mean chiefly to take notice, and which I think are as different from the Torpedo of Europe, as the fiſh is in ſhape, they are as follows.

On touching the fiſh as it lies in the water in a tub provided for it, a ſudden and violent ſhock is received, in all reſpects like that which is felt on touching the prime conductor, when charged with the electrical fluid from the globe; and like that chiefly, affects the ends of the fingers and elbow. Gently holding the tail of the fiſh with one hand and touching the head with the other, a very violent ſhock is felt in both elbows and through the breaſt and ſhoulders. I at firſt imagined that the violence of the ſhock proceeded from both arms receiving it at the ſame time, and that the pain was no more than that of the two ſtrokes added together; but I found myſelf miſtaken. For upon ſeven perſons joining hands, and the firſt taking hold of the tail (which may with more caſe be held than the head) and the ſeventh at the ſame time touching the head, we were all affected in both elbows, and that in the ſame manner as I remember to have been in the electrical experiment, when ſeveral perſons take hold of the wire and the equilibrium is reſtored by the fluids paſſing through their bodies.

I find the ſhock may be received through metallic ſubſtances. On touching the fiſh with an old ſword blade I was ſtrongly affected. But arming it with ſealing-wax and taking hold of that part which was covered with it, the electrical fluid (I cannot help calling it ſo) would not paſs. Neither has it any effect on the body when touched with

Y 2

glafs

glafs bottle, fealing-wax, &c. Yet I cannot obferve the leaft diminution of this quality by placing the tub which contains the fifh on glafs bottles; it continues the fame in all refpects. So that whether it has an unaccountable faculty of collecting a quantity of the fluid from the furrounding waters, or through the body of the perfon touching it, or has in its own body a large fund which it can difcharge at pleafure, I am greatly at a lofs to think or imagine.

Although it has no effect on the human body when touched with a piece of wood, or indeed any other fubflance not metallic ; yet an accident difcovered to me, that on fome occafions the effect would be fenfible through wood. For one morning while I was ftanding by, as a fervant was emptying the tub, which he had lifted intirely from the ground, and was pouring off the water to renew it, and the fifh left almoft dry, the negro received fo violent a fhock as occafioned him to let the tub fall, and calling another to his affiftance, I caufed them both to lift the tub free from the ground, when pouring off the remains of the water they both received fmart fhocks and were obliged to defift from emptying the tub in that manner. This I afterwards tried myfelf and received the like fhock. This fifh indeed was one of the largeft I have feen and but newly caught. For I obferve that after being fometime confined in a tub and wanting perhaps their natural food, they lofe much of the ftrength of this extraordinary quality. I am fometimes apt to conjecture, that this animal has the power of communicating the ftroke when, and with what degree of force it will; and that it ferves him as a weapon of defence againft his enemies. For I have often obferved that on firft taking hold of it, the fhock is tolerable; but as foon as he perceives himfelf the leaft confined, it is much more violent. This I experienced to my coft, as I one day took hold of it, about the middle of the fifh, I lifted it partly out of the water, when on a fudden I received fo fmart a fhock

that

that it occafioned a ftrong contraction in the bending
mufcles of my fingers, and I could not immediately let it
go; but endeavouring to difengage my hand threw it on
the ground; taking hold of it a fecond time, to return it
into the tub, I was more ftrongly affected than at firft, and
that not only in my hands and arms, but throughout my
whole body; the forepart of my head and the back part
of my legs fuffered principally; and in the fame manner
as on receiving a very fmart fhock from a highly charged
phial in electrical experiments.

On obferving that the fenfation occafioned by the fhock
as to the nature and degree of ftrength upon touching different parts of the fifh, was different, I was at firft inclined to think it might be owing to its having an extraordinary faculty of containing more of the fluid in one
part of its body than in another. The tail part to above
one third of its length, occafions rather a numbnefs and
tingling, than pain, but on applying the end of the fingers to the back, head, and under part of its body, it caufes
a fharp pricking pain. This may poffibly be accounted
for by the difference in the texture of the furface of the
fkin, as the manner of the electrical fluids coming from a
glafs tube is different when its furface is altered by being
rubbed with different fubftances, as has been lately taken
notice of in a letter to the Royal Society.

Thefe are the principal obfervations, the fhort time I
refided at Surinam, allowed me an opportunity of making
relating to this extraordinary animal.

N° XIII.

Obſervations on the Numb Fiſh, or Torporific Eel, by
Henry Collins Flagg, *South-Carolina.*

Read March
7th, 1783. I DO myſelf the pleaſure, though late I confeſs, to comply with my promiſe of communicating ſome obſervations on the Numb Fiſh, or *Torporific Eel,* which I think a more proper name. Theſe obſervations are contained in two letters I had the honor to
write to the Rev. Dr. Stiles, a member of your philoſophical ſociety, from Rio Eſſequebo. Pleaſe to accept the
following extracts.

The apparent difference between the torporific eel and
that uſually caught in your harbour is, the former is flatter
on the back and head, the upper part of which is perforated with ſeveral holes*, and has on each ſide, behind, a
ſmall fin which ſome ſay are elevated or depreſſed as the
fiſh is pleaſed or not†; the body I think is larger in proportion to the length, and it has a broad fin connected to
the belly and continued to the tail. I have ſeen this fiſh
four feet long. The ſenſation occaſioned by touching it
appeared to me exactly ſimilar to an electric ſhock. I have
as yet been able to procure only one of theſe eels, and that
was injured by laying too long dry before it came to me.
The following are the remarks I made the little time it
lived. I received the fiſh from a negro in a wicker baſket,
and laying it on the ground felt a conſiderable ſhock, as I
did too when I turned the fiſh out of the baſket into a tub
of

---

* Theſe holes do not penetrate to the mouth, nor could I diſcover the uſe of them. But I
was not ſufficiently exact in my diſſection of the head, or I think I might have found the termination of theſe ducts.
† This is true.

of water.   The fhock is greater if the fifh is enraged; but
whether repeated touches will exhauft this ftrange power,
as frequently repeated bites do the viperine and fome other
poifons for a time, I believe no experiment has yet determined *.   If a perfon hold his finger in the water feveral
inches diftant from the fifh and another touch it, a fhock
equally fevere is felt by him who does not touch it.   The
fame thing happens if the fifh exerts itfelf without being
touched.   If a number of perfons join hands, and one
touch the eel, they are all equally fhocked, unlefs there
fhould happen to be one of the number incapable of being
affected by the eel, which is the cafe of a very worthy
lady of my acquaintance, who can handle this fifh at will.
I am informed fome Indians and negroes can do the fame ;
whether by the affiftance of any means to counteract the
power of the eel, I know not; but am perfuaded it is
fomething in the conftitution of the lady†.   The eel I had
obtained got out of the tub, and it was with fome difficulty I returned it, for the repeated fhocks I received through
a piece of deal board eighteen inches long, with which I
attempted to lift it, made my arms ache very much, and
for a confiderable time.   I think the numbnefs occafioned
by touching this eel continues longer than that from an
electric fhock of the fame degree of force, and I have been
affured by a perfon of good fenfe and veracity, that a negro fellow formerly being bantered by his companions for
his fear of this eel, determined to give a proof of his refolution, and attempted to grafp it with both hands.   The
unhappy confequence was, a confirmed paralyfis of both
arms.   I hear this fellow is ftill living in the ifland of St.
Chriftopher's ; if fo, I can obtain more fatisfaction, for I
have my doubts of the negro's honefty ‡.   But very certain

---

* I am fince convinced they do.

† This lady, when I became acquainted with her, was far gone in an hectic fever.   And I
did not think to enquire if fhe could treat the fifh with fo much familiarity while in a perfect
ftate of health.

‡ This account was afterwards confirmed to me, with the further information, that after feveral years the negro recovered the ufe of his arms by flow degrees, and I think without any
affiftance from medicine.

tain it is, that many perfons have been knocked down by the feverity of the fhock. The languid ftate in which I found the eel the morning after it was taken, gave me an opportunity of obferving that though I could perceive no fhock by touching it on or near the tail; yet applying my finger near the belly, the torporific power was very confiderable, notwithftanding the fifh was now almoft dead. This I repeated feveral times, as a remark of fome confequence in aflifting us to determine whether, or how far, the emiflion of torporific particles depends on the exertion of any mufcular force*; upon which principle Mr. Reamure accounts for the benumbing power of the Torpedo. I much doubt if the moft acute eye can difcern any motion in the eel at the time it fhocks†. I have been fo particular in taking notice of the bafket and deal-board, becaufe it has been aflerted that the eel fhocks only by immediate contact, through metal or very hard wood. This eel is frequently eat by the negroes, and reckoned very delicious. Its common food is fhrimps or any fmall fifh.

I have lately made another experiment upon the torporific eel. It was fuggefted to me by the very great fimilarity between the effects of a fhock from the eel and an electric machine. I held an iron rod between two pieces of glafs and touched the eel with it, but could not perceive the leaft fhock. I held the rod in a filk handkerchief with the fame effect. I repeated thefe experiments on two eels with equal fuccefs. I think this experiment demonftrates that the electric and torporific particles are the fame. I have tried the effects of this fifh upon the needle of a compafs but perceived no influence. I have not, however, done

---

* I have not ventured as yet to give any opinion of the ftrange property by which this fifh becomes the conductor of the electric fluid. But that the emiflion of it depends upon the exertion of mufcular force may, I think, be concluded from hence; that, as has already been determined, repeated exertions will exhauft its power to fhock for a time, and before it can again exert its influence, a frefh quantity of fire muft be collected; nor do I think the experiment I made on the dying eel invalidates this opinion, for to the beft of my recollection it ceafed to fhock fome time before its death.

† I am informed the motion is perceptible, though I confefs I could not diftinguifh it.

done with the eel, and hereafter will repeat all the old and make new experiments upon it*.

This fish raifes its head every few minutes above the water to refpire.

I have feen negroes take hold of it, at firft very cautioufly, receiving many light fhocks, but prefently have grafped it hard and taken it out of the water.

There is a kind of light wood through which the eel cannot fhock.

Mrs. Behn, in her Oroonoko, gives a defcription of this fifh, which fhe calls the numb-eel, and fays it is taken in the river Surinam.

From the above experiments, partial as they are, I leave you, fir, to judge how far the torporific and electric fluids are alike.

I am, with the greateft refpect and efteem,

Your moft humble fervant,

South-Carolina, ꞁ
October 8, 1782. ꞁ   HENRY COLLINS FLAGG.

N° XIV.

To DAVID RITTENHOUSE, *Efquire, from* JOHN PAGE, *Efquire.*

Williamfburg, December 4, 1779.

DEAR SIR,

Read May 2d, 1783. I HAVE often thought there was a ftrong refemblance between fome of the phenomena of electricity and magnetifm, and fancied I faw fomething like the two electricities in the attraction and repulfion of

Z   the

---

* I had not been long in South-America when I made my obfervations; foon after which, the neceffary avocations of my profeffion, together with that relaxation of the mental powers generally confequent upon the laffitude of body incident to the inhabitants of warm climates, indifpofed me to the farther profecution of experiments I am now mortified at not having made.

the two poles. I have amufed myfelf with fuppofing that magnetifm is only a fpecies of electricity, whofe *matter* is as yet not difcovered by human fight; as that of electricity was, when a few years ago, it was perceivable only by its effects in attracting or repelling light bodies, as magnetifm now is in attracting or repelling iron. Experiments by which polarity may be given to needles by means of electricity, perhaps, further improved and clofely attended to, might throw great light on this fubject. I wifh we had more cafes ftated of the effects of lightening and the Aurora Borealis on the needle. But mentioning the Aurora Borealis recalls to my mind, the meteor which was feen at many diftant places in Virginia on the 31ft of October, at about 6^h 10^m P. M. It was what is vulgarly called a falling ftar. It fell as feen at Rofewell about three or four degrees to the north of weft and left a bright trail of light behind it; which extended from the horizon perpendicularly above $7°$; unluckily I loft a view of it when falling, but was called out time enough to fee the grand and beautiful appearance of its trail of light. It was feen for near 15^m, it was as bright as fhining filver, and as broad as the enlightened part of the new moon, when firft vifible, and about $7°$ in length. It might be reprefented by N° 1, when I firft faw it, and by the other figures at intervals of about a minute after. Juft before it difappeared it refembled the edge of a cloud. The fky was remarkably clear and ferene. It appeared in the fame manner exactly to feveral gentlemen above an hundred miles from Rofewell, but on a different point of the compafs. I have not yet had fo accurate an account of its bearing as to afcertain its height and diftance. Did you fee any thing of it?

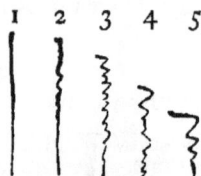

I am, dear fir, yours moft fincerely,
JOHN PAGE.

From DAVID RITTENHOUSE, *Efquire, to* JOHN
PAGE, *Efquire.*

Philadelphia, January 16, 1780.

DEAR SIR,

Read May
2, 1783. I DESIGN to give you my thoughts on Magnetifm in fome future letter, at prefent I fhall
confine myfelf to the fubject of the latter part of yours of
the 4th of December laft.

The extraordinary Meteor you mention was likewife
vifible here, the air being ferene and clear.   I did not fee
it until the bright ftreak was become very crooked, it then
bore S. 70° W. nearly, from Philadelphia, and comparing
this courfe with that obferved by you, I find it muft have
fallen on or near the Ouafiota mountains mentioned in
Lewis Evans's map, about 480 miles from Philadelphia
and 365 from Williamfburg.   And taking its altitude 7,°
as obferved by you, adding $2\frac{1}{4}$ degrees for the depreffion
of that place below your horizon, its entire apparent altitude above the fpot where it fell was $9°\frac{1}{4}$, which, on a
radius of 365 miles, will be 61 miles perpendicular height.
The breadth of the luminous vapour was, I think, in fome
places, when I faw it, not lefs than a quarter of a degree;
this at 480 miles diftance muft have been at leaft two miles.
It was certainly a grand appearance near the place where
it fell, if any human eye was there.

May not thefe fhooting ftars be bodies altogether foreign
to the earth and its atmofphere, accidentally meeting with
it as they are fwiftly traverfing the great void of fpace?
And may they not, either electrically or by fome other
means, excite a luminous appearance on entering our atmofphere? I am inclined to this opinion for the following
reafons: 1ft. It is not probable that meteors fhould be generated in the air at the height of 50 or 60 miles, on account of its extreme rarenefs; and many falling ftars, befides this, are known with certainty to have been at very

great

great heights.   2dly. Their motions cannot be owing to gravity, for they defcend in all directions, and but feldom perpendicularly to the horizon.   Befides, their velocities are much too great.   This meteor would not have fallen by the force of gravity, from the place where it firft appeared, to the earth, in lefs than two minutes of time; nor in lefs than ten feconds, if we fuppofe it impelled by gravity from the remoteft diftance.   They are neverthelefs affected by gravity in fome manner, for I cannot find that any one was ever obferved to afcend upwards in its courfe.

It is true that difficulties will likewife occur, if we fuppofe them to be foreign bodies of fufficient denfity to preferve fuch great degrees of velocity even in paffing through the atmofphere, for it may be afked why do they not frequently ftrike the earth, buildings, &c.

Perhaps they are generally, if not always, exploded in paffing through the air, fomething in the manner that filings of fteel are exploded in paffing through the flame of a candle.   And at the fame time that they afford us occafion to admire the variety and immenfity of the Creator's works, they may perhaps produce fome important and neceffary effects in the atmofphere furrounding this globe, for the welfare of man and its other innumerable tribes of inhabitants.

I am, dear fir, your affectionate friend,

And very humble fervant,

DAVID RITTENHOUSE.

Defcription

N° XV.

Defcription of the Grotto at Swatara, by the Rev. PETER
MILLER, *of Ephrata ; communicated by* WILLIAM
BARTON, *Efquire.*

Read March
7, 1783.
"AS the courfe of my letter now tends this
way, I muſt remind you, if ever you
ſhould publiſh a natural hiſtory of Pennſylvania, not to
confign to oblivion that very curious petrifying cavern, of
which, leſt you ſhould not have ſeen it already, I ſhall
give ſome deſcription.

" It is ſituate on the eaſt fide of Swatara, cloſe to the
river. Its entrance is very ſpacious, and there is ſomewhat of a deſcent towards the other extremity ; inſomuch
that I ſuppoſe the ſurface of the river is rather higher than
the bottom of the cave. The upper part is like an arched
roof, of ſolid lime-ſtone rock, perhaps twenty feet thick.
On entering, are found many apartments, ſome of them
very high, like the choir of a church. There is, as it
were, a continual rain within the cave, for the water drops
inceſſantly from the roof upon the floor ; by which, and
the water petrifying as it falls, pillars are gradually formed to ſupport the roof. I ſaw this cave about thirty years
ago, and obſerved above ten ſuch pillars, each ſix inches
in diameter and ſix feet high ; all ſo ranged that the place
incloſed by them reſembled a ſanctuary in a Roman church :
And I can aſſure you, that no royal throne ever exhibited
more grandeur, than the delightful proſpect of this *luſus
naturæ*. Satisfied with the view of this, we diſcovered the
reſemblances of ſeveral monuments, incorporated into the
walls, as if the bodies of departed heroes were there de-
poſited. Our guide then conducted us to a place, where,
he

he faid, hung the bell : This is a piece of ftone iffuing out of the roof, which when ftruck founds like a bell.

" Some of the ftalactites are of a colour like fugar-candy, and others refemble loaf-fugar ; but it is a pity that their beauty is now almoft deftroyed by the country people. The water, as it falls, runs down the declivity ; and it is both wholefome and pleafant to drink, when it has dif- charged its petrifying matter. It is remarkable that we found feveral holes at the bottom of the cave, going down perpendicularly, perhaps into the abyfs, which renders it dangerous to be without a light. At the end of the cave, there is a pretty run, which takes its courfe through part of it, and then lofes itfelf among the rocks : Here is alfo its exit, by an aperture which is very narrow. Through this the vapours continually pafs outwards, with a ftrong current of air ; and, at night, thefe vapours afcending re- femble a great furnace. Part of thefe vapours and fogs appear, on afcending, to be condenfed at the head of this great alembic, and the more volatile parts to be carried off, through the aperture communicating with the exterior air before mentioned, by the force of the air in its paffage.

" I beg pardon for having troubled you with fuch a long detail. It appears ftrange to me that none of our philo- fophers have hitherto publifhed a true account of this re- markable grotto."

N° XVI.

An Account of fome Experiments on Magnetifm, in a Letter to JOHN PAGE, *Efquire, at Williamsburg.*

DEAR SIR,

Read Feb. 6, 1781.

AGREEABLE to the promife in my laft, I fhall now communicate to you fome conjec- tures and experiments on magnetifm, which may perhaps either

either afford you fome amufement, or induce you to pur-
fue the fubject to more certainty.

I fuppofe then, that magnetical particles of matter are
a neceffary conftituent part of that metal which we call
iron, though they are probably but a fmall proportion of
the whole mafs. Thefe magnetical particles I fuppofe
have each a north and a fouth pole, and that they retain
their polarity, however the metal may be fufed or otherwife wrought. In a piece of iron which fhews no figns of
magnetifm thefe magnetical particles lie irregularly, with
their poles pointing in all poffible directions, they therefore mutually deftroy each other's effects. By giving
magnetifm to a piece of iron we do nothing more than
arrange thefe particles, and when this is done it depends
on the temper and fituation of the iron whether that arrangement fhall continue, that is, whether the piece of
metal fhall remain for a long time magnetical or not.

There is fome power, whencefoever derived, diffufed
through every part of fpace which we have accefs to,
which acts on thefe magnetical particles, impelling one of
their poles in a certain direction with refpect to the earth
and the other pole in the oppofite direction. The direction in which this power acts I take to be the fame with
that of the dipping needle.

By applying a magnet to a piece of iron it becomes
magnetical; for the magnet acting ftrongly on the above
mentioned particles, that action arranges them properly;
overcoming the refiftance of the furrounding parts of the
iron, and this refiftance afterwards ferves to fecure them in
their proper fituations, and prevents their being deranged
by any little accident.

If we place a piece of iron in or near the direction of
the dipping needle, it will in time become magnetical;
that general power producing in this cafe the fame effect
as the application of the magnet, though in a weaker
degree.

Iron

Iron or foft fteel receives magnetifm more eafily than hardened fteel, but will not retain it; may not this be, becaufe the magnetical particles are not fo clofely confined in foft as in hardened fteel, and on that account more eafily admit of arrangement or derangement. By making a piece of fteel red hot, or by twifting it or beating it with a hammer, we may effectually deftroy its magnetifm. Now all thefe operations certainly derange the particles which compofe the bar. By rubbing one piece of fteel with another, magnetifm may be produced, and it is eafy to conceive how this operation, by the tremulous motion which it excites, may contribute to arrange the magnetical particles.

We took a foft fteel ramrod, which did not difcover the leaft fign of magnetifm, and holding it in the direction of the dipping needle, ftruck it feveral fmart blows with a hammer, on one end; then laying it on a watch chryftal it traverfed very well; that end which was held downwards, when ftruck, becoming a north pole, whether the ftroke was applied to the upper or the lower end. By turning the fouth end downwards and ftriking it afrefh, the magnetifm was deftroyed or reverfed, and it was curious to obferve how very nicely you muft adjuft the number and force of the ftrokes, precifely to deftroy the magnetifm before communicated, without giving it anew, in a contrary direction. When we held the ramrod directly acrofs the line of the dipping needle, whilft it was ftruck with a hammer, on many trials it did not difcover any figns of magnetifm. But when held in any other direction, that end which approached neareft to the point which the lower end of the dipping needle tends to, always became the north pole. From all this does it not feem very probable that during the concuffion of the ftroke, and whilft the magnetical particles of the rod were moft difengaged from the furrounding matter, the active power abovementioned feized them and arranged them properly, where being
confined,

confined, the rod afterwards remained magnetical.   All
this is neverthelefs little more than conjecture, until confirmed by further experiments.

I am, dear fir, yours, &c.

DAVID RITTENHOUSE.

N° XVII.

*New Method of placing a Meridian Mark, in a Letter to
the Rev. Dr.* EWING, *Provoft of the Univerfity.   By*
D. RITTENHOUSE, *Efquire.*

DEAR SIR,

Read Nov. SOME time ago I mentioned to you a new in-
1785. vention I had for fixing a Meridian Mark for
my Obfervatory.   This I have fince executed, and as it
anfwers perfectly well, I fhall give you a particular defcription of it.

When my obfervatory was firft erected, I placed a meridian mark to the northward at the diftance of about 1200
feet, my view to the fouth being too much confined by
adjacent buildings, and that to the north was not diftant
enough to have the mark free from a fenfible parallax.
But laft fummer a new brick houfe was built directly north
of the obfervatory, and much too nigh for diftant vifion
with the tranfit inftrument.   Now though a fixed mark is
not abfolutely neceffary where you have a good tranfit inftrument, the pofition of which may be examined and accurately corrected, if neceffary, every fair day, by the
paffage of the pole-ftar above and below the pole, it is neverthelefs very convenient, faves much trouble, and may
fometimes prevent miftakes.   We have an inftance in the
obfervations of the Aftronomer Royal at Greenwich.   His

A a   mark

mark being taken down at repairing the building to which it was secured, the transit instrument was accidentally thrown out of its true position, and the observations with it were continued for a considerable time before the error was detected.. My meridian mark being thus rendered useless, I contrived several other methods of supplying its place, all of which were, on sufficient deliberation, rejected for the following.

I fastened the object glass of a thirty six feet telescope, firmly, to the wall which supports the transit instrument, opposite to and as near as convenient to the object glass of the transit, when brought to a horizontal situation. In the focus of the thirty six feet object glass I screwed fast a piece of brass to a block of marble, supported by a brick pillar built on a good foundation, for this purpose, in my garden. On this piece of brass are several black concentric circles; the rest of the plate is silvered. The diverging rays of light which proceed from every point in these circles, after passing through the thirty-six feet glass become parallel, and entering the transit instrument, an image of the plate and its circles is formed in the same place where the images of stars or the most distant objects are formed. The circles are therefore distinctly seen through the transit, and being placed in the same meridian with the centre of the thirty six feet glass, the innermost circle, about the size of a brevier e, serves for a meridian mark, to the centre whereof the cross hair of the transit may be nicely adjusted.

This mark is in several respects preferable to one placed in the common way. It is entirely free from parallax, which the other cannot be, unless placed at a very great distance, when glasses of great magnifying powers are used. It is not sensibly affected by the undulation of the air, which very often renders it impossible to set the transit accurately to a distant mark. And it can be illuminated at night without difficulty, should the suspicion of any

accident

accident to the tranfit make it neceffary. But it has likewife one difadvantage. Should the pillar in fettling, carry
the mark a little to the eaft or weft, the error will be
greater in proportion to its nearnefs.

I am, dear fir, your humble fervant,

DAVID RITTENHOUSE.

P. S. The great improvement of object glaffes by Dol-
land has enabled us to apply eye glaffes of fo fhort a focus, that it is difficult to find any fubftance proper for the
crofs hairs of fixed inftruments. For fome years paft I
have ufed a fingle filament of filk, without knowing that
the fame was made ufe of by the European aftronomers, as
I have lately found it is by Mr. Hirfchell. But this fubftance, though far better than wires or hairs of any kind,
is ftill much too coarfe for fome obfervations. A fingle
filament of filk will totally obfcure a fmall ftar, and that
for feveral feconds of time, if the ftar be near the pole. I
have lately with no fmall difficulty placed the thread of a
fpider in fome of my inftruments, it has a beautiful effect,
it is not one tenth of the fize of the thread of the filkworm,
and is rounder and more evenly of a thicknefs. I have
hitherto found no inconvenience from the ufe of it, and
believe it will be lafting, it being more than four months
fince I firft put it in my tranfit telefcope, and it continues
fully extended, and free from knots or particles of duft.

N° XVIII.

Account of a Worm in a Horfe's Eye, by F. Hopkinson, *Efquire.*

Read Sep.
26, 1783.

HAVING been myfelf a witnefs to the following curious fact, I thought it fhould

A a 2   not

not pafs unrecorded, efpecially as it occurred in this city, under the immediate notice of the Philofophical Society.

A report prevailed laft fummer that a horfe was to be feen which had a living ferpent in one of his eyes. At firft I difregarded this report, but numbers of my acquaintance, who had been to fee the horfe, confirming the account, I had the curiofity to go myfelf, taking a friend along with me. The horfe was kept in Arch-ftrect and belonged to a free negroe. I examined the eye with all the attention in my power, being no ways difpofed to credit the common report, but rather expecting to detect a fraud or vulgar prejudice; I was much furprifed, however, to fee a real living worm within the ball of the horfe's eye. This worm was of a clear white colour, in fize and appearance much like a piece of fine bobbin; it feemed to be from 2½ to 3 inches in length, which however, could not be duly afcertained, its whole length never appearing at one time, but only fuch a portion as could be feen through the iris, which was greatly dilated. The creature was in a conftant lively vermicular motion; fometimes retiring fo deep into the eye as to become totally invifible, and at other times approaching fo near to the iris as to become plainly and diftinctly feen; at leaft fo much of it as was within the field of the iris. I could not diftinguifh its head, neither end being perfectly exhibited whilft I viewed it, and indeed its motion was fo brifk and conftant, that fo nice a fcrutiny was not to be expected. The horfe's eye was exceedingly enflamed, fwoln and running; I mean the mufcles contiguous to the eye ball, and feemed to give him great pain; fo that it was with much difficulty the eye could be kept open for more than a few feconds at a time; and I was obliged to watch favourable moments for a diftinct view of his tormentor. I believe the horfe was quite blind in that eye, for it appeared as if all the humours were confounded together, and that the worm had the whole orb to range in, which, however, was not

of

of a diameter fufficient for the worm to extend its full length, as far as I could difcover. The humours of the eye were beginning to grow opake like a chilled jelly, and became altogether fo afterwards, as I was informed.

As this is a very uncommon circumftance and may affect fome philofophical doctrines, it is much to be lamented that the horfe had not been purchafed, and the eye diffected for better examination. That there was a living, felf-moving worm within the ball of the horfe's eye, free from all deception or miftake, I am moft confident. How this worm got there, or if bred in fo remarkable a place, where its parents came from, or how they contrived to depofite their femen or convey their egg into the eye of an horfe, I leave for others to determine.

N° XIX.

An improved Method of Quilling a Harpfichord, by F. HOPKINSON, *Efquire.*

Read Dec. 5, 1783.
MUCH of the pleafure and effect in performing on a harpfichord depends on the equality of what is called *the touch ;* and this is principally owing to a continuance of uniformity in the fpring of the little quills, which by their impulfe fet the ftrings in vibration. Thefe quills, in the prefent manner of applying them, will not retain their elafticity for any length of time, but require conftant repair ; which is one of the moft troublefome and difficult operations in keeping the inftrument in order. To remedy this inconvenience, I have fought for a fubftitute for the crow quill, and tried a variety of fubftances, but without fuccefs. I then confidered whether an improvement might not be made in the application of the quills themfelves, and to this purpofe I
examined.

examined the caufe of the quills being fo liable to break, and obferved that the piece of quill is thruft through a fmall hole in the tongue of the jack, projecting only about a quarter of an inch beyond the face of the tongue : That this quill is too fhort to yield in all its parts, and fo act properly as a fpring ; but bends only at the place where it iffues from the hole in the tongue, and works up and down as upon a hinge, in that place; and *there only* is the quill ever known to break.

Thus in Plate III, Figure 6, *a*, is the tongue, *b*, the quill fixed firmly in it, which being too fhort to act fairly as a fpring, will bend only at *c*, when it is forced to pafs the ftring ; and by repeated exercife muft neceffarily break in that part, as any fpring would do if compelled to act in the fame manner.

But if this quill could be made longer, or applied fo that its fpring fhould be part of a curve, it would probably preferve its elafticity for any length of time, as other fprings do.

To effect this I have conftructed the tongue and applied the quill as reprefented in figure 7, where *a*, is the tongue, the top of which is rounded off ; the quill is firmly fixed in the hole at *c*, as ufual, but inftead of paffing through a length fufficient to ftrike the ftring, it is cut off even with the face of the tongue at *f.* The quill thus fixed with its polifhed face downwards, is bent upward round the top of the tongue, and then proceeds horizontally the proper length ;. being kept in the horizontal pofition by the little wire ftaple *e*, being firmly driven into holes drilled for the purpofe, but not fo far as to pinch the quill againft the top of the tongue ; a little fpace being left for the quill to play in.

From this conftruction it is manifeft, that the fpring of the quill will be in its whole length, but chiefly in the curve *c*, *d ;* and that a quill fo applied will act fairly as a fpring, and may be expected to retain its elafticity for

years,

years, fubject to no variations but fuch as may be occafioned by alterations in the ftate of the air, to which all
known fubftances are more or lefs liable.

---

^{Read,} IN the beginning of laft winter, I had the honour to
^{1784.} lay before the fociety an improved method of quilling
a HARPSICHORD. Wifhing to bring my difcovery to the
teft of full experiment and to the judgment of abler critics,
I forwarded a defcription and a model of my improvement
to a friend in London, requefting that it might be fubmitted
to the examination of proper judges, and directing, in
cafe it fhould be approved of, that an inftrument made by
one of the firft artifts and quilled according to my propofed method, fhould be fent to me. I have accordingly
received an excellent double harpfichord, made by Meffrs
Shudi and *Broadwood* of London, and quilled according
to my method; with this difference, I had rounded off the
top of the tongue, and bending the quill over it, kept it in a
horizontal pofition by means of a fmall wire ftaple; as
will be more fully underftood by referring to my former
defcription. But Mr. *Broadwood* has left the tongue of
its full length and ufual form: But made the hole, in
which the quill is commonly fixed tight, fo large, that the
quill has free room to play therein; and then fixing the
quill below, has bent it round and brought it through
this hole; which renders a ftaple unneceffary; the top of
the tongue anfwering the fame purpofe. The principle
on which the improvement depends is the fame in both;
but his is the beft method of executing it.

He informs, however, that one inconvenience occurs
viz. the quills being fo forcibly bent in the curved part,
are liable, in fome inftances, to fpring back, and fo become not only too fhort to reach the ftring it fhould ftrike,
but the projection of the curve will be apt to touch the
ftring behind it, when the ftop is pufhed back.

To

To explain this, let *a*, *b*, figure 8, reprefent the tongue, *c*, *d*, *e*, the quill, firmly fixed at *c*, then bent upwards and brought through a hole, which is large enough for the quill to play freely therein. But the curved part of the quill at *d*, being fo forcibly bent, will in fome inftances fpring back (as reprefented in the figure) not keeping clofe to the back of the tongue, as it fhould do: And as there is no wafte room, the curve *d*, will be apt to touch the ftring behind it, when the ftop is pufhed back, I acknowledge that this inconvenience occurs in fome few inftances in the inftrument Mr. *Broadwood* has fent me; but would ob-ferve that as it does not *always* happen, it is a fault in-the execution and not in the principle. Yet, as it may be dif-ficult to guard againft it, I have confidered how this evil may be effectually prevented.

Inftead of punching the fmall hole, in which the quill is to be fixed, ftraight through the tongue, let it be punch-ed flanting downwards; this will relieve the quill from that ftrained pofition which caufes it to fpring back. Ac-cording to the firft mode of application the curve formed by the quill will be as at *a*, figure 9, in the fecond as at *b*. I have conftructed many tongues in this way, and found none of them liable to the inconvenience complained of, or fhewing any tendency whatever to fpring back; but to remove all jealoufy on this head, fhould any remain, it will be eafy to drive a fmall wire ftaple againft the bottom of the curve behind, which muft effectually retain it clofe to the back of the tongue.

I mention this expedient of the wire ftaple merely with a view of removing all doubt; but I do not think it ne-ceffary; the objection being perfectly remedied by the other method: To, prove this, I have cut out the entire block between the two holes, in the manner of a mortife, and drove a pin acrofs the upper part of it. I then caufed the quill to lie in this flanting mortife, and bending it round brought it over the pin; and I found it would remain

main perfectly at eafe in its birth, although not pinched or
reftrained in any part; *a*, figure 10, reprefents the tongue
in front, and *b*, the mortife, of which the flanting fhape
cannot be feen in this view; but will be better underftood
by obferving the pofition of the quill in figure 11, where
a is a profile of the fame tongue, *b*, *c*, the quill lying in
the mortife, and *d*, the pin over which the top of the quill
paffes.

I have need to apologize to the fociety for directing fo
much of their attention, to an object which may appear to
fome to be of little importance. To the mufical tribe,
however, this improvement will prefent itfelf in a different light. Many perfons who play very well on the
harpfichord, are not able to keep the inftrument in order:
And to fend for a perfon to repair the quills and tune the
inftrument as often as it fhall be neceffary, is not only
troublefome and expenfive, but fuch affiftance is not always to be had, efpecially in the country. And for thefe
reafons many a good harpfichord or fpinnet lies neglected and the fcholar loofes the opportunity of practice. To
fuch perfons a method of quilling that fhall feldom want
repair is a *difideratum* of no fmall importance. And this,
I flatter myfelf I have accomplifhed.

The difficulty of *quilling* being thus removed, I confidered in what manner *tuning* might be made eafy to the
practitioner in mufic. Harpfichords are tuned by means of
fifths and *thirds*; but fuch is the mufical divifion of the
monochord as to make it neceffary, that none of thefe *fifths*
or *thirds* fhould be perfect; an allowance muft be made;
and to do this with judgment, fo that the chords may be
good and the inftrument be in tune, requires much attention and practice. Of the numbers that play, there will
not be found one in an hundred that can tune a harpfichord. To render this tafk eafy, I have procured *twelve*
tuning forks, for the *twelve femitones* of the octave; thefe
I had perfectly tuned; and as they will not be fenfibly af-

B b   fected

fected by any change of weather, they remain as ftandards. I take it for granted that any perfon at all accuftomed to mufical founds can tell when one tone is *in unifon* with another; and that a very little practice will enable him to tune one found *an octave* to another, thefe conchords are fo manifeft that they cannot eafily be miftaken. There is then nothing to be done but to tune the twelve ftrings in unifon with the twelve forks ; this will fix the fcale, or temperature for one octave, which is the whole difficulty ; the reft of the inftrument is eafily tuned by unifons and octaves to the fcale, fo afcertained*.

Having, I hope, fully accomplifhed the defign I had in view when I turned my thoughts to this fubject, I fhall now take leave of it; and fhall be highly gratified if I find others benefited by my attentions, although in a matter of no very ferious import.

Nov. 1784.

Defcription of a further Improvement in the HARP-SICHORD.

Read January
28, 1786.   IN a former paper read before the fociety, refpecting an improved method of quilling a HARPSICHORD, I made fome apology for troubling you with a fubject not ftrictly within the limits of your view as a philofophical fociety, and which might appear to fome of fmall importance. At the fame time I took formal leave of a purfuit which had accidentally engaged my attention, and which I had obtruded upon your's. Notwithftanding this, I find myfelf under a neceffity of again requefting your indulgence, whilft I defcribe a difcovery I made in Auguft laft, of a ftill further improvement to the fame purpofe.

Having

----

* My fet of forks are tuned from the middle C fharp to the C above, inclufive.

Having ſucceeded to the extent of my expeꝗation in a more advantageous way of applying the crow quill in common uſe in a harpſichord, I thought to reſt content with that improvement; which had principally for its objeꝗ the duration of the quill's elaſticity, and of courſe the duration of the equality of touch. But notwithſtanding the long eſtabliſhed prejudice in favour of the crow quill, and the prevailing opinion that no ſubſtance can ſupply its place to advantage, I think a candid critic will allow that one of the following poſitions is founded in faꝗ, and the other in reaſon.

Firſt. Although the three ſtops of a harpſichord ſhould be quilled to the beſt advantage, the reſult of the whole will be an obſervable jingle or tinkling between the quills and wires, which depreciates the dignity and ſweetneſs of the inſtrument. The beſt harpſichords are ſo cenſurable for this imperfeꝗion, that the *Forte Piano*, which is free from it, ſtands a chance of rivalling that noble inſtrument, for this cauſe only; being far inferior in every other reſpeꝗ.

Second. Is it not reaſonable to ſuppoſe that ſo long a ſtring, ſo advantageouſly ſtretched over ſo large a box, ſhould yield a greater body of tone, than that which is produced by the impulſe of a quill? If the quill be made very ſtiff, this will render the touch diſagreeable and encreaſe the jingle, but not add to the *body* of tone. One reaſon why the quill does not draw a fuller tone from the ſtring, I ſuppoſe to be the ſmallneſs of its contaꝗ. The back of a quill is a portion of a circle, the extended ſtring is a right line, and a circle can touch a right line only in a point; the contaꝗ therefore muſt be ſo very ſmall, that mere ſtrength of impulſe is not ſufficient to put the ſtring into full vibration.

The method I am now to deſcribe of quilling, or rather *tonguing* a harpſichord, I have found by experiment, to draw forth the powers of the inſtrument to a ſurpriſing

effeꝗ,

effect, caufing it to yield a full and pure body of tone, free from all jingle and very pleafant to the ear.

N. B. What hath hitherto been called the tongue of the jack, I fhall denominate the *palate*; and the fubftitute I have made for the quill, I fhall call the *tongue*. The propriety of this will appear in the defcription.

Let A, figure 12, reprefent the palate in front, with a mortife cut through it for the tongue to work in. B, is the tongue, having two fmall holes drilled through it, one in the centre of its motion and the other at a little diftance behind, for the reception of one end of a wire fpring hereafter mentioned.

Plate III.

Figure 13, is the palate in profile, with the tongue properly mounted and moveable on the centre pin. This figure alfo fhews how the palate muft be hollowed in behind to expofe the root of the tongue, and the fmall hole in it for the reception of one end of the wire fpring.

Figure 14, is a back view of the palate, fhewing the groove in which the hair fpring of the jack lies, and a fmall wire ftaple at *b*, to which the lower end of the fteel fpring is to be faftened.

Figure 15, is the fpring which is to govern the tongue. It muft be of fine fteel wire, fomewhat annealed by being forcibly rubbed between pieces of leather or cork, and is formed by winding the wire backwards and forwards with a tight hand, over pins driven deep and firm into a piece of wood. As the palate muft play freely within the fork or jaws of the jack, the windings of the fpring muft not exceed the width of the palate. The upper end of the fpring being run through the fmall hole in the root of the tongue and bent round, fo as to fecure it, and the fuperfluous part cut off; the lower end of the fame fpring muft be run under the little ftaple (*b*, figure 14,) and bent upwards with a gentle ftrain, fo as to hook it on and fecure it to that ftaple; the fpring will then operate with all its elafticity, and the tongue will be fubjected to its operation.

Figure

Figure 17, reprefents the palate in a back view with the
zig zag fpring faſtened by one end to the root of the tongue,
and by the other to the little ſtaple.

To prevent the tongue from rifing by the force of the
fpring above a horizontal pofition, there muſt be a wire
ſtaple driven in the front of the palate immediately above
the tongue (as at *a*, in figure 12 and 13;) and the tongue,
if of wood, fhould be armed with a fmall piece of foft leather juſt under the ſtaple, to prevent noiſe.

It muſt be left to future experiment to determine the
moſt proper of all fubſtances of which the tongue fhould
be made; different fubſtances drawing different tones from
the ſtring.   After many effays to this purpofe, I have concluded to furnifh my harpfichord in the following manner.

The tongues of the firſt unifon are of *Ben fole-leather*.
Thofe of the fecond are of a foft leather faced with Morocco, fuch as is frequently ufed in harpfichords, though
applied in a different way, and the tongues of the octave
are of wood, fuch as pear tree, laurel, or any wood of an
even grain and not too hard in fubſtance.   But all mounted on fprings, as above defcribed, and their faces well polifhed with black lead where they come in contact with
the ſtrings.

My reafons are.   The fole-leather produces a full, fweet
and vigorous tone from the firſt unifon.   The fecond unifon, which is the piano of the inſtrument when the pedal
is preffed, is furnifhed with Morocco leather, which draws
a full but more foft and fmothered tone from the ſtring.
And the octave is ſtruck with wooden tongues for the fake
of vivacity or brilliancy, which is the genius of that ſtop;
yet I am not fure but that the octave alfo had better be
ſtruck with fole-leather, like the firſt unifon*.

A harpfichord thus furnifhed, will produce a body or
quantity of found, and a purity of tone, that will aſtonifh
at

* Becaufe, after the ſtroke has been given, the wooden tongue repaſſing the ſtring, yet in
vibration, makes a jingle, which the leather tongues do not.

at the firſt hearing, much reſembling the diapaſon ſtop of an organ. And it is manifeſt that if the touch be well regulated at firſt, it will not afterwards be ſubject to alteration for a long courſe of time. The touch is in part regulated by the ſtrength of the ſerpentine ſpring and the number of its zig zag evolutions; and in part by the manner of rounding off the tip of the tongue; for the tip of the tongue muſt not be cut off ſquare, (in which caſe, the ſtring would leave the tongue too abruptly and cauſe a diſagreeable twang,) but ſhould be ſlanted off from underneath, and its extreme point rounded and well poliſhed by rubbing it very hard with a piece of black lead. As to the ſtrength of the ſpring, four ſizes of wire, viz. from n°· 4 to n°· 8, will be ſufficient for the whole inſtrument; but the touch is more immediately regulated by rounding off the tips of the tongues by the preſſure and poliſh of the black lead, more or leſs, as occaſion ſhall require. When the tongues are of wood, a ſtroke or two of a fine file will be neceſſary to take off the ſquare edge left by the knife, previous to the poliſhing it with the black lead.

After all, a harpſichord juſt furniſhed in this way, will not be ſo pleaſant to the touch or to the ear as it will be after a few weeks uſe; when the ſtrings will, by repeated friction, have rounded off and poliſhed the tips of the tongues, and have made for themſelves a broad bearing or contact, which cannot perhaps be ſo accurately produced by any care of the workman.

Laſtly, it is ſcarce neceſſary to obſerve that the ſerpentine ſpring and the root of the tongue muſt be compriſed within the thickneſs of the jack; otherwiſe they will be apt to interfere with the ſtring behind, when the ſtop is puſhed back.

F. HOPKINSON.

Obſervations

N° XX.

Obſervations on a Comet lately diſcovered; communicated by DAVID RITTENHOUSE, *Eſquire.*

Read Mar. 19, 1784.

ON the 21ſt of January laſt, John Lukens, Eſquire, informed me that he had diſcovered a comet the preceding evening, and on the evening of the ſame day, aſſiſted by Mr. Lukens and Mr. Prior, I obſerved the apparent place of the comet to be in the 15th degree of Piſces, with 16° 6′ ſouth latitude. By ſubſequent obſervations I found its motion to be north eaſterly, with reſpect to the ecliptic, and that its neareſt approach to us had preceded our firſt obſervation. It paſſed the ecliptic on the 31ſt in the 25° of Piſces, and February the 17th it was in Piſces 29° with 13° 10′ north latitude. This was the laſt time I ſaw it, clouds and moonlight having ſince prevented.

The light of this comet was ſo very faint that it was impoſſible to obſerve it with accuracy, at leaſt without better inſtruments than I am poſſeſſed of, eſpecially as the comet was always involved in day light, moonlight or the thick atmoſphere of the horizon. No pains or attention however were wanting, and from the beſt obſervations I could make, I find it paſſed its perihelion about the 20th of January, its diſtance from the ſun being about $\frac{7}{10}$ of the ſun's diſtance from us. The place of its aſcending node is in the 25th deg. of Taurus, and the inclination of its orbit 53°. Its motion is retrograde, that is, contrary to the order of the ſigns. I have ſtill hopes of ſeeing it in the morning, though its diſtance is now ſo very great that it can ſcarcely be viſible to the naked eye.

Extract.

N° XXI.

Extract of a Letter from the Rev. Jeremy Belknap,
containing Observations on the Aurora Borealis.

Dover, New-Hampshire, March 31st, 1783.

Read May
2, 1783. "DID you ever, in observing the Aurora Borealis, perceive a *sound?* I own I once
looked on the idea as frivolous and chimerical, having
heard it at first from persons whose credulity, I supposed,
exceeded their judgment; but, upon hearing it repeatedly, and from some others whom I thought judicious and
curious, I began to entertain an opinion in favour of it.
I was strengthened in this opinion about two years ago,
by listening with attention to the flashing of a luminous
arch which appeared in a calm frosty night, when I thought
I heard a faint rustling noise like the brushing of silk. Last
Saturday evening I had full auricular demonstration of the
reality of this phenomenon. About ten o'clock the hemi-
sphere was all in a glow; the vapours ascended from all
points, and met in a central one in the zenith : All the
difference between the south and north part of the heavens
was, that the vapour did not begin to ascend so near the
horizon in the south as in the north. There had been a
small shower with a few thunder claps, and a bright rain-
bow in the afternoon; and there was a gentle western
breeze in the evening which came in flaws, with intervals
of two or three minutes ; in these intervals I could plainly perceive the rustling noise, which was easily distinguish-
able from the sound of the wind, and could not be heard
till the flaw had subsided. The flashing of the vapour
was extremely quick ; whether accelerated by the wind I
cannot

cannot fay; but from that quarter where the greateft quantity of the vapour feemed to be in motion, the found was plaineft; and this, during my obfervation, was the eaftern. The fcene lafted about half an hour, though the whole night was as light as when the moon is in the quarters."

N° XXII.

A Letter from J. MADISON, *Efq. to* D. RITTENHOUSE, *Efq. containing Experiments and Obfervations upon what are commonly called the Sweet Springs.*

THESE waters rife on the north fide of a large mountain at the foot of it, called the Sweet Spring Mountain, in the county of Botetourt. The fouth fide is covered with ftones of an ocrous appearance. In many places iron ore may be found; but on the north the mountain is fertile, covered with a rich mould, at leaft near the fpring. The remarkable efficacy of thefe waters in many diforders, efpecially, it is faid, in confumptive complaints, firft induced me to attempt their analyfis. Such experiments as I had time and opportunity to make, I fhall faithfully relate, and leave it to others, better qualified than myfelf, to judge of their merits.

Experiment 1. Having plunged a very fenfible mercurial thermometer in the fpring, it ftood at 73° The temperature of air was about 69.

2. A good hydrometer funk one-twentieth of an inch deeper in common mountain water, than in the fpring.

3. Nut-galls mixed with the water in a wine glafs ftruck a palifh brown, which fhewed that there was little or no iron in it.

4. Violets mixed with the water in a wine glafs, turn-

C c

ed it in a fhort time of a reddifh colour. This was a proof that the waters contained fome kind of acid.

5. Having made a folution of filver in the nitrous acid, and mixed a little of it with the water, it immediately became milky, and a white pulvurent precipitate enfued. This experiment fhewed by the whitenefs of the precipitate, that the waters contained nothing fulphureous, and by the pulvurency of the precipitate that the acid contained in the waters was vitriolic.

6. A folution of lead in the nitrous acid being mixed with the water, it became fomewhat milky, and a white precipitate was obferved. This experiment alfo fhews that the waters contain an acid, moft probably the vitriolic, and alfo that they contain calcareous earth. Soap is not readily mifcible with them.

7. A folution of faccharum faturni in the nitrous acid being made, and lines marked upon paper with it, and placed over the water, the lines retained their former colour. This experiment alfo fhews that the water contains nothing fulphureous.

8. Having poured a little of the fpirit of falt into the water, after fome time a coloured precipitate was obferved, but as the waters did not ftrike a green or blue colour, it fhewed that there was no copper in them.

9. A folution of vitriol of copper mixed with the water produced a thick, green, curdly appearance, but did not become bluer. This experiment fhewed that there was no vol. alkali contained in them.

10. The vitriolic acid mixed with the water fuddenly effervefced, and produced a heat which raifed the thermometer from 75 to 83, by applying the bulb to the outfide of the glafs.

11. As the fpring is continually difcharging large bubbles of air, which rifing from the bottom break upon the furface of the water, I was defirous of making fome experiments upon the air, in order to determine whether
the

the acidity of the water might not be owing to it; and also to determine the nature of the air, whether fixed or not. Having therefore caught a quantity of the air in a decanter, I communicated a part of it to an equal bulk of pure mountain water, and after agitating them for some time, gave it to several to taste; who agreed that it had the taste of the spring water. Upon a second trial this experiment did not succeed. I had not an opportunity of trying the nature of the air by means of chalk-water, and was prevented from prosecuting any farther enquiries into the nature of these celebrated waters by a sudden alarm, to which the frontiers were then continually exposed.

These waters have been falsely called *sweet*, for their taste is evidently acidulous. The experiments also shew that they contain an acid. Their taste resembles exactly that of waters artificially impregnated with fixed air, extricated from chalk, by means of the vitriolic acid, and I conceive must be nearly the same with the true Pyrmont water. They have little or no smell, do not form an incrustation, nor do they leave a deposit upon standing many hours. Upon bathing in the morning, the skin has a soapy kind of feel. This was not observed in the evening.

There is near this spring another, a very strong chalybeate.

I am, with great regard, yours,

J. MADISON.

N° XXIII.

A Letter from the Rev. JEREMY BELKNAP, *on the preserving of Parsnips by drying.*

Dover, New-Hampshire, March 5, 1784.

SIR,

Read Apr. 16, 1784.
AMONG the number of esculent roots, the *parsnip* has two singular good qualities.

Cc 2

One

One is that it will endure the fevereft froft and may be taken out of the ground in the fpring, as frefh and fweet as in autum; the other is that it may be preferved by drying to any defired length of time.

The firft of thefe advantages has been known for many years paft; the people in the moft northerly parts of New-England where winter reigns with great feverity, and the ground is often frozen to the depth of two or three feet for four months, leave their parfnips in the ground till it thaws in the fpring, and think them much better preferved than in cellars.

The other advantage never occurred to me till this winter, when one of my neighbours put into my hands a fubftance which had the appearance of a piece of buck's horn.   This was part of a parfnip which had been drawn out of the ground laft April and had lain neglected in a dry clofet for ten months.   It was fo hard as to require confiderable ftrength to force a knife through it crofs-wife; but being foaked in warm water, for about an hour, became tender, and was as fweet to the tafte as if it had been frefh drawn from the ground.

As many ufeful difcoveries owe their origin to accident, this may fuggeft a method of preferving fo pleafant and wholefome a vegetable for the ufe of feamen in long voyages, to prevent the fcurvey and other diforders incident to a fea-faring life, which is often rendered tedious and diftreffing for want of vegetable food; fince I am perfuaded that parfnips dried to fuch a degree, as above related, and packed in tight cafks, may be tranfported round the globe, without any lofs of their flavour or diminution of their nutritive quality.

I am fir, your humble fervant,

JEREMY BELKNAP.

An

N° XXIV.

An Optical Problem, proposed by Mr. HOPKINSON, *and solved by* Mr. RITTENHOUSE.

Philadelphia, March 16th, 1785.

DEAR SIR,

Read Feb. 17, 1786. I TAKE the liberty of requesting your attention to the following problem in *optics*. It is I believe entirely new, and the solution will afford amusement to you and instruction to me.

Setting at my door one evening last summer, I took a silk handkerchief out of my pocket, and stretching a portion of it tight between my two hands, I held it up before my face and viewed, through the handkerchief, one of the street lamps which was about one hundred yards distant; expecting to see the threads of the handkerchief much magnified. Agreeably to my expectation I observed the silk threads magnified to the size of very coarse wires; but was much surprised to find that, although I moved the handkerchief to the right and left before my eyes, the dark bars did not seem to move at all, but remained permanent before the eye. If the dark bars were occasioned by the interposition of the magnified threads between the eye and the flame of the lamp, I should have supposed that they would move and succeed each other, as the threads were made to move and pass in succession before the eye; but the fact was otherwise.

To account for this phenomenon exceeds my skill in *optics*. You will be so good as to try the experiment, and if you find the case truly stated, as I doubt not you will, I shall be much obliged by a solution on philosophical principles. I am sir, with great sincerity,

Your most effectionate friend,

And very humble servant,

F. HOPKINSON.

The Anfwer, by Mr. RITTENHOUSE.

DEAR SIR,

THE experiment you mention, with a filk handkerchief and the diftant flame of a lamp, is much more
curious than one would at firft imagine. For the object
we fee is not the web of the handkerchief magnified, but
fomething very different, as appears from the following
confiderations. 1ft. A diftinct image of any object, placed
clofe to the eye, cannot be formed by parallel rays, or
fuch as iffue from a diftant luminous point : for all fuch
rays, paffing through the pupil, will be collected at the
bottom of the eye, and there form an image of the luminous point. The threads of the handkerchief would only
intercept part of the rays, and render the image lefs bril-
liant. 2dly. If the crofs bars we fee were images of the
filk threads, they muft pafs over the retina, whilft the
threads are made to pafs over the pupil ; but this, as you
obferve, does not happen ; for they continue ftationary.
3dly. If the image on the retina was a picture of the object before the eye, it muft be fine or coarfe, according to
the texture of the handkerchief. But it does not change
with changing the filk, nor does it change on removing
it farther from the eye. And the number of apparent
threads remains the fame, whether 10, 20, or 30 of the
filk threads pafs acrofs the pupil at the fame time. The
image we fee muft therefore be formed in fome different
manner ; and this can be no other than by means of the
inflection of light in paffing near the furfaces of bodies, as
defcribed by NEWTON.

It is well known in optics that different images of the
different points of objects without the eye are formed on
the retina by pencils of rays, which, before they fall on
the eye, are inclined to each other in fenfible angles. And
the great ufe of telefcopes is to encreafe thefe angles, re-
gularly, in a certain ratio ; fuffering fuch rays as were

parallel

parallel before they enter the telefcope to proceed on, parallel, after paffing through it. The extended image which
we fee in this experiment muft therefore be formed by
pencils of rays, which before they entered the eye, had
very confiderable degrees of inclination with refpect to
each other. But coming from a fmall diftant flame of a
lamp, they were nearly parallel before they paffed through
the filk handkerchief. It was therefore the threads of filk
which gave them fuch different directions.

Before the filk is placed to the eye, parallel rays of light
will form a fingle lucid fpot, as at A, Plate III. Figure 16.
And this fpot will ftill be formed afterwards by fuch rays
as pafs through the little mefhes uninfluenced by the
threads. But fuppofe the perpendicular threads by their
action on the rays, to bend a part of them one degree to
the right and left, another part two degrees; there will now
be four new images formed, two on each fide of the original
one at A. By a fimilar action of the horizontal threads, this
line of five lucid points will be divided into five other lines,
two above and two below, making a fquare of twenty-five
bright fpots, feparated by four perpendicular dark lines and
four horizontal ones; and thefe lucid fpots and dark lines
will not change their places on moving the web of filk over
the eye parallel to any of its threads. For the point of the
retina on which the image fhall fall is determined by the
incidence of the rays, with refpect to the axis of the eye, before they enter, and not by the part of the pupil through
which they pafs.

In order to make my experiments with more accuracy,
I made a fquare of parallel hairs about half an inch each
way. And to have them nearly parallel and equidiftant,
I got a watchmaker to cut a very fine fcrew on two pieces
of fmall brafs wire. In the threads of thefe fcrews, 196
of which made one inch, the hairs were laid 50 or 60 in
number. Looking through thefe hairs at a fmall opening
in the window fhutter of a dark room, $\frac{1}{10}$ of an inch wide
and.

and three inches long, holding the hairs parallel to the
flit, and looking toward the sky, I saw three parallel lines,
almoft equal in brightnefs, and on each fide four or five
others much fainter and growing more faint, coloured and
indiftinct, the farther they were from the middle line,
which I knew to be formed by fuch rays as pafs between
the hairs uninfluenced by them. Thinking my apparatus
not fo perfect as it might be, I took out the hairs and put
in others, fomething thicker, of thefe 190 made one inch,
and therefore the fpaces between them were about the $\frac{1}{110}$
part of an inch. The three middle lines of light were now
not fo bright as they had been before, but the others were
ftronger and more diftinct, and I could count fix on each
fide of the middle line, feeming to be equally diftant from
each other, eftimating the diftance from the centre of one
to the centre of the next. The middle line was ftill well
defined and colourlefs, the next two were likewife pretty
well defined, but fomething broader, having their inner
edges tinged with blue and their outer edges with red.
The others were more indiftinct, and confifted each of the
prifmatic colours, in the fame order, which by fpreading
more and more, feemed to touch each other at the fifth or
fixth line, but thofe neareft the middle were feparated from
each other by very dark lines, much broader than the
bright lines.

Finding the beam of light which came through the window fhutter divided into fo many diftinct pencils, I was
defirous of knowing the angles which they made with
each other. For this purpofe I made ufe of a fmall prifmatic telefcope and micrometer, with which I was favoured by Dr. Franklin. I faftened the frame of parallel hairs
before the object glafs, fo as to cover its aperture entirely.
Then looking through the telefcope, I meafured the fpace
between the two firft fide lines, and found the angular
diftance between their inner edges to be $13'$, $15''$; from
the middle of one to the middle of the other $15'$, $30''$, and
from

from the outer edge of one, to the outer edge of the other
17′, 45″. In the firſt caſe I had a fine blue ſtreak in the
middle of the objeĉt, and in the laſt a red ſtreak. The
other lines were too faint, when ſeen through the teleſcope,
to meaſure the angles they ſubtended with accuracy, but
from ſuch trials as I made I am ſatisfied that from the ſecond line on one ſide to the ſecond on the other ſide, and
ſo on, they were double, triple, quadruple, &c. of the firſt
angles.

It appears then that a very conſiderable portion of the
beam of light paſſed between the hairs, without being at
all bent out of its firſt courſe ; that another ſmaller portion was bent at a medium about 7′, 45″ each way ; the
red rays a little more, and the blue rays a little leſs ; another ſtill ſmaller portion 15′, 30″ ; another 23′, 15″, and
ſo on. But that no light, or next to none, was bent in any
angle leſs than 6′, nor any light of any particular colour,
in any intermediate angle between thoſe which ariſe from
doubling, tripling, &c. of the angle in which it is bent
in the firſt ſide lines.

I was ſurprized to find that the red rays are more bent
out of their firſt direĉtion, and the blue rays leſs ; as if the
hairs aĉted with more force on the red than on the blue
rays, contrary to what happens by refraĉtion, when light
paſſes obliquely through the common ſurface of two different mediums. It is, however, conſonant to what Sir
Iſaac Newton obſerves with reſpeĉt to the fringes that
border the ſhadows of hairs and other bodies ; his words
are, " And therefore the hair in cauſing theſe fringes,
" aĉted alike upon the red light or leaſt refrangible rays
" at a greater diſtance, and upon the violet or moſt re-
" frangible rays at a leſs diſtance, and by thoſe aĉtions
" diſpoſed the red light into larger fringes, and the violet
" into ſmaller fringes."

By purſuing theſe experiments it is probable that new
and intereſting diſcoveries may be made, reſpeĉting the

D d   properties

properties of this wonderful fubftance, light, which ani-
mates all nature in the eyes of man, and perhaps above
all things difpofes him to acknowledge the Creator's bounty.   But want of leifure obliges me to quit the fubject for
the prefent.

I am, dear fir, your affectionate friend,
And very humble fervant,
DAVID RITTENHOUSE.

N° XXV.

*An Enquiry into the Caufe of the Increafe of Bilious and
Intermitting Fevers in Pennfylvania, with Hints for
preventing them.   By* BENJAMIN RUSH, M. D. *Profeffor of Chemiftry in the Univerfity of Pennfylvania.*

Read December
16, 1785.
IT has been remarked, that Pennfylvania for
fome years paft has become more fickly than
formerly.   Fevers which a few years ago appeared chiefly
on the banks of creeks and rivers, and in the neighbourhood of mill-ponds, now appear in parts remote from
them all, and in the higheft fituations.   This change with
refpect to the healthinefs of our country, may be traced
to the three following caufes.

1. The eftablifhment and increafe of mill-ponds.   There
are whole counties in Pennfylvania in which intermittents
were unknown, until the waters in them were dammed,
for the purpofe of erecting mill-ponds.

2. The cutting down of wood, under certain circumftances, tends to render a country fickly.   It has been remarked that intermittents on the fhores of the Sufquehan-
nah have kept an exact pace with the paffages which have
been opened for the propagation of marfh effluvia, by
cutting

cutting down the wood which formerly grew in its neighbourhood. I remember the time, when intermittents
were known only within half a mile, in fome places, of
that river. They are now to be met with ten miles from
it in the fame parts of the ftate.

I beg a diftinction to be made here between *clearing* and
cultivating a country. While clearing a country makes
it fickly in the manner that has been mentioned, *cultivating* a country, that is, draining fwamps, deftroying weeds,
burning brufh, and exhaling the unwholfome or fuperfluous moifture of the earth, by means of frequent crops of
grain, graffes, and vegetables of all kinds, render it healthy. I could mention, in fupport of thefe facts, feveral
countries in the United States, which have paffed through
each of the ftages that have been defcribed. The firft fet-
tlers received thefe countries from the hands of nature pure
and healthy*. Fevers foon followed their improvements,
nor were they finally banifhed, until the higher degrees of
cultivation that have been named took place. I confine
myfelf to thofe countries only where the falutary effects of
cultivation were not rendered abortive by the neighbourhood of mill-ponds.

A 3d caufe of the late increafe of bilious and intermitting fevers, muft be fought for in the different and unequal quantities of rain which have fallen within thefe laft
feven years. While our creeks and rivers, from the uniformity of our feafons, were confined to fteady bounds,
there was little or no exhalation of febrile miafmata from
their fhores. But the dry fummers of 1780, 1781, and
1782, by reducing our creeks and rivers far below their
ancient marks ; while the wet fprings of 1784 and 1785,
by fwelling them both beyond their natural heights, have,
when they have fallen, as in the former cafe, left a large

and

---

* A phyfician who travelled through part of Bedford county, in Pennfylvania, in the year
1782, informed me that he was witnefs of fome country people having travelled twenty miles,
to fee whether it was poffible for a German girl who laboured under an intermittent, to be
hot and cold at the fame time.

and extenfive furface of moift ground expofed to the action of the fun, and of courfe to the generation and exhalation of febrile miafmata.   The hiftory of epidemics in
foreign countries, favours this opinion of the caufe of their
increafe in Pennfylvania.   The inhabitants of Egypt are
always healthy during the overflowing of the Nile.   Their
fevers appear only after the recefs of the river.   It is remarkable that a wet feafon is often healthy in low, while
it is fickly in hilly countries.   The reafon is obvious.   In
the former the rains entirely cover all the moift grounds,
while in the latter, they fall only in a fufficient quantity
to produce thofe degrees of moifture which favour febrile
exhalations.   The rains which fall in the fummer are rendered harmlefs only by covering the *whole* furface of
marfhy ground.   The rains which fall in our ftate after
the middle of September, are fo far from producing fevers,
that they generally prevent them.   The extraordinary
healthinefs of the laft autumn, I believe was occafioned
by nothing but the extraordinary quantity of rain that fell
during the autumnal months.   The rain probably acts at
this feafon by diluting, and thus deftroying, the febrile
miafmata that were produced by the heat and moifture of
the preceding fummer.   In fupport of the truth of this
third caufe of the increafe of fevers in Pennfylvania, I have
only to add a fact lately communicated to me by Dr.
Franklin.   He informed me that in his journey from Paffy
to Havre de Grace, laft fummer, he found the country
through which he travelled, unufually fickly with fevers.
Thefe fevers it was generally fuppofed, were produced by
the extraordinary dry weather, of which the public papers
have given us fuch melancholy and frequent accounts.

I come now to fuggeft a few hints for obviating and
preventing fevers, and for rendering our country again
healthy.   For this purpofe I beg leave to recommend in
the firft place, the planting of trees around all our mill-
ponds, (befides cleaning them occafionally) in order to
                                            prevent

prevent the difeafes that have juftly been afcribed to them. Let the trees be planted in the greateft number, and clofeft together, to leeward of the ordinary current of the fummer and autumnal winds. I have known feveral inftances of families being preferved from fevers by an accidental copfe of wood ftanding between a mill-pond and a dwelling houfe, and that in cafes too where the houfe derived no advantage from an high fituation. The trees *around* or *near* a mill-pond, act perhaps in a fmall degree *mechanically*. By fheltering the pond from the action of the fun, they leffen exhalation, as well as obftruct the paffage of the vapors that are raifed to the adjacent parts. But they act likewife *chemically*. It has been demonftrated that trees abforb unhealthy air, and difcharge it in a highly purified ftate in the form of what is now called " de-" flogifticated" air. The willow tree, according to Mr. Ingenhaufz, has been found to purify air the moft rapidly of any tree that he fubjected to his experiments. The rapidity of its growth, its early verdure, and the late fall of its leaf, all feem to mark it likewife as a tree highly proper for this purpofe.

A fecond method of preventing fevers, is to let the cultivation always keep pace with the *clearing* of our lands. Nature has in this inftance connected our duty, intereft and health together. Let every fpot covered with moifture from which the wood has been cut, be carefully drained, and afterwards ploughed and fowed with grafs feed; let weeds of all kinds be deftroyed, and let the waters be fo directed as to prevent their ftagnating in any part of their courfe.

Thefe are the two principal means of extirpating intermitting and bilious fevers from our country, but as thefe means are flow in their operation, I fhall fubjoin a few directions for preventing fevers till the above remedies can take effect.

1. Whether

1. Whether the matter which produces fevers be of an organic, or inorganic nature, I do not pretend to determine, but it is certain, that *fire* or the *smoke* or *heat*, which issue from it, destroy the effects of marsh miasmata upon the human body; hence we find cities more healthy than country places, and the centre of cities more healthy than their suburbs in the sickly months. To derive the utmost possible benefit from this method of preventing sickness, I would advise large fires to be made every evening of brush between the spots from whence the exhalations are derived, and the dwelling house, and as near to the latter as is safe, and not disagreeable. This practice should be continued till the appearance of two or three frosts, for frosts as well as heavy rains in the autumnal months never fail to put a stop to the progress of intermittents.

During the sickly season, fires should be likewise kept in every room in the dwelling house, even in those cases where the heat of the weather makes it necessary to keep the doors and windows open.

2. Let me advise my countrymen in sickly situations, to prefer woolen and cotton to linen clothes in the summer and autumnal months. The most sickly parts of the island of Jamacia have been rendered more healthy, since the inhabitants have adopted the use of woolen and cotton garments instead of linen.

During the late war, I knew many officers both in the British and American armies who escaped fevers in the most sickly places, by wearing woolen shirts, or waistcoats constantly next to their skins. I have heard the present diminution of the human body in strength and size, compared with its ancient vigor and form, ascribed in part to the introduction of linen garments. I am not disposed to controvert this opinion, but I am sure of the efficacy of woolen clothes in wet and cold climates in preventing fevers of all kinds. The parliament of Great
Britain

Britain compels every body that dies within the ifland to be buried in a woolen fhirt or winding fheet. The law would be much wifer if it compelled every body to wear woolen garments next to their fkins during life, and linen after death.

3. The diet in the fickly months fhould be generous. Wine and beer fhould be the drinks of this feafon inftead of fpirits and water. I do not think that fruit and vegetables of any kind produce fevers, but as the feafon of the year produces languor and weaknefs, a larger quantity of animal food than ufual is beft calculated to oppofe them. Salted meat for this reafon is preferable to frefh meat. Food of all kinds eaten during the fickly months fhould be well feafoned.

4. The evening air fhould be avoided as much as poffible. There are at prefent few places in Pennfylvania where it is fafe to fleep, or even to fet, after the going down of the fun, in the fickly months, with the windows open. The morning air before the fun rifes, fhould not be breathed, until the body has been fortified with a little folid aliment, or a *draught* of bitters. Thefe bitters fhould be made of centaury, wormwood, camomile, or the bark of the willow or dogwood trees, infufed in *water*. Bitters made with fpirits, or even wine, cannot be taken in a fufficient quantity to do fervice, without producing intoxication, or the deadly habit of loving and drinking fpirituous liquors.

5. Too much cannot be faid in favour of cleanlinefs, as a means of preventing fevers. The body fhould be bathed or wafhed frequently. It has been proved that in the highlands of Jamaica adding falt to water, renders it more powerful in preventing difeafes when applied to the body. Equal pains fhould be taken to promote cleanlinefs in every fpecies of apparel. Offal matters, efpecially thofe which are of a vegetable nature, fhould be removed from the neighbourhood of a dwelling houfe. The dung of domeftic animals during its progrefs towards manure

may

may be excepted from this direction. Nature, which made man and thefe animals, equally neceffary to each other's fubfiftence, has kindly prevented any inconvenience from their living together. On the contrary, to repay the hufbandman for affording a fhelter to thefe ufeful and helplefs animals, nature has done more. She has endowed their dung with a power of deftroying the effects of marfh exhalations, and of preventing fevers. The miferable cottagers in Europe who live under the fame roof, and in fome inftances in the fame room with their cattle, are always healthy. In Philadelphia, fevers are lefs known in the neighbourhood of livery ftables, than in any other part of the city. I could mention a family that has lived near thirty years near a livery ftable in a fickly part of the city, that has never known a fever but from the meafles or fmall-pox.

N° XXVI.

An Account of the late Dr. Hugh Martin's *Cancer Powder, with brief Obfervations on Cancers. By* Benjamin Rush, M. D. *&c. &c.*

Read February 3, 1786. A FEW years ago a certain Dr. Hugh Martin, a furgeon of one of the Pennfylvania regiments ftationed at fort Pitt, during the latter part of the late war, came to this city, and advertifed to cure cancers with a medicine which he faid he had difcovered in the woods, in the neighbourhood of the garrifon. As Dr. Martin had once been a pupil of mine, I took the liberty of waiting upon him, and afked him fome queftions refpecting his difcovery. His anfwers were calculated to make me believe, that his medicine was of a vegetable nature, and that it was originally an Indian remedy. He

fhewed

shewed me some of the medicine, which appeared to be the powder of a well dried root of some kind. Anxious to see the success of this medicine in cancerous sores, I prevailed upon the doctor to admit me to see him apply it in two or three cases. I observed in some instances, he applied a powder to the parts affected, and in others only touched them with a feather dipped in a liquid which had a white sediment, and which he made me believe was the vegetable root diffused in water. It gave me great pleasure to witness the efficacy of the doctor's applications. In several cancerous ulcers, the cures he performed were complete. Where the cancers were much connected with the lymphatic system, or accompanied with a scrophulous habit of body, his medicine always failed, and in some instances did evident mischief.

Anxious to discover a medicine that promised relief in even a few cases of cancers, and supposing that all the caustic vegetables were nearly alike, I applied the phyto-lacca or poke root, the stramonium, the arum, and one or two others, to foul ulcers, in hopes of seeing the same effects from them which I had seen from Dr. Martin's powder, but in these I was disappointed. They gave some pain, but performed no cures. At length I was furnished by a gentleman from fort Pitt with a powder which I had no doubt, from a variety of circumstances, was of the same kind as that used by Dr. Martin. I applied it to a fungous ulcer, but without producing the degrees of pain, inflammation, or discharge, which I had been accustomed to see from the application of Dr. Martin's powder. After this, I should have suspected that the powder was not a *simple* root, had not the doctor continued upon all occasions to assure me that it was wholly a vegetable preparation.

In the beginning of the year 1784 the doctor died, and it was generally believed that his medicine had died with him. A few weeks after his death, I procured from Mr. Thomas Lieper, one of his administrators, a few ounces of

E e   the

the doctor's powder, partly with a view of applying it to a cancerous fore which then offered, and partly with a view of examining it more minutely than I had been able to do during the doctor's life. Upon throwing the powder, which was of a brown colour, upon a piece of white paper, I perceived diftinctly a number of white particles fcattered through it. I fufpected at firft that they were corrofive fublimate, but the ufual tefts of that metallic falt foon convinced me that I was miftaken. Recollecting that arfenic was the bafis of moft of the celebrated cancer powders that have been ufed in the world, I had recourfe to the tefts for detecting it. Upon fprinkling a fmall quantity of the powder upon fome coals of fire, it emitted the garlic fmell fo perceptibly as to be known by feveral perfons whom I called into the room where I made the experiment, and who knew nothing of the object of my enquiries. After this with fome difficulty I picked out about three or four grains of the white powder, and bound them between two pieces of copper, which I threw into the fire. After the copper pieces became red hot, I took them out of the fire, and when they had cooled, difcovered an evident whitenefs imparted to both of them. One of the pieces afterwards looked like dull filver. Thefe two tefts have generally been thought fufficient to diftinguifh the prefence of arfenic in any bodies, but I made ufe of a third, which has lately been communicated to the world by Mr. Bergman, and which is fuppofed to be in all *cafes* infallible.

I infufed a fmall quantity of the powder in a folution of a vegetable alkali in water for a few hours, and then poured it upon a folution of blue vitriol in water. The colour of the vitriol was immediately changed to a beautiful green, and afterwards precipitated.

I fhall clofe this paper with a few remarks upon this powder, and upon the cure of cancers and foul ulcers of all kinds.

The

1. The use of caustics in cancers and foul ulcers is very ancient, and universal. But I believe *arsenic* to be the most efficacious of any that has ever been used. It is the basis of Plunkett's and probably of Guy's well known cancer powders. The great art of applying it successfully, is to dilute and mix it in such a manner as to mitigate the violence of its action. Dr. Martin's composition was happily calculated for this purpose. It gave less pain than the common or lunar caustic. It excited a moderate inflammation, which separated the morbid from the found parts, and promoted a plentiful afflux of humours to the fore during its application. It seldom produced an escar; hence it insinuated itself into the deepest recesses of the cancers, and frequently separated these fibres in an unbroken state which are generally called the roots of the cancer. Upon this account, I think, in an ulcerated cancer it is to be preferred to the knife. It has no action upon the found skin. This Dr. Hall proved by confining a small quantity of it upon his arm for many hours. In those cases where Dr. Martin used it to extract cancerous or schirrous tumors that were not ulcerated, I have reason to believe that he always broke the skin with Spanish flies.

2. The arsenic used by the doctor was the pure white arsenic. I should suppose from the examination I made of the powder with the eye, that the proportion of arsenic to the vegetable powder, could not be more than $\frac{1}{70}$ part of the whole compound. I have reason to think that the doctor employed different vegetable substances at different times. The vegetable matter with which the arsenic was combined in the powder which I used in my experiments, was probably nothing more than the powder of the root and berries of the solanum lethale, or deadly nightshade. As the principal, and perhaps the only design of the vegetable addition was to blunt the activity of the arsenic, I should suppose that the same propor-

tion

tion of common wheat flour as the doctor ufed of his
cauftic vegetables, would anfwer nearly the fame purpofe.
In thofe cafes where the doctor applied a feather dipped
in a liquid to the fore of his patient, I have no doubt but
his phial contained nothing but a weak folution of arfenic
in water. This is no new method of applying arfenic to
foul ulcers. Dr. Way of Wilmington, has fpoken in the
higheft terms to me of a wafh for foulneffes on the fkin, as
well as old ulcers, prepared by boiling an ounce of white
arfenic in two quarts of water to three pints, and applying it once or twice a day.

3. I mentioned formerly that Dr. Martin was often
unfuccefsful in the application of his powder. This was
occafioned by his ufing it indifcriminately in *all* cafes. In
fchirrous and cancerous tumours, the knife fhould always
be preferred to the cauftic. In cancerous ulcers attended
with a fcrophulous or a bad habit of body, fuch particularly
as have their feat in the neck, in the breafts of females,
and in the axillary glands, it can only protract the patient's mifery. Moft of the cancerous fores cured by Dr.
Martin were feated on the nofe, or cheeks, or upon the furface or extremities of the body. It remains yet to difcover
a cure for cancers that taint the fluids, or infect the whole
lymphatic fyftem. This cure I apprehend muft be fought
for in diet, or in the long ufe of fome internal medicine.

To pronounce a difeafe incurable, is often to render it
fo. The intermitting fever, if left to itfelf, would probably prove frequently, and perhaps more fpeedily fatal than
cancers. And as cancerous tumours and fores are often
neglected, or treated improperly by injudicious people,
from an apprehenfion that they are incurable, (to which
the frequent advice of phyficians " to let them alone," has
no doubt contributed) perhaps the introduction of arfenic
into regular practice as a remedy for cancers, may invite
to a more early application to phyficians, and thereby prevent

vent the deplorable cafes that have been mentioned, which are often rendered fo by delay or unfkilful management.

4. It is not in cancerous fores only that Dr. Martin's powder has been found to do fervice. In fores of all kinds, and from a variety of caufes, where they have been attended with fungous flefh or callous edges, I have ufed the doctor's powder with advantage.

I flatter myfelf that I fhall be excufed in giving this detail of a *quack* medicine, when the fociety reflect that it was from the inventions and temerity of quacks, that phy-ficians have derived fome of their moft active and ufeful medicines.

N° XXVII.

Illuftriffimæ ac celeberrimæ Societati Scientiarum quæ eft Philadelphiæ.

S. P. D.

CHRISTIANUS MAYER Ser^mi Electoris Palatini Aftronomus.

SCRIBENDI occafionem a Cl. D. Ferdinando Far-mer oblatam eo minus negligendam putavi quod hac ratione aliquantum refpondeam honori, quo me illuftriffima focietas affecit, cum me in album fuorum fociorum ad fcripfit. Ex libro Philadelphiæ impreffo & ad me tribus circiter abhinc annis tranfmiffo intellexi non fine magno animi mei fenfu, etiam Philadelphiæ excoli aftronomiam. Libro illo fcriptifque meis aftronomicis infelici incendio abhinc biennio confumtis, de novis meis quibufdam in cœlo inventis ad focietatem illuftriffimam aliquid fcribendum effe, duxi. Speculam novam ad omnes ufus accommoda-tam

tam Manhemii inhabito; nec defunt pretiofiſſima Londi-
nenſia inſtrumenta, in quibus præcipue eminet quadrans
muralis æneus 8 pedum in rhadio a cel. artifici Bird anno
1775 confectus & plane inſigni tubo achromatico inſtruc-
tus, ſolidiſſimeque muro affixus ad plagam cœli meridio-
nalem, quo inſtrumento, quoties cœlum favet, utor quo-
tidie. Adverti autem ſtatim abhinc biennio in ſtellis fixis
plane multis a primo gradu magnitudnis ad ſextum uſque,
diſtingui alias ſtellulas parvulas comites, quarum aliæ ob
lucem tranquillam & obtuſam planetarum ſpeciem referunt,
aliæ teleſcopicam parvitatem non excedunt. Quod maxime
mirabar, illud eſt, quod has ſtellulas comites, paucifſimis
duntaxat exceptis, nullo noto catalogo contineri viderem,
cum tamen earum uſum ad determinandum motum proprium fixarum eſſe plane inſignem evidenter colligerem.
Cum enim ibi, ubi paucorum plerumqe ſecundorum repe-
ritur differentia aſcenſionis rectæ & declinationis inter fixam
lucidiorem, ejuſque comitem, lapſus temporis haud aliam
variationem ſtellæ fixæ, quam ejus comiti inducere poſſit,
unde demum cunque iſta mutatio oriatur, ſive a præceſſi-
one æquinoctiorum, ſive a variatione obliquitatis eclipticæ,
ſive a deviatione inſtrumenti, ſeu ab aberratione luminis
aut nutationis, ſive ab alia quacunque cauſa, quæ pendeat
a mutabili ſtatu atmoſpheræ aut locorum latitudine, con-
tingit ſane, ut omnis mutatio viſa inter fixam, ejuſque
comitem, motusproprii argumentum præbeat certiſſimum,
ſive is fixam ſive ejus comitem afficiat. Noveram Halleum
cel. Angliæ aſtronomum primum fuiſſe, qui anno 1719 ex
inſtituta comparatione obſervationum Flamſteadii cum illis
Ptolomæi in paucis quibuſdam fixis, Syrio, Arcturo &
Aldebaran deprehendit has ſtellas moveri motu ſingulari
proprio. Sed ſimul noveram in Hiſtoria Cœleſti Brittan-
nica Flamſteadii jam anno 1690 uſurpatam fuiſſe a Flam-
ſteadio vocem comitis fixarum, cum vir ſummus nec dum
de motu proprio fixarum cogitaſſet. Aſtronomi reliqui
Halleo poſteriores quotquot in motum proprium fixarum
                                          inquiſiverunt,

inquifiverunt, Hallei methodum fecuti funt, comparando
obfervationes fuas cum obfervationibus antiquorum : methodus hæc prolixos requirit calculorum labores, multifque
dubitationibus manet obnoxia ob incertitudinem, lubricam-
que conditionem inftrumentorum, & obfervationum anti-
quarum ; non item methodus mea nova, qua ex variatione
inter comitem & fixam illuftriorem obfervata, ftatim con-
fequitur dari motum proprium, vel utriufque vel allerutrius
fideris. Itaque ducentos fere diverfarum fixarum comites
a biennio obfervavi, eundem fere paralellum ftatim ante
vel poft fixam decurrentes, & obfervationes hujufmodi
plures cum cel. Angliæ aftronomo Nevil Mafkelyne com-
municavi, qui eas fibi gratiffimas accidiffe refpondet. Ex
multis, obfervationes paucas ad illuftriffimam focietatem
fpeciminis loco tranfmitto, quarum refpondentes in Hifto-
ria Cœlefti Britannica Flamfteadii invenio, unde fimul
patet, quam obfervationes hujufmodi præclare ferviant
motui proprio detegendo. Prima et fecunda columna
finiftima tabulæ fequentis ex titulo facillime intelligitur.
Tertia columna differentiam A. R. in tempore medio in-
dicat inter ftellam ejufque comitem : comes præcedens
fixam, primo loco in tabula fcribitur, comes fequens poft
fixam ponitur. Quarta columna differentiam declinationis
inter fixam ejufque comitem notat, qualem ego Manhemii
obfervavi. Litera A fignificat comitem effe auftraliorem,
litera B magis borealem. Sequentes columnæ, obfervationes.
ejufdem ftellæ factas a Flamfteadio, continent.

	MAYER, Mannheim.			FLAMSTAED, Greenwich.		
	Nomina Fixarum	Diff. A. R. in tempore.	Differ. Declina.	Diff. A. R.	Differ. Declina.	
1777 Die 28 Feb.	ρ Leonis Comes 7æ. five 8væ.	2'. 15".	38'.58".6.A	2'. 18".	38'. 50". A	1690 Die 25 Mar.
1777 28 Feb. item 23 Feb.	Com. γ Leonis 6tæ. γ Leonis 4tæ	5".	21'.57".2.A	2".	22'. 5".	1691 6 Aprilis.
1777 4 Aprilis.	Comes τ Leonis	1'. 5".	8'. 0". 15. B	56.	8'. 30". B	1690 25 Martii.
1777 11 Martii.	Propus Comes 5tæ	5'. 36".	7'. 30."	5'. 38".	7'. 0".	1690 7 Feb.
1777 8 Martii.	Procyon Comes II. 8væ	1'. 40". 5.	3'. 6".2. A	1'. 34".	4'. 40". A	1691 4 Octo.
1777 13 Nov.	Com. 7mæ ε Piscium	51".	2'. 57". 1. B	47".	2'. 30". B	1700 Nov. 13.
1777 Aprilis 6.	Comes Π Cancri	2'. 49".	1'. 40". B	2'. 44".	1'. 12". B	1690 Feb. 18.
1777 Aprilis 8.	Com. 7æ β Leonis	30".	18'.27".1.A	33"5		1692 Aprilis 24.
1776 Mai. 18.	Arcturus Comes.	0. 0. 6".	0. 23. 37. 3	Com. 0. 5". Arcturus.	0. 26. 30.	1690 Febru. 14.
1777 Mart. 11.	Procyon Comes 7æ.	39".	3'. 8". 1. A	35".		1692 22 Janu.
1776 Mai. 18.	Arcturus Comes.	0. 0. 6.	0. 23. 37. 4	MASKELYNE. A. R.		1765 20 Mai.
1777 Aprilis 1.	O Cancri seg. Π Cancri 6.	14'. 56".	32. 29. 6. B	0. 0. 4. 15. 1.	0. 23'.58".8. 32. 25. B	1691 10 Martii.

Apparet ex omnibus Arcturum omnium celerrime ferri motu proprio in occafum, fequidem idem comes, qui tempore Flamfteadii 1690, die 14 Februarii Arcturum præcedebat 5" in tempore nunc 6" poft Arcturum meridianum ingreditur : ex imminuta quoque differentia declinationis inter Arcturum ejufque comitem, patet, Arcturum motu proprio quotannis fere 2" in circulo moveri verfus auftrum. Id ex eo perfpicuum eft, quod declinatio a me obfervata comitis reducta ad parallelum grenovicenfem eandem producat altitudinem poli grenovicenfis, qualis ex obfervatione Flamfteadii eruitur, non item declinatio hodie obfervata Arcturi etiam aberratione & nutatione correcta. Similis indagatio fieri poteft in reliquis fixis, earumque comitibus, atque ex inftituta comparatione cum aliis fixis deprehendi

deprehendi poteft, num fixæ an comiti vel utrique motus proprius tribuendis fit.

Obfervationes omnes in plano meridiani quadrante murali factæ funt Manhemii in nova fpecula a me ædificata S. Electoris Palatini: ejus longitudo ad ortum Grenovicii eft fere 34' 6" in tempore, latitudo fere 49° 27' 50" Gaudebo maxime fi has meas obfervationes illuftriffimæ focietati haud ingratas accidiffe intellexero, cujus benevolentiæ me demififfime commendo.

Illuftriffimæ ac celeberrimæ Societati,
Cuetor et fervus perpetuus,
CHRISTIANUS MAYER, Sereniffimi
Electoris Palatini et Ducis Bavariæ Aftronomus.

Manhemii in Germania, ⎫
  die 24 Aprilis 1778. ⎬

(TRANSLATION.)

To the illuftrious and celebrated Society of Sciences at Philadelphia,

CHRISTIAN MAYER, Aftronomer to his Serene Highnefs the Elector Palatine,

Wifheth Profperity.

I THOUGHT it my duty to embrace the opportunity which my good friend the Rev. Mr. Ferdinand Farmer has procured me of writing to your illuftrious fociety, that I may make fome return to the honour which you have done me by electing and enrolling me among your members. It gave me a very fenfible pleafure to find, by the printed volume of tranfactions, which you fent me about three years ago, that the fcience of aftronomy was cultivated even at Philadelphia. That volume of yours, to-

F f gether

gether with my own aftronomical papers, having been
unhappily deftroyed by fire about two years ago, I have
refolved to give your illuftrious fociety fome fhort account
of certain new celeftial difcoveries which I had made.

My refidence is now at Manheim, in a new obfervatory,
fitted for every aftronomical purpofe; and well furnifhed
with the moft precious and accurate inftruments made at
London; amongft which the chief is a brafs mural quadrant of eight feet radius, the workmanfhip of that celebrated artift Mr. Bird, finifhed in the year 1775, fitted
with an achromatic telefcope, and fixed to a folid wall towards the meridian.   With this inftrument I make daily
obfervations of the heavens, when the weather will permit, and two years ago I diftinctly difcovered, among
many of the *fixed ftars* (from the *firft* to the *fixth* magnitude) other *concomitant* or *attendant little ftars;* fome of
which, from their mild, faint (or unfparkling) light, have
the appearance of planets, while others of them have the
appearance of telefcopic ftars, in refpect to their fmallnefs.

But what furprifed me moft was, that none of thefe
attendant little ftars, a few perhaps excepted, have ever
been noted in any catalogue which I have feen; although
I could clearly collect the fingular ufe which may be made
of them for afcertaining and determining the proper motion of the fixed ftars, as it is called.   When the difference
of right afcenfion and declination between two ftars is at
moft but a few feconds, any variation arifing from the
preceffion of the equinoxes, the variation of the obliquity
of the ecliptic, the deviation of the inftrument, the aberration of light or the nutation, or from any other caufe
depending on the mutable ftate of the air or latitude of
places, muft affect them both equally.   Therefore when
after any length of time a greater variation of right afcenfion or declination is found in one of fuch ftars than in the
other, it affords a certain argument of the proper motion
of one or the other, whether that change affects the fixed
ftar or its attendant.   I know

I know that the celebrated Englifh aftronomer Halley, was the firft who, about the year 1719, by a careful com-parifon of the obfervations of Flamftead with thofe of Ptolemy, refpecting a few fixed ftars, viz. Sirius, Arcturus and Aldebaran, difcovered that thefe ftars had a proper motion of their own.   But I likewife know, that in Flam-ftead's Britifh celeftial hiftory the word *concomitant or at-tendant of fixed ftars* is made ufe of, when that great man had not even thought of a proper motion of the fixed ftars.

The other aftronomers, pofterior to Halley, as far as they inveftigated the proper motion of the *fixed ftars*, fol-lowed the Italian method of comparing their own obfer-vations with thofe of the ancients.   This method requires the labour of prolix calculation, and remains liable to doubts and uncertainty, on account of the inaccuracy of ancient inftruments and obfervations.   My new method is not liable to fuch objections, becaufe from the obferved variation of the attendant ftar and the brighter fixed ftar, it immediately follows that there is a proper motion giv-en, either of the one or the other.

I have, therefore, in the fpace of two years, obferved almoft two hundred attendants of different fixed ftars, running almoft the fame parallel, immediately before or after the fixed ftar; and have communicated many of fuch obfervations to the celebrated Englifh aftronomer Nevil Mafkelyne, who has expreffed his high fatisfaction therewith.

Out of many obfervations, I fend your illuftrious foci-ety a few by way of fpecimen, being fuch whereof I find correfpondent obfervations in the Flamfteadian celeftial hiftory ; whence it appears at once how excellently ob-fervations of this kind ferve for difcovering the proper mo-tion of fuch ftars.

The firft and fecond column of the following table next to the left hand is eafily underftood from its title.   The third column fhews the difference of A. R. in mean time

between the *attendant* and *ſtar*. The attendant which precedes the fixed ſtar occupies the firſt place in the table:
The ſubſequent attendant is placed after the fixed ſtar.
The fourth column ſhews the difference of declination between the fixed ſtar and attendant. The letter A, ſignifies
that the attendant is more ſouth, B, that it is more north
than the ſtar. The ſubſequent columns contain Flamſtead's obſervations of the ſame fixed ſtars.

The TABLE.

By MAYER, at Manheim.				By FLAMSTEAD, at Greenwich.		
Time of Ob-ſervation.	Names of Star.	Diff. A. R. in time.	Differ. of Declina.	Diff. A. R. in time.	Differ. of Declina.	Time of Ob-ſervation.
1777 Februar. 28.	ρ Leonis attendant 7m.	2′. 15″.	38′.58″.6.A	2′. 18″.	38′. 50″. A	1690 March 25.
1777 Feb. 25, 28.	Attend. 6m. γ Leonis	5″.	21′.57″. 2.A	2″.	22′. 5″.	1691 6 April.
1777 April 4.	Attendant, τ Leonis	1′. 5″.	8′. 0″. 15. B	56.	8′. 30″. B	1690 25 March.
1777 March 11.	Propus attendant 5m.	5′. 36″.	7′. 30.″	5′. 38″.	7′. 0″.	1690 7 Feb.
1777 March 8.	Procyon attendant 8m.	1′. 40″. 5.	3′. 6″. 2. A	1′. 34″.	4′. 40″. A	1691 4 Octo.
1777 13 Nov.	Attendant 7m. ι Piſcium	51″.	2′. 57″. 1. B	47″.	2′. 30″. B	1700 Nov. 13.
1777 April 6.	Attendant, Π Cancri	2′. 49″.	1′. 40″. B	2′. 44″.	1′. 12″. B	1690 Feb. 18.
1777 April 8.	Attendant 7m. β Leonis	30″.	18′.27″.1.A	33″½		1692 April 24.
1776 May 18.	Arcturus Attendant,	0. 0. 6″.	0. 23. 37. 3	Com. 0. 5″. Arcturus.	0. 26. 30.	1690 Febru. 14.
1777 March 11.	Procyon Attendant 7m.	39″.	3′. 8″. 1. A	35″.		1692 22 Janu.
1776 May 18.	Arcturus Attendant,	0. 0. 6.	0. 23. 37. 4	MASKELINE. A. R. 0. 0. 4.	0. 23′.58″.8.	1765 20 May.
1777 April 1.	O Cancri Π Cancri 6m.	14′. 56″.	32. 29. 6. B	15. 1.	32. 25. B	1691 10 March.

It appears from every obſervation, that of all the ſtars,
Arcturus, by his proper motion, is carried with the great-
eſt celerity weſtward; ſince the ſame attendant, which in
Flamſtead's

Flamſtead's time, 1690, February 14, preceded Arɛturus 5″ in time, now comes to the meridian 6″ after him. Likewiſe from the very ſmall difference of declination between Arɛturus and his attendant, it appears that Arɛturus by his proper motion moves almoſt 2″ ſoutherly every year in a circle.

N° XXVIII.

Obſervations on the Cauſe and Cure of the Tetanus, by BENJAMIN RUSH, M. D. *Profeſſor of Chemiſtry in the Univerſity of Pennſylvania.*

Read Mar. 17, 1786. **D**URING my attendance upon the military hoſpitals of the United States, in the courſe of the late war, I met with ſeveral caſes of the Tetanus. I had frequently met with this diſorder in private practice, and am ſorry to ſay that I never ſucceeded with the ordinary remedy of opium in any one caſe that came under my care. I found it equally ineffectual in the army. Baffled in my expectations from a remedy that had been ſo much celebrated, I began to inveſtigate more particularly the nature of the diſorder. I found it to be a diſorder of warm climates, and warm ſeaſons. This led me to aſcribe it to relaxation. I reſolved to attempt the cure of it by a ſet of medicines in ſome meaſure the oppoſites of moſt of the medicines that had been employed in that diſorder. Soon after I adopted this reſolution, I was called to viſit Col. John Stone, who was wounded through the foot at the battle of Germantown on the 4th of October 1777. He was in the third day of a Tetanus. His ſpaſms were violent and his pains ſo exquiſite that his cries were heard near a hundred yards from his quarters. His head was thrown a little backwards, and his jaw had become ſtiff and contracted.

He

He was under the care of a fkilful regimental furgeon who was pouring down opium in large quantities without effect.

Duty and friendfhip both led me to do my utmoft to fave the life of this valuable officer. I immediately difmiffed the opium, and gave him large quantities of wine and bark, to the amount of two or three ounces of the latter, and from a bottle to three pints of the former in the day. In a few hours I was delighted with their effects. His fpafms and pains were lefs frequent and violent, and he flept for feveral hours, which he had not done for feveral days and nights before.

With the fame indication in view, I applied a blifter between his fhoulders, and rubbed in two or three ounces of mercurial ointment upon the outfide of his throat. He continued to mend gradually under the operation of thefe medicines, fo that in ten days he was out of danger, although the fpafm continued in his wounded foot for feveral weeks afterwards. In the fummer of the year 1782 I was called to vifit a fervant girl of Mr. Alexander Todd, merchant of this city, who had brought on a Tetanus by fleeping in the evening on a damp brick pavement, after a day in which the mercury in Farenheit's thermometer had flood at near 90°. The cafe was nearly as violent and alarming as the one I have defcribed. I treated her in the fame manner, and with the fame fuccefs. To the above named medicines, I added only the oil of amber which fhe took in large dofes, after I fufpected the tonic powers of the bark and wine began to loofe their effects. The good effects of the oil were very obvious. She recovered gradually and has continued ever fince in good health. In the fummer of the fame year I was called to Alexander Leflie, a joiner, who had run a nail in his foot. I found him the day afterwards in extreme pain, with fmall convulfions and now and then a twinge in his jaw. The wound in his foot was without
fwelling

fwelling or inflammation. I dilated the wound and filled it
with lint moiftened with fpirit of turpentine. This in a
little while produced a good deal of pain and a great inflammation in his foot. While I was preparing to treat him in
the manner I had treated the two former cafes, the pains
and fpafms in his body fuddenly left him, and in twenty-
four hours after I faw him, he complained of nothing but
of the pain and fwelling in his foot, which continued for
feveral weeks and did not leave him till it ended in a fuppuration. From the hiftory of thefe three cafes, I beg
leave to make the following remarks..

1. That the predifpofition to the Tetanus depends upon
relaxation. This relaxation is generally produced by heat;
but exceffive labour, watchings, marches, or fatigue from
any caufe, all produce it likewife, and hence we find it more
frequent from wounds received in battles, than from fimilar wounds received in any other way. Thefe wounds
more certainly produce the Tetanus, if they have been
preceded for fome time with warm weather. Dr. Shoepft,
the phyfician general of the Anfpach troops that ferved at
the fiege of York in the year 1781, informed me of a fingular fact upon this fubject. Upon converfing with the
French furgeons after the capitulation, he was informed
by them that the troops who arrived juft before the fiege
from the Weft-Indies with Count de Graffe, were the only
troops belonging to their nation that fuffered from the
Tetanus. There was not a fingle inftance of that diforder among the troops who had fpent a winter in Rhode-
Ifland.

2. As the Tetanus feems to be occafioned by relaxation, the medicines indicated to cure it are fuch only as are
calculated to remove this relaxation and to reftore a tone to
the fyftem. The bark and wine appear to act in this way.
The operation of the blifters is of a more complicated nature. That they are fedative and antifpafmodic in fevers
is univerfally acknowledged, but in the peculiar ftate of
irritability

irritability which occurs in the Tetanus, perhaps their effects are more fimply ftimulating. But I will go one ftep further. In order to cure this diforder, it is neceffary not only to produce an ordinary tone in the fyftem, but fomething like the inflammatory diathefis. The abfence of this diathefis is taken notice of by all authors, particularly by Dr. Cullen*.

Mercury appears to act only by promoting this diathefis. Hence it. never does any fervice unlefs it be given time enough to produce a falivation. The irritation and inflammation produced in the mouth and throat, feldom fail to produce the inflammatory diathefis, as blood drawn in a falivation has repeatedly fhewn.

I apprehend that the oil of amber acts as a ftimulant chiefly in this diforder. I have heard of a Tetanus being cured in the ifland of Grenada by large dofes of muftard. Dr. Wright, lately of the ifland of Jamaica, relates in the 6th volume of the London Medical Effays, feveral remarkable cafes of the Tetanus being cured by the cold bath. Both thefe remedies certainly act as ftimulants and tonics. By reafoning *à priori*, I conceive that electricity would be found to be an equally powerful remedy in this diforder.

As a general inflammatory diathefis difpofes to topical inflammation, fo topical inflammation difpofes to general inflammatory diathefis. Wounds upon this account are lefs apt to inflame in fummer than in winter. In the Tetanus I have uniformly obferved an abfence of all inflammation in the wounds or injuries that produced it. A fplinter under the nail produces no convulfions, if pain, inflammation and fuppuration follow the accident. It is by exciting pain and inflammation I apprehend that the fpirit of turpentine acts in all wounds and punctures of nervous and tendinous parts. I have never known a fingle inftance of a Tetanus from a wound, where this remedy had been applied in time. It was to excite an inflammation in the foot of Mr. Leflie, that I dilated the wound

and

* Firft Lines, Vol. III.

and filled it with the fpirit of turpentine.   I was not furprifed at its good effects in this cafe, for I was prepared
to expect them.

I find a remarkable cafe related in Dr. W. Monroe's
Thefis, publifhed in Edinburgh in the year 1783, of a
black girl who had a Tetanus from running a nail in her
foot, being perfectly cured by deep and extenfive incifions
being made in the wounded part by Dr. John Bell, of the
ifland of Grenada.

It is by producing inflammation in a particular part,
and tone in the whole fyftem, I apprehend that the amputation of a wounded limb fometimes cures a Tetanus;
and it is becaufe the degrees of both are too inconfiderable
to oppofe the violence of the fpafms in the advanced ftages
of the Tetanus, that amputation often fails of fuccefs.

I have been informed by a phyfician who refided fome
time at St. Croix, that the negroes on that ifland always
apply a plaifter made of equal parts of falt and tallow to
their frefh wounds, in order to prevent a locked jaw.
The falt always produces fome degree of inflammation.

If the facts that have been ftated are true, and the in-
ferences that have been drawn from them are juft, how
fhall we account for the action of opium in curing this
diforder?   I do not deny its good effects in many cafes, but
I believe it has failed in four cafes out of five in the hands
of moft practitioners.   It is remarkable that it fucceeds
only where it is given in very large dofes.   In thefe cafes
I would fuppofe that its fedative powers are loft in its ftimulating.   It is upon a footing, therefore, in one refpect,
with the ftimulating medicines that have been mentioned;
but from its being combined with a fedative quality, it is
probably inferior to moft of them.   I am the more inclined to adopt this opinion, from an account I once received
from Dr. Robert, of the ifland of Dominique, who informed me that after having cured a negro man of a Tetanus with large dofes of opium, he was afterwards feized

G g   with

with a diforder in his ftomach, of which he died in a few
days. Upon opening him, he found his ftomach inflamed and mortified. I do not forbid the ufe of opium altogether in this diforder. I think fmall dofes of it may be
given to eafe pain, as in other fpafmodic diforders ; but as
its qualities are complicated, and its efficacy doubtful, I
think it ought to yield to more fimple and more powerful
remedies.

To the cafes that have been mentioned, I could add
many others, in which I have reafon to believe that the
excitement of a topical inflammation by artificial means,
has effectually prevented a Tetanus.

To this account of the Tetanus, I beg leave to fubjoin
a few words upon a diforder commonly called the jaw-fall
in infants, or the Trifmus Nafcentium of Dr. Cullen,
which is nothing but a fpecies of Tetanus.

I have met with three cafes of it in this city, all of
which proved fatal. The ftage of the diforder in which
I was confulted, and the age and weaknefs of the infants,
forbad me to attempt any thing for their relief. I have
introduced the fubject of this diforder in children, only
for the fake of mentioning a fact communicated to me by
the late Dr. Cadwalader Evans of this city. This gentleman practifed phyfic for feveral years in Jamaica, where
he had frequent opportunities of feeing the Tetanus in
the black children. He found it in every cafe to be incurable. He fuppofed it to be occafioned by the retention
of the meconium in the bowels. This led him invaria-
bly to purge every child that was born upon the eftates
committed to his care. After he adopted this practice,
he never met with a fingle inftance of the Tetanus among
children.

Perhaps it may tend to enlarge our ideas of the Tetanus, and to promote a fpirit of enquiry and experiment, to
add, that this diforder is not confined to the human fpecies.
I have known feveral inftances of it in horfes from nails
running

running in their feet, and other accidents. It is attended with a rigidity of the muscles of the neck, a stiffness in the limbs, and such a contraction of the jaw as to prevent their eating. It is generally fatal. In two cases I had the pleasure of seeing the disease perfectly cured by applying a potential caustic to the neck under the mane, by large doses of oil of amber, and by plunging one of them into the river, and throwing buckets of cold water upon the other.

How far the reasonings contained in this paper may apply to the hydrophobia, I cannot determine, having had no opportunity of seeing the disease since I adopted these principles; but from the spasmodic nature of the disorder, from the season of the year in which it generally occurs, and above all, from the case related by Dr. Fothergill, of a young woman having escaped the effects of the bite of a mad cat by means of the wound being kept open, (which from its severity was probably connected with some degrees of inflammation) is it not probable that the same remedies, which have been used with success in the Tetanus, may be used with advantage in the hydrophobia?—In a disease so deplorable, and hitherto so unsuccessfully treated, even a conjecture may lead to useful experiments and enquiries.

N° XXIX.

To His Excellency BENJAMIN FRANKLIN, *Esq. L. L. D. President of the State of Pennsylvania, and of the American Philosophical Society, &c.*

SIR,   Philadelphia, January 12, 1786.

Read March 17, 1786.   THE subject of smoky chimneys, of which I had the honor of conversing with you at your own house last evening, is of so much importance to

G g 2   every

every individual, as well as to every private family, that
too much light cannot be thrown upon it.

A fmoky houfe and a fcolding wife,
Are (faid to be) two of the greateft ills in life.

And however difficult it may be to remedy one of thofe
ills, yet any advances we may be able to make towards
removing the inconveniencies arifing from the other, cannot fail to be favourably received by the public. As they
are fhortly to be favoured with your fentiments on that
fubject, poffibly the following obfervations, which were
in fact occafioned by neceffity, and are the refult of my
own experience, may not be altogether undeferving of
notice.

When I left London and went to live in Devonfhire in
the latter end of the year 1777, it happened to be my lot
to dwell in an old manfion which had been recently mo-
dernifed, and had undergone a thorough repair. But as
in moft of the old houfes in England, the chimneys, which
were perhaps originally built for the purpofe of burning
wood, though they had been contracted in front, fince coal
fires came into general ufe, to the modern fize, yet they
were ftill, above, out of fight, extravagantly large. This
method of building chimneys may perhaps have anfwered
well enough while it was the cuftom to fit with the doors
and windows open; but when the cuftoms and manners
of the people began to be more polifhed and refined, when
building and architecture were improved, and they began
to conceive the idea of making their chambers clofe, warm,
and comfortable, thefe chimneys were found to fmoke
abominably, for want of a fufficient fupply of air. This
was exactly the cafe with the houfe in which I firft lived,
near Exeter, and I was under the neceffity of trying every
expedient I could think of to make it habitable.

The firft thing I tried, was that method of contracting
the chimneys by means of earthen pots, much in ufe in
England,

England, which are made on purpofe, and which are put upon the tops of them; but this method by no means anfwered.   I then thought of contracting them below, but as the method of contracting them in front to the fize of a fmall coal-fire grate has an unfightly appearance, as it makes a difagreeable blowing like a furnace, and as it is the occafion of confuming a great deal of unneceffary fuel, the heat of which is immediately hurried up the chimney, I rejected this method, and determined to contract them above, a little out of fight.   For this purpofe I threw an arch acrofs, and alfo drew them in at the fides. This had fome effect, but as this contraction was made rather fuddenly, and the fmoke, by ftriking againft the corners that were thereby occafioned, was apt to recoil, by which means fome part of it was thrown out into the room ; I determined to make the contraction more gradually, and therefore run it up at the back, where the depth of the chimney would admit of it, and alfo fhelving or floping in a conical kind of direction at the fides, as high as a man, ftanding upright, could conveniently reach, and by this means brought the cavity within the fpace of about twelve by fourteen or fixteen inches, which I found fufficiently large to admit a boy to go up and down to fweep the chimnies.   This method I found to fucceed perfectly well, as to curing the chimneys of fmoking, and it had this good effect of making the rooms confiderably warmer ; and as this experiment fucceeded fo well, fince the only ufe of a chimney is to convey away the fmoke, I determined to carry it ftill farther, in order to afcertain with precifion, how much fpace is abfolutely neceffary for that purpofe, becaufe all the reft that is fhut up, muft be fo much gained in warmth.   Accordingly I laid a piece of flate acrofs the remaining aperture, removable at pleafure, fo as to contract the fpace above two thirds, leaving about three inches by twelve remaining open ; but this fpace, except when the fire burnt remarkably clear, was

fcarcely

scarcely sufficient to carry away the smoke. I therefore
enlarged it to half the space, that is, to about six by seven
or eight inches, which I found fully sufficient to carry
away the smoke from the largest fires.

When I removed into the Bedford Circus in Exeter,
though the house was modern, and almost perfectly new,
yet the chimneys were large ; in consequence of which almost every room of it smoked.   My predecessor, who was
the first inhabitant, had been at great expence in patent
stoves, &c. but without effect ; but by adopting the method I have just now described, I not only cured every
chimney of smoking, but my house was remarked for being one of the warmest and most comfortable to live in of
any in that large and opulent city.

The house I now live in, in Philadelphia, I am told,
has always had the character of being both cold and
smoky ; and I was convinced, as soon as I saw the rooms
and examined the chimneys, that it deserved that character ; for though the rooms were close, the chimneys were
large : And we shall ever find, that if our chimneys are
large, our rooms will be cold even though they should be
tolerably close and tight ; because the constant rushing in
of the cold air at the cracks and crevices, and also at
every opening of the door will be sufficient to chill the air,
as fast as it is heated, or to force the heated air up the
chimney ; but by contracting the chimneys I have cured
it of both these defects.   There was one remarkable cir-
cumstance attending the contraction of the chimney in
the front parlour, which deserves to be attended to ;
which was, that before I applied the cast iron plate, which
I made use of instead of slate, to diminish the space requi-
site for a chimney sweeper's boy to go up and down, the
suction or draught of air was so great, that it was with
difficulty I could shut the door of the room, insomuch that
I at first thought it was owing to a tightness of the hinges,
which I imagined must be remedied, but upon applying
                                                    the

the iron plate, by which the fpace was diminifhed one half, the door fhut to with the greateft eafe. This extraordinary preffure of the air upon the door of the room, or fuction of the chimney, I take to be owing in fome meafure to the unufual height of the houfe.

Upon the whole, therefore, this fact feems clearly afcertained, viz. That the flue or fize of the chimney, ought always to be proportioned to the tightnefs and clofenefs of the room, fome air is undoubtedly neceffary to be admitted into the room in order to carry up the fmoke, otherwife as you juftly obferved we might as well expect fmoke to arife out of an exhaufted receiver; but if the flue is very large, and the room is tight, either the fmoke will not afcend, in confequence of which will be, that the air of your room will be fo frequently and fo conftantly changed that as faft as it is heated, it will be hurried away, with the fmoke, up the chimney, and of courfe your room will be conftantly cold.

One great advantage attending this method of curing fmoky chimneys is, that, in the firft place, it makes no aukward or unfightly appearance, nothing being to be feen but what is ufual to chimneys in common; and in the fecond place that it is attended with very little expence, a few bricks and mortar with a plate or covering to the aperture, and a little labour, being all that is requifite. But in this new country where crops of houfes may be expected to rife almoft as quick as fields of corn, when the principles upon which chimneys ought to be thoroughly underftood, it is to be hoped, that not only this expence, fmall as it is, but that all the other inconveniencies we have been fpeaking of, will be avoided, by conftructing the flues of the chimneys fufficiently fmall.

From your humble fervant,

THOMAS RUSTON..

N° XXX.

Obſervations on the annual Paſſage of Herrings, by Mr. JOHN GILPIN.

A S this very uſeful part of the finny race has never been found in the freſh rivers, or waters of Europe, it remains a query amongſt the naturaliſts, where they go to ſpawn and perpetuate their ſpecies. I apprehend this query may be anſwered to the ſatisfaction of the curious by an account of their annual progreſs, from which it will appear they are a fiſh of paſſage, and obſerve one regular annual rout in the ſea, ſhifting their climate with the ſun, and that it is the ſame ſcoole which is found at different times about Britain and in America. This opinion is founded on obſervations made on ſeeing them caught at Whitehaven and in this country, from which I have not obſerved that there is any viſible difference in the fiſh in the different places, except that thoſe at Whitehaven are fatter and rounder than thoſe in America; but this difference is not ſo great as that between the ſpring and fall mackarel, and which I conceive might be accounted for from the time of the year, and manner in which they appear on each coaſt. For they are found on the other ſide the Atlantic, or rather in the North ſea, in the favourable month of June about the iſlands of Shetland, from whence they proceed down to the Orkneys, and then dividing, they ſurround the iſlands of Great-Britain and Ireland, and unite again off the Land's End in the Britiſh channel in September, from whence this grand united ſcoole ſteers ſouth-weſt, and is not found any more on that ſide or in the Atlantic, until the ſame time the enſuing year, but appear next on the American coaſts.

coafts. They arrive in Georgia and Carolina the latter
end of January, and in Virginia in February; and coafting from thence eaftward to New-England, they divide
and go into all the bays, rivers, creeks and even fmall
ftreams of water in amazing quantities, and continue
fpawning in the frefh water until the latter end of April,
when the old fifh return into the fea, where they change
their latitudes by a northward direction and arrive at Newfoundland in May; after which we neither hear or fee any
thing more of them in America, until their return amongft
us the enfuing fpring, and bring with them a providential
bleffing to the poor. Their coming fooner or later up our
rivers depends on the warmth or coolnefs of the feafon: And
it is further obferved that if a few warm days invite them
up, and cool weather fucceeds, it totally checks their paffage
until more warm weather returns. From all which circumftances it appears probable there is a certain degree of
warmth particularly agreeable to them, which they endeavour to enjoy by changing their latitude according to
the diftances of the fun. Thus they are found in the Britifh channel in September, but leave it when the fun is at
too great a diftance from them in the fouthern hemifphere,
and pufh for a more agreeable climate; and when the
weather in America becomes too warm in May, (after
having depofited their eggs in fhallow water and fecured
their young fry from the fifh of prey,) fteer the courfe
which leads to the cooler northern feas, and by that prudent change of place perpetually enjoy the temperature of
climate beft adapted to their nature; which from the table
hereto annexed, fhewing the places and times of their vi-
fitation, and the calculation of the diftance of the fun at
thofe times from them, is that degree of warmth which
is produced by the mean diftance between 37 to 43 degrees; except whilft they are fpawning; during which
they bear a greater degree of heat from the neceffity of
remaining in it a fhort time to fpawn; and alfo on the
other extreme, when detained at too great a diftance by
the ifland of Great-Britain and its dependencies.

H h

Here

Here another query occurs, what becomes of the young
fry, the produce of the spawn they left in the fresh waters
of America? We know they do not follow the old ones
the first season, because they are found in great scooles in
all the American bays during the summer, and disappear
in the fall, from whence it may rationally be supposed that
from their natural propensity to keep at a certain distance
from the sun, the season leads them to a different course
from the old ones, by which they meet their parentage
about the latitude 23° N. and 70° W. longitude, and there
tack about and follow the older ones; which, being larger
and stronger than the younger, come first into our harbours,
but are fewer in number than the lesser, probably from
having suffered great loss and pillage in their long rout
from the fish of prey, and their greater enemies the fish-
ermen in the different parts of the world.

*A Table shewing nearly about the place of the grand scoole
of herrings, and their mean distance from the sun.*

* Place and Time.		Latitude.	Longitude.	Sun's De-clination.	The Mean Distance.
I.	January,	23	70	20 S.	43
II.	February,	32	79	12	44
III.	March,	36	75	0	36
IV.	April,	39	72	10 N.	29
V.	May,	49	50	19	30
VI.	June,	65	15	23	42
VII.	July,	58	0	21	37
VIII.	August,	52	0	14	38
IX.	September,	48	6	0	48
X.	October,	35	22	9	44
XI.	November,	22	40	18	40
XII.	December,	18	52	23	41

* See Map B, in Plate V.

Some Obfervations and Reafons given for the courfe of the Herrings, and the variation in their Mean Diftance from the Sun in different months of the year.

[See Map B, Plate V.]

JANUARY. In this month the herrings are fuppofed to be returning from too warm a climate and the approaching fun, from which they retreat faft.

FEBRUARY. The time of fpawning now drawing nigh, the herrings, in this month pafs through the gulph ftream, and fall on the coaft of America, in order to depofit their fpawn in frefh fhoal water.

MARCH. Now being the beginning of the time of fpawning, the largeft and ftrongeft fifh, which perhaps are the oldeft, rufh up into the bays, inlets and frefh water ftreams.

APRIL. In this month the leffer, weaker, and perhaps younger fifh, rufh up even to the heads of fmall ftreams, as far as it is poffible for them to get, and lay their fpawn. Thefe are twice as numerous as the other.

MAY. Having been detained by the fpawning feafon, they are overtaken by the fun, and nearer to it now than at any other time; they therefore haften out of the rivers in this month, and make great way towards the North fea.

JUNE. Now having by a rapid progrefs pufhed into a cold climate, on a chilly, icy coaft, and the fun beginning to draw towards the fouth, they whirl round eaftward.

JULY. The coldnefs of this fea, and the fun's declination towards the fouth, now inclines them that way, in which they fall on the Orkneys, and the fcoole divides.

AUGUST. The grand fcoole being divided, now furround the whole ifland of Great-Britain and Ireland, and are caught on every fide.

SEPTEMBER. Having been detained the laft month by their obftruction amongft the iflands, and being harraffed by the fifhermen, their mean diftance is now the greateft; they collect into one body and haften to the fouthward.

OCTOBER. Being now under great way, they leffen their mean diftance, and by the courfe which they fteer, which perhaps is inclined more weftward by the current of the trade wind, they pafs the Atlantic.

NOVEMBER. Being now more in the trade, and having approached a warmer climate, their motion is fuppofed to incline more weftward.

DECEMBER. The fun now beginning to return, they are fuppofed to incline more northward, to the place where we began; where they are fuppofed to meet their young fry.

N° XXXI.

Obfervations on a Solar and a Lunar Eclipfe, communicated to the Society by M. M. DE GRAUCHAIN, *Major General of the French Squadron.*

(*Tranflated from the French.*)

GENTLEMEN, Newport, 5th December, 1780.

THE ftudy of aftronomy having often occupied my leifure during the peace, I could not refufe myfelf even in the midft of the preparations for war, an oppor-

tunity

tunity which prefented of making two important obfervations, which I have the honour of fending you.

Eclipfes form the bafis of chronology ; this may one
day ferve to fix the epocha of the independence of America, one of the moft interefting in the hiftory of mankind. This is a motive to dedicate thefe obfervations to
you ; and I pay this refpect with the greateft pleafure to
an illuftrious fociety, whofe members know how at the
fame time to enlighten their country by their knowledge
in mathematics and philofophy, and to ferve them fuccefsfully in their councils and armies.

I am, &c.

De GRAUCHAIN, Major General
of the French Squadron.

MESSIEURS,

L'ETUDE de l'aftronomie ayant fouvent occupé mon loifir pendant la paix, je n'ai pu
me refufer, même au milieu de l'appareil de la guerre, a l'occafion qui fut prefentée de
faire deux obfervations importantes et j'ai l'honneur de vous les adreffer. Les eclipfes forment
la bafe de la chronologie, et celles cy pourront un jour fervir a fixir l'epoque de l'independance
de l'Amerique l'une des plus interreffantes de l'hiftoire du genre humain. C'eft un motif
pour vous en dedier les obfervations, meffieurs, et je rends cet hommage avec le plus grand
plaifir a une focieté illuftre dont les membres fcavant en même temps eclaires leur patrie par
leur connoiffances dans les mathematiques et dans la phifique, et la fervir utilement dans les
confeils et dans les armées.

Je fuis avec refpect, Meffieurs,

Votre tres humble et tres obeiffant ferviteur,

DE GRAUCHAIN, Major general de l'efcadre Francoife.

A Newport le 5 Novembre, 1780.

An

An Obfervation of an Eclipfe of the Sun on the 27th of October, 1780, at Newport in the State of Rhode-Ifland.

	Time by the Clock.			True Time.		
	h.	′	″	h.	′	″
The time that the eclipfe was perceived to begin,	9	24	32	11	0	12*
The preceding limb of the fun at the vertical,	11	21	39	0	57	27
The upper edge of the fun at the horizontal,		11	54		57	42
The upper horn of the moon at the horizontal,		22	3		57	51
The edge of the moon at the vertical, - -		22	45		58	33
The upper horn at the vertical, - - -		23	7		58	55
The lower horn at the vertical, - - -		23	35		59	23†
The lower horn at the horizontal, - - -		29	31	1	5	20
The lower limb of the fun at the horizontal, -		31	2		6	51†
The preceding limb of the fun at the vertical,	11	37	12	1	13	1
The upper limb ditto at the horizontal, - -		37	59		13	48
The upper horn ☽ at the horizontal, - -		38	52		14	21
The limb ditto at the vertical, - - -	not obferved.					
The upper horn ditto at the vertical, - -		38	57		14	16
The lower horn ditto at the vertical, - -		39	19		15	8
The lower horn ditto at the horizontal, - -		43	38		19	8
The lower limb of the fun at the horizontal, -		45	27		21	17
The preceding limb ☉ at the vertical, - -	11	47	8	1	22	58
The upper edge of ditto at the horizontal, -		48	17		24	7
The limb of the ☽ at the vertical, - - -		49	0		24	50
The upper horn at the vertical, - - -		49	5		24	55
The upper horn at the horizontal, - -		47	7		24	57
The lower limb of ☉ at the horizontal, - -		55	2		30	52
The end of the Eclipfe, - - - -	12	4	50	1	40	41

	At Noon.		
The rate of the clock, October 21,	10	35	12,8
24,	10	29	42,0
25,	10	27	52,3
27,	10	24	15,8

* When the fun was perceived to be indented, it was about 1′ 20″ after the eclipfe began; therefore the true time of beginning was at 10h. 58′ 52″.
† Uncertain.
‡ The fuperior limb is called the inferior, &c. as the glafs of the quadrant inverted the objects.

The latitude of the place of obfervation on Goat-Ifland, 41° 30′ 20″ N.

An.

An Obfervation of the Eclipfe of the Moon on the 11th of Nov. 1780, at Newport in the State of Rhode-Ifland.

	Time by the Clock.			True Time.		
	h.	′	″	h.	′	″
The beginning of the Eclipfe, - - - -	7	40	5	10	24	39
Immerfion of Grimaldi begins, - - -	7	48	50	10	33	25
Ditto, - - - ends, - - -	7	51	25	10	36	10
Immerfion of Tycho begins, - - -	8	0	36	10	45	12
Ditto, - - ends, - - -	not obferved.					
The fhadow to Gallileo, - - -	8	3	42	10	48	18
Immerfion of Copernicus begins, - -	8	27	54	11	12	31
Ditto, - - - ends, - - -	8	32	35	11	17	12
The fhadow in the middle of Dionyfius, - -	8	46	55	11	31	33
The fhadow of the Pointed Promontary, - -	8	55	42	11	40	21
Copernicus begins to appear, - - -	9	17	54	12	2	34
Grimaldi - ditto, - - -	9	22	2	12	6	42
Copernicus wholly appears, - - -	9	23	35	12	8	15
Grimaldi - ditto, - - -	9	26	45	12	11	26
The Pointed Promontary appears, - - -	9	51	12	12	35	55
Tycho wholly appears, - - -	10	10	6	12	54	51
The end of the Eclipfe, - - -	10	32	10	13	16	57
The rate of the Clock, November 11,	At Noon.					
9	16	15,7				
12,	9	14	30,7			

Remarks upon the Obfervation of the Eclipfe of the Sun.

THE clock by which the time was obferved, is a pendulum one with a verge of compenfation, made by Mr. Earthond, a celebrated clock maker at Paris. It was regulated many days before and after the obfervation by correfponding altitudes taken with a quadrant of Ramfden, having a radius of one Englifh foot; it is a very good one and well graduated.

The fame quadrant ferved to obferve the time when the horns and limbs of the moon and fun arrived at the hori-

Eclairciffements fur l'obfervation de l'eclipfe de Soleil.

LA pendule dont on s'eft fervi pour obtenir l'heure eft une pendule a verge de compenfation faite par M. Earthond celebre horloger de Paris, elle a été reglée plufieurs jours avant et apres l'obfervation par des hauteurs correfpondantes prifes avec un quart de cercle de Ramfden d'un pied anglois de rayon tres bon, et tres bien divifé.

Le même quart de cercle a fervi pour les obfervations des paffages des cornes et des bords du foleil et de la lune au fil horifontal, et au fil vertical de la lunette qui y eft adaptée.

L'obfervateur qui en embarquant des inftruments d'aftronomie n'avoit eu pour objet que de regler des montres marines, n'etoit pas aufli bien pourvu de lunettes que de pendules et de quart de

horizontal and vertical threads of the glaſs which is fitted to the quadrant.

The obſerver who provided and ſhipped the inſtruments, had no other objeƈt in view but to reƈtify the clock belonging to the ſhip, which was the cauſe that he was not ſo well provided with teleſcopes as with clocks and quadrants, he was therefore obliged to make uſe of a ſimple achromatic ſea-glaſs of four feet focus, to obſerve the beginning and end of the eclipſe.

Yet he believes he can anſwer for the end of the eclipſe within about four or five ſeconds. The inſtant of time which it began is much more uncertain. The ſun was already indented when it was firſt perceived, but in order that he might eſtimate groſsly the true time of its beginning, he has eſtimated pretty nearly the diſtance of the horns, the moment when the ſun's limb was firſt perceived to be indented. By comparing the time elapſed after the end of the eclipſe to the inſtant when the diſtance of the horns of the moon were ſenſibly the ſame, hence he judged that it ſhould have been about 1′ 20″ from the true time in which the eclipſe began until the obſerved time.

At

de cercle, et il a eté obligé de ſe ſervir pour les obſervations du commencement et de la fin de l'eclipſe d'une ſimple lunette achromatic de mer de quatre pieds de foyer.

Cependant on croit pouvoir repondre de la fin de l'eclipſe a quatre ou cinq ſecondes pres ; l'inſtant du commencement eſt beaucoup plus incertain ; le ſoleil etoit deja conſiderablement entamé, lors qu'on s'en eſt apperçu : pour conclure au moins groſſierement l'inſtant vrai du commencement de l'eclipſe, on a eſtime a peu pres quelle etoit la diſtance des cornes au moment ou on s'eſt apperçu que le diſque du ſoleil etoit entamé, et vers la fin de l'eclipſe on a examine combien il s'eſt ecoulé de tems depuis l'inſtant ou la diſtance des cornes a eté ſenſiblement la même juſqu'a la fin de l'eclipſe.   C'eſt de cette maniere que l'on a jugé qu'il devoit s'etre ecoulé environ 1′ 20″ depuis l'inſtant vrai du commencement de l'eclipſe, juſqu'à celui ou on s'eſt apperçu, quelle etoit commencée.

On a dabord crû inutile de chercher a obſerver la grandeur de l'eclipſe avec le quart de cercle, a cauſe de la lenteur du mouvement des deux aſtres dans le ſens vertical, cependant a la reflexion on a penſé que les paſſages des cornes et des bords du ſoleil et de la lune au fil vertical ſeulement fulliroient pour donner les differences de hauteur et d'azimuth des centres des deux aſtres, et par conſequent leur difference de latitude et de longitude.   On les a donc obſervès vers la fin de l'eclipſe, et en même tems on a obſervé les paſſages au fil horiſontal, mais ſans eſperer quils puſſent etre d'un grand ſecours pour calculer la diſtance des centres.

Dans la premiere obſervation le paſſage de la corne ſuperieure au fil vertical eſt un peu douteux.   On penſe donc qu'il eſt a propos d'employer de preference dans le calcul de cette obſervation les paſſages du bord de la lune, et de la corne inferieure au même fil vertical.   De cette maniere on connoitra immediatement les lignes N B et C O dont la premiere combinée avec les deux diametres L N et S T donnera L E ; difference d'azimuth des centres des deux aſtres. On obtiendra auſſi facilement la difference apparente de hauteur S E des mêmes centres en calculant

At firſt it was thought uſeleſs to endeavour to obſerve the magnitude of the eclipſe with the quadrant, becauſe of the ſlow movement of the two planets vertically, yet upon reflection he thought that the paſſage of the horns and limb of the ſun and moon to the vertical thread only, would be ſufficient to give the differencies of the altitude and azimuth of the centers of the ſun and moon, and of courſe their difference of latitude and longitude. He then obſerved them towards the end of the eclipſe, and at the ſame time obſerved the time of their arrival at the horizontal thread, but without any expectation of their being of great ſervice to calculate the diſtance of the centers from.

In the firſt obſervation the paſſage of the upper horn to the vertical thread, is a little doubtful ; at the time it was thought proper to give the preference to the paſſages of the limb and lower horn of the moon to the ſame vertical thread, in making the calculations from this obſervation; by this means we may find the lines

Plate III.
Figure 18.

N B and C O, the firſt of which combined with the two diameters L N and S T will give L E, the difference of azimuths and of the centers of the two planets; the apparent difference of the altitude from the ſame centers may be eaſily obtained, by calculating S F and C M, ſides of the right-angled triangles C S F and C L M, in which are known the other two ſides.

In

culant S F et C M cotes des triangles rectangles C S F et C L M dans les quels on connoit deja les deux autres cotés.

Dans la ſeconde obſervation on a obmis par diſtraction, l'inſtant du paſſage du bord de la lune au fil vertical, on ſe ſervira donc pour la calculer des paſſages des cornes au même fil les quels donneront immediatement C A et C O d'ou ſouſtrayant S T, on aura C D et C F connoiſſant ces deux lignes et le demi-diametre du ſoleil on calculera les angles C S D, C S F ſouſtrayant leur ſomme de 180°, on aura l'angle C S L partageant cet angle par la moitié on aura l'angle C S L du triangle C L S, on connoitra donc aiſement S L coté de ce triangle et du triangle S L E calculant enfin ce dernier triangle S L E dans le quel on connoit deux angles et un côté on obtiendra L E; difference d'azumuth et S E ; difference apparente de hauteur des centres des deux aſtres.

La derniere obſervation etant plus complette on pourra la calculer indifferement de l'une ou l'autre maniere. On pourra même faire uſage du paſſage au fil horiſontal pour conclure la difference de hauteur attendu que le movement des deux aſtres dans le ſens vertical commencoit a devenir moins lent lorſque cette obſervation a eté faite.

In the fecond obfervation was omitted, by inattention, the inftant of the arrival of the limb of the moon to the vertical thread, which however may be calculated by the arrival of the horns to the fame thread, by which CA and CO are obtained : By fubtracting S T from thefe, the remainder will be CD and CF, having thefe two lines and the femi-diameter of the fun, the angles C S D, C S F, may be had, and fubtracting their fum from 180° the remainder will be the angle C S C, the half of which is the angle C S L ; from the triangle C S L you may readily obtain S L, a fide of this triangle, and of the triangle S L E ; from thefe at length this laft triangle S L E may be calculated, in which are had two angles and one fide, from which may be obtained L E the difference of azimuth, and S E the apparent difference of altitude of the centers of the fun and moon.

My laft obfervation being more complete, might be calculated either from the one or the other method, and the paffage to the horizontal thread might even be ufed to determine the difference of the altitude of the centers, as the motion of thefe planets with refpect to the vertical, began to be quicker when this obfervation was made.

If we are defirous to afcertain the time of the paffage of the upper horn of the moon to the vertical thread in the firft obfervation, or to know in the fecond obfervation the time of the paffage of the limb of the moon by the fame thread, they may eafily be calculated by the help of the quantities already found. Perhaps it might be ufeful to make this calculation, to determine the variation which ought to have place in the pofition of the two points obferved,

I i relatively

Si l'on vouloit dans la premiere obfervation veriffier l'inftant du paffage de la corne fuperieure au fil vertical, ou connoitre dans la feconde obfervation l'inftant du paffage du bord de la lune au même fil on pourroit aifément les calculer avec le focours des quantites deja connues. Il fera peutetre même utile de faire ce calcul pour fe mettre en etat de determiner la variation qui a du avoir lieu dans la pofition des deux points obfervér relativement l'un a l'autre, pendant l'efpace de tems ecoulé entre leurs paffages au même fil.

Obfervation

relatively to each other during the time elapfed between their paffage to the fame thread.

Obfervation de l'èclipfe de Lune.

ON a fait ufage dans cette obfervation de la même quart de cercle, et de la même lunette qui avoient fervi pour l'obfervation de l'éclipfe de foleil. La marche de la pendule etoit cependant un peu differente parce qu'on y avoit touché.

N° XXXII.

An Account of the Tranfit of Venus over the Sun, June 3d, 1769, as obferved at Newbury, in Maffachufetts; by the Rev. Samuel Williams, A. M.

THE tranfit of Venus over the fun, being one of the moft uncommon and ufeful phenomena in aftronomy, I determined to make as careful an obfervation of it as I could. Early in May I received an invitation from *Triftram Dalton*, Efq. a gentleman of Newbury-Port, to obferve it with him. He had a feat at Newbury, in a high elevated fituation, very convenient for this purpofe, at which we agreed to make the obfervation. The weather for feveral days had been dull and rainy, but clearing up on Tuefday evening I went early on Wednefday to put every thing in readinefs. The regulation of our clock being an article of great importance, I was very careful to have it thoroughly examined, and well fitted up. To adjuft it to apparent time we took correfponding altitudes of the fun, both before and on the day of the tranfit. In thefe obfervations, it was eafy to arrive to a pretty great exactnefs; and as they were very numerous, the going of the clock was well afcertained by them, and found to be fteady and regular. The telefcope we had prepared was a reflector made by *Nairne*, magnifying about 55 times; a good inftrument, but not fitted with a
micrometer,

micrometer, or with vertical and horizontal hairs, as we could have wifhed.

The third of June proved favourable to our wifhes. The air was uncommonly clear, and the fky ferene. About twenty minutes before the tranfit, I began to keep my eye fteadily fixed on that part of the fun's limb, on which the planet by calculation was to enter; an affiftant counting the clock in the mean time, while another ftood by to write down the obfervations. Thus prepared, we waited with a kind of agreeable anxiety for the high fatisfaction of feeing Venus on the fun; a fatisfaction I had once before enjoyed in viewing the tranfit of 1761*, and which I knew muft end with that of 1769! The firft impreffion of Venus on the fun, I expected would not appear like a diftinct well defined black fpot coming on as it were in an inftant, but rather like an ill defined mixture of limbs. The event was agreeable to the conjecture, for at 2ʰ 30′ 14″, apparent time, I imagined I faw *a fmall difturbance* on the fun's limb; but the impreffion was then fo fmall, irregular and ill defined, that it was not till after feveral feconds that I was certain the tranfit was begun. But the impreffion increafing and growing more diftinct, I fixed on the time mentioned above as the time of the *external contact*. To obfervers with telefcopes and eyes equally good, and fixed on that part of the fun on which the planet entered, I conceive this firft impreffion might have been obferved to an agreement of 5 or 6 feconds. Though perhaps it might be the contact of the atmofphere, rather than of the body of Venus with the fun.

In about ten minutes after the *external*, I began to look for the *internal contact*. From the form in which Venus appeared, being furrounded with a glimmering light, not very diftinctly defined, I concluded it would be difficult if not impoffible to fix upon the precife moment when her

I i 2   limb

---

* At St. *John's*, in *Newfoundland*.

limb would be exactly coincident with that of the fun; and therefore determined to wait till there fhould appear a fmall thread of light between them. As the contact drew near, the thread of light began to form, and feemed to dart on each fide of the planet for feveral feconds without being fixed or fettled. At 2^h $48'$ $44''$, with a feeming uncertainty of not more than $7''$ it became clofed and fixed; Venus then appeared wholly within the fun, feparated from its limb by a fine ftream of light flowing gently round it. This I fixed upon as the *internal contact*, though this might alfo be the contact not of Venus but of her atmofphere with the fun. Not having a *micrometer* or *hairs* fixed in the reflector, inftead of making any further obfervations, we could only enjoy the pleafure of viewing this curious phenomenon, and fhowing it to a number of gentlemen that had affembled on the occafion.

To determine the latitude of the place, we took the meridian altitude of the fun on the day of the tranfit, by tranfmitting his rays from a ftyle 10 feet high, upon a large horizontal platform. From this obfervation our latitude came out $43°$ $2'$ north. Sufpecting the obfervation was not fufficiently accurate, I have fince carefully examined the matter, and from feveral obfervations which nearly agree, I find it to be but $42°$ $57'$. With regard to our longitude, the mean of fix or feven obfervations of the eclipfes of Jupiter's firft fatellite, gives it about 4^h $42'$ $30''$ weft from *Greenwich*.

In the above account of the *contacts*, the duration of the ingrefs, or paffage of Venus over the fun's limb, is $18'$ $30''$; near a minute longer than in moft of the *American* obfervations. By theory it fhould be $18'$ $56''$, but as this muft have been contracted at the place of obfervation, $15''$, by parallax, the apparent duration of the ingrefs, would be but $18'$ $41''$; that is, $11''$ longer than it was made by obfervation. I much doubt whether it was poffible to difcern the planet fo foon as $11''$ after the

firft

firſt contact, when not a ſecond of its diameter had entered upon the ſun. It is moſt probable that the *internal
contact* was paſt before the thread of light appeared to
me to be compleated. It ſeems as though ſomething of
the ſame kind, muſt alſo have been the caſe in moſt of the
European obſervations; as they make the ingreſs near a
minute longer, than it was ſeen by moſt of the *American*
obſervers, when by theory it muſt rather have been ſhorter. But the different appearances of Venus, different
ideas of the contacts, with the unavoidable difference of
eyes, teleſcopes, the ſtate of the atmoſphere and the like,
might eaſily occaſion ſuch differences in the obſervations.
Though in the ſame circumſtances, it can hardly be
thought but that the *European* and the *American* obſervations would have more nearly agreed.

*An Account of the Tranſit of Mercury over the Sun, No-
vember 9th, 1769, as obſerved at Salem, in Maſſachuſetts; by the Rev. SAMUEL WILLIAMS, A. M.*

THE tranſits of Mercury, though they are not of equal
uſe in aſtronomy with thoſe of Venus, are yet of great advantage to perfect the elements of his theory, and to determine the longitude of places on the earth. I had an
opportunity to obſerve one of theſe tranſits, November 9,
1769, in company with *Andrew Oliver*, Eſq. at *Salem.*
Mr. Oliver had a good reflector, magnifying about ſixty
times. But his clock not being in ſo good order as was
to be wiſhed, and not having any inſtrument to take altitudes, I was obliged to have recourſe to the following
method to determine the time. The day before the tranſit I drew a meridian line, with which I examined the
going of the town clock on the day of the tranſit, and on
the day after, and found it had kept time very well.
Comparing my watch with the clock, the time was pointed out to minutes pretty exactly. Taking the minutes
from

from the watch, I endeavoured to count the feconds, which by a perſon uſed to it may be done pretty near the truth. This method of determining the time, though ſuch as an aſtronomer would by no means chuſe, was the only one that I could make uſe of; and from the pains I took to be exact, I believe it might be depended upon to eight or ten feconds.

At the *firſt contact* I expected *Mercury* would have appeared as Venus had done, ſomething irregular, uneven, and not very diſtinctly defined. But at 2ʰ 54′ 40″ apparent time, I was agreeably diſappointed by ſeeing the planet come on as it were in an inſtant, in the form of a clear, regular, well defined black ſpot. The *internal contact* was equally inſtantaneous; at 2ʰ 56′ 0″ the thread of light cloſed to appearance in a moment, without a ſeeming uncertainty of a ſecond. The ſky being perfectly clear and ſerene, nothing could be better defined than the limbs of Mercury and the ſun. There was no appearance of any thing like an atmoſphere round the planet, but all the time the ſun was viſible, Mercury appeared like a ſteady diſtinct black ſpot, much leſs than ſome that were then upon the ſun. Not having a micrometer, it was not in our power to make any further obſervations, either on the diameter of the ſun or Mercury, or of the leaſt diſtance of their limbs.

An Obſervation of an Eclipſe of the Sun, November 6th, 1771, at Bradford, in Maſſachuſetts; by the Rev. SAMUEL WILLIAMS, A. M.

FROM the beginning of the year 1769 till the end of 1771, there were but two eclipſes that could be obſerved at *Bradford.* One of theſe was a total eclipſe of the moon, June 19th, 1769; of this I had no obſervation, being prevented by an indiſpoſition. The other was an eclipſe of the ſun, November 6th, 1771. The weather for ſeveral

ral days before, was fo cloudy that I attempted in vain to
regulate my clock, though I watched every favourable
opportunity. On the day of the eclipfe I got it pretty
well adjufted by feveral correfponding altitudes of the fun.
About 1^h P. M. the clouds gathered fo much round the
fun, that I was apprehenfive they would prevent any obfervation. But being pretty much fcattered, at 1^h 36′ 42″
apparent time, I could very plainly perceive that the
eclipfe was juft begun. This I judged was very near the
beginning, if not exactly fo, though it was attended with
fome uncertainty. In a few minutes the fun was wholly
covered with the clouds, and remained thus till 3$\frac{1}{4}$^{h}, when
they began again to fcatter, and left that part of the heavens in which the fun appeared, perfectly clear. The
weather continued thus till the end of the eclipfe, which
by a good obfervation was at 3^h 47′ 2″. Thefe obfervations were made with a reflector made by *Nairne*, magnifying as near as I could judge about fixty times ; but as
to the *quantity* of the eclipfe, no obfervation could be made;
the fun being obfcured by the clouds the biggeft part of
the time.

N° XXXIII.

*An eafy and accurate Method of finding a true Meridian
Line, and thence the Variation of the Compafs.*
By ROBERT PATTERSON.

Read Apr.
7, 1786. OF the various methods which aftronomers
employ for finding a true meridian line,
none feems fo well adapted, as could be wifhed, to the
common ufe of furveyors, in finding the variation of the
Compafs.

To find the azimuth of the fun by a fingle obfervation
of his altitude, befides a quadrant which is neceffary fo
thi�

this purpofe, requires the previous knowledge either of the latitude of the place, or hour of the day, at the time of obfervation; neither of which can, by the common apparatus of a furveyor, be found with fufficient accuracy.

The fun's azimuth may, it is true, be found without knowing either the latitude of the place or hour of the day, by taking equal altitudes before and after noon; but this requires time, attention and inftruments, which furveyors can but feldom command.

That method, which is perhaps the moft exact, viz. meafuring the time between the paffage of two ftars which differ confiderably, in declination and but little in right afcenfion, over the fame vertical circle, is ftill farther out of the reach of common furveyors.

The following table of the pole ftar will, it is prefumed, furnifh a more eafy, and yet fufficiently accurate method of determining this problem; free from all the above inconveniencies, and requiring no difficult calculation, nor any other inftrument than the common theodolite, or circumferentor. For though the latitude of the place fhould not be known within a whole degree, nor the hour of the night within 2 or 3 minutes, this table, by a fingle obfervation of the magnetic azimuth or bearing of the pole ftar, will generally give the variation of the needle true to a fingle minute of a degree. Nay if the obfervation be made (as it may be every night) when the ftar is near its greateft elongation, an error of 10, or even 20 minutes in time will, as is plain from the table, produce little or no fenfible error in the azimuth. And as thefe obfervations may be repeated at pleafure during the night, and a mean of all taken, the variation may, by this means, be found to any degree of accuracy that can be defired. Befides, the needle is not at this time affected with any diurnal variation; which in the day-time is very uncertain, and frequently amounts to more than one quarter of a degree.

The

The beſt inſtrument for obſerving the ſtar's magnetic azimuth is a theodolite, furniſhed with ſpirit-levels, and a ſmall teleſcope with a perpendicular wire. A common circumferentor may, however, anſwer the purpoſe. When this inſtrument is uſed, a fine thread or hair muſt be ſtretched along from the top of one ſight to that of the other, directly over the center of the compaſs; and the obſerver muſt be very careful to place the ſights perpendicular to the horizon when he makes the obſervation; for this purpoſe a ſmall pocket ſpirit-level, in the form of a carpenter's ſquare, would be very convenient.

By the common circumferentor we cannot, indeed, take the bearing of an object with very minute accuracy ; for though the eye can very well judge of the coincidence of two lines, or of the point of the needle with any whole degree on the compaſs, yet the parts of a degree cannot readily be obſerved to greater exactneſs than one third or one fourth of the whole. This inconvenience may, however, be eaſily remedied, and at a very trifling expence, in the following manner.

Let one of the ſights, by means of a ſcrew, be made movable at right angles to the index ; and on the end of the index, cloſe to the movable ſight, ſet off, on each ſide of the central line, the tangent of three degrees to a radius equal to the whole length of the index, or diſtance between the two ſights. Let each of theſe degrees be divided into ſix equal parts; then will a nonius diviſion on the ſight, where ten equal parts muſt correſpond with eleven on the index, ſubdivide theſe parts into minutes of a degree.

It will be unneceſſary to make the ſight move in the arch of a circle, the difference between this and the tangent, in ſo ſmall an arch, being quite imperceptible. With this ſimple improvement the common circumferentor will take the bearing of an object true to a minute, thus : Let the end of the needle be made exactly to coincide with the

K k   neareſt

neareſt whole degree, then move the ſcrew till the object appears in the direction of the ſights, and the nonius on the movable ſight will point out the odd minutes.

Explanation and Uſe of the TABLE.

The left hand double column of the table contains the time before the ſtar's paſſage over the meridian above the pole, for every twenty minutes of its whole diurnal circuit. The firſt column, under each particular latitude, ſhews the azimuth of the ſtar at theſe times, reſpectively, in degrees, minutes and tenths of a minute. The ſecond column ſhews the difference of azimuth in every twenty minutes of intermediate time, in minutes and tenths.

To find the true azimuth of the ſtar in any latitude, at any given time.

From the ſtar's right aſcenſion, viz. $0^h \, 49^m$, increaſed by 24^h if neceſſary, ſubtract the right aſcenſion of the ſun computed to the time of the ſtar's paſſage over the meridian, above the pole, nearly, the remainder will be the time of ſaid paſſage, reckoned from noon. From which, increaſed by 24^h if neceſſary, ſubtract the time of the obſervation, reckoned alſo from noon, the remainder will ſhew the time before the ſtar comes to the ſaid meridian. Look for this time in the left hand column of the table, oppoſite to which in the column of azimuth, under the proper latitude, you will have the true azimuth of the ſtar at that time.

If the time before the ſtar comes to the meridian be leſs than 12 hours, its azimuth will be eaſterly; but if more than 12 hours, its azimuth will be weſterly.

If the magnetic azimuth, and the true azimuth at the time of the obſervation, be both eaſterly or both weſterly, their difference will be the variation of the needle. But if one be eaſterly and the other weſterly, their ſum will be

be the variation.   And if the magnetic be to the weftward of the true azimuth, the variation will be wefterly ; but if to the eaftward, the variation will be eafterly.

If the time before the ftar's paffage over the meridian be fome intermediate minute, or the latitude of the place fome intermediate degree, not found in the table, a proportional intermediate azimuth, by means of the differences, muft be taken.

The right-afcenfion of the pole ftar annually increafes 10 feconds of time, and its polar diftance decreafes 20 feconds of a degree, therefore to its prefent right afcenfion (in 1785,) viz. $0^h 49^m$, muft be added one minute every year; and from its prefent polar diftance ($1° 50'.5$) one minute muft be fubtracted, and a proportional part from all the numbers in the columns of azimuth, every three years.   The effect of aberration and nutation may be fafely neglected; as the error arifing from thefe caufes can never amount to more than half a minute of a degree in azimuth.

In computing the fun's right afcenfion to the time of the ftar's paffage over the meridian nearly, the following little table will be ufeful.

K k 2   TABLE.

T A B L E.

Time.		Star paſſes Meridian nearly at
April	2	Noon
	19	11 A. M.
May	5	10
	20	9
June	4	8
	18	7
July	3	6
	17	5
Auguſt	2	4
	17	3
September	3	2
	19	1
October	6	Midnight
	22	11 P. M.
November	6	10
	21	9
December	5	8
	19	7
January	1	6
	15	5
	29	4
February	13	3
March	1	2
	17	1

EXAMPLE I.

Suppoſe on the 12th of September 1785, at 8 o'clock in the evening, in the latitude of 40° N. the magnetic azimuth of the pole-ſtar had been obſerved to be 0° 38′ eaſterly; required the variation of the needle at the time and place of obſervation.

Star's

	H.	M.
Star's R. A. increased by 24 hours, -	24	49
Sun's R. A. computed to 1ʰ A. M. (taken from the nautical almanac, or any other table of the sun's R. A.) subtract -	11	25

	H.	M.
True time of star's passage over meridian, reckoned from noon, - -	13	24
Hour of the night subtract, - -	8	0
Time before star's passage, - -	5	24

Which corresponds to true azimuth, 2° 23′ E.
Magnetic azimuth,   -   -   0 38 E.

Variation of the needle,   -   1 45 W.

EXAMPLE II.

In the latitude of about 32° north, on the 4th of July 1785, at 48 minutes after 10 o'clock at night, suppose the magnetic azimuth of the pole star, to be 2° 40′ east; required the variation of the needle.

	H.	M.
Star's R. A. + 24ʰ, - - -	24	49
Sun's R. A. - - - -	6	54
Time of star's passing meridian, -	17	55
Time of observation, - - -	10	48
Time before star comes to meridian, -	7	7

Which corresponds to true azimuth, 2° 4′ E.
Magnetic azimuth,   -   -   2 40 E.

Variation,   -   -   0 38 E.

Ex-

EXAMPLE III.

Latitude of the place 42° north, time of obfervation,
January 17th 1785, at 2ʰ 40ᵐ A. M.   Magnetic azimuth, 1° 5′ eafterly.

	H.	M.
Star's R. A. + 24ʰ - - - -	24	49
Sun's R. A. - - - -	20	1
Time of ftar's paffing the meridian, -	4	48
	24	
	28	48
Time of obfervation reckoned from noon,	14	40
Time before ftar comes to meridian, -	14	8

Correfponding to true azimuth,   1° 16′ W.
Magnetic azimuth,   -   -   1   5 E.

Variation,   -   -   -   2 21 E.

A TABLE

A TABLE of the Azimuth of the Pole-star for every 20 Minutes of its diurnal Motion round the Pole.

Time before the star comes to the meridian above the pole.		Latitude 30°		Latitude 35°		Latitude 40°		Latitude 45°		Latitude 50°		Latitude 55°	
H. M.	H. M.	Star's azimuth	Diff.	Star's azimuth	Diff.	Star's azimuth	Diff.	Star's azimuth	Diff.	Star's azimuth	Diff.	Star's azimuth	Diff.
0 0	24 0	0 0.0	11.3	0 0.0	12.0	0 0.0	12.9	0 0.0	14.1	0 0.0	15.6	0 0.0	17.6
0 20	23 40	11.3	11.3	12.0	12.0	12.9	12.8	14.1	13.9	15.6	15.4	17.6	17.4
0 40	23 20	22.6	11.1	24.0	11.7	25.7	12.6	28.0	13.7	31.0	15.2	35.0	17.2
1 0	23 0	33.7	10.7	35.7	11.5	38.3	12.3	41.7	13.4	46.2	14.8	52.2	16.7
1 20	22 40	44.4	10.4	47.2	11.0	50.6	11.9	55.1	12.9	1 1.0	14.3	1 8.9	16.0
1 40	22 20	54.8	10.0	58.2	10.6	1 2.5	11.3	1 8.0	12.3	15.3	13.6	24.9	15.4
2 0	22 0	1 4.8	9.5	1 8.8	10.0	13.8	10.9	20.3	11.8	28.9	12.9	40.3	14.5
2 20	21 40	14.3	8.9	18.8	9.4	24.7	10.0	32.1	10.9	41.8	12.0	54.8	13.5
2 40	21 20	23.2	8.2	28.2	8.8	34.7	9.3	43.0	10.1	53.8	11.2	2 8.3	12.5
3 0	21 0	31.4	7.6	37.0	7.8	44.0	8.5	53.1	9.1	2 5.0	10.0	20.8	11.2
3 20	20 40	39.0	6.7	44.8	7.1	52.5	7.5	2 2.2	8.2	15.0	9.0	32.0	10.0
3 40	20 20	45.7	5.9	51.9	6.3	2 0.0	6.3	10.4	7.2	24.0	7.7	42.0	8.7
4 0	20 0	51.6	5.0	58.2	5.2	6.7	5.5	17.6	6.0	31.7	6.6	50.7	7.3
4 20	19 40	56.6	4.1	2 3.4	4.3	12.2	4.5	23.6	4.9	38.3	5.4	58.0	6.6
4 40	19 20	2 0.7	3.1	7.7	3.3	16.7	3.6	28.5	3.7	43.7	4.0	3 4.6	3.6
5 0	19 0	3.8	2.2	11.0	2.3	20.3	2.4	32.2	2.5	47.7	2.6	8.2	3.0
5 20	18 40	6.0	1.3	13.3	1.4	22.7	1.3	34.7	1.4	50.3	1.4	11.2	1.4
5 40	18 20	7.3	.7	14.7	.6	24.0	.9	36.1	1.0	51.7	1.1	12.6	1.5
6 0	18 0	7.6	1.7	14.8	1.9	24.2	2.0	36.2	2.2	51.8	2.5	12.5	2.9
6 20	17 40	6.9	2.5	14.2	2.8	23.3	3.0	35.2	3.3	50.7	3.9	11.0	4.3
6 40	17 20	5.2	3.5	12.3	3.8	21.3	4.1	33.0	4.5	48.2	4.9	8.1	5.6
7 0	17 0	2.7	4.5	9.5	4.6	18.3	5.0	29.7	5.5	44.3	6.2	3.8	7.0
7 20	16 40	1 59.2	5.1	5.7	5.6	14.2	6.0	25.2	6.5	39.4	7.1	2 58.2	8.2
7 40	16 20	54.7	6.2	1.1	6.4	9.2	6.9	19.7	7.5	33.2	8.4	51.2	9.3
8 0	16 0	49.6	6.8	1 55.5	7.3	3.2	7.6	13.2	8.5	26.1	9.2	43.0	10.4
8 20	15 40	43.4	7.5	49.1	7.9	1 56.3	8.5	2 5.7	9.2	17.7	10.2	33.7	11.5
8 40	15 20	36.6	8.2	41.8	8.7	48.7	9.4	1 57.2	9.9	2 8.5	11.0	23.3	12.1
9 0	15 0	29.1	8.8	33.9	9.2	40.2	9.9	48.0	10.8	1 58.3	11.7	11.8	13.2
9 20	14 40	20.9	9.3	25.2	9.8	30.8	10.4	38.1	11.3	47.3	12.4	1 59.7	13.8
9 40	14 20	12.1	9.7	16.0	10.3	20.9	11.0	27.3	11.8	35.6	12.9	46.5	14.5
10 0	14 0	2.1	10.2	6.2	10.7	10.5	11.7	16.0	12.3	23.2	13.4	32.7	14.9
10 20	13 40	0 53.1	10.5	0 55.9	11.2	0 59.5	12.0	4.2	12.7	10.3	14.0	18.2	15.6
10 40	13 20	42.1	10.7	45.2	11.4	48.1	12.1	0 51.9	11.9	0 56.9	14.2	3.3	15.7
11 0	13 0	32.4	10.8	34.2	11.5	36.4	12.2	39.2	13.1	42.9	14.3	0 47.7	15.9
11 20	12 40	21.7	10.9	22.9	11.5	24.4	12.2	26.3	13.2	28.7	14.4	32.0	16.1
11 40	12 20	10.9	10.9	11.5	11.5	12.2	12.2	13.2	13.2	14.4	14.4	16.1	16.1
12 0	12 0	0.0		0.0		0.0		0.0		0.0		0.0	

N° XXXIV.

Astronomical Observations, communicated by Mr. RIT-
TENHOUSE.

By Mr. *James Six*, of Canterbury.

Geocentric place of the New Planet.

April 1st, 1782,   29° 5′ 30″ in ♏ lat. 13′ N.
October 15th,   7 21 18 ♋ nearly stationary.
December 26th,   5 2 30 in opposition.
March 10th, 1783,   3 15 0 stationary.
October 15th,   11 53 10 stationary.
December 30th,   9 47 25 in opposition.
March 14th, 1784,   7 46 0 stationary.

Lat. 23 N.

By *D. Rittenhouse*, at Philadelphia.

Transit of Mercury over the sun's disk, Nov. 12th, 1782.

First external contact,   9ʰ 34′ 50″ morn. ⎫
Internal, uncertain,   40 0   ⎬ Mean Time.
Second internal,   10 51 30   ⎪
Last contact,   57 35   ⎭

Greatest distance of ☿ center from sun's limb, 31″.

1784,		On Meridian.
Jan. 29th.	ɣ Gemino	9ʰ 49′ 20″
	‘ Gem.	9 54 45
	New Planet	10 1 48
	ζ Gem.	10 15 19
Feb. 12th.	ɣ Gem.	8ʰ 54′ 19″
	New Planet,	9 4 54
	ζ Gem.	9 20 18

1785.
January 26th.

On Meridian.

		h	'	"
January 26th.	ζ Gemino	10	24	14
	New Planet	10	31	22
	δ Gem.	10	40	7
February 4th.	ζ Gem.	9	48	48
	New Planet	9	54	32
	δ Gem.	10	4	41

Feb. 12th. Observed zenith distance,

	°	'	"
ζ Gemino	19	5	7
New Planet	16	40	45
δ Gem.	17	35	33

		h	'	"
Febr. 17th.	ζ Gem.	8	57	42
	New Planet	9	1	46
	δ Gem.	9	13	35

zenith distance, 16° 40' 42"
ditto, 17 35 40

		h	'	"
Febr. 27th.	ζ Gem.	8	18	34
	New Planet	8	21	32
	δ Gem.	8	34	27
March 12th.	ζ Gem.	7	27	14
	New Planet	7	29	41½
	δ Gem.	7	43	6¼
March 15th.	Sirius	6	59	51
	ζ Gemino	7	15	30
	New Planet	7	17	54
	δ Gem.	7	31	23
March 17th.	Sirius	6	51	58
	ζ Gem.	7	7	37
	New Planet	7	9	59
March 22d.	Sirius	6	32	18
	ζ Gem.	6	47	56
	New Planet	6	50	19
March 27th.	Sirius	6	12	38
	ζ Gem.	6	28	16
	New Planet	6	30	45
28th.	ζ Gem.	6	24	19
	New Planet	6	26	50¼

1786,

		h	'	"	Micrometer measure of Z. D.		Difference in min. & secc.
January 25th.	δ Gemino	10	45	1			
	New Planet	10	56	48			
26th.	δ Gem.	10	41	5	+	r. 1	d. 35
	New Planet	10	52	44	—	4	37½

Difference, 6 24½ = 20' 59"

1786,		On Meridian.			Micrometer measure of Z. D. r. d.		Difference in min. & secs.	
January 27th.	♂ Gemino	10ʰ	37′	8″	+ 1	34		
	New Planet	10	48	37	— 4	34		
					Diff. 6	29	= 21′	17″
31ſt.	♂ Gem.	10	21	24				
	New Planet	10	32	13				
February 1ſt.	♂ Gem.	10	17	28 } Diff. 7 0			= 22	33
	Pluto	10	28	7				
2d.	μ Gem.	9	16	23½				
	♂ Gem.	10	13	33	8	40		
	New Planet	10	24	2	16	0		
					Diff. 7	8	= 23	5
3d.	♂ Gem.	-	-	-	8	39		
	New Planet	-	-	-	16	3½		
					Diff. 17	12½	= 23	24
6th.	♂ Gem.	9	57	50	8	39¾		
	New Planet	10	7	43	16	17		
					Diff. 7	25¼	= 24	7
10th.	μ Gem.	-	-	-	13	21½		
	♂ Gem.	9	42	7				
	New Planet	9	51	24	16	29½		
					Diff. 3	8	= 10	13
21ſt.	♂ Gem.	8	58	52				
	New Planet	9	6	46				
March 10th.	♂ Gem.	7	52	2	12	5½		
	New Planet	7	58	31	21	21		
					Diff. 9	15½	= 30	3
11th.	μ Gem.	6	50	55				
	♂ Gem.	7	48	5	12	5		
	New Planet	7	54	31	21	20½		
					Diff. 9	15¾	= 30	4
12th.	♂ Gem.	7	44	9	13	17½		
	New Planet	7	50	32	22	34½		
					Diff. 9	17	= 30	9
18th.	μ Gem.	6	23	23				
	♂ Gem.	7	20	33	13	16½		
	New Planet	7	26	43½	22	35½		
					Diff. 9	18½	= 30	16

1786,		On Meridian.				Micrometer meaſure of Z. D. r.	d.		Difference in min. & ſeco.	
March 19th.	δ Gem.	7	16	37½		14	36			
	New Planet	7	22	47½		24	8¼			
					Diff.	9	20¼	=	30	24
21ſt.	δ Gem.	7	8	46		5	18			
	New Planet	7	14	53		14	37¼			
					Diff.	9	19¼	=	30	18
23d.	δ Gem.	7	0	54½		3	28½			
	New Planet	7	7	1½		12	47			
					Diff.	9	18½	=	30	15
24th.	δ Gem.	6	56	59		8	14¾			
	New Planet	7	3	6		17	34			
					Diff.	9	19¼	=	30	18
25th.	δ Gem.	6	53	3						
	New Planet	6	59	16						
27th.	δ Gem.	6	45	11		8	13¾			
	New Planet	6	51	18		17	31			
					Diff.	9	17¼	=	30	10
April 2d.	δ Gem.	6	21	36						
	New Planet	6	27	53						

N. B. In theſe obſervations the declination of the New Planet was conſtantly greater than that of δ Geminorum, but leſs than μ.

N° XXXV.

A Letter from Mr. OTTO, *to* Dr. FRANKLIN, *with a Memoir on the Diſcovery of America.*

New-York, 1ſt April, 1786.

SIR,

Read Apr. 7, 1786.

ALMOST all the authors who have written upon the diſcovery of America, make mention of ſome information which Chriſtopher Columbus procured at Madeira, upon the exiſtence of a weſtern continent; but they do not tell us, poſitively, how far this in-

 formation

formation aſſiſted him, or from what ſource he derived it. I have always been curious to clear up this intereſting part of hiſtory; and in running over many ancient hiſtorians, as well German as Spaniſh, I have found ſome circumſtances, which have appeared to me to eſtabliſh, in the cleareſt manner, a diſcovery anterior to that of Columbus. I have the honor to ſend you the reſult of my enquiries; and if you think this piece worthy of being ſubmitted to the conſideration of the Philoſophical Society, I beg you to preſent it to them as a mark of my homage, and of the deſire which I have of being of ſome ſervice.

I have the honor to be, with reſpectful attachment,

Your excellency's very humble and

Moſt obedient ſervant,

OTTO.

His excellency Dr. Franklin.

A New-York, le 1 Avril, 1786.

MONSIEUR,

PRESQUE tous les auteurs qui ont ecrit ſur la decouverte de l'Amerique, ſont mention de quelques renſeignemens que Chriſtophe Colomb s'eſt procurés dans l'iſle de Madere ſur l'exiſtence d'un continent occidental, mais ils ne nous diſent pas poſitivement juſqu'à quel point ces relations ont pu lui être utiles, ou quelle en a été la ſource. J'ai toujours été curieux de debrouiller cette partie intéreſſante de l'hiſtoire; et en parcourant pluſieurs anciens hiſtoriens, tant Allemans qu'Eſpagnols, j'ai trouvé quelques détails qui m'ont paru établir d'une maniere indubitable une decouverte anterieure à celle de Colomb. J'ai l'honneur de vous en adreſſer le reſumé, et ſi vous croyés que cette piece ſoit digne d'être miſe ſous les yeux de la ſociété philoſophique, je vous ſupplie de la lui preſenter comme une marque de mon hommage et du deſir que j'ai de lui être de quelqué utilité.

J'ai l'honneur d'être avec un reſpectueux attachement,

MONSIEUR,

De votre Excellence,

Le très humble et très obeiſſant ſerviteur,

OTTO.

S. E. M. FRANKLIN.

Memoir upon the Discovery of America.

IT has always been looked on as a piece of injustice, not to have given the name of Columbus to that valuable part of the world which he discovered; and that Americanus Vespucius, who did nothing but follow his footsteps, has had the good fortune of having his name handed down to the most distant posterity, to the prejudice of his predecessor. What then will be said, if it shall be proved, that neither of those celebrated navigators were the first discoverers of this immense country, and that this honor belongs to a man scarcely known in the republic of letters. This, however, is what I shall attempt in the following paper; and if the obscurity of cotemporary writers and the distance of time, do not afford arguments sufficient for an absolute demonstration, there will however be enough to call in question the pretensions of Christopher Columbus.

I shall not here enter into an examination of the reveries of some historians, on the voyages of the Carthaginians, the Atlantis of Plato, the bold expedition of Madoc prince of Wales and son of Owen Guinnedd, of which Hackluyt has preserved some account, nor on the voyages of Bacchus, or the land Ophir of Solomon. Conjectures of this kind, whether true or false, cannot lessen the glory of Columbus, were there not proof that he received, just before

MÉMOIRE SUR LA DÉCOUVERTE DE L'AMÉRIQUE. Mars 1786.

ON a regardé jusqu'ici comme une injustice qu'on n'ait point donné le nom de Christophe Colomb à la belle partie du monde qu'il a découverte, et qu'Americ Vespuce, qui n'a fait que marcher sur ses traces, ait eu le bonheur de faire passer son souvenir à la postérité la plus éloignée au préjudice de son prédécesseur. Que diroit 'on s'il étoit prouvé qu'aucun de ces grands navigateurs n'a le merite de la premiere découverte de ce pays immense, et que l'honneur en est dû à un homme presqu'inconnu dans la republique des lettres ? C'est ce que je me propose de faire dans ce mémoire, et si l'obscurité des écrivains contemporains et l'éloignement des époques ne me permettent pas de pousser mes argumens jusqu'à l'évidence, ils suffiront au moins pour établir des doutes fondés sur la prétendue découverte de Christophe Colomb.

Nous n'examinerons point ici les rêves de quelques historiens sur la navigation des Carthaginois, sur l'Atlantide de Platon, sur les expeditions hardies de Madox, prince de Galles, et fils d'Owen Guynet, dont Hakluit nous a conservé les détails, ni sur les voyages de Bacchus ni sur l'Ophir de Salomon ; ces conjectures vraies ou fausses ne sauroient diminuer la glorie de Christophe

before his expedition, the charts and journal of a learned aftronomer who had been in America.

Garcilaſſo de la Vega, born at Cuſco in Peru, has given us an hiſtory of his country, in which, to take from Columbus the merit of the diſcovery of America, and to give the honor of it to the Spaniards, he aſſures us, that this navigator had been informed of the exiſtence of another continent by Alonzo Sanchez de Huelva, who in his voyage to the Canaries had been driven by a gale of wind to the Antilles; but that his chief information was procured from a celebrated geographer of the name of Martin Behenira. Garcilaſſo ſays nothing more of this Behenira; and ſince we know of no Spaniſh geographer of this name, Garcilaſſo has been ſuſpected of making a ſacrifice of truth to the deſire of wreſting from a Genoeſe the glory of diſcovering the new world.

On looking over, with attention, a liſt of all the learned men of the fifteenth century, I find the name of Martin Behem, a famous geographer and navigator. The chriſtian name is the ſame with that mentioned by Garcilaſſo, and I find that the ſyllables *ira*, added to his name, are owing to a particular circumſtance; namely, the honor conferred on him by John II. king of Portugal. It is then poſſible, that this Martin Behem is the ſame perſon as Martin Behenira mentioned by Garcilaſſo; but this vague conjecture will receive the ſtamp of truth by the following detail.   The

Chriſtophe Colomb, s'il n'étoit prouvé, que, peu de tems avant ſon expédition, un aſtronome ſavant avoit été en Amérique, et lui avoit communiqué ſes cartes et ſes journaux.

Garcilaſſo de la Vega, né à Cuſco en Perou, nous a donné une hiſtoire de ſa patrie dans laquelle, pour oter à Colomb le merite de la decouverte de l'Amerique, et pour en faire honneur aux Eſpagnols, il aſſure que ce navigateur avoit été inſtruit de l'exiſtence d'un autre continent par Alonzo Sanchez de Huelva, qui faiſant route pour les Canaries avoit été pouſſé aux Antilles par un coup de vent; mais *qu'il avoit ſur tout tiré grand parti des informations d'un celebre geographe nommé Martin Behenira*. Garcilaſſo ne nous dit rien de plus ſur ce *Behenira*, et comme on ne connoit point de géographe Eſpagnol de ce nom, on a ſoupçonné de la Vega d'avoir ſacrifié la verité au deſir de ne pas laiſſer à un Génois la gloire d'avoir decouvert le nouveau monde.

En parcourant avec attention la liſte de tous les ſavans du XV ſiecle, je trouve le nom de *Martin Behem*, grand géographe et navigateur, je trouve que le nom de batême eſt conferme à celui qui eſt cité par Garcilaſſo, que les ſyllabes *ira* ajoutées à ſon nom doivent être dues à une circonſtance particuliere, et cette circonſtance je la trouve dans la confiance dont il a été honoré par Jean II roi de Portugal. Il eſt donc poſſible que ce *Martin Behem* ſoit le même homme que ce *Martin Behenira* mentionné par Garcilaſſo; mais cette conjecture vague aura tous les caracteres de l'évidence par les détails ſuivans.

                                                L'hiſtoire

The literary hiftory of Germany gives an account of a Martin Behem, Beheim, or Behin, who was born at Nurenburgh, an imperial city of the circle of Franconia, of a noble family, fome branches of which are yet extant. He was much addicted to the ftudy of geography, aftronomy and navigation, from his infancy. At a more mature age he often thought on the poffibility of the exiftance of the Antipodes and of a weftern continent. Filled with this great idea, he paid a vifit in 1459 to Ifabella daughter of John the I. king of Portugal and regent of the duchy of Burgundy and Flanders. Having informed her of his defigns, he procured a veffel, in which he made the difcovery of the ifland of Fayal in 1460. He there eftablifhed a colony of Flemings, whofe defcendants yet exift in the Azores; which were, for fome time called the Flemifh iflands. This circumftance is proved, not only by the writings of cotemporary authors, but alfo by the manufcripts preferved in the records of Nurenburg, from which the following is copied. "Martin Behem tender-
"ed his fervices to the daughter of John king of Lufita-
"nia, who reigned after the death of Philip of Burgun-
"dy firnamed the Good, and from her procured a fhip,
"by means of which, having failed beyond all the then
"known limits of the weftern ocean, he was the firft who,
"in the memory of man, difcovered the ifland of Fayal,
"abound-

L'hiftoire litteraire de l'Allemagne nous apprend que *Martin Behem*, *Beheim* ou *Behin* eft né à Nurenberg, ville imperiale du cercle de Franconie, d'une famille noble dont quelques branches exiftent encore aujourdhui. Dès fa plus tendre jeuneffe il fe livra à l'étude de la geographie, de l'aftronomie et de la navigation. Parvenu à un age mur il reflechit beaucoup fur la poffibilité de l'exiftence des Antipodes et d'un continent occidental. Rempli de cette grande idée, il fut trouver en 1459 Ifabelle fille de Jean I. roi de Portugal et regente du duché de Bourgogne et de l'landre. Après lui avoir fait part de fes projets, il en obtint un vaiffeau avec lequel il fit, en 1460, la decouverte de l'ifle de Fayal. Il y établit une colonie Flamande, dont les defcendans exiftent encore aujourdhui aux Açores, qu'on a appellées pendant quelque tems les ifles Flamandes. Cette circonftance eft prouvée, non feulement par les auteurs contemporains, mais par des manufcrits confervés dans les archives de Nurenberg, dont voici la copie : " Martinus " Behemus, Joaunis Lufitaniæ regis filiæ, quæ poft obitum Philippi Burgundi cognomento " boni, rerum dominabatur, operam fuam addixit, et ab ea navim impetravit, qua occidentalis " oceani hactenus cognitos terminos et fines prætervectus *primus* poft hominum memoriam " *Fayalem* infulam, *Fago* arbore, quam Lufitani *Faye* vocant, ac unde appellatio ei hafit abun- " dantem

" abounding with beachtrees, which the people of Lufita-
" nia call Faye; whence it derived its name. After this
" he difcovered the neighbouring iflands, called by one
" general name *the Azores*, from the multitude of hawks
" which build their nefts there (for the Lufitanians ufe
" this term for hawks, and the French too ufe the word
" *Effos* or *Efores* in their purfuit of this game) and left
" colonies of the Flemifh on them; when they began to
" be called Flemifh iflands, &c." Although this record is
contrary to the generally received opinion, that the Azores
were difcovered by Gonfalva Velho, a Portuguefe, yet its
authenticity cannot be doubted; it is confirmed by feveral
cotemporary writers, and efpecially by Wagenceil, one of
the moft learned men of the laft century; who after having travelled into Africa, and throughout all Europe, was
made doctor of laws at Orleans and chofen fellow of the
academy of Turin and Padua, although he was a German by birth. The particulars are to be found in his
univerfal hiftory and geography. I have moreover received, from the records of Nurenberg, a note written in
German on parchment, which contains the following facts.
" Martin Behem, efquire, fon of Mr. Martin Behem of
" Schroperin, lived in the reign of John II. king of Portu-
" gal, in an ifland which he difcovered, and called the ifland
" of Fayal, one of the Azores, lying in the weftern ocean."
After having obtained from the regent Ifabella a grant
of Fayal, and refided there about twenty years, during
which

" dantem reperit, nec minus poftea finitimas infulas, uno nomine ab accipitrum ibi nidifican-
" tium multitudine *Açores* dictas (Lufitani enim hoc vocabulo *accipitres* efferunt, et Galli quo-
" que in aucupiis verbum *Effos* et *Effores* adhibent) detexit, ac flandrorum colonias in iis re-
" liquit, unde et infulæ illæ Flandriæ vocari cæperunt, &c." Quoique ce monument foit con-
traire à l'opinion généralement reçue que les Açores ont été decouvertes par un Portugais
nommé Gonzalve Velho, on ne fauroit douter de fon authenticité ; il fe trouve confirmé par
plufieurs auteurs contemporains, et furtout par Wagenfeil, un des plus grands favans du dernier
fiecle, qui après avoir voyagé par l'Afrique et par toute l'Europe, a été fait docteur en droit à
Orleans, et academicien à Turin et à Padoue, quoiqu'il fut né Allemand. On en trouve des
détails dans fon hiftoire univerfelle et dans fa geographie. On m'a d'ailleurs communiqué dans
les archives de Nurenberg une note en Allemand écrite fur parchemin, contenant les faits
fuivans : " M. Martin Beham, ecuyer, fils de M. Martin Beham de Scopperin, a vecu fous le
" regne de Jean II. roi de Portugal, dans une ifle qu'il a trouvée lui même, et qu'il a appellée
" ifle de Fayal; elle eft fituée aux Açores dans l'océan occidental."
Après avoir obtenu de la regente Ifabelle la propriété de Fayal, et après y avoir employé environ

which time he was bufied in making frefh difcoveries in
geography, by fmall excurfions, which need not be mentioned, Behem applied in 1484 (which was eight years
before Columbus's expedition) to John II. king of Portugal, to procure the means of undertaking a great expedition towards the fouth-weft. This prince gave him fome
fhips, with which he difcovered that part of America,
which is now called Brazil; and he even failed to the
ftreights of Magellan, or to the country of fome favage
tribes, whom he called Patagonians, from the extremities
of their bodies being covered with a fkin more like a bear's
paws than human hands and feet. This fact is proved by
authentic records, preferved in the archives of Nurenberg.
One of which in particular deferves attention " Martin
" Behem, traverfing the Atlantic ocean for feveral years,
" examined the American iflands, and difcovered the
" ftrait which bears the name of Magellan, before either
" Chriftopher Columbus or Magellan failed thofe feas;
" and even mathematically delineated on a geographical
" chart for the king of Lufitania, the fituation of the
" coaft, around every part of that famous and renowned
" ftrait." This affertion is fupported by Behem's own
letters, written in German and preferved in the archives
of Nurenberg, in a book which contains the birth and illuftrious actions of the nobility of that city. Thefe let-

M m   ters

viron 20 années à faire des recherches ulterieures fur la géographie, dans de petites excurfions
que ne meritent par d'être rapportées ici; Behem s'adreffa en 1484, c'eft à dire huit années
avant l'expedition de Chriftophe Colomb, à Jean II. roi de Portugal, pour obtenir de lui les
moyens d'entreprendre une grande expedition vers le fud-oueft. Ce prince lui confia quelques
vaiffeaux avec lefquels il decouvrit la partie de l'Amerique connue fous le nom de Brefil, et
il étendit meme fa navigation jufqu'au détroit de Magellan, ou à la terre de quelques hordes
fauvages qu'il appella Patagons, puifque les extremités de leurs corps couvertes de peaux reffem-
bloient plutôt à des pattes d'ours qu'à des pieds et à des mains. Ce fait eft prouvé par des do-
cumens authentiques dépof's dans les archives de Nurenberg. Il y en a un furtout qui merite
notre attention : " Martinus Behemus per oceanum Atlanticum huc illuc annos plufculos
" oberrans, ante Chriftophorum Columbum Americæ infulas, ante Fernaidum Magellanum,
" fretum quod ab eo cognomentum habet perveftigavit, unde et in tab.la geographica projiu
" quam Magellanes de expeditione fua cogitaffet, omnem circa infigne clariffimumque fretum
" illud oræ habitudinem Lufitaniæ regi radio delineavit." Cette affertion fe trouve appuyée
par des lettres de Behem ecrites en Allemand, et confervées dans les archives de Nurenberg,
dans un volume contenant l'origine et les actions éclatantes des patriciens de cette ville. Ces
lettres

ters are dated in 1486; that is, fix years before the expedition of Columbus. This wonderful difcovery has not
efcaped the notice of cotemporary writers. The following paffage is extracted from the chronicle of Hartman
Schedl: "In the year 1485, John the fecond, king of
" Portugal, a man of a magnanimous fpirit, furnifhed
" fome gallies with provifions, and fent them to the fouth-
" ward beyond the ftraits of Gibraltar. He gave the com-
" mand of this fquadron to James Canus, a Portuguefe,
" and Martin Behem a German of Nurenberg in Upper
" Germany, defcended of the family of Bonna, a man
" very well acquainted with the fituation of the globe,
" bleffed with a conftitution able to bear the fatigues of
" the fea, and who by actual experiments and long fail-
" ing, had made himfelf perfectly mafter with regard to
" the longitudes and latitudes of Ptolemy, in the weft.
" Thefe two, by the bounty of Heaven, coafting along the
" fouthern ocean, and having croffed the æquator, got
" into the other hemifphere, where facing to the eaft-
" ward, their fhadows projected towards the fouth and
" right-hand. Thus, by their induftry, they may be faid
" to have opened to us another world hitherto unknown,
" and for many years attempted by none but the Genoefe,
" and by them in vain. Having finifhed this cruife in the
" fpace of twenty-fix months, they returned to Portugal,
" with the lofs of many of their feamen, by the violence
" of the climate."   This

---

lettres font datées de 1486, c'eft à dire fix années avant l'expédition de Chriftophe Colomb.
Quelques auteurs contemporains n'ont pas manqué de faire mention d'une decouverte auffi
étonnante.   Je trouve entre autres dans la chronique de Hartman Schedl le paffage fuivant :
" Anno Domini 1485, Johannes fecundus Portugalliæ rex, altiffimi vir cordis, certas galeas
" omnibus ad victum neceffariis inftruxit, eafque ultra columnas Herculis ad meridiem mifit.
" Præfecit autem his patronos duos Jacobum Canum Portugallenfem et Martinum Behemum,
" hominem Germanum ex Nurimberga fuperioris Germaniæ de Bonna familia natum, hominem
" inquam in cognofcendo fitu terræ peritiffimum, marifque patientiffimum, qui Ptolomæi lon-
" gitudines et latitudines in occidente ad unguem experimento longævaque navigatione novit.
" Hi duo, bono Deorum aufpicio mare meridionale fulcantes a littore non longe evagantes
" fuperato circulo æquinoctiali in alterum orbem excepti funt, ubi ipfis ftantibus orientem
" verfus umbra ad meridiem et dexteram projiciebatur.   Aperuere igitur fua induftria aliam
" orbem hactenus nobis incognitum, et multis annis a nullis quam a Januenfibus licet fruftra tentatum ;
" peracta autem hujufmodi navigatione viciffimo fexto menfe reverfi funt in Portugalliam,
" pluribus ob aeris impatientiam mortuis."

Cequi

This paſſage becomes more intereſting, from being quoted in a book on the ſtate of Europe during the reign of the emperor Frederick III. by the learned hiſtorian Æneas Sylvius, afterwards pope Pius II. This hiſtorian died before the diſcoveries of Behem were made, but the publiſhers of his works, thought the paſſage in Hartman Schedl ſo important, that they inſerted it in the hiſtory. We alſo find the following particulars, in the remarks made by Petrus Matæus, on the canon law, two years before the expedition of Columbus: " The firſt chriſtian " voyages to the newly diſcovered iſlands became fre- " quent, under the reign of Henry ſon of John king of " Luſitania. After his death, Alphonſus the fifth proſecut- " ed the deſign, and John who ſucceeded him followed " the plan of Alphonſus by the aſſiſtance of Martin Bœhm, " a very experienced navigator, ſo that, in a ſhort time, " the name of Luſitania become famous over the whole " world." Cellarius, one of the moſt learned men of his age, ſays expreſsly: " Bœhm did not think it enough to " ſurvey the iſland of Fayal, which he firſt diſcovered, or " the other adjacent iſlands which the Luſitanians call " Azores, *and we after the example of Bœhm's companions*, " *call Flemiſh iſlands;* but advanced ſtill farther and far- " ther ſouth, until he arrived at the remoteſt ſtrait, be- " yond which, Ferdinand Magellan, following his tract, " afterwards ſailed and called it after his own name."

M m 2

All

Ce qui rend ce paſſage plus intereſſant encore, c'eſt qu'il eſt cité dans l'ouvrage du ſavant hiſ- torien *Æneas Sylvius*, depuis pape ſous le nom de Pie II. ſur l'état de l'Europe du tems de l'empereur Frederic III. Cet hiſtorien eſt mort avant les decouvertes de Behem, mais les copiſtes de l'ouvrage d'Æneas Sylvius ont trouvé le paſſage de Hartman Schedl ſi intéreſſant qu'ils l'ont inſeré dans le corps de cette hiſtoire. Nous trouvons d'ailleurs dans les notes que Petrus Matæi a faites ſur le droit canon, deux ans avant l'expedition de Colomb, les détails ſuivans : " Primæ navigationes chriſtianæ ad novas inſulas eluceſcere ceperunt ſub Henrico " Johannis Luſitaniæ regis filio, &c. illo mortuo Alphonſus V. cœpta proſecutus eſt; Al- " phonſum Johannes imitatus opera *Martini Bohemi*, hominis in curſu navium peritiſſimi, ut " brevi tempore nihil celebrius per totum orbem audiretur ipſo Luſitaniæ nomine." Cel- larius, un des plus grands ſavans de ſon ſiecle, dit expreſſement : " Behaimius non modo " Fagalem inſulam, quam primus invenit, aut alias circumjectas quas Azores Luſitani, nos " *Flandrias a Bohaimi comitibus*, nominant, perluſtrandas ſibi cenſuit, verum etiam in auſtrum " magis et magis progreſſus uſque ad ultimum fretum, quod Ferdinandus Magellanus hujus " ductum ſecutus, pertranſiit et de ſuo id nomine appellavit."

Toutes

All thefe quotations, which cannot be thought tedious, fince they ferve to prove a fact almoft unknown, feem to demonftrate, that the firft difcovery of America is due to the Portuguefe, and not to the Spaniards; and that the chief merit belongs to a German aftronomer. The expedition of Ferdinand Magellan, which did not take place before the year 1519, arofe from the following fortunate circumftance. This perfon, being in the apartment of the king of Portugal, faw there a chart of the coaft of America, drawn by Behem, and at once conceived the bold project of following the fteps of this great navigator. Jerome Benzon, who publifhed a defcription of America in 1550, fpeaks of this chart, a copy of which, fent by Behem himfelf, is preferved in the archives of Nurenberg. The celebrated aftronomer Riccioli, though an Italian, yet does not feem willing to give his countryman the honor of this important difcovery. In his geography reformed, book III. page 90, he fays: " Chriftopher Columbus never thought " of an expedition to the Weft Indies, until fome time " before, while in the ifland of Madeira, where amufing " himfelf in forming and delineating geographical charts, " he obtained information from Martin Bœhm, or as the " Spaniards fay, from Alphonfus Sanchez de Huelva, a " pilot, who by meer chance had fallen in with the ifland " afterwards called Dominica." And in another place, " let Bœhm and Columbus have each their praife, they " were

---

Toutes ces citations qui ne fauroient être trop longues, parcequ'elles fervent à prouver un fait prefqu'inconnu, paroiffent demontrer que la premiere decouverte de l'Amerique eft due aux Portugais, et non aux Efpagnols; et que c'eft un aftronome Allemand qui étoit à leur tête. L'expedition de Ferdinand Magellan, qui n'a eu lieu qu'en 1519, eft due à un heureux hazard. Ce navigateur fe trouvant dans l'appartement du roi de Portugal, y vit une carte des cotes de l'Amerique tracée par Behem, et conçut dès lors le projet hardi de fuivre la route de ce grand navigateur. Jerome Benzon, qui a donné en 1550, une defcription de l'Amerique, fait mention de cette carte, dont on a confervé une copie dans les archives de Nurenberg, où Behem l'avoit envoyée lui-même; et celte re aftronome Riccioli, qui étoit lui-même Italien, ne paroit pas cependant vouloir attribuer à fon compatriote cette importante decouverte; il dit dans fa geographie reformée, livre 3. p. 90. " Chriftophorus Columbus, cum " prius in Madera infula, ubi conficiendis et delineandis chartis geographicis verfabar, initio ha- " bito a Martino Bohemo, aut et Hifpani dictant ab Alphonfo Sanchez de Huelva, nauclero " qui forte incidert in infulam, poftea Dominicam dictam, cogitavit de navigatione in indiam " occidentalem." Et dans un autre endroit, " Sit fua laus Behemo, et fua laus Columbo, " ambo

" were both excellent navigators; but Columbus would
" never have thought of his expedition to America, had
" not Bœhm gone there before him. His name is not fo
" much celebrated as that of Columbus, Americus or Ma-
" gellan, although he is fuperior to them all."

But the moft pofitive proof of the great fervices rendered to the crown of Portugal by Behem, is the recompence beftowed on him by king John, who in 1485 knighted him in the moft folemn manner, in the prefence of all
his court. I have before me a German paper extracted
from the archives of Nurenberg to the following purpofe. " In the year 1485, on the 18th of February, in
" Portugal, in the city of Allafavas, and in the church of
" St. Salvador, after the mafs, Martin Behem of Nurenberg,
" was made a knight by the hands of the moft puiffant
" lord, John the fecond king of Portugal, Algarve, Afri-
" ca and Guinea; and his chief fquire was the king him-
" felf, who put the fword in his belt; and the duke of Begia
" was his fecond fquire, who put on his right fpur; and
" his third fquire was count Chriftopher de Mela, the
" king's coufin, who put on his left fpur; and his fourth
" fquire was count Martini Marbarinis who put on his
" iron helmet; and the king himfelf gave him the blow
" on the fhoulder, which was done in the prefence of all
" the princes, lords and knights of the kingdom : and he
                                            " efpoufed

" ambo fuerunt magni navarchi, fed nunquam de fua in Americam expeditione cogitaffet
" Columbus nifi Bohemum habuiffet prædecefforem. Hujus nomen non tantopere celebra-
" tur quanto Columbi, Americi et Magellani, quamvis his tribus fit præferendus."

Mais ce qui prouve plus que toute autre chofe les grands fervices rendus par Behem à la
couronne de Portugal, c'eft la reconnoiffance du roi Jean, qui en 1485, le fit lui-même chevalier, de la manière la plus folemnelle, et en préfence de toute fa cour. J'ai fous mes yeux
un document Allemand, tiré des archives de Nurenberg, de la tenur fuivante : " En 1485,
" le 18 Fevrier, en Portugal dans la ville d'Allafavas, et dans l'églife de Santo Salvador,
" après la meffe, a été fait chevalier Martino Behem, de Nurenberg, par la main du très
" puiffant feigneur roi Jean fecond de Portugal, roi d'Algarve, roi d'Afrique et roi de
" Guinée; et fon premier ecuyer etoit le roi lui-même, qui mit fon épée à fon ceinturon; et
" le duc de Begia étoit fon fecond ecuyer qui lui mit fon éperon droit; et fon troifième
" ecuyer étoit le comte Chriftophe de Mela coufin du roi, qui lui mit fon éperon gauche; et
" fon quatrieme ecuyer étoit le comte Martini Marbarinis, qui lui mit fon cafque de fer; et
" le roi lui donna lui-même un coup fur l'epaule; ce qui fe paffa en préfence de tous les princes
" et de tous les feigneurs et chevaliers du royaume ; et il a efpoufé la fille d'un grand feigneur
                                            " en

" efpoufed the daughter of a great lord, in confideration
" of the important fervices he had performed, and he was
" made governor of the ifland of Fayal." Thefe marks
of diftinction conferred on a ftranger, could not be meant
as a recompence for the difcovery of the Azores, which was
made 20 years before; but as a reward for the difcovery of
Congo, from whence the chevalier Behem had brought gold
and different kinds of precious wares. This difcovery made
much greater impreffion than that of a weftern world, made
at the fame time, but it neither increafed the wealth of the
royal treafury, nor fatisfied the avarice of the merchants.

In 1492 the chevalier Behem, crowned with honors
and riches, undertook a journey to Nurenberg, to vifit his
native country and his family. He there made a ter-
reftrial globe, which is looked on as a mafter-piece for
that time, and which is ftill preferved in the library of
that city. The tract of his difcoveries may there be feen
under the name of weftern lands, and from their fituation
it cannot be doubted, that they are the prefent coafts of
Brazil and the environs of the ftraits of Magellan. This
globe was made in the fame year that Columbus fat out
on his expedition, from whence it is not poffible that
Behem could have profited by the works of this navigator, who befides, went a much more northerly courfe.

After having performed feveral other interefting voyages, the chévelier Behem died at Lifbon in July 1506,
regretted

" en confidération des fervices qu'il a rendus, et il a été fait gouverneur de l'ifle de Fayal."
Cette grande diftinction accordée à un étranger, ne pouvoit être la recompenfe de la decouverte
des Açores, qui avoit eu lieu plus de 20 ans auparavant ; mais elle étoit le pris de la decouverte
du Congo, d'ou le chevalier Behem avoit apporté de l'or et plufieurs marchandifes précieufes.
Cette decouverte fit beaucoup plus d'impreffion que celle d'une terre occidentale faite dans le
meme tems, mais qui n'offroit aucun benefice au tréfor royal ni à la cupidité des marchands.

En 1492, le chevalier Behem, comblé d'honneur et de richeffes, entreprit un voyage à Nurenberg, pour revoir fa patrie et fa famille. Il y compofa un globe terreftre, qui eft regardé
comme un chef d'œuvre de fon tems, et qui eft encore confervé dans la bibiliotheque de cette
ville.   On y voit la trace de fes decouvertes fous le nom de terres occidentales, et par leur fituation on ne peut difconvenir qu'elles ne foient les cotes actuelles du Brefil et les environs du
détroit de Magellan.   Ce globe eft fait dans la même année où Colomb a commencé fon
expedition ; il eft donc impoffible que Behem ait profité du travail de ce navigateur, qui d'ailleurs a dirigé fa courfe beaucoup plus au nerd.

Après avoir achevé plufieurs autres voyages intéreffans, le chevalier Behem mourut à Lif-
bonne

regretted by every body, but leaving behind him no other work than the globe which we have juft been fpeaking of. It is made from the writings of Ptolemy, Pliny, Strabo, and efpecially from the account of Mark Paul the Venetian, a celebrated traveller of the XIIIth century, and of John Mandeville, an Englifhman, who, about the middle of the XIVth century, publifhed an account of a journey of 33 years in Africa and Afia. He has alfo added the important difcoveries made by himfelf on the coafts of Africa and America.

From thefe circumftantial accounts, little known to modern writers, we muft conclude that *Martin Behenira*, of whom Garcilaffo makes mention, is the fame chevalier Behem, upon being the place of whofe birth Nurenberg prides itfelf fo much. It is probable, that as foon as he was knighted in Portugal, he thought it neceffary to give a Portuguefe termination to his name, to make it more fonorous and more conformable to the idiom of the country. Garcilaffo, deceived by this refemblance of found, has made him a Spaniard, in order to deprive Chriftopher Columbus of the honor of having procured to his country fo great an advantage. And what ought to confirm us in this opinion is, that we neither find in Mariana nor any other Spanifh hiftorian, the name of this Martin Behemira, who was certainly a man of too much importance not to have had a diftinguifhed place in hiftory. Befides, the Spanifh pride

bonne en Juillet 1506, generalement regretté, mais ne laiffant à la pofterité d'autre ouvrage que le globe dont nous venons de parler. Il eft fait d'après les ecrits de Ptolomée, de Pline, de Straton, et furtout d'après les relations du Venitien Marc Paul, voyageur celebre du XIII fiecle, et de Jean Mandeville, Anglois, qui au milieu du XIV fiecle a publié les détails d'un voyage de 33 années en Afrique et en Afie; il y a ajouté, les grandes decouvertes qu'il a faites lui-même fur les cotes d'Afrique et d'Amérique.

D'après ces détail peu connus des écrivains modernes, nous devons conclure que *Martin Behenira*, dont Garcilaffo fait mention, eft ce même chevalier Behem que la ville de Nurenberg fe glorifie d'avoir vu naitre dans fes murailles. Il eft vraifemblable qu'au moment où il fut creé chevalier en Portugal, il a cru devoir donner une terminaifon Portugaife à fon nom, pour le rendre plus fonore et plus conforme à l'idiome du pays. Garcilaffo trompé par cette reffemblance de fon, en a fait un Efpagnol pour enlever à Chriftophe Colomb la gloire d'avoir procuré à fa metropole un auffi grande acquifition. Ce qui doit nous confirmer dans cette opinion, c'eft que nous ne trouvons ni dans Mariana ni dans aucun autre hiftorien Efpagnol le nom de ce *Martin Behenira* qui auroit dû être un homme trop important pour ne pas occuper

pride would have been flattered in giving to a native thofe laurels with which it crowned Chriftopher Columbus.

It is then very unlikely, that this navigator was treated as an enthufiaft, when he offered to the court of Portugal to make difcoveries in the weft. The fearch after unknown countries was at that time the reigning paſſion of this court; and even if the chevalier Behem had not offered the interefting ideas which he had procured, the novelty of the project had undoubtedly engaged king John to give into the views of Columbus; but it appears that this prince declined it, becaufe all his thoughts were turned at that time to the coaft of Africa, and the new paffage to the Indies, from whence he promifed himfelf great riches; whilft the fouthern coaft of Brazil and the territories of the Patagonians, feen by Behem, offered to him only barren lands, inhabited by unconquerable favages. The refufal of John II. very far from weakening the teftimony of Behem's difcoveries, is then rather a proof of the knowledge, which this politic prince had already procured, of the exiftence of a new continent; and it was only in 1501, that is to fay three years after the voyage of Vafco de Gama to the Indies, that Emanuel thought proper to take advantage of the difcoveries of Behem, by fending Albarez Cabral to Brazil; a meafure which was perhaps rather owing to the jealoufy which has always exifted between Portugal and
Spain,

cuper une place diftinguée dans l'hiftoire. La fierté Efpagnole auroit d'ailleurs été flattée d'accorder à un national les lauriers dont elle a couronné Chriftophe Colomb.

Il eft donc peu vraifemblable que ce navigateur ait été traité comme un extravagant quand il offrit à la cour de Portugal de faire des découvertes dans l'oueft. La recherche des pays inconnus étoit alors la paffion dominante de cette cour, et quand même le chevalier Behem n'auroit pas donné les notions importantes qu'il s'étoit procurées, la nouveauté du projet eut indubitablement engagé le roi Jean à fe prêter aux vues de Colomb; mais il paroît que ce prince s'y eft refufé, puifque toutes fes vues portoient alors fur la cote d'Afrique et le nouveau paffage dans l'Inde, d'où il fe promettoit de tirer de grandes richeffes, tandifque les cotes meridionales du Brefil et la terre des Patagons, vues par Behem, ne lui offroient que des terres fteriles, habitées par des fauvages incomptables. Le refus de Jean II. bien loin d'affoiblir l'evidence des découvertes de Behem, eft donc plutot une preuve des connoiffances que ce prince habile s'étoit déja procurées fur l'exiftence d'un nouveau continent; et ce n'eft qu'en 1501, c'eft à dire trois ans après l'expedition de Vafco de Gama dans l'Inde, qu'Emanuel jugea à propos de tirer parti des découvertes de Behem, en envoyant au Brefil Albarez Cabral; mefure qui étoit peut être plutot une fuite de cette jaloufie qui a toujours exifté entre
le

Spain, than to a defire of making advantageous eſtabliſh-
ments, for which the Indies were much more proper than
this part of America.

If any doubts yet remain reſpecting the important difcovery made by the chevalier Behem, it is particularly
the authority of Dr. Robertſon, which attacks the teſti-
mony of the different authors we have tranſcribed. This
learned writer treats the hiſtory of Behem as a fiction of
ſome German authors, who had an inclination to attribute to one of their countrymen, a diſcovery, which has
produced ſo great a revolution in the commerce of Europe.
But he acknowledges nevertheleſs, with Herrera, that Behem had ſettled at the iſland of Fayal, that he was the
intimate friend of Chriſtopher Columbus, and that Magellan had a globe made by Behem, by the help of which
he undertook his voyage to the South ſea; a circumſtance
which proves much in favor of our hypotheſis. He relates alſo, that in 1492, this aſtronomer paid a viſit to his
family at Nurenberg, and left there a map drawn by him-
ſelf, which Dr. Forſter procured him a copy of, and
which, in his opinion, partakes of the imperfection of the
coſmographical knowledge of the fifteenth century; that
he found in it, indeed, under the name of the iſland of St.
Brandon, land which appears to be the preſent coaſt of
Guiana, and lies in the latitude of cape Verd, but that
there is reaſon to believe, that this fabulous iſland, which

N n   is

le Portugal et l'Eſpagne, que du deſir de faire des établiſſemens avantageux aux quels l'Inde
étoit beaucoup plus propre que cette partie de l'Amerique.
    S'il nous eſt permis de douter encore de l'importante decouverte faite par le chevalier Be-
hem, c'eſt ſurtout l'autorité du Dr. Robertſon, qui doit porter atteinte aux témoignages des
différens auteurs que nous avons tranſcrits.   Ce ſavant écrivain traite l'hiſtoire de Behem
comme une fiction de quelques auteurs Allemans, qui deſiroient d'attribuer à un de leurs com-
patriotes une decouverte qui a produit une ſi grande revolution dans le commerce de l'Europe.
Mais il avoue cependant, d'après Herrera, que Behem étoit établi à l'iſle de Fayal, qu'il étoit
l'ami intime de Chriſtophe Colomb, et que Magellan avoit eu un globe compoſé par Behem, d'après
lequel il avoit entrepris ſon expedition dans la mer du Sud ; circonſtance qui prouve beaucoup
en faveur de notre hypotheſe.   Il rapporte de plus qu'en 1492, cet aſtronome a été voir ſa
famille à Nurenberg, et qu'il y a laiſſé une carte delinée par lui-même ; que le Dr. Forſter
lui a procuré une copie de cette carte, qui ſuivant lui ſe reſſent de l'imperfection des connoiſ-
ſances coſmographiques du XV ſiecle ; qu'il y a trouvé à la verité ſous le nom de l'iſle de St.
Brandon, une terre qui paroit être la cote actuelle de la Guyane, et qui eſt placée dans la la-
                                                                                    titude

is found in many ancient maps, merits no more attention
than the childish legend of St. Brandon himself. Although
Dr. Robertson does not appear difpofed to grant to Behem
the honor of having difcovered the new continent, we find
the means of refuting him in his own hiftory. He allows
that Behem was very intimate with Chriftopher Columbus,
that he was the greateft geographer of his time, and fcholar of the celebrated John Muller or Regiomontanus ; that
he had difcovered, in 1483, the kingdom of Congo upon
the coaft of Africa ; that he made a globe, which Magellan made ufe of; that he drew a map at Nurenberg containing the particulars of his difcoveries, and that he
placed in this chart land which is found to be in the latitude of Guiana. Dr. Robertfon afferts, without any proof,
that this land was but a fabulous ifland; we may fuppofe,
upon the fame foundation, that the chevalier Behem, engaged in an expedition to the kingdom of Congo, was
driven by the winds to Fernambouc, and from thence, by
the currents, very common in thofe latitudes, towards the
coaft of Guiana ; and that he took for an ifland the firft
land which he difcovered. The courfe which Chriftopher
Columbus afterwards fteered, makes this fuppofition ftill
more probable ; for if he knew only of the coaft of Brazil,
which they believe to have been difcovered by Behem, he
would have laid his courfe rather to the fouth-weft. The
expedition

titude du cap Verd; mais qu'il y a lieu de croire, que cette ifle fabuleufe, qui fe trouve fur plufieurs anciennes cartes, ne merite pas plus d'attention que la legende puerile de St. Brandon
lui-même. Quoique le Dr. Robertfon ne paroiffe pas difpofé d'accorder à Behem la gloire
d'avoir decouvert le nouveau continent, nous trouvons dans fon hiftoire même des armes pour
le combattre. Il convient que Behem étoit très lié avec Chriftophe Colomb, qu'il étoit le
plus grand geographe de fon tems, et difciple du celebre Jean Muller ou Regiomontanus;
qu'il a decouvert en 1483, le royaume de Congo, fur la cote d'Afrique; qu'il a compofé un
globe dont s'eft fervi Magellan ; qu'il a deffiné à Nurenberg, une carte contenant des détails
fur fes decouvertes, et qu'il a marqué fur cette carte une terre qui fe trouve dans la latitude
de la Guyane actuelle. Le docteur Robertfon admet fans aucune preuve, que cette terre
n'étoit qu'une ifle fabuleufe ; nous pouvons fuppofer avec autant de fondement, que le chevalier Behem faifant fon expedition dans le royaume de Congo, ait été pouffé par les vents vers
Fernambouc, et de là par des courans très communs dans ces parages vers les cotes de la
Guyane, et qu'il ait pris pour une ifle la premiere terre qui s'eft offerte à fes yeux. La route
qu'a pris dans la fuite Chriftophe Colomb rend cette fuppofition encore plus vraifemblable,
car s'il n'avoit eu connoiffance que des cotes du Brefil, que l'on croit avoir été reconnues par
Behem, il auroit dirigé fa navigation plutôt vers le fud-oueft. L'expedition au Congo a eu
lieu

expedition to Congo took place in 1483 ; it is then poffible, that, at his return, Behem propofed a voyage to the
coafts of Brazil and Patagonia, and that he requefted the
affiftance of his fovereign, which we have mentioned
above.   It is certain, that we cannot have too much deference for the opinion of fo eminent a writer as Robertfon, but this learned man not having it in his power to
confult the German pieces in the original, which we have
quoted, we may be allowed to form a different opinion
without being too prefumptuous.

But fhould it be afked, why we take from Chriftopher
Columbus the reputation which all Europe has to this day
allowed him? Why we are fearching in the archives of
an imperial city, for the caufes of an event which took
place in the moft weftern extremity of Europe? Why the
enemies of Chriftopher Columbus, who were numerous,
did not take advantage of the pretended chevr. Behem,
to leffen his confequence at the Spanifh court? Why Portugal, jealous of the difcovery of the new world, had not
protefted againft the affertions of the Spaniards? Why
Behem, who died only in 1506, had not left to pofterity
any writing to confirm to himfelf fo important a difcovery?

To anfwer all thefe queftions, I fhall fubmit to the impartial reader, the following remarks:

N n 2   1. Before

---

lieu en 1483, il eft donc poffible qu'à fon retour Behem ait projetté une expedition vers les
cotes du Brefil et des Patagons, et qu'il ait demandé à fon fouverain les fecours dont nous
avous parlé plus haut. Il eft fur qu'on ne fauroit avoir trop de déference pour l'opinion d'un
écrivain tel que Robertfon, mais ce favant n'ayant pu avoir connoiffance des pieces Alle-
mandes originales que nous avous citées, nous pouvons avoir un avis different du fien fans
nous rendre coupable de prefomption.

Mais, dira-ton, pourquoi enlever à Chriftophe Colomb une gloire que toute l'Europe lui a
accordée jufqu'ici? Pourquoi chercher dans les archives d'une ville imperiale les caufes d'un
évenement qui a eu lieu à l'extremité la plus occidentale de l'Europe? Pourquoi les ennemis
de Chriftophe Colomb, qui étoient en grand nombre, n'ont ils pas tiré parti des prétendues
decouvertes du Chevalier Behem pour diminuer fon importance à la cour d'Efpagne? Pourquoi le Portugal, jaloux de la decouverte du nouveau monde, n'at'il pas protefté contre les
affertions des Efpagnols? Pourquoi Behem qui n'eft mort qu'en 1506, n'at'il pas laiffé lui
même à la pofterité un écrit pour s'attribuer une decouverte auffi importante?

Pour repondre à toutes ces queftions je foumettrai au lecteur impartial les remarques
fuivantes:

1. Avant

1. Before Columbus, the great merit of a navigator confifted rather in conceiving the poffibility of the exiftence of a new continent, than in fearching for lands in a region where he was fure to find them. If it is then certain that Behem had conceived this bold idea before Columbus, the fame of the latter muft be confiderably diminifhed.

2. The hiftorical proofs, which we have given above, leaving us no doubt of the fact, we have only to explain the moral caufes of the filence of the Spanifh and Portuguefe authors, of the enemies of Columbus, and of Behem himfelf.

3. It is well known, that previous to the reign of Charles V. there was little communication between the learned men of different nations. Writers were fcarce, excepting fome monks who have related, well or ill, the events which came to their knowledge, in chronicles which are no longer read; or they had but little idea of what paffed in foreign countries. Gazettes and journals were unknown, and the learned obliged to travel to inform themfelves of the progrefs of their neighbours. Italy was the center of the arts and what are called fcience at that time. The frequent journies of the German emperors to Rome gave them an opportunity of knowing perfons of merit, and of placing them in the different univerfities of the empire. It is to this circumftance that we

ought

---

1. Avant Colomb le grand merite d'un navigateur confiftoit plutôt à conçevoir la poffibilité de l'exiftence d'un nouveau continent, qu'à chercher des terres dans une region où il etoit fur d'en trouver. S'il eft donc certain que Behem a eu cette idée hardie avant Colomb, la gloire de ce dernier en eft fingulierement diminuée.

2. Toutes les preuves hiftoriques que nous avons donnés ci deffus ne nous laiffent aucun doute fur le fait, il s'agit feulement d'expliquer les caufes morales du filence des auteurs Efpagnols et Portugais, des ennemis de Colomb, et de Behem lui-même.

3. On fait qu'avant Charles quint il y avoit très peu de communication entre les favans des differentes nations. Les ecrivains étoient fort rares, à l'exception de quelques moines qui ont rapporté bien ou mal les evenemens qui étoient à leur portée dans des chroniques qu'on ne lit plus, ou n'avoit que peu de notions fur ce qui fe paffoit en pays étranger ; les gazettes, les journaux étoint inconnus, et les favans étoient obligés de voyager pour voir de leurs propres yeux les progrés de leurs voifins. L'Italie étoit le centre des arts et de ce qu'on appelloit fcience dans ce tems-là. Les frequens voyages des empereurs d'Allemagne à Rome leur donna la facilité de connoitre des gens de merite, et de les placer dans les differentes univerfités

de

ought to attribute the great progrefs which the Germans made, particularly in mathematics, from the fourteenth to the fixteenth century; during which time they had the beft geographers, the beft hiftorians, and the moft enlightened politicians. They were particularly attentive to what paffed in Europe, and the multiplied conne&ions of different princes with foreign powers, affifted them greatly in colle&ing in their archives the original pieces of the moft important events of Europe. It is to this fpirit of criticifm and enquiry, that we are indebted for the reformation of Luther, and we cannot deny, that particularly in the fifteenth century, there was more hiftorical and political knowledge in Germany than in all the reft of Europe, Italy excepted. It is not then aftonifhing, that we fhould find, in the archives of one of the moft ancient imperial cities, the particulars of an expedition, planned upon the banks of the Tagus by a German, a man of great repute in his own country, and whofe every a&ion became very interefting.

4. It was different in Portugal, where the whole nation, except the king, was plunged in the moft profound ignorance. Every body was either fhopkeeper, failor or foldier; and if this nation has made the moft important difcoveries, we muft afcribe them rather to avarice than to a defire of knowledge. They were fatisfied with fcraping

ing

de l'empire. C'eft à cette circonftance que l'on doit attribuer les grands progrés que les Allemans ont faits furtout dans les mathematiques, depuis le XIV. jufqu'au XVI. fiecle; ils avoient les meilleurs géographes, les meilleurs hiftoriens et les politiques les plus éclairés. Ils étoient attentifs fur tout ce qui fe paffoit en Europe, et les liaifons multipliées des differens princes avec les puiffances étrangeres, leur donnoient une grande facilité de raffembler, dans leurs archives, les pieces originales des evenemens les plus importans de l'Europe. C'eft a cet efprit de critique et de recherche qu'eft due en grande partie la reformation de Luther, et on ne peut fe diffimuler, que, furtout dans le XV. fiecle, il n'y ait eu plus de connoiffances hiftoriques et politiques en Allemagne que dans tout le refte de l'Europe, à l'exception de l'Italie. Il n'eft donc pas étonnant que nous trouvions dans les archives d'une des plus anciennes villes imperiales des détails fur une expedition, projetté fur les bords du Tage par un Allemand, par un homme très confidéré dans fon pays, et dont par confequent toutes les demarches devenoient intereffantes.

4. Il n'en étoit pas de même du Portugal, où toute la nation à l'exception du fouverain, étoit plongée dans la plus profonde ignorance. Tout le monde y étoit ou marchand, ou matelot, ou foldat; et fi ce peuple a fait les decouvertes les plus importantes, il faut en chercher le motif dans fa cupidité, et non dans fon defir de s'inftruire. Il fe contenta d'amaffer de l'or

dans

ing together gold in every quarter of the known world,
whilft the German and the Italian took up the pen, to
tranfmit to pofterity the remembrance of their riches and
cruelties. The Spaniards were not much more informed
before Charles V. introduced at Madrid the learned men
of Flanders and Germany. It is then very poffible, that
the chevr. Behem made very interefting difcoveries in
geography, in 1485, without the public's being acquainted with them. If he had brought back from his expedition, gold or diamonds, the noife would have been fpread
in a few weeks; but fimple geographical knowledge was
not of a nature to intereft men of this turn of mind.

5. The long ftay which Chriftopher Columbus made
at Madeira, makes his interview with Behem more than
probable. It is impoffible that he fhould have negleted
feeing a man fo interefting, and who could give him every
kind of information, for the execution of the plan which
he had formed. The mariners who accompanied the
chevr. Behem, might alfo have fpread reports at Madeira
and the Azores, concerning the difcovery which they had
been witneffes of. What ought to confirm us in this, is,
that *Mariana* fays himfelf (book 26. chap. III.) that a *certain* veffel going to Africa, was thrown by a gale of wind
upon certain unknown lands, and that the failors at their
return to Madeira had communicated to Chriftopher Columbus

dans toutes les parties du monde connu, tandifque l'Allemand et l'Italien tenoient la plume
pour tranfmettre à la pofterité le fouvenir de fes richeffes et de fes cruautés. Les Efpagnols
n'étoient par beaucoup plus inftruits, avant que Charlesquint eut amené à Madrid des favons
de Flandres et d'Allemagne. Il eft donc très poffible que le chevalier Behem ait fait en
1485, des decouvertes très intéreffantes pour la géographie, fans que le public en ait été in-
ftruit. S'il eut rapporté de fon expedition de l'or ou des diamans, le bruit s'en feroit répandu
en peu de femaines, mais de fimples notions géographiques n'étoient pas de nature à intéref-
fer des hommes de cette trempe.
    5. Le long féjour qu'a fait Chriftophe Colomb à Madere, rend fon entrevue avec Behem
plus que vraifemblable. Il eft impoffible qu'il ait négligé de voir un homme auff intéreffant,
et qui pouvoit lui donner toutes fortes de confeils fur l'execution du plan qu'il avoit formé.
Les marins qui ont accompagné le chevalier Behem pouvoient d'ailleurs repandre à Madere,
et aux Açores, des bruits concernant les decouvertes dont ils avoient été témoins. Ce qui
doit nous confirmer dans cette opinion, c'eft que *Mariana* dit lui-même (livre 26, chap. .)
qu'un *certain* batiment allant en Afrique, avoit été jetté par un corp de vent fur de certaines
terres inconnues; et que les matelots après leur retour à Madere, avoient communiqué à
                                                                        Chriftophe

Iumbus the circumftances of their voyage. All authors agree that this learned man had fome information refpecting the weftern fhores, but they fpeak in a very vague manner. The expedition of the chevr. Behem explains this myftery.

6. This aftronomer could not be jealous of the difcoveries of Columbus, becaufe the laft had been farther north, and that in a time when they did not know the whole extent of the new world, and when geographical knowledge was extremely bounded, it might be believed, that the country difcovered by Columbus, had no connection with that difcovered by Behem.

It appears however, certain, that Behem difcovered this continent before Columbus, and that this queftion, which is only curious in Europe, becomes interefting to the American patriot. The Grecians have carefully preferved the fabulous hiftory of their firft founders, and have raifed altars to them; why are not Behem, Chriftopher Columbus and Vefpucius, deferving of ftatues, in the public fquares of American cities? Thefe precious monuments would tranfmit to pofterity the gratitude which the names of thefe benefactors of mankind fhould infpire. Without knowing it, they have laid the foundation of the happinefs of many millions of inhabitants; and Sefoftris, Phul, Cyrus, Thefeus and Romulus, the founders of the

greateft

Chriftophe Colomb les circonftances de leur navigation. Tous les auteurs s'accordent en général, que ce favant avoit eu quelques renfeignemens fur des terres occidentales, mais ils ne nous en parlent que d'une manière très vague. L'expedition du chevalier Behem nous explique ce myftere.

6. Cet aftronome ne pouvoit être jaloux des decouvertes de Colomb, puifque celui-ci a été beaucoup plus nord; et que dans un tems où l'on ne connoiffoit par toute l'étendue du nouveau monde, et où les connoiffances géographiques étoient extrêmement bornées, ou pouvoit croire que le pays trouvé par Colomb n'avoit aucun rapport avec celui de Behem.

Quoiqu'il en foit, il paroit certain que Behem a decouvert ce continent avant Colomb, et que cette queftion qui n'eft que de pure curiofité en Europe, devient intéreffante pour le patriote Américain. Les Grecs ont confervé foigneufement l'hiftoire fabuleufe de leurs premieres fondateurs, ils leur ont élevé des autels; pourquoi Behem, Chriftophe Colomb et Vefpuce ne mériteroient'-ils pas des ftatues fur les places publiques des villes Américaines? Ces monumens précieux tranfmettroient à la pofterité la reconnoiffance que doivent infpirer les noms de ces bienfaiteurs du genre humain. Sans le favoir ils ont jetté les fondemens du bonheur de plufieurs millions d'habitans; et Sefoftris, Phul, Cyrus, Thefée, Romulus, les

fondateurs

greateſt empires, will be forgotten, before the ſervices rendered by theſe illuſtrious navigators can be effaced from
the memory of man.

fondateurs des plus grands empires, feront oubliés, avant que les fervices rendus par ces navigateurs illuſtres, puiſſent s'effacer de la memoire des hommes.

N° XXXVI.

*The antiſeptic Virtues of Vegetable Acid and Marine Salt
combined, in various Diſorders accompanied with Pu-
tridity ; communicated in a Letter to* JOHN MORGAN,
*M. D. F. R. S. and Profeſſor of the Theory and Practice
of Phyſic at Philadelphia, by* WILLIAM WRIGHT, M.
D. of Trelawney in Jamaica.

HAVING experienced the virtues of vegetable acid
and marine ſalt, when combined ; I beg leave to
lay before you a few obſervations on the uſe of this ſimple
medicine in ſeveral diſeaſes.   It is my ſincere wiſh, that
it may prove as beneficial to mankind in general, as it has
been to many of my patients in this part of the country.

Take of lime-juice or lemon-juice three ounces, of marine ſalt as much as the acid will diſſolve ; of any ſimple
diſtilled cordial water one pint ; and of loaf ſugar a ſufficient quantity to ſweeten it.   The doſe of this mixture
muſt be proportioned to the age, ſex, and violence of the
diſeaſe.   A wine glaſs-ful may be given to adults every
two, four or ſix hours.

By Geoffroy's table it appears, that the foſſil alkali has
a greater affinity with the marine, than with the vegetable acid.   However, marine ſalt diſſolves readily in the
lime-juice, throws up a white ſcum to the ſurface, and on
applying the ear near the veſſel where the experiment is
made, a ſmall hiſſing may be heard, ſimilar to that when
acids

acids and alkalies are mixed. It would feem probable that part of the marine falt is hereby decompofed.

That vegetable acids and marine falt are antifeptics, has long been known, but their effects when mixed I apprehend to be but lately difcovered.

Without farther preface, I fhall proceed to the particular difeafes in which they have been adminiftered, prepared as above.

Of the DYSENTERY.

The dyfentery is a very frequent diforder in this and other Weft-India iflands; and fometimes is epidemic, particularly in the rainy feafons, or when provifions are fcarce. Amongft other caufes of dyfenteries, I have often known the eating of yams not arrived at maturity, as alfo unripe alligator pears, produce a bloody flux.

Dyfenteries commonly begin with frequent loofe ftools for a day or two, attended with gripings: by degrees, the gripes grow more fevere, nothing is voided by ftool but a fmall quantity of mucus, mixed with blood ; a tenefmus comes on and is exceedingly troublefome.

The appetite fails, the patients are low fpirited, and fuffer a great proftration of ftrength. The mouth and tongue are much furred and flimy, and the tafte is like that of rotten butchers meat. The defire of drink is fometimes exceffive, but for the moft part very moderate. The pulfe is very low, feeble and undulating; and rarely rifes fo high, as to indicate the ufe of a lancet. Such was the dyfentery in 1771. It proved fatal to many people, both old and young, though treated according to the moft approved methods of cure, and the lofs of feveral patients of mine, convinced me of the neceffity of ufing antifeptics early in this difeafe.

A vomit feemed neceffary to clear the ftomach, and fome gentle purge, to carry off part of the offending mat-

ter

ter by ſtool. But the action of theſe, however mild, often increaſed the proſtration of ſtrength, and rendered the ſtools ſooner bloody. Nor was opium of any real uſe. A tea made of Simarouba and given to ſome, had a very ſalutary effect, whilſt, if given to others, it would by no means lye on their ſtomachs.

From a conſideration of the antiſeptic quality of both the ſal: marin: and of the vegetable acid, I was induced to make trial of their effects united in the manner above mentioned. It acted like a charm, and I find that from the uſe of it, the frequency of ſtools, gripes and teneſmus, have ſoon worn off; the ſtools gradually become of a natural conſiſtence and quantity; the ſpirits, ſtrength and appetite returned, and the patient has been reſtored to perfect health in a very few days.

When the dyſentery was of long ſtanding, ſtarch clyſters, with a ſmall portion of opium, abated the teneſmus.

This medicine was equally ſerviceable in diarrhœas.

DIABETES.

As I had ſucceeded ſo well in the cure of dyſenteries, I was determined to try its effects in the diabetes : ſeveral opportunities ſoon offered; but as theſe caſes were accompanied with other complaints, eſpecially with fevers of the remitting kind, it will be proper firſt to ſpeak of

THE REMITTENT FEVER.

This by far the moſt common fever within the tropics, is the leaſt underſtood, and conſequently for the moſt part badly treated. Strangers, who walk much, or work hard in the heat of the ſun, are more ſubject to it than ſeaſoned Europeans or natives of the country.

Dr. Cleghorn's deſcription of this fever is accurate and juſt. His method of cure, ſimple and eaſy. Every phyſician

fician, who would wifh to practice with fuccefs, fhould be well acquainted with that valuable performance, as alfo with what Dr. Lind has faid on the fubject.

It is then fufficient here, to obferve that remittent fevers are often attended with diarrhœas, the diabetes, and fometimes with a copious difcharge of faliva, as if mercury had been previoufly given. In fuch circumftances I never found the bark of fervice; a few glaffes of the above mixture fully anfwered the intention, not only by removing thefe fymptoms, but the fever at the fame time.

The Peruvian bark afterwards, taken out of fome of the fame mixture, effectually fecured the patient from a return of this dangerous malady.

The mixture rarely acted as an aftringent in this or any other diforder. But when this effect took place, the interpofition of fome lenient purge was deemed neceffary.

BELLY-ACH.

The belly-ach with inflammatory fymptoms has frequently occured in the courfe of my practice; they yielded with difficulty to bleeding, fmall dofes of emetic tartar, a mercurial pill, repeated dofes of caftor oil, diluting drinks, with nitre, fomentations and glyfters. A copious difcharge of fœtid excrement for the moft part gives immediate relief.

I have obferved in many cafes, after moft excruciating bellya-chs, that the ftools were liquid, white, fmall in quantity, and very fœtid. The patients being worn out with pain, grew difpondent, did not care to fpeak, fell into cold clammy fweats and were very reftlefs. They complained of an ill tafte in their mouths. Their tongues were much furred. Their breath offenfive, and they had a great propenfity to vomit.

Formerly I attempted the relief of thofe threatening fymptoms with the bark, in various forms, as well as

claret,

claret, and often faved my patient; fometimes however
I failed of fuccefs.   When fuch cafes fall now under my
care, I have immediate recourfe to the antifeptic mixture ;
nor have I been hitherto difappointed : the ftools becoming lefs frequent on the ufe of it, and of a better confiftence ; the cold fweats alfo difappear, and the fpirits foon
return, together with an appetite for food.

The PUTRID SORE THROAT.

In June 1770, the putrid fore throat made confiderable
havock amongft adults and children.   It attacked thofe of
a lax habit, who for a few days had flight head-achs,
chillinefs and heats alternately, and an uneafinefs about
their throats, but not fo much as to hinder their fwal-
lowing.

On examination, the mouth, tongue and gums were
foul and flimy ; the tonfils and uvula covered with white
fpecks or floughs ; the breath was hot and offenfive ; the
fkin felt hot and pungent to the touch; the pulfe low and
quick ; a diarrhœa often attended, and the patients were
in general much dejected.

Antimonial wine with cordials and nourifhing diet fucceeded beft, till the floughs or fpots were removed and
feparated ; then the bark completed the cure.   When a
diarrhœa accompanied this diforder, I gave the mixture
with fuccefs.

In all diforders where a gargle is neceffary, I make ufe
of the above mixture in preference to any other ; and I
find it fpeedily cleanfes the tongue, gums and fauces, and
fweetens the breath.

Where lemons or limes cannot be had, vinegar or
cremor tartar may be fubftituted in their room.

From what has been faid, it is evident, that the medicine is poffeffed of confiderable antifeptic powers, and its
virtue

virtue confifts in correcting the peccant matter in the ftomach and inteftinal canal.

All the difeafes in which I have given it, had a putrid tendency. I fhall be happy to hear of its fuccefs in your weftern hemifphere.

And am, with efteem,

SIR,

Your moft humble fervant,

WILLIAM WRIGHT.

N° XXXVII.

Medical Hiftory of the Cortex Ruber, or Red Bark; communicated to JOHN MORGAN, M. D. Profeffor of the Theory and Practice of Phyfic at Philadelphia, and F. R. S. London, &c.

^{Read Feb.}
^{20, 1784.} I HAVE lately received the following communications upon the Cortex Ruber, which I have found fo efficacious in the cure of obftinate remittent and bilious fevers, that I think it my duty to lay them before this fociety, in hopes of fo valuable a medicine being thereby better known, and introduced more generally into practice.

Extract of a Letter from Thomas S. Duché, *dated London, Auguft 9, 1783.*

" I was lately at a lecture delivered at Guy's hofpital, by Dr. Saunders, upon the cure of intermittent fevers, and obferving the doctor fpoke very much in favour of a new fpecies of bark which he had introduced into the practice of phyfic, I procured a fpecimen of it for you, thinking

thinking it might be agreeable to you to hear of any new improvements in the healing art. It is called *Red Bark*. According to his account it poffeffes fo much virtue, and is of fuch certain efficacy, that, compared with it, the common bark is an inert mafs. It contains a much larger portion of refin, has a much ftronger aromatic tafte than the common bark, and does not require half the quantity for a dofe. Amongft other particulars, he mentioned the following proof of its fuperior virtue, namely, that of this medicine, when adminiftered in a fimple cold infufion, any given quantity is much ftronger and effectual to remove the fever than a chemical extract from the fame quantity of the other. I now fend you a fpecimen, by which you will be able to make a trial and form fome judgment of its virtues."

T. S. Duché.

Soon after the receipt of the foregoing letter, I received the following valuable communication from Dr. George Davidfon of St. Lucia, which it affords me great pleafure to lay before this fociety.

St. Lucia, Auguft 29, 1783.

To Doctor John Morgan, at Philadelphia.

Sir,
IF the fubject upon which I have the honour to write you, fhould be found to merit attention, and prove in any refpect ufeful and advantageous to mankind, I fhall eafily ftand excufed in addreffing you, perfonally unacquainted as I am.

I have by this opportunity fent a fmall fpecimen of the Cinchona of this ifland, refembling the Peruvian bark in its botanical character, and from the trial made here furpaffing it in medical virtues. It is now nearly four years fince the Caribæan bark was difcovered upon the heights
adjoining

adjoining Morne Fortuné, and introduced into practice by
Dr. Young, phyfician to his Britannic majefty's troops.
The frefhnefs of the bark, the little attention beftowed in
drying it, and the large dofes in which it was exhibited,
produced alarming fits of vomiting and purging, and de-
terred us, at that time, from the further profecution of the
fubject, until the other day that a treatife upon the red
bark, by Dr. Saunders of London, and a belief which we
entertained that this was the fame bark which he defcribes,
induced us again to make a trial of it.   Having properly
dried it, and given it in the cold infufion with greater
caution and in lefs dofes than at the firft effay, we are now
happy in affuring the public, that in moft inftances it has
not difappointed us.   Still, however, notwithftanding the
utmoft care in drying it, in fome cafes it ftill feems to retain its emetic and purgative qualities, as the ftomach and
firft paffages, in complaints here, are loaded with a quantity of putrid bile.   Thefe are not its leaft valuable properties.   It will, however, be neceffary when thefe effects
are produced, to check them afterwards by opiates.

With regard to its preparations: I have generally given
it in the cold infufion either made with lime or cinnamon
water.   An extract made with fpirits and water fits eafily on the ftomach and can be given in larger quantities.

In fome late cafes of tertians, where I have been called to the patient during the fecond fit; without watch-
ing for its going off, I have begun with this bark, which
effectually cleanfed the ftomach and bowels, and paved
the way for its future adminiftration.

In putrid dyfenteries, and in a remarkable fpecies of
dyfentery, conjoined with an intermittent fever, which I
have met with here, the bark has done more than all the
remedies which I have feen employed.   The purgative
effects which it produced enabled us to throw it in earlier; the hardened fcybula, the fupport of the difeafe, were
removed.

removed, the ftomach and bowels braced up, and, by the interpofition of opiates, the fpafms were removed.

Having fent feveral fpecimens of the bark for a trial to different parts of the continent of America, and particularly to my worthy friend Doctor Hall of Peterfburgh Virginia, I impatiently wait the refult of your trials, and will efteem myfelf particularly obliged by your communication. If you chufe, I fhall fend you fome of the young trees planted in tubs, with fome of the feeds.

Should it be found to anfwer my expectation, the pleafure refulting from the thoughts of having communicated fomething ufeful, will be to me ample enough recompenfe. I have the honor to be,

With the utmoft refpect,

Your moft obedient humble fervant,

GEORGE DAVIDSON.

P. S. Dr. Wright of Jamaica (in fifth vol. of medical commentaries,) defcribes a fpecies of Cinchona, with only one flower on a footftalk; the fame was likewife found at the Havanna. It differs in that particular from the old bark, which refembles the St. Lucia bark, in having feveral flowers on each footftalk.

The following is a Defcription of the Cinchona Caribæa Sanctæ Luciæ.

The tree is commonly found in ravines, near fprings, under the fhade of a larger tree. It delights in places well fhaded, and defended from the north-eaft trade wind. The foil is commonly a ftiff red earth with a clayey fubftratum; quantities of fmall beautiful chryftals, of a regular angular form, are found intermixed.

The tree is about the fize of the cherry tree; feldom exceeding the thicknefs of the thigh, and twenty-five feet in height.

The

The flowers begin to appear at the commencement of the rainy feafon in beautiful tufts, upon pannicles branched out in threes and fours.   I have never feen that fpecies defcribed by Jacquin and found at the Havannah, *pedunculis unifloris*.

Before the corolla is fully expanded, and the ftamina make their appearance without the tube of the corolla, the flower is white, but it afterwards turns to a beautiful purple.   Then dropping off, the germen enlarges to the fize of an hazle-nut, oblong and round.   It gradually dries, burfts in two, and fcatters the feeds, which fall to the ground and again take root.

The wood of the tree is light, fpongy, and fit for no ufeful purpofe.   It has not the bitter tafte of the bark. The leaves are very bitter, and the flowers, feeds, &c. feem to poffefs the bitternefs and aftringency in a more eminent degree.

An ounce of the bark in fine powder infufed in a quart of cold water for twenty-four hours, and the infufion afterwards filtered, appears higher coloured than a decoction made with double the quantity of the old bark.   The colour which it ftrikes with the *tinct. flor. martial.* and *fal martis*, is likewife of a deeper black.   The fpirituous tincture is of a deep red colour, and ftrikes a deep black by the addition of the preparations of iron.

The tafte of the Cinchona Caribæa is manifeftly more aftringent than the tafte of the old bark ; an inference may therefore, *à priori*, be made, that its tonic powers are greater.

The quantity of refin which it yields is much more confiderable, and an extract made with both fpirits and water, feems to poffefs the whole virtues of the bark.

N° XXXVIII.

A Letter from Dr. BENJAMIN FRANKLIN, *to* Mr. ALPHONSUS le ROY, *Member of several Academies, at Paris. Containing sundry Maritime Observations.*

At Sea, on board the London Packet, Capt. Truxton, Auguſt 1785.

SIR,

Read Dec. 2, 1785.

YOUR learned writings on the navigation of the antients, which contain a great deal of curious information; and your very ingenious contrivances for improving the modern ſails (*voilure*) of which I ſaw with great pleaſure a ſucceſsful trial on the river Seine, have induced me to ſubmit to your conſideration and judgment, ſome thoughts I have had on the latter ſubject.

Thoſe mathematicians who have endeavoured to improve the ſwiftneſs of veſſels, by calculating to find the form of leaſt reſiſtance, ſeem to have conſidered a ſhip as a body moving through one fluid only, the water; and to have given little attention to the circumſtance of her moving through another fluid, the air. It is true that when a veſſel ſails right before the wind, this circumſtance is of no importance, becauſe the wind goes with her; but in every deviation from that courſe, the reſiſtance of the air is ſomething, and becomes greater in proportion as that deviation increaſes. I wave at preſent the conſideration of thoſe different degrees of reſiſtance given by the air to that part of the hull which is above water, and confine myſelf to that given to the ſails; for their motion through the air is reſiſted by the air, as the motion of the hull through the water is reſiſted by the water, though with leſs force as the air is a lighter fluid. And to ſimplify the diſcuſſion as much as poſſible, I would ſtate one ſituation only, to wit, that of the wind upon the beam, the ſhip's courſe being directly acroſs the wind; and I would

ſuppoſe

ſuppoſe the ſail ſet in an angle of 45 degrees with the keel, as in the following figure; wherein

A B repreſents the body of the veſſel, CD the Plate IV. Figure 1. poſition of the ſail, E E E the direction of the wind, M M the line of motion. In obſerving this figure it will appear, that ſo much of the body of the veſſel as is immerſed in the water, muſt, to go forward, remove out of its way what water it meets with between the pricked lines F F. And the ſail, to go forward, muſt move out of its way all the air its whole dimenſion meets with between the pricked lines C G and D G. Thus both the fluids give reſiſtance to the motion, each in proportion to the quantity of matter contained in the dimenſion to be removed. And though the air is vaſtly lighter than the water, and there-fore more eaſily removed, yet the dimenſion being much greater its effect is very conſiderable.

It is true that in the caſe ſtated, the reſiſtance given by the air between thoſe lines to the motion of the ſail is not apparent to the eye, becauſe the greater force of the wind which ſtrikes it in the direction E E E, overpowers its effect, and keeps the ſail full in the curve a, a, a, a, a. But ſuppoſe the wind to ceaſe, and the veſſel in a calm to be impelled with the ſame ſwiftneſs by oars, the ſail would then appear filled in the contrary curve b, b, b, b, b, when prudent men would immediately perceive that the air reſiſted its motion, and would order it to be taken in.

Is there any poſſible means of diminiſhing this reſiſt-ance, while the ſame quantity of ſail is expoſed to the ac-tion of the wind, and therefore the ſame force obtained from it? I think there is, and that it may be done by di-viding the ſail into a number of parts, and placing thoſe parts in a line one behind the other; thus inſtead of one ſail extending from C to D, figure 2, if four ſails containing together the ſame quantity of canvas, were placed as in figure 3, each having one quarter of the dimenſions

menſions of the great ſail, and expoſing a quarter of its
ſurface to the wind, would give a quarter of the force; ſo
that the whole force obtained from the wind would be the
ſame, while the reſiſtance from the air would be nearly
reduced to the ſpace between the pricked lines *a b* and *c d*,
before the foremoſt ſail.

It may perhaps be doubted whether the reſiſtance from
the air would be ſo diminiſhed; ſince poſſibly each of the
following ſmall ſails having alſo air before it, which muſt
be removed, the reſiſtance on the whole would be the
ſame.

This is then a matter to be determined by experiment.
I will mention one that I many years ſince made with
ſucceſs for another purpoſe; and I will propoſe another
ſmall one eaſily made. If that too ſucceeds, I ſhould
think it worth while to make a larger, though at ſome
expence, on a river boat; and perhaps time and the improvements experience will afford, may make it applicable
with advantage to larger veſſels.

Having near my kitchen chimney a round hole of eight
inches diameter, through which was a conſtant ſteady
current of air, increaſing or diminiſhing only as the fire
increaſed or diminiſhed, I contrived to place my jack ſo
as to receive that current; and taking off the flyers, I fixed in their ſtead on the ſame pivot a round tin plate of
near the ſame diameter with the hole; and having cut it
in radial lines almoſt to the centre, ſo as to have ſix equal
vanes, I gave to each of them the obliquity of forty-five
degrees. They moved round, without the weight, by the
impreſſion only of the current of air, but too ſlowly for
the purpoſe of roaſting. I ſuſpected that the air ſtruck by
the back of each vane might poſſibly by its reſiſtance retard the motion; and to try this, I cut each of them into
two, and I placed the twelve, each having the ſame obliquity, in a line behind each other, when I perceived a great
augmentation in its velocity, which encouraged me to divide

vide them once more, and, continuing the fame obliquity, I placed the twenty-four behind each other in a line, when the force of the wind being the fame, and the furface of vane the fame, they moved round with much greater rapidity, and perfectly anfwered my purpofe.

The fecond experiment that I propofe, is, to take two playing cards of the fame dimenfions, and cut one of them tranfverfely into eight equal pieces; then with a needle ftring them upon two threads one near each end, and place them fo upon the threads that, when hung up, they may be one exactly over the other, at a diftance equal to their breadth, each in a horizontal pofition; and let a fmall weight, fuch as a bird-fhot, be hung under them, to make them fall in a ftraight line when let loofe. Sufpend alfo the whole card by threads from its four corners, and hang to it an equal weight, fo as to draw it downwards when let fall, its whole breadth preffing againft the air. Let thofe two bodies be attached, one of them to one end of a thread a yard long, the other to the other end. Extend a twine under the ceiling of a room, and put through it at thirty inches diftance two pins bent in the form of fifh-hooks. On thefe two hooks hang the two bodies, the thread that connects them extending parallel to the twine, which thread being cut, they muft begin to fall at the fame inftant. If they take equal time in falling to the floor, it is a proof that the refiftance of the air is in both cafes equal. If the whole card requires a longer time, it fhows that the fum of the refiftances to the pieces of the cut card is not equal to the refiftance of the whole one*.

This principle fo far confirmed, I would proceed to make a larger experiment, with a fhallop, which I would rig in this manner.

A B is

---

* The motion of the veffel made it inconvenient to try this fimple experiment, at fea, when the propofal of it was written. But it has been tried fince we came on fhore, and fucceeded at the other.

Plate IV.
Figure 4. A B is a long boom, from which are hoifted feven jibs, a, b, c, d, e, f, g, each a feventh part of
the whole dimenfions, and as much more as will fill the
whole fpace when fet in an angle of forty-five degrees, fo
that they may lap when going before the wind, and hold
more wind when going large. Thus rigged, when going right before the wind, the boom fhould be brought at
right angles with the keel, by means of the fheet ropes
C D, and all the fails hauled flat to the boom.

These pofitions of boom and fails to be varied as the
wind quarters. But when the wind is on the beam, or
when you would turn to windward, the boom is to be
hauled right fore and aft, and the fails trimmed according
as the wind is more or lefs againft your courfe.

It feems to me that the management of a fhallop fo rigged would be very eafy, the fails being run up and down
feparately, fo that more or lefs fail may be made at pleafure; and I imagine, that there being full as much fail
expofed to the force of the wind which impells the veffel
in its courfe, as if the whole were in one piece, and the
refiftance of the dead air againft the forefide of the fail being diminifhed, the advantage of fwiftnefs would be very
confiderable; befides that the veffel would lie nearer the
wind.

Since we are on the fubject of improvements in navigation, permit me to detain you a little longer with a fmall
relative obfervation. Being, in one of my voyages, with
ten merchant-fhips under convoy of a frigate at anchor in
Torbay, waiting for a wind to go to the weftward; it
came fair, but brought in with it a confiderable fwell. A
fignal was given for weighing, and we put to fea all together; but three of the fhips left their anchors, their cables parting juft as the anchors came a-peak. Our cable
held, and we got up our anchor; but the fhocks the fhip
felt before the anchor got loofe from the ground, made
me reflect on what might poffibly have caufed the breaking

ing of the other cables; and I imagined it might be the
fhort bending of the cable juft without the haufe-hole,
from a horizontal to an almoft vertical pofition, and the
fudden violent jerk it receives by the rifing of the head of
the fhip on the fwell of a wave while in that pofition.
For example, fuppofe a veffel hove up fo as to have her
head nearly over her anchor, which ftill keeps its hold,
perhaps in a tough bottom; if it were calm, the cable ftill
out would form nearly a perpendicular line, meafuring the
diftance between the haufe-hole and the anchor; but if
there is a fwell, her head in the trough of the fea will fall
below the level, and when lifted on the wave will be as
much above it.   In the firft cafe the cable will hang loofe
and bend perhaps as in figure 5.   In the fecond cafe figure
6, the cable will be drawn ftraight with a jerk, muft fuftain
the whole force of the rifing fhip, and muft either loofen the
anchor, refift the rifing force of the fhip, or break.   But
why does it break at the haufe-hole?

Let us fuppofe it a cable of three inches diameter, and
reprefented by figure 7.   If this cable is to be bent round the
corner A, it is evident that either the part of the triangle
contained between the letters a, b, c, muft ftretch confiderably, and thofe moft that are neareft the furface; or that
the parts between d, e, f, muft be compreffed; or both,
which moft probably happens.   In this cafe the lower half
of the thicknefs affords no ftrength againft the jerk, it not
being ftrained, the upper half bears the whole, and the
yarns near the upper furface being firft and moft ftrained,
break firft, and the next yarns follow; for in this bent
fituation they cannot bear the ftrain all together, and each
contribute its ftrength to the whole, as they do when the
cable is ftrained in a ftraight line.

To remedy this, methinks it would be well to have a
kind of large pulley wheel, fixed in the haufe-hole, fuppofe of two feet diameter, over which the cable might
pafs; and being there bent gradually to the round of the
wheel,

wheel, would thereby be more equally ftrained, and better able to bear the jerk, which may fave the anchor, and by that means in the courfe of the voyage may happen to fave the fhip.

One maritime obfervation more fhall finifh this letter. I have been a reader of news-papers now near feventy years, and I think few years pafs without an account of fome veffel met with at fea, with no foul living on board, and fo many feet of water in her hold, which veffel has neverthelefs been faved and brought into port: and when not met with at fea, fuch forfaken veffels have often come afhore on fome coaft. The crews who have taken to their boats and thus abandoned fuch veffels, are fometimes met with and taken up at fea by other fhips, fometimes reach a coaft, and are fometimes never heard of. Thofe that give an account of quitting their veffels, generally fay, that fhe fprung a leak, that they pumped for fome time, that the water continued to rife upon them, and that defpairing to fave her, they had quitted her left they fhould go down with her. It feems by the event that this fear was not always well founded, and I have endeavoured to guefs at the reafon of the people's too hafty difcouragement.

When a veffel fprings a leak near her bottom, the water enters with all the force given by the weight of the column of water, without, which force is in proportion to the difference of level between the water without and that within. It enters therefore with more force at firft, and in greater quantity, than it can afterwards when the water within is higher. The bottom of the veffel too is narrower, fo that the fame quantity of water coming into that narrow part, rifes fafter than when the fpace for it to flow in is larger. This helps to terrify. But as the quantity entering is lefs and lefs as the furfaces without and within become more nearly equal in height, the pumps that could not keep the water from rifing at firft, might afterwards be able to prevent its rifing higher, and the people might

might have remained on board in fafety, without hazard-ing themfelves in an open boat on the wide ocean. (Fig. 8.)

Befides the greater equality in the height of the two furfaces, there may fometimes be other caufes that retard the farther finking of a leaky veffel. The rifing water within may arrive at quantities of light wooden work, empty chefts, and particularly empty water cafks, which if fixed fo as not to float themfelves may help to fuftain her. Many bodies which compofe a fhip's cargo may be fpecifically lighter than water, all thefe when out of wa-ter are an additional weight to that of the fhip, and fhe is in proportion preffed deeper into the water; but as foon as thefe bodies are immerfed, they weigh no longer on the fhip, but on the contrary, if fixed, they help to fupport her, in proportion as they are fpecifically lighter than the water. And it fhould be remembered, that the largeft body of a fhip may be fo balanced in the water, that an ounce lefs or more of weight may leave her at the furface or fink her to the bottom. There are alfo certain heavy car-goes, that when the water gets at them are continually diffolving, and thereby lightening the veffel, fuch as falt and fugar. And as to water cafks mentioned above, fince the quantity of them muft be great in fhips of war where the number of men confume a great deal of water every day, if it had been made a conftant rule to bung them up as faft as they were emptied, and to difpofe the empty cafks in proper fituations, I am perfuaded that many fhips which have been funk in engagements, or have gone down afterwards, might with the unhappy people have been faved; as well as many of thofe which in the laft war foundered, and were never heard of. While on this to-pic of finking, one cannot help recollecting the well known practice of the Chinefe, to divide the hold of a great fhip into a number of feparate chambers by partitions tight caulked, (of which you gave a model in your boat upon the Seine) fo that if a leak fhould fpring in one of them

Q q   the

the others are not affected by it; and though that cham--
ber should fill to a level with the sea, it would not be sufficient to sink the vessel.   We have not imitated this practice.   Some little disadvantage it might occasion in the
stowage is perhaps one reason, though that I think might
be more than compensated by an abatement in the insu-
rance that would be reasonable, and by a higher price
taken of passengers, who would rather prefer going in such
a vessel.   But our seafaring people are brave, despise danger, and reject such precautions of safety, being cowards
only in one sense, that of *fearing* to be *thought afraid.*

I promised to finish my letter with the last observation,.
but the garrulity of the old man has got hold of me, and
as I may never have another occasion of writing on this
subject, I think I may as well now, once for all, empty
my nautical budget, and give you all the thoughts that
have in my various long voyages occurred to me relating
to navigation.   I am sure that in you they will meet with
a candid judge, who will excuse my mistakes on account
of my good intention..

There are six accidents that may occasion the loss of
ships at sea.. We have considered one of them, that of
foundering by a leak.   The other five are, 1. Oversetting
by sudden flaws of wind, or by carrying sail beyond the
bearing. 2. Fire by accident or carelessness.. 3. A heavy
stroke of lightning, making a breach, in the ship, or
firing the powder.   4. Meeting and shocking with other
ships in the night.   5. Meeting in the night with islands
of ice.

To that of oversetting,. privateers in their first cruize
have, as far as has fallen within my knowledge or information, been more subject than any other kind of vessels..
The double desire of being able to overtake a weaker flying
enemy, or to escape when pursued by a stronger, has induced
the owners to overmast their cruizers, and to spread too
much canvas; and the great number of men, many of
them.

them not feamen, who being upon deck when a fhip heels fuddenly are huddled down to leeward, and increafe by their weight the effect of the wind. This therefore fhould be more attended to and guarded againft, efpecially as the advantage of lofty mafts is problematical. For the upper fails have greater power to lay a veffel more on her fide, which is not the moft advantageous pofition for going fwiftly through the water. And hence it is that veffels which have loft their lofty mafts, and been able to make little more fail afterwards than permitted the fhip to fail upon an even keel, have made fo much way, even under jury mafts, as to furprize the mariners themfelves. But there is befides, fomething in the modern form of our fhips that feems as if calculated exprefsly to allow their overfetting more eafily. The fides of a fhip inftead of fpreading out as they formerly did in the upper works, are of late years turned in, fo as to make the body nearly round, and more refembling a cafk. I do not know what the advantages of this conftruction are, except that fuch fhips are not fo eafily boarded. To me it feems a contrivance to have lefs room in a fhip at nearly the fame expence. For it is evident that the fame timber and plank confumed in raifing the fides from a to b, and from d to c, would have raifed them from a to e, and from d to f, fig. 9. In this form all the fpaces between e, a, b, and c, d, f, would have been gained, the deck would have been larger, the men would have had more room to act, and not have ftood fo thick in the way of the enemy's fhot; and the veffel the more fhe was laid down on her fide, the more bearing fhe would meet with, and more effectual to fupport her, as being farther from the center. Whereas in the prefent form, her ballaft makes the chief part of her bearing, without which fhe would turn in the fea almoft as eafily as a barrel. More ballaft by this means becomes neceffary, and that finking a veffel deeper in the water occafions more refiftance to her going through it. The

Bermudian

Bermudian floops ftill keep with advantage to the old
fpreading form.   The iflanders in the great Pacific ocean,
though they have no large fhips, are the moft expert boat-
failors in the world, navigating that fea fafely with their
proas, which they prevent overfetting by various means.
Their failing proas for this purpofe have outriggers generally to windward, above the water, on which one or
more men are placed to move occafionally further from
or nearer to the veffel as the wind frefhens or flackens.
But fome have their outriggers to leeward, which refting
on the water fupport the boat fo as to keep her upright
when preffed down by the wind.   Their boats moved by
oars or rather by paddles, are, for long voyages, fixed two
together by crofs bars of wood that keep them at fome
diftance from each other, and fo render their overfetting
next to impoffible.   How far this may be practicable in
larger veffels, we have not yet fufficient experience.   I
know of but one trial made in Europe, which was about
one hundred years fince by, Sir William Petty.   He built a
double veffel, to ferve as a pacquet boat between England
and Ireland.   Her model ftill exifts in the mufeum of the
Royal Society, where I have feen it.   By the accounts we
have of her, fhe anfwered well the purpofe of her conftruction, making feveral voyages; and though wrecked
at laft by a ftorm, the misfortune did not appear owing
to her particular conftruction, fince many other veffels of
the common form were wrecked at the fame time.   The
advantage of fuch a veffel is: That fhe needs no ballaft,
therefore fwims either lighter or will carry more goods;
and that paffengers are not fo much incommoded by her
rolling: to which may be added, that if fhe is to defend
herfelf by her cannon, they will probably have more effect, being kept more generally in a horizontal pofition,
than thofe in common veffels.   I think however that it
would be an improvement of that model, to make the fides
                                                        which

which are oppofed to each other perfectly parallel, though the other fides are formed as in common thus, figure 10.

The building of a double fhip would indeed be more expenfive in proportion to her burthen; and that perhaps is fufficient to difcourage the method.

The accident of fire is generally well guarded againft by the prudent captain's ftrict orders againft fmoking between decks, or carrying a candle there out of a lanthorn. But there is one dangerous practice which frequent terrible accidents have not yet been fufficient to abolifh; that of carrying ftore-fpirits to fea in cafks. Two large fhips, the Seraphis and the Duke of Athol, one an Eaft-Indiaman, the other a frigate, have been burnt within thefe two laft years, and many lives miferably deftroyed, by drawing fpirits out of a cafk near a candle. It is high time to make it a general rule, that all the fhip's ftore of fpirits fhould be carried in bottles.

The misfortune by a ftroke of lightning I have in my former writings endeavoured to fhow a method of guarding againft, by a chain and pointed rod, extending, when run up, from above the top of the maft to the fea. Thefe inftruments are now made and fold at a reafonable price by *Nairne and Co.* in London, and there are feveral inftances of fuccefs attending the ufe of them. They are kept in a box, and may be run up and fixed in about five minutes, on the apparent approach of a thunder guft.

Of the meeting and fhocking with other fhips in the night, I have known two inftances in voyages between London and America. In one both fhips arrived though much damaged, each reporting their belief that the other muft have gone to the bottom. In the other, only one got to port; the other was never afterwards heard of. Thefe inftances happened many years ago, when the commerce between Europe and America was not a tenth part of what it is at prefent, fhips of courfe thinner fcattered, and the chance of meeting proportionably lefs. It has long

been

been the practice to keep a *look-out before* in the channel, but at fea it has been neglected. If it is not at prefent thought worth while to take that precaution, it will in time become of more confequence; fince the number of fhips at fea is continually augmenting. A drum frequently beat or a bell rung in a dark night, might help to prevent fuch accidents.

Iflands of ice are frequently feen off the banks of Newfoundland, by fhips going between North-America and Europe. In the day-time they are eafily avoided, unlefs in a very thick fog. I remember two inftances of fhips running againft them in the night. The firft loft her bowfprit, but received little other damage. The other ftruck where the warmth of the fea had wafted the ice next to it, and a part hung over above. This perhaps faved her, for fhe was under great way; but the upper part of the cliff taking her foretopmaft, broke the fhock, though it carried away the maft. She difengaged herfelf with fome difficulty, and got fafe into port; but the accident fhows the poffibility of other fhips being wrecked and funk by ftriking thofe vaft maffes of ice, of which I have feen one that we judged to be feventy feet high above the water, confequently eight times as much under water; and it is another reafon for keeping a good *look-out before*, though far from any coaft that may threaten danger.

It is remarkable that the people we confider as favages, have improved the art of failing- and rowing-boats in feveral points beyond what we can pretend to. We have no failing boats equal to the flying proas of the fouth feas, no rowing or paddling boat equal to that of the Greenlanders for fwiftnefs and fafety. The birch canoes of the North-American Indians have alfo fome advantageous properties. They are fo light that two men may carry one of them over land, which is capable of carrying a dozen upon the water; and in heeling they are not fo fubject to take in water as our boats, the fides of which are
                                                                loweft

loweſt in the middle where it is moſt likely to enter, this being higheſt in that part, as in figure 11.

The Chineſe are an enlightened people, the moſt anti-ently civilized of any exiſting, and their arts are antient, a preſumption in their favour: their method of rowing their boats differs from ours, the oars being worked either two a-ſtern as we ſcull, or on the ſides with the ſame kind of motion, being hung parallel to the keel on a rail and always acting in the water, not perpendicular to the ſide as ours are, nor lifted out at every ſtroke, which is a loſs of time, and the boat in the interval loſes motion. They ſee our manner, and we theirs, but neither are diſpoſed to learn of or copy the other.

To the ſeveral means of moving boats mentioned above, may be added the ſingular one lately exhibited at Javelle, on the Seine below Paris, where a clumſy boat was moved acroſs that river in three minutes by rowing, not in the water, but in the air, that is, by whirling round a ſet of windmill vanes fixed to a horizontal axis, parallel to the keel, and placed at the head of the boat. The axis was bent into an elbow at the end, by the help of which it was turned by one man at a time. I ſaw the operation at a diſtance. The four vanes appeared to be about five feet long, and perhaps two and a half wide. The weather was calm. The labour appeared to be great for one man, as the two ſeveral times relieved each other. But the ac-tion upon the air by the oblique ſurfaces of the vanes muſt have been conſiderable, as the motion of the boat appear-ed tolerably quick going and returning; and ſhe returned to the ſame place from whence ſhe firſt ſet out, notwith-ſtanding the current. This machine is ſince applied to the moving of air balloons: An inſtrument ſimilar may be contrived to move a boat by turning under water.

Several mechanical projectors have at different times propoſed to give motion to boats, and even to ſhips, by means of circular rowing, or paddles placed on the circumference:

ference of wheels to be turned conftantly on each fide of
the veffel; but this method, though frequently tried, has
never been found fo effectual as to encourage a continuance
of the practice.   I do not know that the reafon has hitherto been given.   Perhaps it may be this, that great part of
the force employed contributes little to the motion.   For
inftance, (fig. 12.) of the four paddles a, b, c, d, all under
water, and turning to move a boat from X to Y, c has the
moft power, b nearly though not quite as much, their
motion being nearly horizontal; but the force employed
in moving a, is confumed in preffing almoft downright
upon the water till it comes to the place of b; and the
force employed in moving d is confumed in lifting the
water till d arrives at the furface; by which means much
of the labour is loft.   It is true, that by placing the wheels
higher out of the water, this wafte labour will be diminifhed in a calm, but where a fea runs, the wheels muft unavoidably be often dipt deep in the waves, and the turning of them thereby rendered very laborious to little
purpofe.

Among the various means of giving motion to a boat,
that of M. Bernoulli appears one of the moft fingular,
which was to have fixed in the boat a tube in the form of
an L, the upright part to have a funnel-kind of opening
at top, convenient for filling the tube with water; which
defcending and paffing through the lower horizontal part,
and iffuing in the middle of the ftern, but under the furface of the river, fhould pufh the boat forward.   There
is no doubt that the force of the defcending water would
have a confiderable effect, greater in proportion to the
height from which it defcended; but then it is to be confidered, that every bucket-full pumped or dipped up into
the boat, from its fide or through its bottom, muft have its
vis inertiæ overcome fo as to receive the motion of the
boat, before it can come to give motion by its defcent;
and that will be a deduction from the moving power.

                                                          To

To remedy this, I would propofe the addition of another fuch L pipe, and that they fhould ftand back to back in the boat thus, figure 13. the forward one being worked as a pump, and fucking in the water at the head of the boat, would draw it forward while pufhed in the fame direction by the force at the ftern. And after all it fhould be calculated whether the labour of pumping would be lefs than that of rowing. A fire-engine might poffibly in fome cafes be applied in this operation with advantage.

Perhaps this labour of raifing water might be fpared, and the whole force of a man applied to the moving of a boat by the ufe of air inftead of water; fuppofe the boat conftructed in this form, figure 14. A, a tube round or fquare of two feet diameter, in which a pifton may move up and down. The pifton to have valves in it, opening inwards to admit air when the pifton rifes; and fhutting, when it is forced down by means of the lever B turning on the center C. The tube to have a valve D, to open when the pifton is forced down, and let the air pafs out at E, which ftriking forcibly againft the water abaft muft pufh the boat forward. If there is added an air-veffel F properly valved and placed, the force would continue to act while a frefh ftroke is taken with the lever. The boatman might ftand with his back to the ftern, and putting his hands behind him, work the motion by taking hold of the crofs bar at B, while another fhould fteer; or if he had two fuch pumps, one on each fide of the ftern, with a lever for each hand, he might fteer himfelf by working occafionally more or harder with either hand, as watermen now do with a pair of fculls. There is no pofition in which the body of a man can exert more ftrength than in pulling right upwards.

To obtain more fwiftnefs, greafing the bottom of a veffel is fometimes ufed, and with good effect. I do not know that any writer has hitherto attempted to explain this. At firft fight one would imagine, that though the friction of a hard body fliding on another hard body, and

l   R r   the

the refiftance occafioned by that friction, might be diminifhed by putting greafe between them, yet that a body
fliding on a fluid, fuch as water, fhould have no need of
nor receive any advantage from fuch greafing. But the
fact is not difputed. And the reafon perhaps may be this.
The particles of water have a mutual attraction, called the
attraction of adhefion. Water alfo adheres to wood, and
to many other fubftances, but not to greafe: On the
contrary they have a mutual repulfion, fo that it is a
queftion whether when oil is poured on water, they ever
actually touch each other; for a drop of oil upon water,
inftead of fticking to the fpot where it falls, as it would if
it fell on a looking-glafs, fpreads inftantly to an immenfe
diftance in a film extremely thin, which it could not eafily
do if it touched and rubbed or adhered even in a fmall degree to the furface of the water. Now the adhefive force of
water to itfelf, and to other fubftances, may be eftimated
from the weight of it neceffary to feparate a drop, which
adheres, while growing, till it has weight enough to force
the feparation and break the drop off. Let us fuppofe the
drop to be the fize of a pea, then there will be as many
of thefe adhefions as there are drops of that fize touching
the bottom of a veffel, and thefe muft be broken by the
moving power, every ftep of her motion that amounts to
a drop's breadth : And there being no fuch adhefions to
break between the water and a greafed bottom, may occafion the difference.

So much refpecting the motion of veffels. But we have
fometimes occafion to ftop their motion ; and if a bottom
is near enough we can caft anchor : Where there are no
foundings, we have as yet no means to prevent driving in
a ftorm, but by lying-to, which ftill permits driving at
the rate of about two miles an hour; fo that in a ftorm
continuing fifty hours, which is not an uncommon cafe,
the fhip may drive one hundred miles out of her courfe ;
and fhould fhe in that diftance meet with a lee fhore, fhe
may be loft.   To

To prevent this driving to leeward in deep water, a fwimming anchor is wanting, which ought to have thefe properties.

1. It fhould have a furface fo large as being at the end of a haufer in the water, and placed perpendicularly, fhould hold fo much of it, as to bring the fhip's head to the wind, in which fituation the wind has leaft power to drive her.

2. It fhould be able by its refiftance to prevent the fhip's receiving way.

3. It fhould be capable of being fituated below the heave of the fea, but not below the undertow.

4. It fhould not take up much room in the fhip.

5. It fhould be eafily thrown out, and put into its proper fituation.

6. It fhould be eafy to take in again, and ftow away.

An ingenious old mariner whom I formerly knew, propofed as a fwimming anchor for a large fhip to have a ftem of wood twenty-five feet long and four inches fquare, with four boards of 18, 16, 14, and 12, feet long, and one foot wide, the boards to have their fubftance thickened feveral inches in the middle by additional wood, and to have each a four inch fquare hole through its middle, to permit its being flipt on occafionally upon the ftem, and at right angles with it; where all being placed and fixed at four feet diftance from each other, it would have the appearance of the old mathematical inftrument called a foreftaff. This thrown into the fea, and held by a haufer veered out to fome length, he conceived would bring a veffel up, and prevent her driving, and when taken in might be ftowed away by feparating the boards from the ftem. Figure 15. Probably fuch a fwimming anchor would have fome good effect, but it is fubject to this objection, that lying on the furface of the fea, it is liable to be hove forward by every wave, and thereby give fo much leave for the fhip to drive.

Two

Two machines for this purpofe have occurred to me, which though not fo fimple as the above, I imagine would be more effectual, and more eafily manageable. I will endeavour to defcribe them, that they may be fubmitted to your judgment, whether either would be ferviceable; and if they would, to which we fhould give the prefer-ence.

The firft is to be formed, and to be ufed in the water on almoft the fame principles with thofe of a paper kite ufed in the air. Only as the paper kite rifes in the air, this is to defcend in the water. Its dimenfions will be different for fhips of different fize.

To make one of fuppofe fifteen feet high; take a fmall fpar of that length for the back-bone, A B, figure 16, a fmaller of half that length C D, for the crofs piece. Let thefe be united by a bolt at E, yet fo as that by turning on the bolt they may be laid parallel to each other. Then make a fail of ftrong canvas, in the fhape of figure 17. To form this, without wafte of fail-cloth, few together pieces of the proper length, and for half the breadth, as in figure 18, then cut the whole in the diagonal lines a, b, c, and turn the piece F fo as to place its broad part op-pofite to that of the piece G, and the piece H in like man-ner oppofite to I, which when all fewed together will ap-pear as in figure 17. This fail is to be extended on the crofs of figure 16, the top and bottom points well fecured to the ends of the long fpar; the two fide points d, e, faftened to the ends of two cords, which coming from the angle of the loop (which muft be fimilar to the loop of a kite) pafs through two rings at the ends of the fhort fpar, fo as that on pulling upon the loop the fail will be drawn to its extent. The whole may, when aboard, be furled up, as in figure 19, having a rope from its broad end, to which is tied a bag of ballaft for keeping that end down-wards when in the water, and at the other end another rope with an empty keg at its end to float on the furface;

this

this rope long enough to permit the kite's defcending into the undertow, or if you pleafe lower into ftill water. It fhould be held by a haufer. To get it home eafily, a fmall loofe rope may be veered out with it, fixed to the keg. Hauling on that rope will bring the kite home with fmall force, the refiftance being fmall as it will then come endways.

It feems probable that fuch a kite at the end of a long haufer would keep a fhip with her head to the wind, and refifting every tug, would prevent her driving fo faft as when her fide is expofed to it, and nothing to hold her back. If only half the driving is prevented, fo as that fhe moves but fifty miles inftead of the hundred during a ftorm, it may be fome advantage, both in holding fo much diftance as is faved, and in keeping from a lee fhore. If fingle canvas fhould not be found ftrong enough to bear the tug without fplitting, it may be doubled, or ftrengthened by a netting behind it, reprefented by figure 20.

The other machine for the fame purpofe, is to be made more in the form of an umbrella, as reprefented, figure 21. The ftem of the umbrella a fquare fpar of proper length, with four moveable arms, of which two are reprefented C, C, figure 22. Thefe arms to be fixed in four joint cleats, as D, D, &c. one on each fide of the fpar, but fo as that the four arms may open by turning on a pin in the joint. When open they form a crofs, on which a four fquare canvas fail is to be extended, its corners faftened to the ends of the four arms. Thofe ends are alfo to be ftayed by ropes faftened to the ftem or fpar, fo as to keep them fhort of being at right angles with it: And to the end of one of the arms fhould be hung the fmall bag of ballaft, and to the end of the oppofite arm the empty keg. This on being thrown into the fea, would immediately open; and when it had performed its function, and the ftorm over, a fmall rope from its other end being pulled on, would turn it, clofe it, and draw it eafily home to the fhip. This machine feems more fimple in its ope-ration,,

ration, and more eafily manageable than the firft, and perhaps may be as effectual.*

Veffels are fometimes retarded, and fometimes forwarded in their voyages, by currents at fea, which are often not perceived. About the year 1769 or 70, there was an application made by the board of cuftoms at Bofton, to the lords of the treafury in London, complaining that the packets between Falmouth and New-York, were generally a fortnight longer in their paffages, than merchant fhips from London to Rhode-Ifland, and propofing that for the future they fhould be ordered to Rhode-Ifland inftead of New-York. Being then concerned in the management of the American poft-office, I happened to be confulted on the occafion; and it appearing ftrange to me that there fhould be fuch a difference between two places, fcarce a day's run afunder, efpecially when the merchant fhips are generally deeper laden, and more weakly manned than the packets, and had from London the whole length of the river and channel to run before they left the land of England, while the packets had only to go from Faimouth, I could not but think the fact mifunderftood or mifreprefented. There happened then to be in London, a Nantucket fea-captain of my acquaintance, to whom I communicated the affair. He told me he believed the fact might be true; but the difference was owing to this, that the Rhode-Ifland captains were acquainted with the gulf ftream, which thofe of the Englifh packets were not. We are well acquainted with that ftream, fays he, becaufe in our purfuit of whales, which keep near the fides of it, but are not to be met with in it, we run down along the fides, and frequently crofs it to change our fide: and in croffing it have fometimes met and fpoke with thofe packets, who were in the middle of it, and ftemming it. We have informed them that they were

* Captain Truxton, on board whofe fhip this was written, has executed this propofed machine; he has given fix arms to the umbrella, they are joined to the ftem by iron hinges, and the canvas is double. He has taken it with him to China. February 1786.

were ftemming a current, that was againft them to the
value of three miles an hour; and advifed them to crofs
it and get out of it; but they were too wife to be coun-
felled by fimple American fifhermen. When the winds
are but light, he added, they are carried back by the
current more than they are forwarded by the wind: and
if the wind be good, the fubtraction of 70 miles a day
from their courfe is of fome importance. I then obferved
that it was a pity no notice was taken of this current upon the charts, and requefted him to mark it out for me,
which he readily complied with, adding directions for a-
voiding it in failing from Europe to North-America. I
procured it to be engraved by order from the general poft-
office, on the old chart of the Atlantic, at Mount and Page's,
Tower-hill; and copies were fent down to Falmouth for
the captains of the packets, who flighted it however; but
it is fince printed in France, of which edition I hereto annex a copy.

This ftream is probably generated by the great accumulation of water on the eaftern coaft of America between
the tropics, by the trade winds which conftantly blow
there. It is known that a large piece of water ten miles
broad and generally only three feet deep, has by a ftrong
wind had its waters driven to one fide and fuftained fo as
to become fix feet deep, while the windward fide was laid
dry. This may give fome idea of the quantity heaped up
on the American coaft, and the reafon of its running down
in a ftrong current through the iflands into the bay of
Mexico, and from thence iffuing through the gulph of
Florida, and proceeding along the coaft to the banks of
Newfoundland, where it turns off towards and runs down
through the Weftern iflands. Having fince croffed this
ftream feveral times in paffing between America and Europe, I have been attentive to fundry circumftances relating to it, by which to know when one is in it; and befides the gulph weed with which it is interfperfed, I find
that

that it is always warmer than the sea on each side of it, and that it does not sparkle in the night: I annex hereto the observations made with the thermometer in two voyages, and possibly may add a third. It will appear from them, that the thermometer may be an useful instrument to a navigator, since currents coming from the northward into southern seas, will probably be found colder than the water of those seas, as the currents from southern seas into northern are found warmer. And it is not to be wondered that so vast a body of deep warm water, several leagues wide, coming from between the tropics and issuing out of the gulph into the northern seas, should retain its warmth longer than the twenty or thirty days required to its passing the banks of Newfoundland. The quantity is too great, and it is too deep to be suddenly cooled by passing under a cooler air. The air immediately over it, however, may receive so much warmth from it as to be rarified and rise, being rendered lighter than the air on each side of the stream; hence those airs must flow in to supply the place of the rising warm air, and meeting with each other, form those tornados and water-spouts frequently met with, and seen near and over the stream; and as the vapour from a cup of tea in a warm room, and the breath of an animal in the same room, are hardly visible, but become sensible immediately when out in the cold air, so the vapour from the gulph stream, in warm latitudes is scarcely visible, but when it comes into the cool air from Newfoundland, it is condensed into the fogs, for which those parts are so remarkable.

The power of wind to raise water above its common level in the sea, is known to us in America, by the high tides occasioned in all our sea-ports when a strong north-easter blows against the gulph stream.

The conclusion from these remarks is, that a vessel from Europe to North-America may shorten her passage by avoiding to stem the stream, in which the thermometer will

be

Plate 1.

be very ufeful; and a veffel from America to Europe may
do the fame by the fame means of keeping in it.   It may
have often happened accidentally, that voyages have been
fhortened by thefe circumftances.   It is well to have the
command of them.

But may there not be another caufe, independent of
winds and currents, why paffages are generally fhorter
from America to Europe than from Europe to America?
This queftion I formerly confidered in the following fhort
paper.

On board the Pennfylvania Packet, Capt. Ofborne,
At fea, April 5, 1775.

" Suppofe a fhip to make a voyage eaftward from a
place in lat. 40° north, to a place in lat. 50° north, diftance
in longitude 75 degrees.

" In failing from 40 to 50, fhe goes from a place where
a degree of longitude is about eight miles greater than in
the place fhe is going to.   A degree is equal to four minutes of time; confequently the fhip in the harbour fhe
leaves, partaking of the diurnal motion of the earth, moves
two miles in a minute fafter, than when in the port fhe
is going to; which is 120 miles in an hour.

" This motion in a fhip and cargo is of great force; and
if fhe could be lifted up fuddenly from the harbour in
which fhe lay quiet, and fet down inftantly in the latitude
of the port fhe was bound to, though in a calm, that force
contained in her would make her run a great way at a
prodigious rate.   This force muft be loft gradually in her
voyage, by gradual impulfe againft the water, and probably thence fhorten the voyage.   Query, In returning does
the contrary happen, and is her voyage thereby retarded
and lengthened?" *

Would it not be a more fecure method of planking fhips,
if inftead of thick fingle planks laid horizontally, we were

S s   to

---

* Since this paper was read at the Society, an ingenious member, Mr. Patterfon, has convinced the writer that the returning voyage would not, from this caufe, be retarded.

to use planks of half the thickness, and lay them double and across each other as in figure 23 ? To me it seems that the difference of expence would not be confiderable, and that the ship would be both tighter and ftronger.

The fecuring of the ship is not the only neceffary thing; fecuring the health of the failors, a brave and valuable order of men, is likewife of great importance. With this view the methods fo fuccefsfully practifed by Captain Cook in his long voyages, cannot be too clofely ftudied or carefully imitated. A full account of thofe methods is found in Sir John Pringle's fpeech, when the medal of the Royal Society was given to that illuftrious navigator. I am glad to fee in his laft voyage that he found the means effectual which I had propofed for preferving flour, bread, &c. from moifture and damage. They were found dry and good after being at fea four years. The method is defcribed in my printed works, page 452, fifth edition. In the fame, page 469, 470, is propofed a means of allaying thirft in cafe of want of frefh water. This has fince been practifed in two inftances with fuccefs. Happy if their hunger, when the other provifions are confumed, could be relieved as commodioufly; and perhaps in time this may be found not impoffible. An addition might be made to their prefent vegetable provifion, by drying various roots in flices by the means of an oven. The fweet potatoe of America and Spain, is excellent for this purpofe. Other potatoes, with carrots, parfnips and turnips, might be prepared and preferved in the fame manner.

With regard to make-fhifts in cafes of neceffity, feamen are generally very ingenious themfelves. They will excufe however the mention of two or three. If they happen in any circumftance, fuch as after fhipwreck, taking to their boat, or the like, to want a compafs, a fine fewing-needle laid on clear water in a cup will generally point to the north, moft of them being a little magnetical, or may be made fo by being ftrongly rubbed or hammered,

ed, lying in a north and fouth direction. If their needle is too heavy to float by itfelf, it may be fupported by little pieces of cork or wood. A man who can fwim, may be aided in a long traverfe by his handkerchief formed into a kite, by two crofs fticks extending to the four corners; which being raifed in the air, when the wind is fair and frefh, will tow him along while lying on his back. Where force is wanted to move a heavy body, and there are but few hands and no machines, a long and ftrong rope may make a powerful inftrument. Suppofe a boat is to be drawn up on a beach, that fhe may be out of the furf, a ftake drove into the beach where you would have the boat drawn; and another to faften the end of the rope to, which comes from the boat, and then applying what force you have to pull upon the middle of the rope at right angles with it, the power will be augmented in proportion to the length of rope between the pofts. The rope being faftened to the ftake A, and drawn upon in the direction C D, will flide over the ftake B; and when the rope is bent to the angle A D B, reprefented by the pricked line in figure 24, the boat will be at B.

Some failors may think the writer has given himfelf unneceffary trouble in pretending to advife them; for they have a little repugnance to the advice of landmen, whom they efteem ignorant and incapable of giving any worth notice; though it is certain that moft of their inftruments were the invention of landmen. At leaft the firft veffel ever made to go on the water was certainly fuch. I will therefore add only a few words more, and they fhall be addreffed to paffengers.

When you intend a long voyage, you may do well to keep your intention as much as poffible a fecret, or at leaft the time of your departure; otherwife you will be continually interrupted in your preparations by the vifits of friends and acquaintance, who will not only rob you of the time you want, but put things out of your mind, fo

that

that when you come to fea, you have the mortification to recollect points of bufinefs that ought to have been done, accounts you had intended to fettle, and conveniencies you had propofed to bring with you, &c. &c. all which have been omitted through the effect of thefe officious friendly vifits. Would it not be well if this cuftom could be changed; if the voyager after having, without interruption, made all his preparations, fhould ufe fome of the time he has left, in going himfelf to take leave of his friends at their own houfes, and let them come to congratulate him on his happy return.

It is not always in your power to make a choice in your captain, though much of your comfort in the paffage may depend on his perfonal character, as you muft for fo long a time be confined to his company, and under his direction; if he be a fenfible, fociable, good natured, obliging man, you will be fo much the happier. Such there are; but if he happens to be otherwife, and is only fkilful, careful, watchful and active in the conduct of his fhip, excufe the reft, for thefe are the effentials.

Whatever right you may have by agreement in the mafs of ftores laid in by him for the paffengers, it is good to have fome particular things in your own poffeffion, fo as to be always at your own command.

1. Good water, that of the fhip being often bad. You can be fure of having it good only by bottling it from a clear fpring or well and in clean bottles. 2. Good tea. 3. Coffee ground. 4. Chocolate. 5. Wine of the fort you particularly like, and cyder. 6. Raifins. 7. Almonds 8. Sugar. 9. Capillaire. 10. Lemons. 11. Jamaica fpirits. 12. Eggs greas'd. 13. Diet bread. 14. Portable foup. 15. Rufks. As to fowls, it is not worth while to have any called yours, unlefs you could have the feeding and managing of them according to your own judgment under your own eye. As they are generally treated at prefent in fhips, they are for the moft part fick, and their flefh

tough

tough and hard as whitleather. All feamen have an opinion, broached I fuppofed at firft prudently, for faving of
water when fhort, that fowls do not know when they
have drank enough, and will kill themfelves if you give
them too much, fo they are ferved with a little only once
in two days. This is poured into troughs that lie flope-
ing, and therefore immediately runs down to the lower
end. There the fowls ride upon one another's backs to
get at it, and fome are not happy enough to reach and
once dip their bills in it. Thus tantalized, and torment-
ed with thirft, they cannot digeft their dry food, they fret,
pine, ficken and die. Some are found dead, and thrown
overboard every morning, and thofe killed for the table
are not eatable. Their troughs fhould be in little divifions like cups to hold the water feparately, figure 25. But
this is never done. The fheep and hogs are therefore
your beft dependance for frefh meat at fea, the mutton
being generally tolerable and the pork excellent.

It is poffible your captain may have provided fo well
in the general ftores, as to render fome of the particulars
above recommended of little or no ufe to you. But there
are frequently in the fhip poorer paffengers, who are
taken at a lower price, lodge in the fteerage, and have no
claim to any of the cabbin provifions, or to any but thofe
kinds that are allowed the failors. Thefe people are
fometimes dejected, fometimes fick, there may be women
and children among them. In a fituation where there
is no going to market, to purchafe fuch neceffaries, a
few of thefe your fuperfluities diftributed occafionally may
be of great fervice, reftore health, fave life, make the miferable happy, and thereby afford you infinite pleafure.

The worft thing in ordinary merchant fhips is the
cookery. They have no profeffed cook, and the worft
hand as a feaman is appointed to that office, in which he
is not only very ignorant but very dirty. The failors
have

have therefore a faying, that *God fends meat and the devil cooks.* Paffengers more pioufly difpofed, and willing to believe heaven orders all things for the beft, may fuppofe that knowing the fea-air and conftant exercife by the motion of the veffel would give us extraordinary appetites, bad cooks were kindly fent to prevent our eating too much; or, that forefeeing we fhould have bad cooks, good appetites were furnifhed to prevent our ftarving. If you cannot truft to thefe circumftances, a fpirit-lamp, with a blaze-pan, may enable you to cook fome little things for yourfelf; fuch as a hafh, a foup, &c. And it might be well alfo to have among your ftores fome potted meats, which if well put up will keep long good. A fmall tin-oven to place with the open fide before the fire, may be another good utenfil, in which your own fervant may roaft for you a bit of pork or mutton. You will fometimes be induced to eat of the fhip's falt beef, as it is often good. You will find cyder the beft quencher of that thirft which falt meat or fifh occafions. The fhip bifcuit is too hard for fome fets of teeth. It may be foftened by toafting. But rufk is better; for being made of good fermented bread, fliced and baked a fecond time, the pieces imbibe the water eafily, foften immediately, digeft more kindly and are therefore more wholfome than the unfermented bifcuit. By the way, rufk is the true original bifcuit, fo prepared to keep for fea, bifcuit in French fignifying twice baked. If your dry peas boil hard, a two-pound iron fhot put with them into the pot, will by the motion of the fhip grind them as fine as muftard.

The accidents I have feen at fea with large difhes of foup upon a table, from the motion of the fhip, have made me wifh that our potters or pewterers would make foup-difhes in divifions, like a fet of fmall bowls united together, each containing about fufficient for one perfon, in fome fuch form as fig. 26; for then when the fhip fhould make a fudden heel, the foup would not in a body flow

over

over one fide, and fall into people's laps and fcald them,
as is fometimes the cafe, but would be retained in the feparate divifions, as in figure 27.

After thefe trifles, permit the addition of a few general
reflections.   Navigation when employed in fupplying neceffary provifions to a country in want, and thereby preventing famines, which were more frequent and deftruc-
tive before the invention of that art, is undoubtedly a
bleffing to mankind.   When employed merely in tranfporting fuperfluities, it is a queftion whether the advantage of the employment it affords is equal to the mif-
chief of hazarding fo many lives on the ocean.   But when
employed in pillaging merchants and tranfporting flaves, it
is clearly the means of augmenting the mafs of human
mifery.   It is amazing to think of the fhips and lives
rifqued in fetching tea from China, coffee from Arabia,
fugar and tobacco from America, all which our anceftors
did well without.   Sugar employs near one thoufand fhips,
tobacco almoft as many.   For the utility of tobacco there
is little to be faid; and for that of fugar, how much more
commendable would it be if we could give up the few minutes gratification afforded once or twice a day by the tafte
of fugar in our tea, rather than encourage the cruelties
exercifed in producing it.   An eminent French moralift
fays, that when he confiders the wars we excite in Africa
to obtain flaves, the numbers neceffarily flain in thofe wars,
the many prifoners who perifh at fea by ficknefs, bad provifions, foul air, &c. &c. in the tranfportation, and how
many afterwards die from the hardfhips of flavery, he cannot look on a piece of fugar without conceiving it ftained
with fpots of human blood! Had he added the confideration of the wars we make to take and retake the fugar
iflands from one another, and the fleets and armies that
perifh in thofe expeditions, he might have feen his fugar
not merely fpotted, but thoroughly dyed fcarlet in grain.
It is thefe wars that make the maritime powers of Europe,
            the

the inhabitants of London and Paris, pay dearer for fugar than thofe of Vienna, a thoufand miles from the fea ; becaufe their fugar cofts not only the price they pay for it by the pound, but all they pay in taxes to maintain the fleets and armies that fight for it.

With great efteem, I am, Sir,

Your moft obedient humble fervant,

B. FRANKLIN.

Obfervations

Observations of the warmth of the sea-water, &c. by Fahrenheit's thermometer, in crossing the Gulph stream; with other remarks made on board the Pennsylvania packet, Capt. Osborne, bound from London to Philadelphia, in April and May 1775.

Date	Hour	Temp. of Air.	Temp. of Wat.	Wind.	Course.	Distance.	Latitude N.	Longitude W.	Remarks.
April 10		60	64						
11		60	61						
12		70	64						
13		67	65						
14		63	65						
26	8 A.M.	65	70	S s E	W b S	34	37 39	60 38	Much gulph weed; saw a whale.
27	6 P.M.	66	70	S W	W N W	44	37 13	62 29	Colour of water changed.
28	8 A.M.	64	64	N E	W	57	37 48	64 35	No gulph weed.
—	5 P.M.	62	71	N E W b N	W b S	69			Sounded, no bottom.
29	11 dit.	64	72	N E	W b S	24	37 26	66 0	Much light in the water last nig.
—	8 A.M.	65	66		E b S	43			Water again of the usual deep sea colour, little or no light in it at night.
—	12	68	70	E S E	W b N	35	37 20	68 53	Frequent gulph weed, water continues of sea colour, little light.
—	6 P.M.	65	72	S	W N W	60			Much light.
30	10 dit.	64	65	S S W	W b N	44	38 13	72 23	Much light all last night.
—	7 A.M.	62	63	S W	W N W	21			Colour of water changed.
—	4 P.M.	60	56	W S W	N W	31	38 43	74 3	Much light.
May 1	8 A.M.	64	57	N W	W S W	18			Much light. Thunder-gust.
—	12	65	53	N b W	W b N	18	38 30	75 0	
—	6 P.M.	6.	53			15			
—	10 dit.		55			10			
—	- A.M.		54			30			

Observations

Observations of the warmth of the sea-water, &c. by Fahrenheit's thermometer; with other remarks made on board the Reprisal, Capt. Wycks, bound from Philadelphia to France, in October and November 1776.

Date.	Hour A.M.	Hour P.M.	Temp. of Air.	Temp. of Water.	Wind.	Course.	Distance.	Latit. N.	Long. W.	Remarks.
Oct. 31	10	4	76	70	S S E	E b S	135	38 12	70 30	Left the capes Thursday night, October 29, 1776.
Nov. 1	10	4		71	W S W	E ½ N	109	No ob.	68 12	
	8		71	78						
	12		71	81						
2				75.	N		141	ditto.	65 23	Some sparks in the water these two last nights.
	8		67	78	N W	E S E ½ E				
	12			76		E b S				
3	8		70	76		N b E	160	37 0	62 7	
	12		68	76						
4	9	4		76		N E	194	36 26	58 8	Ditto.
		1	68	76						
5	8	4 8	68	76			163	35 21	55 3	Ditto.
	12		70	75						
6	8	4 8		75	E b N	S 50 E	75	35 33	53 52	
	12			76						
7	8			77	S E b E	N 30 W	108	36 6	52 46	
	12			77						
8	9	4	75	77	S b E	N 49 E	175	38 2	50 1	
	12			77						
9	9	4	75	77	S W	N 33 E	175	39 39	46 55	
	12		75	70						

Obſervations made on board the Repriſal, continued.

Date.	Hour A.M.	Hour P.M.	Temp. of Air.	Temp. of Water.	Wind.	Courſe.	Diſtance.	Latit. N.	Long. W.	Remarks.
Novem. 9	8	4	70	71, 68	E	N 17 E	64	40 39	46 27	
10	12			64, 63	S E	N 8 E	41	41 19	46 19	
11	8	4		61, 59	N N W	N 80 E	120	41 39	43 42	
12	12	Noon	56	69, 68	E	S 81 E	69	41 29	42 10	
13	all day	4		70, 72	E S E	N 74 E	111	42 0	39 57	
14	8	Noon	70	71	W S W	N 70 E	186	43 3	35 51	Some gulph weed.
15	8	4	61	69	S W	N 67 W	48	43 22	34 50	
16	8	Noon	65	68, 67	E S E	N 19 E	56	44 15	34 25	
17	all day			67, 63	S b W	N 75 E	210	45 6	29 43	
18	8	4	65	63	S W	N 80 E	238	45 46	24 2	
19				65	N	S 80 E	155	45 19	20 30	
20				64	S	N 88 E	94	45 22	18 17	
21	9	Noon	60	62	S S W	S 89 E	133	45 19	15 19	
22	10	do.		60	W S W	S 86 E	194	45 6	10 35	
23		do.		62	N N E	N 78 E	191	45 46	6 10	
24		do.		61	N E	S 76 E	125	45 4	3 23	
25		do.		60	E	N 73 E	31	45 13	2 20	
26		do.		60						
27		do.	56	58						Soundings off Belliſle.
28		do.	54	56						

1785. A Journal of a voyage from the Channel between France and England towards America.

N. B. Longitude is reckoned from London, and the Thermometer is according to Fahrenheit.

Dates.	Latit. N.	Long. W.	Therm. A.M. Air	Therm. A.M. Water	Therm. P.M. Air	Therm. P.M. Water	Winds.	Course.	Distance Miles.	Variation of the Needle West.	Therm. Noon A.	Therm. Noon W.
July 29	49 15	4 15	62	57	63	58	East	S W ¼ W	60	22° 0	77	78
30	48 28	8 58	62	58	62	62	E S E	W b S ¼ S	174		81	79
31	47 0	12 13	60	58	60	64	N E	S W b W	160		79	79
August 1	47 0	15 43	63	62	64	63	N W b W	S W ½ W	190		81	80
2	45 5	15 25	64	64	omitted	66	N E	S W b S	131	20 0	80	78
3	43 3	17 3	66	67	dn.	68	N E	S W ¼ S	166	16 30	79	79
4	41 45	19 44	67	66	65	69	N E	S S W ¼ W	165	11 30	77	77
5	38 42	21 34	70	65	71	70	N E	W S W ¼ S	149	11 15	77	75
6	36 40	23 10	70	68	68	72	N E	W S W ¼ W	137		80	75
7	35 0	25 0	72	70	73	74	N W	S W ¼ W	76		omitted	
8	35 0	27 0	73	71	73	75	North	W ¼ S	112		75	74
9	33 51	28 42	71	73	77	77	North	W ½ S	143		80	76
10	33 30	31 32	74	74	76	76	N E	W ¼ N	103		80	76
11	33 17	33 31	76	75	78	78	S S E	S W ¼ W	50		78	78
12	33 22	34 31	76	76	81	79	W N W	W ½ N	35		78	78
13	33 45	35 0	78	76	81	80	West	N N W ½ N	38		80	80
14	34 14	36 30	79	78	80	78	W S W	N N W ¼ N	75		80	80
15	35 37	36 4	80	78	78	77	N W b W	W N W ¼ N	65		83	80
16	36 7	37 16	78	77	omitted	77	W S W	N W ¼ W	49		84	81
17	36 38	38 0	78	76	78	76	West	N ¼ W	62		83	81
18	37 38	38 6	73	74	80	77	W N W	S b W	82		82	81
19	35 15	38 26	79	76	78	75	W b S	S S W	38	8	78	80
20	35 40	40 44	77	76	75	74	North	W ¼ S	100		78	80
21	35 35	40 52	75	76	80	76	W N W	S W b W	41		75	80
22	35 12	41 31	79	77	81	78	W b N	W N W ¼ N	60		78	73
Septem. 1	34 5	51 4	80	79	81	79	East	W ¼ S	129			
2	34 20	52 47	81	80	omitted		S S W	W ¼ S	86	6 0		

OBSERVATIONS.

July 31. At one P. M. the Start bore W N W. diſtant ſix leagues.
Auguſt 1. The water appears luminous in the ſhip's wake.
—2. The temperature of the water is taken at eight in the morning and at eight in the evening.
—6. The water appears leſs luminous.
—7. Formegas S W. diſt. 32½ deg. St. Mary's S W ¼ S 33 leagues.
—8. From this date the temperature of the water is taken at eight in the morning and at ſix in the evening.
—10. Moonlight, which prevents the luminous appearance of the water.
—11. A ſtrong ſoutherly current.
—12. Ditto. From this date the temperature of the air and water was taken at noon, as well as morning and evening.
—16. Northerly current.
—19. Firſt ſaw gulph weed.
—21. Southerly current.
—22. Again ſaw gulph weed.
—24. The water appeared luminous in a ſmall degree before the moon roſe.
—29. No moon, yet very little light in the water.
—30. Much gulph weed to-day.
—31. Ditto.
Sept. 1. Ditto.
—2. A little more light in the water.
—4. No gulph weed to-day. More light in the water.
—5. Some gulph weed again.
—6. Little light in the water. A very hard thunder-guſt in the night.
—7. Little gulph weed.
—8. More light in the water. Little gulph weed.
—9. Little gulph weed. Little light in the water laſt evening.
—10. Saw ſome beds of rock-weed; and we were ſurpriſed to obſerve the water ſix degrees colder by the thermometer than the preceding noon.

This day (10th) the thermometer ſtill kept deſcending, and at five in the morning of the 11th, it was in water as low as 70, when we ſtruck ſoundings. The ſame evening the pilot came on board, and we found our ſhip about five degrees of longitude a-head of the reckoning, which our captain accounted for by ſuppoſing our courſe to have been near the edge of the gulph ſtream, and this an eddy-current always in our favour. By the diſtance we ran from Sept. 9, in the evening, till we ſtruck ſoundings, we muſt have been at the weſtern edge of the gulph ſtream, and the change in the temperature of the water was probably owing to our ſuddenly paſſing from that current, into the waters of our own climate.

On the 14th of Auguſt the following experiment was made. The weather being perfectly calm, an empty bottle, corked very tight, was ſent down 20 fathoms, and it was drawn up ſtill empty. It was then ſent down again 35 fathoms, when the weight of the water having forced in the cork, it was drawn up full; the water it contained was immediately tried by the thermometer, and found to be 70, which was ſix degrees colder than at the ſurface : The lead and bottle were viſible, but not very diſtinctly ſo, at the depth of 12 fathoms but when only 7 fathoms deep, they were perfectly ſeen from the ſhip. This experiment was thus repeated Sept. 11, when we were in ſoundings of 18 fathoms. A keg was previouſly prepared with a valve at each end, one opening inward the other outward ; this was ſent to the bottom in expectation that by the valves being both open when going down, and both ſhut when coming up, it would keep within it the water received at bottom. The upper valve performed its office well, but the under one did not ſhut quite cloſe, ſo that much of the water was loſt in hauling it up the ſhip's ſide. As the water in the keg's paſſage upwards could not enter at the top, it was concluded that what water remained in it was of that near the ground, and on trying this by the thermometer, it was found to be at 58, which was 12 degrees colder than at the ſurface.

This laſt Journal was obligingly kept for me by Mr. J. Williams, my fellow-paſſenger in the London Packet, who made all the experiments with great exactneſs.

Two

N° XXXIX.

Two Hearts found in one Partridge.

ALL the works of nature are linked the one to the other and form a whole, in the immenſity of which we only perceive ſome points which appear to us detached, becauſe ţhoſe which unite them are concealed from us.

The reſult of this connection is, that no work of nature ought to be neglected, that there is not one which may not derive ſome direct or indirect utility to man.

That which appears futile, ſhould be graſped like the others, and in poſſeſſing ourſelves of it we ſhould be aſſured that we have hold of a chain, the precious links of which will be diſcovered by time[a]. If thoſe links which are wanting leave vacancies, the intermediate links are every day preſented to us by the hand of chance; and it is the buſineſs of the naturaliſt to arrange them. Let us then offer

DEUX COEURS TROUVÉS DANS UNE PERDRIX.

TOUS les faits de la nature ſont liés les uns aux autres, et forment un tout, dans l'immenſité duquel nous n'appercevons que quelques points, qui nous paroiſſent iſolés parce-que ceux qui les uniſſent nous ſont cachés. Il reſulte de cet enchainement qu'aucun fait de la nature ne doit être négligé, qu'il n'en eſt pas un qui ne puiſſe devenir de quelque utilité pour l'homme, ſoit directe ou indirecte. Celui qui paroit le plus futile doit être recueilli comme les autres ; en le ſaiſiſſant on doit être aſſuré qu'on tient une chaine ou le temps découvrira des chainons precieux`. Si ceux qui manquent y laiſſent des lacunes, ces chainons intermediaires nous ſont tous les jours preſentés par la main du hazard, et celle du naturaliſte les met à leurs places.
Offrons

(a) We here ſee women ſit quiet in their houſes whilſt thunder is rumbling over their heads; would they, at this day, enjoy this happy ſecurity, if a man had not obſerved, ſome thouſand years ago, that a piece of amber when rubbed attracted light bodies which are near it. It is he who put into the hands of modern philoſophers the chain in which Franklin was to find the link, from which his imagination took the hint of his conductor.

* *Nous voyons ici les femmes tranquilles dans leurs maiſons lorſque la tonnerre gronde ſur leur tête. Jouiroient elles aujourd'hui de cette heureuſe ſécurité, ſi un homme n'avoit obſervé il y a quelques milliers d'années, qu'un morceau d'ambre frotté ottire les corps legers qui l'avoiſinent ? C'eſt lui qui a mis dans les mains des phyſiciens modernes la chaine ou Franklin devoit trouver le chainon dont il eſt parti pour imaginer ſon conducteur.*

fer him all thofe which we meet with. It increafes the mafs of human knowledge, and enriches a ftore-houfe which is very precious to man; a ware-houfe belonging to all nations and to all ages. Not to lodge every new difcovery in this common ftore, is to fquander away riches which we held only in truft, and in which the moft diftant generations have an intereft. This is criminally depriving humanity of a bleffing which is intended for the good of fociety.

The foregoing reflections induce me to publifh the following fact. Monfieur Vergé, fenior furgeon of the artillery, lodged next door to me, and came into my room with the entrails of a partridge which he had juft opened, and fhewed me two hearts attached to one lung by blood veffels. I requefted him to go immediately to the chev. de Chaftellux, knowing that the phenomenon would be interefting to him. But wifhing firft to ftep home, and not being able with one hand to open the padlock which faftened his door, he put down the faucer which contained the entrails; his dog who had followed, fuppofing it was a mefs for himfelf, foon emptied the faucer.

The chevalier de Chaftellux called on me an hour afterwards to fee a male opoffum, of which I fpoke to him on account

Offrons lui donc tous ceux que nous rencontrons, c'eft groffir la maffe des connoiffances humaines, et enrichir le magazin le plus précieux à l'homme, magazin qui appartient à toutes les nations et à tous les fiecles. Ne pas rapporter à ce depôt commun les faits nouveaux que l'on découvre, c'eft perdre des richeffes dont on étoit dépofitaire, et fur lefquelles les générations les plus reculées avoient intérêt. C'eft fe rendre coupable envers l'humanité, en la fruftrant d'un bien dont on lui étoit comptable.

Ce font ces réflexions qui m'engagent à rendre publique le fait fuivant.

Le Sieur Vergé, chirurgien major de l'artillerie, logé à coté de chèz moi, entra il y a quelques jours dans ma chambre, tenant dans fes mains les entrailles d'une perdrix qu'il venoit d'ouvrir, et m'y fit remarquer deux coeurs qui tenoient à un même poumon par des vaiffeaux fanguins. Je le priai d'aller fur le champ les faire voir à Mr. le Chevr. de Chaftellux, que je favois que ce phénomene interefferoit. Mais ayant voulu auparavant rentrer chez lui, et ne pouvant d'une main ouvrir le cadenat qui ferme fa porte, il pofa a terre la foucoupe fur laquelle etoient ces entrailles. Son chien, qui l'avoit fuivi, crut que c'etoit pour lui, et eut bientôt vidé la foucoupe. Mr. le Chevr. de Chaftellux vint une heure aprés chez moi, voir un opoffum mâle, dont je lui avois parlé à caufe de la fingularité des organes de la génération de
ces

account of the fingularity of his organs of generation[b].
I mentioned to him the two hearts, he could not comprehend me. I fent to afk of the fenior furgeon why he did
not do what I requefted of him; he came and related
the accident of the faucer. The chevalier de Chaftellux
judged there was no other way of repairing the lofs but by
a certificate, ftating what we had feen; but every thing
confpired againft the defire the chevalier de Chaftellux
and I had to perpetuate the phenomenon; the dog had deprived us of the monument; the mafter refufed us his
certificate, faying, one cannot be too circumfpect in affirm-
ing a fact which we ought not to judge of from external
appearances; but to be convinced that that which appeared
to us as two hearts were really fo, they ought to have been
diffected, &c. One cannot too much applaud the fcruples
of Mr. Vergé; but regarding as much my veracity as Mr.
Vergé his, I am not afraid to hazard an exact relation of
what I have feen, without alteration or exaggeration. I
faw, then, two flefhy fubftances of a brown violet colour,
of an oblong form, thicker at one end than the other, nearly
round taken tranfverfely. Thefe two fubftances refembled
each

cet animal†. Je lui parlai des deux cœurs; il ne feut ce que je lui voulois dire: J'énvoyai de-
mander au chirurgèon major pourquoi il n'avoit pas exécuté ce que je lui avoit dit; il vint nous
raconter l'accident de la foucoupe. Mr. le Chevr. de Chaftellux jugea qu'l n'y avoit pas
d'autre moyen de réparer cette perte, que par un proces verbal, qui conftata ce que nous avions
vu. Mais tout confpiroit contre le defir que Mr. le Chevr. de Chaftellux et moi avions de
perpétuer le fouvenir de ce phenomene: Le chien nous a privé du monument; le maitre nous
refufe fon atteftation, difant, *qu'on ne peut être trop circonfpect à affirmer un fait; qu'il ne faut pas
juger fur des apparences exterieurs; que pour etre affure que ce qui nous a paru des cœurs fuffent reellement
des cœurs, qu'il eut fallu les avoir ouverts, &c.* On ne peut qu'aplaudir aux fentimens qui rendent
M. Vergé fi fcrupuleux. Mais en me piquant d'autant de véracité que M. Vergé, je ne
crains point de la compromettre en rendant exactement ce que j'ai vu, fans altération et fans
exagération. Or j'ai vû deux corps charnus d'un violet brun, de forme un peu oblongue,
plus gros par un bout que par l'autre, un peu plus convexe d'un coté que de l'autre, a peu
près ronds confidérés tranfverfalement. Ces deux corps etoient abfolument femblables l'un a
l'autre

(b) It has nothing external except the two tefticles placed under the belly; the male and the
female have but one orifice placed under the tail, which ferves them to void their excrements,
their urine, and probably for generation. It is not known whether a penis comes out of this
orifice, or whether there is nothing but an opening of the two orifices in the act of copulation.

† *Il n'a d'exterieur que deux tefticules placées fous le ventre, le male et la femelle n'ent qu'un orifice
placé fous la quéue qui leur fert a vider les excréments, leur urine, et probablement à la génération. On
ignore fi par ce clouque le mâle fort une verge, ou s'il ne fe fait qu'un aboutement des deux orifices lors
de la copulation.*

each other exactly in fize, form and colour. From their thicker ends came out feveral veffels, among them I obferved one to each of the bodies pretty large and paler than the reft; a part of this veffel was faftened to the lungs in fuch a manner, that by taking hold of only the lungs, thefe two bodies in queftion were both fufpended at the fame diftance from the lungs. In placing thefe vifcera on the hand in fuch a manner that the refembling fides of thefe two bodies faced each other, the veffels which were fufpended appeared uniformly difpofed, which makes me imagine that the two bodies were uniformly difpofed in the body of the animal[c]. However, the above obfervations being frefh in my memory, I ordered the entrails of four dozen of partridges of the fame fpecies[d], juft taken out, to be brought me; and I found in each a body like the double body which had been found in the bird of Mr. Vergé, having fimilar veffels, fome of which were paler than others, adhering in the fame manner to the lungs, and this body was certainly a heart or my partridges had none. I neverthelefs leave every one at liberty to judge which

U u

l'autre, en volume, en forme, et en couleur; de leur gros bout fortoient plufieurs vaiffeaux, parmi lefquels j'en remarquai un à chacun de ces corps, afsèz gros et de couleur plus pale que les autres; une partie de ces vaiffeaux tenoient au poumon, de manière que faififfant feulement le poumon, les deux corps dont il s'agit y reftoient fufpendus tous deux a la même diftance du poumon. En arrangeant ces vifceres fur la main, de manière que les cotes femblables de ces deux corps fe regardaffent, les vaiffeaux qui y tenoient fe trouvoient fimetriquement difpofés; ce qui me fait juger que ces deux corps devoient fe trouver dans l'animal fimetriquement placés[*]. Enfin ayant encore la memoire fraiche des obfervations fufdites, je me fis apporter les entrailles de quatre douzaines de perdrix de la même efpece[†] que l'on venoit de vider, et j'ai vû qu'il fe trouvoit dans chacune un corps en tout femblable à celui qui s'etoit trouvé double dans la perdrix de M. Vergé, ayant de pareils vaiffeaux, dont un plus pâle que les autres, tenant de la même manière au poumon, et ce corps etoit certainement un cœur, ou mes perdrix n'en avoient pas. Je laiffe maintenant chacun libre de juger lequel paroit le plus vraifemblable, qu'une perdrix eut deux cœurs, ou qu'il ne s'en trouva pas un feul dans quarante

[*] Je prefume qu'ils occupoient les deux cotés du thorax, et que les veines de l'un s'anaftomofit't aux artères de l'autre et reciproquement.

(c) I prefume that they occupied the two fides of the thorax, and that the veins of the one anaftamofed with the arteries of the other, and vice verfa.

[†] Elle eft un peu plus petite que celle qu'on appelle en France perdrix de paffage ou raquette, elle fe perche de même.

(d) It appears rather fmaller than that which, in France, is called perdrix de paffage, or raquette; they fit on a tree in the fame manner.

which was the moſt probable, that one partridge had two hearts, or that forty-eight had none at all. It may indeed be objected, that the firſt might have a true and a falſe one. Mr. Voltaire, who believes that nature amuſes herſelf in making concha veneris, might alſo believe that ſhe diverted herſelf in imitating two hearts. I ſhould therefore be as circumſpect as Mr. Vergé, and not affirm sooner than him that his partridge had two hearts, for I may be miſtaken. I am, however, infinitely more certain of it than that it had but one.

D'ABOVILLE.

Williamſburgh, Feb. 15, 1782.

I the ſubſcriber, ſenior ſurgeon of the regiment of Auxonne, and of the artillerymen of the king's army in America, do declare, that the 10th of this month, having taken out the entrails of the body of a partridge, there appeared to me two hearts. However, during the ſhort time that I had to inſpect them, I was ſo aſtoniſhed with ſo ſurprizing a phenomenon, that I fear my eyes may have deceived me, and I dare not to affirm what I believe I ſaw. I went immediately to a merchant, who lodged next door to me, to ſhow him this miracle, and alſo to Mr. Aboville. The latter has juſt read to me the account he has written of this phenomenon as it appeared to him. I hereby certify that

I ſaw

quarente huit perdrix. Il reſtera à dire que la premiére pouvoit en avoir un vrai et un faux. M. de Voltaire, qui croyoit que la nature s'amuſe a imiter des conqua véneris, auroit pu croire qu'elle s'amuſe auſſi a contrefaire des cœurs; je ferai donc auſſi circonſpect que M. Vergé, et n'affirmerai pas plus que lui que ſa perdrix avoit deux cœurs, car je pourrois me tromper; j'en ſuis cependant infiniment plus certain que je ne le ſuis de n'en avoir qu'un.
A Williamſburg en Virginie, le 15 Fev. 1782.
(Signé) d'Aboville.

JE ſouſſigné, chirurgien major du régiment d'Auxonne, et de l'equipage d'artillerie de l'armée du roi en Amerique; déclare, que le dix de ce mois ayant retiré les entrailles du corps d'une perdrix, il me parut qu'il s'y trouvoit deux cœurs. Mais pendant le peu de temps que j'ai pu les conſidérer, j'étois tellement ebloui d'un phénomene auſſi ſurprenant, que je crains que mes yeux ne m'ayent trompé, et n'oſe affirmer ce que je crois avoir vû. Je fus ſur le champ montrer cette merveille a un marchand qui loge a coté de chez moi, et à M. d'Aboville; ce dernier vient de me lire l'expoſé qu'il a écrit de ce phénomene, tel qu'il s'eſt preſenté

I faw nothing contrary to the obfervations contained in this account.

Williamfburgh, Feb. 15, 1782.   VERGÉ.

I the fubfcriber, merchant at Williamfburgh, refiding next door to Mr. Vergé, fenior furgeon of artillery, do certify that the 10th of this month, this furgeon came to fhew me the entrails of a partridge, and pointed out to me two hearts very diftinct, adhering by their blood-vef-fels to the fame lung. I moreover certify that Mr. Abo-ville has read me the account he has given thereof, and that I find nothing in it contrary to what I faw.

THOMAS BENTLEY.

Williamfburgh, Feb. 18, 1782.

fenté a fes yeux. Je certifie n'avoir rien obfervé qui ne foit conforme aux obfervations con-tenues dans cet expofé.

A Williamfburg, le 18 Fev. 1782.
(Signé) Vergé.

Je fouffigné marchand demeurant à Williamfburg à coté de chez M. Vergé, chirurgien major de l'artillerie, certifie, que le dix de ce mois ce chirurgien vint me montrer les entrailles d'une perdrix, et qu'il m'y fit remarquer deux cœurs, bien diftincts, tenans tous les deux par leurs vaiffeaux fanguins, à un même poumon. Je certifie en outre que M. d'Aboville vient de me lire l'expofé qu'il en a fait, et que je n'y ai rien trouvé que de conforme à ce que j'avois vû.

A Williamfburg, le 18 Fev. 1782.
(Signé) Thomas Bentley.

N° XL.

Conjectures concerning Wind and Water-Spouts, Tornados and Hurricanes. Communicated by Dr. JOHN PERKINS, *of Bofton, to* JOHN MORGAN, *M. D. of Philadelphia, Profeffor of the Theory and Practice of Phyfic; and F. R. S. London, &c.*

WITH refpect to water-fpouts what I am about to confider is whether water afcends or defcends in

U u 2   thefe

thefe bodies? A queftion which it is reafonable to think fhould be determined by facts, and the nature of things; and concerning which, if we wifh to attain to any certainty, we muft be careful not to be mifled by fuch appearances and imaginations, as have hitherto commanded the general belief.

Agreeable to this method of inquiry, I fhall in the firft place produce the obfervations of three or four perfons, in whom I can confide for fimplicity and honefty of intention.

The firft is that of captain Melling, formerly of Bofton, who informed me that in a voyage from our Weft-India iflands, in the month of Auguft, in a warm day juft at evening, a fpout fell clofe by the veffel, and in two or three feconds of time came acrofs the ftern where he then was. A flood of water, as he expreffed it, poured upon him and almoft beat him down, fo that he was obliged to lay hold of what was neareft to him, to prevent being wafhed overboard, which in his fright he was apprehenfive of. But the fpout immediately paffed off with a roaring noife into the fea. I afked him if he tafted the water? Tafte it faid he! I could not help tafting it, it ran into my mouth, nofe, eyes and ears. Was it then frefh or falt? as frefh, faid he, as ever I tafted fpring water in my life.

The next account I had was from captain John Wakefield, alfo of Bofton, which was, that being juft within the ftraits of Gibraltar, a fpout fell clofe by his fhip with a great roaring which he heard as he was fetting in the cabbin, the men upon deck immediately crying out for him to come up, which he inftantly did, and faw it travelling away before the fhip, fo near that he plainly faw the water defcend. His men affured him that it did fo from the beginning. He told me the wind was very fmall during the operation of it.

Captain John Howland, of the fame town, told me that in paffing the calm latitudes, a fpout fell fo near that
he

he evidently faw the water defcend, very contrary to his former opinion concerning thefe bodies.

Mr. Samuel Spring, of the fame town, told me that in a voyage from India, in paffing the ftraits of Malacca, a fpout fell by eftimation about fifty yards from their fhip; the appearance of which was that of a column of water; or rather a ftream of almoft contiguous drops, from the cloud down into the fea, making a great froth in the place like water falling among rocks, as he expreffed it. He faid it was extremely plain that the water defcended. One of the fhip's crew was with him when he gave me this account, and confirmed it.

Many other accounts I have had from thofe who have feen fpouts, but fo indeterminate as not to be worth much notice; I therefore content myfelf with the above, which fpeak for themfelves.

In the next place I fhall make a few remarks on Mr. Stuart's figures of fpouts, which he took in the Mediterranean, as they are to be feen in the philofophical tranfactions of London, Le Motte's abridgement; particularly on the pointing to the place of fpattering in the water, and the great roar that attends the operation of a large fpout; the bufh about the foot or bafe of a great fpout; the break or partition in the trunk of it at the top of the bufh; and the pillar-like appearance within the bufh.

Firft I fhall endeavour to give fome idea of the nature and caufe of the pointing by the external and apparent means that nature ufes in the production of a fpout; for as to the intimate operations of nature our faculties cannot reach them. Two or three obfervations I fuppofe will readily be granted, and fhorten my work.

One is that thofe places where the lower region of air is drawn away on one or both fides, either by the heat of neighbouring continents, or in the calm latitudes, from which it paffes away into, and for the fupply of the equatorial

torial expence, are likely to be the places moft liable to
fpouts.

In the next place I expect it will be granted that the air is
much colder in the upper regions, and of confequence fpecifically heavier than that near the furface, by which
when there are little or no differing motions of the air,
(i. e. winds) in or about the region of the clouds, particular
fpots of air and vapour in the cloud, may be difpofed to
defcend, and, when fo, will take very aptly a particular
channel downwards.   Thefe things being granted what is
of a like kind will readily be fo difpofed too, as when the
atmofphere is full of vapours condenfing into clouds, this
condenfation may be quicker in one place than in another,
which by the acquired cold will become more weighty
and prefs moft in a particular point.   Thus it may defcend
through the more rarified and yielding fubjacent region, the
firft drops piercing and making a channel may facilitate the
defcent of the vapour, till it puts on what Stuart calls a
fword-like appearance.   The agitation caufed by defcending will accelerate condenfation, which together with the
drops paffing through the vapour in this channel, may at
every ftop in the paffage be wafting the vapour, by taking
it up into leffer maffes of water till it ends in a point,
which it will in this cafe naturally do, becaufe the fwifteft
motion down is in the center of the pointing body.

Such a fpout may increafe fo as to form maffes of water, the fubftance of the cloud, all obftacles removed, paffing down in greater abundance, and ftill more fwiftly
condenfing; or it may prefently ceafe when it has but juft
appeared, or inftead of this, make, as it were, feveral attempts for completing a fpout, the vapour teat advancing
and retiring alternately, but which finally fail, without
producing effect.   Thus it has done, as it feems, when
the cloud has not had fufficient fupplies for it to fucceed
in a complete and opaque fpout.   Such are the appearances of Mr. Stuart's figures, &c.   The obliquity of the
                                                    pointing

pointing is owing to the courfe of the air, as the bend is to two different ones at different heights.

The next thing propofed to be confidered, was the great roar that attends a complete fpout while it lafts; and it is the fame as that in cataracts or falls of water from great eminencies. This kind of roar could not exift in any way of afcent, being very different from that of a whirlwind, which is no other than that of any other ftrong wind.

Mr. Stuart's figures of the great fpouts are drawn with the appearance of a bufh round their bafes : The cafe is fuch, that great falls of waters muft make a proportionable fpray; fo that the appearance is natural, and indeed a neceffary confequence. It rifes up from the foot of the fpout and falls back in a parabolic manner into the fea. As was faid of the roar juft now, fo it may be faid of this, that it could not have exifted in any conceivable way of afcent; while on the contrary it is perfectly agreeable to nature on the principle of defcent. It continues the whole time of a large fpout, increafing and diminifhing as that does.

The appearance of a break or partition in the trunk of the fpout, at the top of the bufh, is a very curious phenomenon : It is not real but apparent, and could not have happened without the bufh; it being caufed by a refraction of rays from the drops that conftitute the top of the bufh; whence a divergency and fo much lofs of vifion.

In great fpouts there is alfo a pillar-like appearance, being a part of the trunk within the bufh, and by another refraction through the fide of the bufh; by which it appears much bigger than it is, and limited in altitude by the break. The three laft are agreeable to the laws of optics; and all the five particulars being attendants on the greater or the fmaller fpouts, are to me undeniable evidences of the univerfal defcent of waters in thefe bodies. I pafs from Mr. Stuart's figures to that of Mr. Maine, which is not lefs curious.

Mr.

Mr. Maine, in the fame philofophical tranfactions, has given us the figure of a fpout that fell at Topfham, near Exeter. He has depicted it in the act of ftriking a boat as it paffed a creek ; from the bottom of which he has drawn a rebound of the whole body of the fpout projected from it to a large diftance ; evidently proving the defcent : And which, while he is arguing for the afcent, it would have much become him to have accounted for, and to have fhown how it agreed with the doctrine of afcent. The fpout proceeding paffed on to the land, and brake off the limbs of a tree, beat the thatch off of a houfe, and did perhaps various other damage ; but we hear nothing of its carrying up any of the light fubftances and dropping them at great diftances, far from any environs of the place, which it would moft certainly have done had there been a whirlwind, or any fupernal fuction employed in the operation.

The fupernal fuction which fome have mentioned I fuppofe I may pafs over without more than the bare mention of it, but whirlwinds we know there are frequently, and fome of confiderable ftrength; fo that it being the general opinion that fpouts are formed by them, it may not be amifs to examine a little what force they may reafonably be allowed to have, and the limits of it.

Their genuine caufe, fuppofing them to be natural productions, is no other than the afcent of the heated and confequently lighter air, at the furface, into, or through the colder and confequently heavier regions of the atmofphere above : And in proportion to the different degrees of heat in one of thefe, and cold in the other, may the ftrength of thefe be, but no more.

Dr. Arbuthnot, in his treatife on the air, tells us, that the rarification of the air in the hotteft day in fummer renders it but one-tenth lighter than that of the coldeft in winter, or in words to this purpofe, if I remember right, for I have not his book by me. Suppofing then the upper region the fame at all times as the lower one in winter

ter when a whirlwind happens, it cannot have any greater force than the weight of one-tenth of the atmofphere,
and confidering the refiftance to its rifing which it muft en-
counter, and the friction by the way, not fo much; by which
the ftrength may not be equal to three feet of water.   It is
undoubtedly nine parts in ten too weak to make a vacuum,
and having a column of water two miles high to fupport,
befides the additional neceffity of ftill more force to drive
it fwiftly up, would require an atmofphere two thoufand
times more weighty than ours to raife water to the clouds.

Mr. Stuart fays he faw the water afcend in the heart of
a fpout; which feems to have been an unlucky expreffion.
The bodies of large fpouts are too grofs and opaque for
any one to fee to the center of them; and no one has ever
pretended to have feen water afcend in the fmall ones.
His imagination therefore muft have been too ftrong for
any one to confide in, fo far as was he prejudiced; and
at leaft one of his views was to prove the afcent; which,
had he underftood nature in a tolerable degree, he would
have renounced.

That there is a gyrating appearance in the great fpouts,
feems to have been matter of obfervation; nor is there any
improbability in the thing.   As air paffing up in whirlwinds, fo water, or air, paffing down may gyrate; and no
doubt it does.   The cafe is, that fome have imagined the
gyration to have been upwards: but the appearance of gyration up or down may eafily deceive, as any one may be
convinced by obferving the fwift turning of artificial
fcrews, in which the direction will appear as the perfon is
difpofed to fancy it.

We are told the Chinefe failors anfwer to the queftion,
what are you afraid of in fpouts, is, that they may break
in their decks.   Which fhows they take them to be defcents; and their knowledge is from obfervation and experience.

I conclude with one fhort remark, viz. That to believe water afcends in thefe bodies, to the region of the

clouds, is virtually to admit of real and effential miracle, without fufficient proof; and contrary to every idea we can form, of a divinely wife intention.

Tornados and hurricanes I take to be of the fame gene-ral nature, although differing in fome circumftances and appearances.

By the term tornado, or wind-fpout, I mean a violent wind which has been obferved in thefe northern colonies a few times fince they were difcovered and fettled by our people. But perhaps no part of the terraqeous globe is en-tirely free from fomething of the like kind, as the atmof-phere is every where liable to fimilar commotions.

The Spanifh term of tornado, feems to have been chiefly ufed for a violent ftorm at fea, of larger extent than what I am about to explain, which is of a more contracted na-ture, and confined to a narrow fphere of action; fo that it requires a particular and fignificant name, fuch as wind-fpout, till a more fuitable one is found for it.

Defcription of one. It begins of a fudden; more or lefs of clouds having been drawn together, a fpout of wind coming from it ftrikes the ground in a round fpot of a few rods or perches diameter, with a prone direction, in the courfe of the wind of the day, and proceeds thus half a mile or a mile. The pronenefs of its defcent makes it re-bound from the earth, throwing fuch things as are move-able before it, but fome fideways from it. A vapour, mift or rain defcends with it, by which the path of it is mark-ed and wet.

I fhall produce the inftance of that at Leicefter, a town about fifty miles from Bofton, a few years fince, which being more violent than ufual, may give fome idea of the thing.

It happened in the month of July, on a hot day about four o'clock P. M. A few clouds having gathered weft-ward and coming over head, a fudden motion of their running together in a point being obferved, immediately a fpout of wind ftruck the ground at the weftern end of a
houfe

houfe, and inftantly carried it away, with a negro fellow
in it, who was afterwards found dead in the path of it.
Two men and a woman, by the breach of the floor, fell
into the cellar; one man was driven forceably up into the
chimney-corner.   Thefe were preferved, though much
bruifed; they were wet with a vapour or mift, as were the
remains of the floor and the whole path of the fpout.

This wind raifed boards, timbers, &c. and carried them
before it.   A joift was found on one end driven near three
feet into the ground.   I imagine the fpout took it in its
elevated ftate and drove it forceably down.   By what I
can learn of its procedure, it continued but three or four
feconds of time in a place, paffing along with the celerity
of a middling wind, conftantly declining in ftrength till
it ceafed.

There feems to have been fuch a guft as this at cape
Cod, about forty years ago, of which I received an account from two men who lived in the neighbourhood of
the place.   It came on of a fudden, and was fo violent that
it threw down a young woman who happened to be in the
way of it; fhe was forced to lay hold on the bufhes which
happened to be within her reach, to prevent her being carried away by it.   It paffed a pond of water, and the people
wondered it did not fuck up the water, as they conceived it
to be a water-fpout, but it did not.   The young woman
was however wet with the vapour that accompanied it.

Of Hurricanes, particularly thofe of the Weft-India Iflands.

To account fatisfactorily for thefe convulfions of our
atmofphere, requires a greater number and more circumftantial obfervations than we are at prefent furnifhed with;
fo that all that can at prefent be faid of their origin and
caufes muft be very conjectural.   However, fince an attempt to explain them may give occafion to further and
more exact obfervations, I fhall proceed to offer my prefent thoughts concerning them.

I believe

I believe thofe of the Weft-India iflands to be owing to
fome occafional obftruction in the ufual and natural procedure of the equatorial trade. This I conjecture from
the more than ufual preceding calms. In the natural courfe
of this trade the air rifes up in the line and paffes off towards the poles, and, in the more contracted degrees of the
greater latitudes, proves the courfe of their weftern trades :
So that could this afcent be prevented through the whole
circle of that zone, there would be no more wefterly winds
in thefe latitudes than any others.

Over violent rains and cold naturally tend to check the
afcent of air out of this circle, rather making it defcend.
And as there are annual rains in the equator over againft
thofe iflands, and in fome years more than others, it is eafy
to conceive fuch an effect, and the confequences. Great
clouds and over-much vapour generate cold and weight,
while at the fame time the rains are beating down the air ;
and as thefe prevent the rifing of the air out of the line,
fo they hinder its ufual progrefs to it from the tropics on
both fides. Thus calms muft take place ; by which the
natives ufed to predict approaching hurricanes, without
underftanding the reafon of the thing.

Much of calms in the inter-tropical climates caufe ra-
rifactions, and afcents of air into the upper regions, inftead
of its being carried to the line to be difpofed of in the
grand circulation of the atmofphere; this will be the cafe
more efpecially among the iflands, which increafe the heat
of the atmofphere. Then by thefe afcents there will be ac-
cumulations of air above, which becoming cold in the higher regions will acquire a greater fpecific weight, and be difpofed to defcend on the firft giving way of the more rarified and yielding fubjacent region ; and this will be the
cafe when there happens not to be fufficient motions of
air in the middle region to keep fmooth and even the ftra-
tums of the more and the lefs rarified regions ; and fo
prevent particular portions and places from bending downwards;

wards; and it is this alone that does prevent it. By a failure in this, a defcent once begun, the confequences cannot be prevented: The heavy quantity above will continue to defcend till all the upper cold regions are exonerated to many hundreds of miles round; and all their contents fhifted into the place of the rarified and lighter air below.

Such are my ideas of the caufes and operations of a hurricane in thofe climates. I have only to add here, that the rains in thefe violent ftorms are, as I think, a ftrong confirmation of the doctrine of defcent; as they are in that kind of hurricane called by failors the Ox's Eye, on the coaft of Guinea; and the like happens under various names in different parts of our globe. Even the wind in our thunder-gufls is from defcent; the air in the cloud being rendered denfe and weighty, defcends, and flows in the direction of the wind of the time, and with the more violence, by the warm air at the furface giving way to it. Thefe are fometimes ftrong, but feldom attended with danger or damage.

What objections may be raifed againft thefe opinions, fhall be candidly attended to; in the mean time there is one objection that muft be obviated, the argument being fomewhat interefted in it. It is as follows.

Having expreffed my opinion that hurricanes and tornados or wind fpouts have the fame general nature, while we fee a great difparity in their magnitude and procedure; fome explanation feems neceffary to prevent miftakes; I think a little confideration of the place, climate, and circumftances may remove the difficulty.

The earth is an oblate fpheroid, its diameter many miles greater at the equator than at the poles, caufed by its diurnal centrifugal force. If this then has fo great an effect on terraqueous matter, it cannot have lefs on our air, but if any difference, rather more; efpecially if we confider, that the atmofphere makes a larger diameter, and yet revolves

volves in the fame time, fo that its centrifugal force muft be proportionably greater. The diurnal motion of the earth tends to throw a vaft furplus of air on the equator, by which there is probably more air between the tropics than on the reft of the globe. But this is a matter of conjecture not to be perceived by any fort of preffure any more than by the barometer, for reafons obvious to thofe converfant in the nature and effect of the feveral principles. However it might not be amifs to obferve whether there be any difference in the height of the mercury before any of thefe ftorms. But to return.

Although the air in the intert-ropical latitudes is in the general lighter than in the remote ones, yet when the upper air has obtained a paffage downward, it being vaft in quantity, and occupying great fpace, it will be long in accelerating and paffing down. The paffage is long, fo that it will gain a great deal of the force we find it has by the length of defcent. Neither will the middle region be difpofed to fhut up without a brifk wind in it, before the whole, even to remote regions, is difcharged through the large hiatus, as before mentioned and now repeated, to account for the duration and extent of thefe otherwife wonderful winds, with fuch unrelenting violence.

Far different is the cafe of the high latitude tornados in their circumftances and their manner, although agreeing in their general nature. The centrifugal force here has extremely little effect, unlefs to caft the atmofphere toward the equator inftead of raifing or increafing its quantity over any given place on either fide. Befides there is the attraction of the fun, moon, and all the other planets for ever within the tropics attracting the atmofphere that way and leffening the height of the high latitude atmofphere, which therefore may be fuppofed not a fourth fo high from the furface as that.

Since then the atmofphere is vaftly lefs in height, and alfo much lefs in quantity than toward the line, the defcents
muft

muſt naturally be very different.   Here are no accumula-
tions aloft.   The quantity ready for a diſcharge downward
is vaſtly leſs, and the paſſage narrow and contracted ; and
by the almoſt conſtant motions of air, were there more
ſupplies it would ſoon ſhut up.   Beſides there is little apt-
neſs to flow from ſurrounding regions by reaſon of the
ſmallneſs of their depth, &c.   And yet ſo great is the ſpe-
cific weight of what deſcends, that the firſt aſſault has been
known to equal the greateſt violence of the proper hurricanes in their moſt powerful moments.

N° XLI.

The whole Proceſs of the Silk-Worm, from the Egg to the
Cocon ; communicated to Dr. JOHN MORGAN, *Phyſici-*
an at Philadelphia, in two Letters from Meſſrs HARE
and SKINNER, *Silk Merchants in London,* July 27,
1774, *and February* 24, 1775.

Read July
8, 1775.

IT is ſome time ſince we were honored with your
eſteemed letter of 27th September laſt.   We
ſhould not have delayed ſo long acknowledging its receipt,
if it had been in our power to have ſent you before this
time the manuſcript you will receive herewith ; but it is
only lately we have been able to procure it from one of
the firſt houſes in Italy.   It contains an exact account of
the Italian moſt improved method of making raw ſilk.
We flatter ourſelves it may prove of ſome ſervice to your
new eſtabliſhed manufactory, for whoſe uſe ſolely we ſent
for it to Italy.

The large quantity of raw ſilk that continually arrives
from China every year, being moſtly of a round or large
ſize, will a good deal interfere with the ſale of yours,
provided

provided you make it of the fame ; therefore we by all means recommend your reeling yours of the finenefs of five to fix cocons, no coarfer at any rate if avoidable. And we further beg leave to recommend your giving orders to your workmen to be extremely careful in afforting the filk, obferving that all that is put into one parcel be exactly, if poffible, of the fame finenefs ; for if it is not, it will very much prejudice its fale; a neglect in this particular is complained of in all the filk that has hitherto been received from America. If the filk, which was very good in itfelf that we received from Georgia, had been properly afforted, we certainly fhould have fold it 1/6 or 2f. per *lb.* better than we did. If you reel your filk fine the China filk rather promotes its fale than otherwife, as it is neceffary to have fine filk to work up with that of China.

We fhall at all times be very ready to communicate to you any intelligence in our power.

We are, with refpect,

Sir,

Your moft obedient fervants,

HARE & SKINNER.

Chap. I. *Of the Silk-Worm.*

THE perfon who purpofes raifing a quantity of filkworms, and preferving good eggs, muft begin a year before hand. He muft choofe a certain number of good cocons, or filk cods, the fuperficies of which, he flightly pierces with a needle and thread and ftrings them by fcores ; which done, he hangs them up in a convenient room, this being the moft proper pofition for them. After the moths or butterflies contained in the cocon, have eaten their way through their natural inclofure, (which is generally about four days after the cocon is finifhed*) you

may

---

* It happens fometimes the butterfly is longer before its birth, i. e. from 15 to 30 days if the weather is chilly. They generally come out in the morning.

may place them on a linen cloth difpofed vertically, as against a wall, or on a line, &c. where they couple and are joined during twenty-four hours. This over, the female lays her eggs during other twenty-four hours; after which fhe dies, as does the male; this their fecond life, if I may be permitted the term, is only of forty-eight hours duration. When the eggs are new laid, they are about the bignefs of a common pin's head, and of a ftraw colour; by degrees they become black, affume more folidity, lofing at the fame time part of their bulk.

When they are arrived at this point, you muft feparate them from the cloth; to effect which, you muft dip them into a large pan filled with one half water and the other half wine, rather more than lukewarm; when your cloth has foaked in this liquor a little while, you may feparate them from the cloth with a filver fpoon and dry them in a funny place, and take them away when they begin to be whitifh.

When you have thus detached your eggs, you muft keep them till the next year in a cool damp place to preferve them from hatching during the great heat, which would ruin the project.

On the arrival of the fpring, you muft obferve when the mulberry tree begins to put forth its leaves, which muft be your fignal to expofe your eggs in a very warm place, that they may all hatch at once, otherwife they would only hatch by little and little, and in proportion as each individual would be arrived at the point of its natural maturity. In which cafe the pains required to feparate their different claffes would be exceffive, not to fay impoffible. To hatch your eggs you muft carry them about you nine or ten days, keeping them in your bofom, or other parts near the body; in the night you may put them between the matraffes of the bed. You may likewife hatch them by the heat of an oven, but this method is dangerous, becaufe you may poffibly burn the worm

Y y   contained

contained in the egg, and thereby deſtroy all your future
hopes.

II. The worm is entirely black at its birth, and is about
as long as an ant. He is rolled up in the egg, which
otherwiſe could not contain him. He preſerves this black
colour eight or nine days. After your worms are hatched
you muſt put them on wicker ſhelves, which are covered
firſt with paper and afterwards with a bed of the youngeſt
and moſt tender mulberry leaves; you may place ſeveral
ranges of them in the ſame chamber, one above another,
provided you leave at leaſt a foot and a half between each
range; that the ſcaffolding be in the middle of the room,
and that your wicker ſhelves be not too broad, but juſt ſo
as to reach on each ſide conveniently to the middle. By
degrees the worm grows and requires more room. It muſt
be your care to thin them, and keep thoſe of the ſame ſize
as near as you can on one row; for which reaſon you muſt
always leave ſome ſhelves vacant for that purpoſe.

The worm continues feeding during eight days after
its birth, at the end of which he has three lines in length
or the fourth part of an inch. He is then attacked with
his firſt ſickneſs, which conſiſts in a kind of lethargic ſleep
for three days together, during which ſpace he changes
his ſkin, ſtill preſerving the ſame bulk.

This ſleep being over, he begins to eat again during
five days, at which term he is grown to the ſize of ſeven
lines in length, after which follows a ſecond ſickneſs*, in
every reſpect like the former. He then feeds during other
five days, and is now about nine lines in length, when
he is attacked with his third ſickneſs; which over, he continues to eat again five days more, which are followed by
his fourth ſickneſs, at which time he is arrived at his full
growth, i. e. about fourteen lines in length and two in
diameter.

He

---

* You muſt obſerve that theſe ſickneſſes are much longer, and laſt ſeven or eight days when
the weather is cold.

He then feeds during five days with a moft voracious
appetite; after which he difdains his food, becomes tranfparent a little on the yellow caft, and leaves his filky
traces on the leaves where he paffes; thefe figns denote
that he is ready to begin his cocon.

You muft then furnifh him with little bufhes of heath,
broom or other like twigs, fticking the bundles upright
in rows between the fhelves, and forcing them a little that
they may not fall; he remains ftill two days to climb up
the twigs, and fettle himfelf on a good place, after which
he begins to lay the foundation of his lodge, and is five
days in fpinning his cocon. He remains generally about
the fpace of forty-feven days.

III. You muft keep your worms in a dry place, fheltered and fhut up clofe, provided it be not too hot. If the
weather be cold you muft make a fmall fire. When you
furnifh them with leaves, take great care that they be
thoroughly dry and ftrew them lightly over your worms.
You muft obferve to take away their dung very frequently. When the worms are ready to mount (in order to
fpin) if the weather be ftifling hot attended with thunder,
you will fee them in a languifhing condition; your care
muft then be to revive them, which is effected thus.

Take a few eggs and onions and fry them in a pan
with fome ftale hog's lard, the ranker the better, and
make pancake; which done, carry it fmoaking hot into
the room where they are kept, and go round the chamber
with it. You will be furprized to fee how the fmell revives
them, excites thofe to eat who have not done feeding, and
makes the others that are ready to fpin, climb up the twigs.

Thefe little creatures require a great deal of care in the
management; one or other muft attend them day and
night; you muft be very dexterous and gentle in handling
them; and, as I may fay, the whole fuccefs depends on the
care you obferve and pains you take in rearing them.

The worms cannot fuffer ftrong fmells, fuch as tobacco

and the like, for which reafon you muft avoid offending
their delicate organs.

In many parts of Italy, amongft others Romagna and
La Marche of Ancona, they have two filk racoltas, or har-
vefts. They keep the eggs in very cool places, and when
the mulberry tree begins to bud again (for during the racolta it is ftripped of its leaves for food for the worms)
they expofe their eggs to hatch. Sometimes they give
rofe leaves to the young worms, when there are no young
mulberry leaves. The cocons of this fecond racolta are
rather inferior to thofe of the firft. The filk worm is generally fourteen lines in length and two in diameter and
fix and two-fevenths in circumference. He is either of
a milk or pearl colour or blackifh: thefe laft are the beft.
His body is divided into feven rings, to each of which are
joined two very fhort feet. He has a fmall point like a
thorn, exactly above the anus. The fubftance which
forms the filk, is in their ftomach, which is very long;
wound up as it were on two fpindles and furrounded
with a gum, commonly yellow, fometimes white, not often
greenifh. When the worm fpins his cocon, he winds off
a thread from each of his fpindles, and joins them, afterwards, by means of two hooks which are placed in his
mouth; fo that the cocon is compofed of a double thread.
Having opened a filk worm you may take out the fpindles which are folded up in three plaits, and on ftretching
them out and drawing each extremity, you may extend
them to near two ells in length. If you then fcrape the
thread fo ftretched out with your nail, you will fcratch off
the gum, which is very much like bees-wax, and performs
the fame office to the filk it covers, as a gold leaf does to the
ingot of filver it furrounds, when drawn out by the wire-
drawer; the filk then remains of a pearl colour. This
thread which is extremely ftrong and even is about the
thicknefs of a middling pin.

Three things very remarkable in this infect, are,

1. They

1. They defcribe a femicircle in eating.

2. Their excrement has perfectly the form of a mulberry.

3. They have no fex before their metamorphofis.

Chap. II. *Of the Cocons.*

I. IT is almoft a general rule to wait fix or feven days after all the cocons feem to be formed, before you take them off the boughs in order to give the worms time to bring them to perfection. It is then proper from that time to give fome air to the room in which you have kept them, in order to diffipate a confiderable dampnefs which the worms exhale on their mounting, (when they have not been well fed and kept, for when they have been properly nurfed this dampnefs is not to be found) and which is of great detriment to the cocons, either by rotting them, rendering them foft, or covering them with fpots.

The cocons may be divided into two general claffes, the white and the yellow, in the yellow you meet with all the fhades from a bright yellow diminifhing at laft to white, fome few are of a pale green. We reckon nine forts of cocons, viz.

1. The good cocons are thofe which are brought to their perfection, ftrong and little, and not at all fpotted.

2. The pointed cocons are thofe, one of whofe extremities rifes up in a point. After having afforded a little filk, the point, which is the weaker part, breaks or tears, and it is impoffible to continue winding that cocon any longer, becaufe when the thread comes round to the hole it is of confequence broke.

3. The cocalons are a little bigger than the other, yet they do not contain more filk, becaufe the contexture is not fo ftrong. In winding they are to be feparated from the reft, becaufe they require to be wound in cooler water, otherwife they furze out in winding.

4. The

4. The dupions, or douple cocons, are so called becaufe they contain fometimes two and fometimes three worms, who have jointly formed one fingle cocon. They interlace their threads, for which reafon they are to be kept afunder from the reft; they make the filk we call dupions.

5. The foufflons are cocons very imperfect, whofe contexture is loofe, fometimes to that degree that they are tranfparent, and bear the fame proportion to the others, as a gauze to a fattin. Thefe cannot be wound.

6. The perforated cocons are fo called, becaufe they have a hole at one end, for which reafon they alfo cannot be wound.

7. The calcined cocons are thofe whofe worm, after the formation of the cocon, is attacked with a ficknefs which fometimes petrifies it, and at others reduces it to a fine white powder, without in the leaft endamaging the filk; on the contrary, thefe cocons produce more filk than the others, becaufe the worm is confiderably lighter. They are to be diftinguifhed by the noife the petrified worm makes when you fhake the cocon. In Piedmont they fell for half as much again as the others. It is very rare to fee a parcel of 25 *lb.* of them at a time: 63 *lb.* of thefe cocons have produced 1 *lb.* 1 *oz.* of fine filk of five to fix cocons.

8. The good choquette confifts in thofe cocons whofe worm dies, before he has brought it to its perfection. They are to be known by the worms fticking to one fide of the cocon, which is eafily to be perceived when on fhaking it you do not hear the chryfalis rattle. Thefe cocons are of as fine filk as the others, but they are to be wound feparately becaufe they are fubject to furze out, and the filk has not fo bright a colour, neither is it fo ftrong and nervous.

9. The bad choquette is compofed of defective cocons, fpotted or rotten. They wind many of thefe cocons together. It makes a very foul bad qualified filk of a blackifh colour.

II. To

II. To know whether a cocon be good or not you muſt obſerve if it be firm and ſound, or not, if it has a fine grain,
and if the two ends are round and ſtrong.   The cocons
of a bright yellow yield more ſilk than the others, becauſe
they contain a greater quantity of gum; but the advantage accrues to the winder only, becauſe all this gum is
loſt in the dying.   For which reaſon, as well as for certain colours they take better, the pale ſilks are preferred,
becauſe having leſs gum they loſe leſs in boiling.

In the number of cocons that are bought, there ought
to be neither ſoufflons, nor perforated cocons; becauſe
the ſeller is obliged to keep them apart and to ſell them
as ſuch; notwithſtanding which, you may always reckon
on half profit of theſe ſorts that remain with the others,
and if to theſe you add the dupions and choquette, you
may calculate them at ten per cent.

The cocons of the mountains are better than thoſe of
the plain; there is a greater quantity of white amongſt
them.   'Tis true they are not ſo large as thoſe of the plain,
but the worm, at the ſame time, is proportionably leſs.
The reaſon of which is, that the air of the mountains being ſharper, the worm labours with greater vigour.   They
ſucceed, likewiſe, better in the dry plains than in the damp
and marſhy parts, becauſe the leaf is more nouriſhing.
Five or ſix days after the cocon has been detached from
the branches, it is your buſineſs to prevent the birth of
the worm, who would, otherwiſe, pierce through the ſhell,
and thereby render the cocon uſeleſs.   To prevent which
you muſt put your cocons in long ſhallow baſkets, and
fill them up within an inch of the top.   You then cover
them with paper and a wrapper over that.   Theſe baſkets
are to be diſpoſed in an oven, whoſe heat is as near as can
be that of an oven from which the bread is juſt drawn
after being baked.   After your cocons have remained
therein near an hour, you muſt draw them out, and to ſee
whether all the worms are dead, draw out a dupion from
the

the middle of your baſket and open it, if the worm be dead, you may conclude all the reſt are ſo; becauſe the contexture of the dupion being ſtronger than that of the other cocons, it is conſequently leſs eaſy to be penetrated by the heat. You muſt obſerve to take it from the middle of the baſket, becauſe in that part the heat is leaſt perceptible; after you have drawn your baſkets from the oven, you muſt firſt cover each of them with a woolen blanket or rug, leaving the wrapper beſides, and then you pile them one on the other. If your baking has ſucceeded, your woolen cover will be all over wet with a kind of dew, the thickneſs of your little finger. If there be leſs, it is a ſign your cocons have been too much or too little baked. If too much baked, the worm being over dried, cannot tranſpire a humour he no longer contains, and your cocon is then burnt. If not enough baked, the worm has not been ſufficiently penetrated by the heat to diſtil the liquor he contains, and in that caſe is not dead.

You muſt let your baſkets ſtand thus covered five or ſix hours if poſſible, in order to keep in the heat, as this makes an end of ſtifling thoſe worms, which might have avoided the firſt impreſſion of the fire.

You are likewiſe to take great care to let your cocons ſtand in the oven the time that is neceſſary; for if they do not ſtand long enough your worm is only ſtunned for a time and will afterwards be revived. If on the other hand, you leave them too long in the oven you burn them, many inſtances of theſe two caſes are frequently to be met with.

It is a good ſign when you ſee ſome of the butterflies ſpring out from among the cocons which have been baked, becauſe you may be certain they are not burnt. For if you would kill them all to the laſt worm you would burn many cocons, which might be more expoſed to the heat than that particular worm.

III. When

III. When you put your cocons into the oven, you muſt be very careful in picking out all the ſpotted ones, other-wiſe they communicate their ſpots by the great perſpirati-on occaſioned in them by the heat. If you have a parcel of ſtrong and another of weak cocons, and you can only wind a part of them freſh (i. e. without baking) give the preference to the weak cocons, and bake your ſtrong ones, becauſe the latter, containing more gum, ſupport the baking much better and ſuffer leſs than the weak ones.

As faſt as the cocons you buy are brought in, put them in baſkets and expoſe them to the ſun, if it ſhines, in caſe your oven be full, in order at leaſt to ſtun the worm and prevent his working to pierce his cocon during that time.

It is very proper likewiſe that they be a little in the air before you put them in the oven; becauſe the peaſants bring them in baſkets heaped one on the other, which heats them and renders them extremely ſoft, but the air brings them to their proper tone again.

Sometimes the peaſants ſell you the cocons ready baked when they have been obliged to keep them ſometime. It is eaſy to know them, becauſe the worms when baked, being dry, make a louder noiſe on rattling them than when they are freſh.

When your cocons are fully baked, and have ſtood long enough, you muſt ſpread them half a foot thick on broad ozier ſhelves, which are diſtributed into as many ſtories as the height of the room will admit of, two or three feet diſtant one from the other; taking care to turn them every day, and to change their places, for otherwiſe there are many inconveniencies that would ariſe from ſuch a neglect. They would become mouldy and the moths would eat them. Beſides this, it is abſolutely neceſſary in order to ſeparate the ſpotted cocons, or the bad choquette, which would ſpread to all the cocons that are near them, and muſt be wound immediately to prevent their damaging any further.

Z z

The

The building where you fpread your cocons is called
the Coconiere, and confifts of one or more large rooms, in
which are diftributed as many ranges as you can conveniently place, taking care that the fupporters touch neither the roof nor the wall, becaufe if there were any rats in
the Coconiere they would come down the poles, and deftroy the cocons, they being very greedy of the worm contained in them.

A middling cocon has about thirteen lines in its greater diameter, by eight lines the leffer diameter, fome are
larger, fome are fmaller; but this is the general fize.
The dupion has generally fifteen lines great diameter by
nine leffer diameter.

The cocon is compofed of feveral ftrata or furfaces applied one on the other; notwithftanding they all communicate, otherwife it would be impoffible to wind them off.
It is an eafy matter to take off one or more of thefe furfaces, the uppermoft of which is coarfer, lefs gummed,
and higher coloured than the undermoft. Finally, thefe
furfaces are compofed of a fine fort of faliva, whofe texture has a tolerable refemblance to the thin fkin you find
joined to the infide of a hen's egg.

The cocons produce a thread of a very unequal length,
you may meet fome that yield twelve hundred ells, whilft
others will fcarcely afford two hundred ells. In general
you may calculate the production of a cocon, from five
hundred to fix hundred ells in length.

IV. The worm or chryfalis, as he is inclofed in his cocon is fhrunk up into himfelf, fo that it is but half as
long in his primitive ftate, but it is on the contrary as
thick again.

He is of a cinnamon colour, and full of liquor, rather
clear, which forms the feed in the males, and the eggs
in the females. Though he feems to be infenfible in
that ftate, yet you may perceive he is not wholly fo, for
on piercing him with a pin flightly, you will fee him
move,

move, and we make ufe of thefe experiments to fee if they have been killed in the oven.

The worm dries the older it grows, fo that the fame quantity, or the fame number of cocons decreafes daily in weight. The cocons which enclofe the male butterfly have more filk at the extremities, than thofe which contain the females; but it is very difficult to perceive this difference, the moft fkilful connoiffeurs will miftake at leaft twenty in a hundred.

When the worm wants to break his way through, he pierces the cocon, firft wetting it a little in order to gnaw it the more eafily ; he has then only to ftrip off his upper coat, under which he has another quite white, with wings.

When he comes out, his wings, which at firft appear very fmall, open and difplay themfelves by little and little, and are entirely at liberty in an hour or two. As foon as born he feeks a female, and one would fay he is born again merely to propagate his fpecies, for he expires a very little time after having performed his function.

CHAP. III. *Of Cocons Royal, Perforated Cocons, and Soufflons.*

THE royal cocons are thofe which you have kept for feed. The worm makes a hole in them for his paffage, fo that they cannot be wound, and are in the fame clafs with the perforated cocons.

Neither can the foufflons be wound, becaufe their thread being the produce of a weak, fick worm, it has not the gum it ought to contain. Befides they cannot be wound off, their thread being interlaced and entangled.

The ufes you may make of thefe cocons are the following ; and firft for the

Soufflons ; you muft let them boil for about half an hour in common water, after which you muft dry them. When they are quite dry you muft threfh them on the

Z z 2

floor

floor with a flail, to bring out the worm, which is reduced
to aſhes by the fire and air. Afterwards you put them
on a diſtaff and open them; to effect which you muſt take
them by the two ends and ſtretch them out at arms length,
you may then faſten them on your diſtaff.

2. The perforated cocons; you muſt obſerve the ſame
method as for the ſoufflons, except that you muſt let them
boil three-quarters inſtead of half an hour, becauſe they
contain a greater quantity of gum.

3. The cocons royal. As it is natural to ſuppoſe you
keep the flower of your cocons for ſeed; they are fuller
of gum than the others, for which reaſon you muſt let
them boil an hour; after which you muſt not threſh them
as the former, becauſe they contain no worm, neither is
it neceſſary to ſtay till they are quite dry before you ſpin
them; on the contrary, they open more eaſily when damp.
The produce of theſe three ſorts of cocons, when worked,
makes what we call *fleuret*.

After you have boiled the cocons and threſhed them
well, to ſhake out the worm they contain, you may card
them inſtead of opening them as above, you will then
make a much more beautiful fleuret, and of a brighter
colour, but it will at the ſame time come conſiderably
dearer, becauſe of the waſte in carding. A good ſpinſter
performs a very reaſonable days work if ſhe can ſpin an
ounce of fleuret.

To ſum up the whole, and give you a notion of the value of theſe three ſorts of cocons, you may calculate thus.

If the good cocons are worth one hundred, the perforated are worth thirty-three one third, the ſoufflons twenty-five, the royal cocons two hundred and fifty; but if
your royal cocons are not choſen ones for ſeed, they are
worth but two hundred.

The beſt fleuret is that which proceeds from the royal
cocons, afterwards that of the perforated cocons unchoſen,
laſt of all that of the ſoufflons.

CHAP.

CHAP. IV. *Of the Filature, or Winding from the Worm.*

Although the fresh cocons, that is to say, those that have not been baked in the oven, yield a brighter silk than those that have, and at the same time yield better weight, by reason of part of their gum which they have not lost by the fire, yet most people prefer those that are baked, in order to have a silk more even in its colour; unless you could have a considerable quantity of fresh cocons, and time to wind them so; for otherwise it is undeniable, that the fresh would be much more advantageous, as well for the reason above mentioned as because they are easier to wind, not having been dried by the fire.

Before you begin to wind, you must prepare your cocons as follows.

1. In stripping them of that waste silk that surrounds them, and which served to fasten them to the twigs. This burr is proper to stuff quilts, or other such uses; you may likewise spin it to make stockings, but they will be coarse and ordinary.

2. You must sort your cocons, separating them into different classes in order to wind them apart. These classes are,

> The good white cocons:
> The good cocons of all the other colours.
> The dupions.
> The cocalons, among which are included the weak cocons.
> The good choquette; and, lastly,
> The bad choquette.

In sorting the cocons, you will always find some perforated cocons amongst them, whose worm is already born; those you must set apart for fleuret. As I have described above, you will likewise find some soufflons, but very few; for which reason you may put them among the bad choquette, and they run up into waste.

The

The good cocons, as well white as yellow, are the eafieſt to wind ; thoſe which require the greateſt care and pains are the cocalons; you muſt wind them in cooler water than the others, and if you take care to give them to a good windſter, you will have as good ſilk from them as the reſt. You muſt likewiſe have careful windſters for the dupions and choquettes. Theſe two articles require hotter water than the common cocons.

The good cocons are to be wound in the following manner. Firſt chooſe an open convenient place for your filature, the longer the better, if you intend to have many furnaces and coppers. This building ſhould be high and open on one ſide and walled on the other, as well to ſcreen you from the cold winds and receive the ſun, as to give a free paſſage to the ſteam of your baſons or coppers.

Theſe coppers or baſons are to be diſpoſed (when the building will admit of it) in a row on each ſide of the filature, as being the moſt convenient method of placing them, for by that means in walking up and down you ſee what every one is about. And theſe baſons ſhould be two and two together, with a chimney between every couple.

Having prepared your reels, (which are turned by hands and require a quick eye) and your fire being a light one under every baſon, your windſter muſt ſtay till the water is as hot as it can be without boiling. When every thing is now ready, you throw into your baſons two or three handsful of cocons, which you gently bruſh over with a wiſk about ſix inches long, cut ſtumpy like a broom worn out: by theſe means the threads of the cocons ſtick to the wiſk. You muſt diſengage theſe threads from the wiſk, and purge them by drawing theſe ends with your fingers till they come off entirely clean. This operation is called la Battüe.

When the threads are quite clear, you muſt paſs four of them (if you will wind ſine ſilk) through each of the holes in a thin iron bar that is placed horizontally at the
edge

edge of your bafon; afterwards you twift the two ends
(which confift of four cocons each) twenty or twenty-five
times, that the four ends in each thread may the better join
together in croffing one another, and that yo ur filk may be
plump, which otherwife would be flat.

Your windfter muft always have a bowl of cold water
by her, to dip her fingers in, and to fprinkle very often,
the faid bar, that the heat may not burn the thread.

Your threads, when thus twifted, go upon two iron
hooks called rampins, which are placed higher, and from
thence they go upon the reel. Now at one end of the
axis of the reel is a cog-wheel, which catching in the teeth
of the poft-rampin, moves it from the right to the left,
and confequently the thread that is upon it; fo that your
filk is wound on the reel crofs-ways, and your threads
form two hanks of about four fingers broad.

As often as the cocons you wind are done, or break or
diminifh only, you muft join frefh ones to keep up the
number requifite, or the proportion; I fay the proportion,
becaufe as the cocons wind off, the thread being finer,
you muft join two cocons half wound to replace a new
one: Thus you may wind three new ones and two half
wound, and your filk is from four to five cocons.

When you would join a frefh thread, you muft lay one
end on your finger, which you throw lightly on the other
threads that are winding, and it joins them immediately,
and continues to go up with the reft. You muft not wind
off your cocons too bare or to the laft, becaufe when they
are near at an end, the bairré, as we call it, that is the
hufk, joins in with the other threads and makes the filk
foul and gouty.

When you have finifhed your firft parcel, you muft
clean your bafons, taking out all the ftriped worms, as well
as the cocons, on which there is a little filk, which you
firft open and take out the worm and then throw them into a bafket by you, into which you likewife caft the loofe
filk that comes off in making the battüe. **You**

You then proceed, as before, with other two or three handsful of cocons; you make a new battüe; you purge them, and continue to wind the fame number of cocons or their equivalent, and fo to the end.

As I faid above, your windfter muft always have a bowl of cold water by her, to fprinkle the bar, to cool her fingers every time fhe dips them in the hot water, and to pour into her bafon when neceffary, that is, when her water begins to boil. You muft be very careful to twift your threads a fufficient number of times, about twenty-five, otherwife your filk remains flat, inftead of being round and full; befides when the filk is not well croffed it never can be clean, becaufe a gout or nub that comes from a cocon will pafs through a fmall number of thefe twifts, though a greater will ftop it. Your thread then breaks and you pafs what foulnefs there may be in the middle of your reel, between the two hanks, which ferves for a head band to tie them.

You muft mind your water be juft in a proper degree of heat. When it is too hot the thread is dead and has no body; when it is too cold, the ends which form the thread do not join well, and form a harfh ill-qualified filk.

You muft change the water in your bafon four times a day, for your dupions and choquette, and twice only for good cocons when you wind fine filk, but if you wind coarfe filk it is neceffary to change it three or four times. For if you was not to change the water the filk would not be fo bright and gloffy, becaufe the worm contained in the cocons foul it very confiderably. You muft endeavour as much as poffible to wind with clear water, for if there are too many worms in it, your filk is covered with a kind of duft, which attracts the moth and deftroys your filk.

You may wind your filk of what fize you pleafe, from one cocon to a thoufand; but it is difficult to wind more than thirty in a thread. The nicety, and that in which

consists

confifts the greateft difficulty, is to wind even, becaufe as the cocon winds off, the end is finer, and you muft then join other cocons to keep up the fame fize. This difficulty of keeping the filk always even is fo great, that (excepting a thread of two cocons, which we call fuch) we do not fay a filk of three, of four, or of fix cocons, but a filk of three to four, of four to five, of fix to feven cocons. If you proceed to a coarfer filk you cannot calculate fo nicely as to one cocon more or lefs. We fay for example, from twelve to fifteen, from fifteen to twenty, and fo on.

It is eafy to conceive, that it is more difficult to wind a coarfe filk even, than a fine one, becaufe it is harder to keep a great number of cocons always to the fame fize, than a fmall one.

The dupions which you defign for rondelette, or ordinary fewing filk, are to be wound from fifteen to twenty. The reft you may wind as coarfe as poffible, i. e. from forty to fifty: they ferve to cover and fill up in coarfe ftuffs, and may likewife be ufed for fome fort of fewing filk.

The good choquette is to be wound according to the ufes to which you intend to apply it; however not finer than from feven to eight. The bad choquette you may wind from fifteen to twenty cocons.

In winding the good cocons, you will always meet with fome defect've, which will not wind off, or are full of gouts and nubs. Thefe you muft take out of your bafon and keep by themfelves. They are called *baffinats*. They are to be wound apart as coarfe as you can. They make a foul, dirty filk. To have a good filk, you muft wind in fine weather. If the wind be high it fhakes your filk, and prevents its lying fmooth on the reel, forms ftrings of threads, which make it very difficult to wind on bobbins. If the weather is rainy the filk is damp, and has not that luftre it ought to have, or which it has when it dries, as it goes upon the reel. You muft mind not to hank it when damp, but let it dry on the reel; otherwife it would be furzy.

A a a

I have

I have now only to fpeak of the wafte that comes from the battüe, and the hufks of the cocons, that have ftill fome filk upon them, which are thrown into bafkets in winding, and are what we call *morefques*. Thefe you firft dry in the fun, then threfh, and afterwards card and fpin them to make fleuret. One hundred and fifty ounces of good cocons yield about eleven ounces of filk from five to fix cocons; if you wind coarfer, fomething more. You may wind about eleven or twelve ounces of filk from five to fix cocons in fourteen hours.

The filk which is made of baffinats and bad choquette ferves to make ftockings and coarfe heavy ftuffs, fuch as fattinades and damafks for hangings, &c. &c.

N° XLII.

The Art of making Anatomical Preparations by Corrofion. By John Morgan, *M. D. Profeffor of the Theory and Practice of Phyfic in the Univerfity of Pennfylvania, Member of the Royal College of Phyficians at Edinburgh, and F. R. S. at London, &c.*

AS no branch of fcience more certainly leads to an intimate acquaintance with the functions of the animal body, (which is the foundation of all rational knowledge of the caufes and cure of difeafes) than that of the ftructure of the vafcular fyftem, the origin, divifions, different ramifications and numerous inofculations of the veffels into, and their communication with each other, I have always thought this field of ufeful information deferved to be cultivated with great induftry and attention. In effect it brings us immediately, and in the moft compendious way, to acquire a knowledge of the nature, and of the motions of the fluids which circulate through them, of their diftribution throughout the different parts of the

body,

body, and of the action and ufes of the veffels containing, as well as of the humours contained in them. In particular, it behoves every practitioner of phyfic to ftudy the vafcular texture and compofition of the vifcera, for upon their healthful action the continuance of life, free from difeafe, principally depends; and the more their functions are injured, the more dangerous difeafes are thereby generated. From a relaxation of them arife atonia and weaknefs, and from obftruction of them infarctions, inflammations, tumors and fchirri are produced. To an acquaintance with their ftructure and anaftomofes, and the fluids they carry, we muft be chiefly indebted for our knowledge of the doctrines of refolution and fuppuration, and for the indications that point out to the phyfician by what means to accomplifh thefe defirable events, according to circumftances.

The little progrefs which practical anatomy has hitherto made in America, and the great confequence it may be of to the rifing ftudents of phyfic and furgery, to employ more of their attention on this ufeful fubject, are my motives for laying before you this effay, in hopes through this channel to ftir them up to profecute it with more zeal and ardor. This becomes the more neceffary, becaufe, owing to the late revolution, the fubjects of North-America having eftablifhed themfelves into independent ftates, have at prefent lefs commerce and lefs intercourfe with the learned and polifhed nations of Europe. At leaft fewer ftudents from America have recourfe to them for improvement in the knowledge of their profeffion than formerly, in as much as medical fchools and colleges have been founded in feveral of thefe different ftates, fince the author of this effay firft recommended and affifted in carrying into execution the plan of tranfplanting phyfic, as a fcience, from acrofs the ocean, by inftituting medical fchools on this weftern fide of the Atlantic*.

A a a 2

Upon

* See his difcourfe on the inftitution of medical fchools in America, delivered at a public commencement in the college of Philadelphia, May 1765.

Upon our own exertions muſt we therefore chiefly depend for building up the medical fabric, erecting uſeful temples of the healing arts, and diffuſing the lights
we can kindle through this new world. I know no one
ſtep that can be more uſeful to accompliſh this undertaking, than to teach the art of inveſtigating the ſtructure of
the different parts of the animal body, by injections and
corroſions, and other preparations of wax.

Such is the preſent ſtate of anatomy in this country
that there are at preſent but very few, I believe I may ſay
no ſuch preparations worth mentioning to be met with
here, that have been made in America. Doctor Chovet,
now reſident in this city has indeed a good collection of
wax preparations, of different parts of the human body,
which he made in his younger days and brought hither
from Europe. But nothing of this kind has hitherto
been practiſed, or it has been ſo taught as never to have
been of laſting uſe to any that I know of.

Being well acquainted with the general deſire that fills
the breaſts of my countrymen, to acquire and improve
every kind of ſcience that is uſeful, which is properly laid
before them, I truſt this attempt will ſtir up many to
learn and practiſe thoſe leſſons which, for their particular
benefit, I now unfold to them; nor do I doubt in a little time
but we ſhall ſee ſuch an emulation kindled for improving
on theſe hints, that all kinds of uſeful preparations will be ſo
common after a while, as not only to give riſe to anatomical cabinets and repoſitaries for ſpecimens of the animal, vegetable and foſſil kingdoms, as will tend to throw
great light upon philoſophy in general, but contribute to lay
a ſolid and uſeful foundation of natural hiſtory in America.

The firſt rudiments of this art that I acquired was
from the two Hunters, known through all Europe for
their ſuperior ſkill in anatomy, and acting as practical diſ-
fector to the celebrated doctors Colignon and Smith, pro-
feſſors of anatomy in the univerſities of Cambridge and Ox-
ford,

ford, which I further improved by practice at Paris with
Monf. Süe, to whom I am wholly indebted for my knowledge of anatomical preparations in wax.

The kind of preparations of thofe parts of the animal
body which admit of it that I now propofe to explain,
namely by injection and corrofion, exceeds in beauty,
nicety and ufefulnefs, that which is commonly called diffection.

In fact, in this latter, we can trace nature but very im-
perfectly, becaufe by diffection, the larger veffels only are
preferved from the knife, and for the moft part all the
fmaller are unavoidably cut away.

On the contrary, in anatomical preparations by corrofion, even the very fmall veffels may be kept entire, and
we can fee, at a caft of the eye, the courfe and diftribution of all the vafcular fyftem even to the fize of an hair,
called capillary veffels, and thofe too difengaged from the
furrounding parts, which otherwife wholly conceal, or
make them difficult to be perceived. It is impoffible that
with only the affiftance of a diffecting knife, any perfon
fhould be able to lay open to view all thofe fmaller veffels,
however fkilful and experienced the hand may be that
directs it. The exact and perfect imitation of nature
which this fort of preparations prefents, the eafe with
which they are made, and their extraordinary beauty and
neatnefs, render a knowledge of this art fo much the
more defirable.

The art of injecting the very fine veffels of the body
with common injection, was well known to the celebrated
Ruyfch, the moft famous anatomift, in that way, of any
living in Europe in his day; and therefore it has been
fometimes called the Ruyfchian art, but it fell fhort of the
one I now undertake to explain, becaufe in his preparations the minute veffels only become vifible, fo far as
the fubftance through which they proceed was tranfparent, but our art extends to the removal of every furrounding

rounding fubftance, and leaves them entirely naked and perfectly expofed to the eye. I once fhewed a preparation of the veffels of a kidney I had thus executed at Paris, to a meeting of the French academy of furgery in the year 1764, who allowed it to be curious and quite new to them. I think none of the members prefent at that meeting, except Monf. Morand, fecretary of that academy, who had been in England and was acquainted with doctor Hunter, alledged their having ever feen a fimilar preparation. At their requeft I prefented a memoir on the fubject, and fince that time Monf. Süe has beftowed one entire fection in treating exprefsly upon it, with a polite acknowledgement of his having acquired his knowledge from me, only with the particularity of naming me as one of the faculty of Edinburgh, without taking any notice of my being a Pennfylvanian by birth, or native of America, which have led fome into miftakes concerning the author of that piece. The reafon may be that Americans before the revolution, being but little confidered in any other light than as colonifts, their nation was feldom taken notice of, and I was introduced to him firft as a graduate of the univerfity of Edinburgh, and known to him afterwards as a member of the royal college of phyficians of that place.

Thefe preparations are, fince that period, become common in France, and the art is now well known, and cultivated fuccefsfully by Monf. Süe and others; but it was unknown there till I communicated it, firft at Paris, and afterward in the fouth of France; where I had the honour of explaining it to the illuftrious Monf. Imbert, chancellor of the univerfity at Montpelier, and to Monf. Bourgelas, principal of the Ecole veterenaire, or academy eftablifhed at Lyons for the improvement of the fcience of horfeman-fhip, juftly celebrated for his very elegant preparations of the anatomy of horfes, &c. But what gave me equal pleafure and furprize, was the admiration excited on my

presenting

prefenting only a part of the vafcular preparation of a
kidney by corrofion, (the reft being broke down in a journey by land of above a thoufand miles) which was expreffed by the celebrated Morgagni, illuftrious profeffor
of anatomy in the univerfity of Padua. He had kept up
a literary correfpondence with Ruyfch when alive, had
been favoured with fpecimens of this great man's preparations, and declared that in comparifon to the preparation
I gave him, they were " *rudis indigeflaque moles.*" From
this fmall fpecimen, he faid, " ex ungue leonem," he could
readily comprehend that the ufefulnefs of this kind of
knowledge amongft the learned in anatomy, muft become
great and extenfive.

I mention thefe anecdotes merely to fhow how recent,
or at leaft how confined the knowledge of this ufeful art
then was, being limited, as far as I know, to Great-Britain only. I fuppofe it to be owing to this circumftance,
viz. that real practical anatomifts who have excelled in
their preparations, have too generally kept fecret the methods and arts they employed in making thofe preparations. For this reafon, much I think is due to the memory of the great Profeffor Monro, of Edinburgh, who
has publifhed a paper upon the art of making injections.

So far as I can learn, this art cannot be traced farther
back than to the learned Dr. Nichols of London, who formerly gave lectures in anatomy both there and at Ox-
ford, and from whom Dr. Hunter acknowledged to his
pupils that he received his firft information. He then deferves to be looked upon as the author and inventor of
this art. When Dr. Nichols declined the bufinefs, Dr.
Hunter and his brother Mr. Hunter, took up the profeffion
of anatomy. Without doubt, thofe unrivalled brothers in
anatomical fkill, made confiderable improvements in the
art of injecting and diffecting animal bodies ; and it is likely improved the compofition of injections for corrofion.

My

My well meant intention of marking the rife and progrefs of this art, and of exciting an emulation in my
countrymen to profecute and improve it, will, I hope, not
only excufe but juftify both the matter and length of my
introduction.

Thefe preliminaries being thus fettled, I now proceed
to the main object of this communication. Without ex-
patiating upon the advantages that will attend an accurate
knowledge of this art, for the fake of perfpicuity I fhall
here reftrict myfelf to laying the following obfervations
before you, reduced to general heads, in as few words,
and in as concife a manner as I am able. They may be
ufeful to thofe who wifh to put them in practice, and will
perhaps give occafion to perfons who are curious in making
experiments in anatomy, to light up fome new difcovery.

The art of making anatomical preparations by corrofion, depends on the following principles.

1. We ought for the matter of injection to make ufe of
a fubftance that is poffeffed of a fuitable degree of confiftence, and fine enough to penetrate into the minuteft veffels, and which at the fame time has fuch a firmnefs of
texture as not to alter with the changes of the temperature
of the atmofphere, that is, it ought not to be fubject to
melt with the fummer's heat, nor to break down from its
brittlenefs on being gently handled in the winter.

2. The colours to be employed for fake of diftinguifh-
ing the different orders of veffels, whether arterial, venal,
tracheal or others, ought to be of fuch a nature as not to
be changed upon application of the menftruum.

3. We ought to make ufe of a menftruum that is capable of confuming the mufcular, parenchymatous, cellular
or fatty parts that furround the veffels, without affecting
the fubftance that we ufe for injection to fill the veffels.

4. Care and addrefs are neceffary in the perfon who
makes the injection.

5. Laftly, great attention is requifite in removing the
loofe and corroded parts, and in feparating them from the
injected

injected veffels without breaking them down by the force applied in cleanfing them.

The following directions will ferve to guide the operator in thefe different manœuvres.

The common injections are compofed of wax and fuet, or of wax and oil; the fuet or oil is made ufe of to foften the wax, and to give it the neceffary confiftence. We cannot employ fuch a compofition in our corroded preparations, being oppofed to the third principle laid down; becaufe the menftruum we ufe for deftroying the parts that furround the veffels, will alfo attack and confume the fat and animal fubftances which enter into the compofition of the injection. But we may employ the following compofitions, the goodnefs whereof has been proved by repeated trials, viz.

FIRST RECEIPT.

Take of white or the beft yellow wax and purified rofin each equal parts, e. g. ten or twelve ounces; melt them together and add a fufficient quantity of fpirit of turpentine, to give a due confiftence, that is from fix to eight ounces.

It is advifeable to melt the rofin firft, and ftrain it through a piece of fine linen; becaufe, in the ftate it is bought out of the fhops, it is often mixed with foreign fubftances.

I am of opinion this injection will turn out to be finer than the following, that is, it will penetrate into ftill fmaller veffels, but it is thought to have the inconvenience of being more brittle; fo that after corrofion, the moft flender of the veffels are more liable to break down in handling the preparation.

The following is the receipt which the celebrated Meffrs Hunter of London, have commonly made ufe of. It is lefs brittle and produces a firmer cohefion of parts, with nearly the fame confiftence as the former. Befides, it enters very fufficiently into the capillary veffels.

SECOND RECEIPT.

Take of pure rofin eight ounces, of wax four ounces, of Venice turpentine a fufficient quantity, that is, about

eleven

eleven or twelve ounces, to procure a proper confiſtence to the injection.

The method of aſcertaining the due confiſtence and the neceſſary firmneſs of the injection, is by taking up any quantity of it, whilſt melted, with a ſmall wooden ſpatula, and then letting it fall drop by drop on the ſurface of cold water. This immediately ſpreads and forms into a thin plate. By rolling it between your thumb and finger firſt moiſtened, or in the palm of one hand with the fingers of the other, both previouſly made wet to prevent ſticking, turn it into the ſhape of a cylinder or ſmall blood-veſſel, then throw it into a baſon of cold water, and let it remain till it is quite cold. If it is then of ſuch a confiſtence as not to yield to a very ſlight force, when preſſed between your thumb and finger, and yet ſo ſoft as to be capable of bending readily without breaking, it has the due medium of firmneſs and flexibility which is deſired. If it appears to be too ſoft, a further quantity of wax and roſin are to be added in the above mentioned proportion, till it acquires the wiſhed for confiſtence. If, on the other hand, it is too hard, a proportionably larger quantity of the Venice turpentine is to be added. The ſame precaution is to be obſerved, if we make uſe of roſin, wax and ſpirit of turpentine, as directed in the firſt receipt.

Operators ſeldom are at the trouble of weighing the ingredients; they generally judge of the reſpective weights and proportions of each by the eye. This method of determining them will anſwer very well for perſons who have acquired experience; for the different ſeaſon of the year when the injection is made, and the different confiſtence or purity of the wax and roſin, with other little circumſtances which ſometimes happen, occaſion ſome little variation. In general there is not ſo great danger of ſpoiling the preparation, by making the compoſition a little ſofter than is required, rather than harder, becauſe it grows ſome what harder by time, and alſo by ſteeping
the

the parts injected in water, for the fake of wafhing off the menftruum that we have made ufe of for performing the neceffary corrofion.

Thefe injections are well fuited to make corroded preparations of the vifcera, as of the heart, lungs, liver and kidneys. Yet I doubt not but perfons of ingenuity, who fhall be at the pains to render themfelves converfant in the art of injection, by giving attention to every circumftance, will acquire further fkill and may find other fubftances, equally fit for injection without being fo liable to become brittle, which thofe compofitions I have given above are, in fome degree, even when made with the utmoft care and exactnefs.

To know whether any fubftance of which a perfon wifhes to make a trial for injection, will withftand the action of the menftruum he means to employ, it is fufficient to put a piece of the compofition to be ufed as an injection into a fmall quantity of the menftruum, and let it remain in it for a week or fortnight; by that means he can judge of its goodnefs, before he is at the trouble of making, or of fpoiling an injection, as the cafe may happen.

Of the COLOURS.

The colours we commonly ufe to diftinguifh the different orders of veffels are, 1ft. Vermilion for colouring the injection for the arteries. 2d. Blue verditure, or what is called Pruffian blue, for the injection to be thrown into the veins. 3d. For colouring the injections to be thrown into the ureters and pelvis of the kidneys, and the tracheal veffels of the lungs, what are called in Englifh king's yellow and flake white are moftly ufed. A variety of other colours may be employed, but thefe are the principal and the beft.

We fhould obferve to melt the wax thoroughly over a flow fire, and the colouring powders fhould be added by degrees, ftirring them well in at the fame time, before the

other

other ingredients are added. This method prevents any effervefcence, which often happens when there is too great a fire, or when all the ingredients are mingled together before the colouring powders are added, efpecially the two laft. The quantity is judged of by trial.

Of the proper MENSTRUUM.

I now pafs to the third head, viz. to confider what fubftances will anfwer, for confuming all the parts furrounding the injection, and leaving the matter in the veffels themfelves untouched.

The beft I have yet tried is the concentrated fuming acid of marine falt, which comes over in the diftillation employed in the procefs for making glaubers falt; it fhould not be diluted with water, nor be dulcified, otherwife it becomes too weak to anfwer the purpofe, or at leaft the time required for compleating the corrofion is thereby protracted beyond what is needful.

The concentrated acids of vitriol and of nitre, are no lefs powerful to deftroy all the animal fubftance, furrounding the injected veffels, but the objection to which, from feveral trials, they appear to be liable, is that they are fuppofed to crifp the veffels ; at leaft the fpirit of fea-falt has been moft ufed, and concluded to be the leaft exceptionable menftruum for this operation.

Such were the fentiments I communicated, in my memoir to the royal academy of furgery at Paris in the year 1764, fince which, Monf. Süe, royal profeffor of anatomy in the fchools of furgery, and in the royal academy of painting and fculpture at Paris, having honoured my communication to the abovementioned academy, with a fection in his treatife entitled Anthropotomie, chap. 2. fect. 25. from page 70 to page 84 ; after acknowledging that he received the art of making thofe preparations from me, thus adds. " Since that time my nephew and I, having worked at them a great deal, and with abundant fuccefs,

cefs, we have difcovered, that we may change the menftruum, without injuring the preparation at all, and employ aqua fortis, or the nitrous acid in place of the fuming fpirit of falt; and that aqua fortis is even a more
perfect menftrum, than the fpirit of falt, in as much as
the colour of the injection is thereby lefs changed, and
the fmall veffels better preferved. Befides the difference
of expence is confiderable, as the fpirit of falt is worth
eighteen livres a pint, whilft the aqua fortis cofts at moft
but two livres, and the effect is the fame for quantity. I
have alfo employed the fpirit of nitre for the fame purpofe, with great fuccefs*."

*In refpect to the fourth Principle, namely, the Addrefs of
the Operator, and wherein it confifts.*

He ought to guard againft cutting away or removing
the cellular and other furrounding parts, before he has
made the injection. In fact, thefe give firmnefs to the
veffels, and prevent their ftretching unnaturally, or affuming forms contrary to nature, from the impulfe of the injection when drove into them by the hand of the anatomift. Thefe fubftances enable them to refift the too great
extenfion and yielding to the force applied.

The injecting pipes ought to be proportioned to the fize
of the veffels through which the injection is to be made.

It is proper to foak thofe parts in warm water, which
we are about to inject, for a fhorter or longer fpace of time,
as well to wafh them clean, as to carry off the blood and
other fluids, and the better to difpofe thofe parts to receive
the injection, with which they are to be filled.

The

* Monf. Morgan, Docteur en medicine de la faculté d'Edinbourg, en a donné une defcription exacte à l'Academie royale de la chirurgie, et c'eft de lui que je tiens l'art de préparer ces
parties; mais depuis après y avoir beaucoup travaillé, mon neveu et moi, et y avoir eu beaucoup de fuccès, nous avons decouvert qu'on pouvoit changer le menftrue, fans préjudicier
en rien à la preparation, et employer, au lieu de fel fumant, l'eau forte, qui eft même un
menftrue plus parfait, que l'efprit de fel, puifque la couleur de l'injection eft moins changée,
et que les petits vaiffeaux font mieux confervès. D'ailleurs la difference eft encor bien grande
pour la dépenfe, puifque l'efprit de fel vaut 18 liv la pinte, au lieu que l'eau forte ne coûte
tout au plus que 2 liv, et que la quantité eft la même pour l'effet. J'ai employè auffi avec
beaucoup de fuccès l'efprit de nitre. Anthropotomie, pag. 83. 84.

The fubftance employed for the injection ought to be entirely melted over a moderate fire, and be heated to the exact degree that will not permit the cooling of it too faft, upon coming into contact with the parts into which it is impelled, nor ought it to be fo great, on the other hand, as to burn or crifp the veffels, or prove troublefome to the operator in handling the fyringe or pipes, whilft he is making the injection.

The injection fhould be thrown into the part to be prepared, at one uniform impulfe, made flowly and evenly, with a fteady hand, and with fo little force as not to endanger a rupture of the veffels in the foft parts. When the injection is finifhed, the pipes fhould be corked or otherwife clofed, and the parts injected fhould be fuffered to cool by degrees. If they are plunged at once into cold water, before the fubftance of them has acquired a certain degree of hardnefs and firmnefs, a contraction in the elaftic coats of the veffels may be produced, fufficient to occafion a rupture, efpecially in the capillaries, which will always be followed by an extravafation of the injected fubftance.

Having expofed the injected parts to the air during an hour or two, it is proper to commit them to cold water all night, to cool and to harden them thoroughly. After taking them out of the containing veffel and abforbing the water from their furface with a fpunge gently applied, or fuffering it to run off by draining, they fhould be put into a fufficient quantity of the menftruum to cover the preparation entirely.

The next confideration is how to make ufe of the menftruum for corroding the parts to be diffolved and removed from the veffels. For this purpofe the operator fhould be furnifhed with a china bowl or a ftone veffel, on which the menftruum can make no impreffion; or what will anfwer ftill better, a glafs veffel with a mouth fufficiently large to put in and take out the injected parts, without any difficulty.

difficulty. It would be well to furnifh it with a proper cover to reftrain the acid fumes from efcaping. I have always ufed a cover of cork lined with wax, into which, whilft it is in a melted ftate, the inferior fide of the cover may be dipped; and this cover muft be cut fo as to fit exactly the mouth of the veffel. The great advantage of a glafs veffel over the others is its tranfparency, whereby we are able to fee how the corrofion goes on, and to judge when it is finifhed. This takes up from fix or feven days to a fortnight or three weeks, according to the nature of the part to be prepared, and to the quantity and concentricity of the menftruum employed, in which it ought to be entirely covered. When the acid is very dilute, it proves rather antifeptic and a preferver of animal fubftances, than a corrofive menftruum.

Of difengaging the Corroded Subftance.

Fifthly. The laft part of the operation confifts in difengaging the loofened and corroded fubftance from that of the injection. In this piece of bufinefs we ought to take the greateft care, if we wifh to avoid breaking down the beautiful fmall veffels of the part. With this view the acid fpirit employed as a menftruum fhould be decanted from the injection with great caution, whenever the corrofion of the furrounding fubftance is complete, fo that it no longer adheres to the veffels. In place of the corroding menftruum, foak the preparation in fimple water for three or four days. The loofe fubftance may be removed from the veffels, by pouring frefh water over the preparation flowly, and in fmall quantity at a time; or otherwife we may put the preparation in a veffel pierced with holes, like a cullender, and place this in fuch a manner as to receive a gentle current or ftream of water. If we fhould place the veffel near the nofel of a pump, and under the droppings or fmalleft ftream which we can procure to fall from it, the preparation may be thus cleanfed from the loofe corroded matter with which it is encompaffed.

But

But the method I have difcovered, and always practifed as the fafeft and beft, is to make ufe of a fmall fyringe, the pifton whereof works eafily, with which, whilft the preparation is covered three or four inches over with water, I fyringe gently, fo as to wafh and clean it entirely from the corroded fubftance which is but loofely attached to it. In this manner, ufing proper care, it may be performed perfectly without breaking down any, even the fineft parts, of the tender veffels.

But if more force than needful is employed, even the droppings of a pump from a too great height, when the preparation is taken out of the water, will fometimes break down the extremities of the fmall veffels, and mar the beauty of it..

After all thefe directions have been well executed, the preparation is to be fufpended for fome time in a fafe place, till it is dry ; then it is to be fixed on a wooden pedeftal, having a focket like a candleftick, in which it may be faftened with a little glue or melted wax. Then let it be covered with a tranfparent glafs in form of a globe or bell, with the mouth downward, to guard it from accidents. This finifhes the work.

Thefe preparations give us a moft exact knowledge of all the ramifications and anaftomofes of the veffels, and often of the junction of the arterial and venal fyftem, when the injection is fine enough, and fo fuccefsfully thrown from the arterial trunk as to penetrate into the veins and fill that fyftem of veffels in the organ prepared, completely, at one and the fame time. Thus I have filled both the emulgent arterial and venal fyftem of veffels, in a kidney, at one coup de main, through a fingle pipe fixed in the great trunk of the emulgent artery, the correfponding trunk of the vein being fhut up with a ligature. But it is more common for the injection made by the artery to ftop at the extremities of the evanefcent branches, and to fill the venal fyftem by a fecond injection, drove through the great trunk of the emulgent vein.

Upon

Upon the whole, thefe teach us, in the beſt manner poſſible, the true and intimate ſtructure of the viſcera in general, and of every particular part; from whence we may aſſert, without fear of any juſt cenſure, that prepara- tions thus executed are exceedingly uſeful, and enrich the cabinet with choice and beautiful ſpecimens of anatomy.

I have only to add that, in order to enable the artiſt to ſucceed and puſh his diſcoveries, it behoves him to learn the art of preparing the ſubject by diſſection. This is a new branch, though intimately connected with the foregoing: There are few books that teach it; but one very excellent treatiſe on the ſubject is publiſhed in French by Monſ. Süe, already quoted by the title of anthropotomy, or the art of diſſecting, injecting, embalming and preſerv- ing the parts of the human body; which, as I think it will greatly contribute to improve anatomy, I have ſome thoughts, at my leiſure, to tranſlate into Engliſh, for the benefit of the ſtudents of anatomy, phyſic and ſurgery in America.

I here ſubjoin the manner of making Wax Preparations by Monſ. Süe.

"WHEN we have a mind to make any prepara- tion of wax, we ought to begin by moulding the part we wiſh to imitate with freſh plaiſter of Paris made very fine, taking care to oil it previous to the appli- cation of the plaiſter.

"When the plaiſter laid on the ſurface of the part is cold, remove all the pieces that compoſe the mould one after another, taking care not to break any of them.

C c c   After

MANIERE DE FAIRE LES PREPARATIONS EN CIRE.

LORSQU'ON veut faire quelque preparation en cire, il faut commencer par mouler la partie que l'on veut imiter avec du platre frais et bien fin, ayant l'attention de bien huiller la partie avant que d'appliquer le platre. Lorſque le platre ſera refroidi de deſſus la partie, alors on otera toutes les pieces qui compoſent le moule, l'une après l'autre, prenant garde qu'aucuno

After leaving them to dry for fome time, they may be fafely ufed. For this purpofe, melt a fufficient quantity of virgin wax in a fkillet, over a gentle fire, and colour it according to the colour of the part which is to be imitated, with carmine, or other paint; or if the piece to be imitated has feveral parts of different colours, we muft not then colour the whole piece at once, but are to place the colour required upon each part, after the piece has been melted.

" Whilft the wax melts, prepare the mould, which we muft be careful to oil well with a little brufh to prevent fticking; then join all the pieces of the mould together, which muft be tied faft with fmall cords or twine; and that the air may not pafs through the cracks or joinings of the pieces of the mould, place fome clay on the outfide, by way of luting.

" The mould being thus prepared, and having taken care to leave an opening, we pour the wax into the mould through it, and then carefully turn the mould every way, in order that the wax may fpread equally through all the interior parts, of it until it is cold. If it be found that the piece is not thick enough, we are to pour on more melted wax, and turn it as before; then let the piece cool in the mould: afterwards, with proper precaution, we are to take the pieces of the mould apart, one after the other. The preparation being taken out of the mould entire, we muft take off the fuperfluous portions of wax which penetrated the

qu'aucune ne caffe. On le laiffe fecher pendant quelque tems. Enfuite on peut s'en fervir.
Pour cet effet on fait fondre de la cire vierge dans un poulon à petit feu, et on le colore, fuivant la couleur de la partie qu'on veut reprefenter, avec du carmin, ou quelque autre couleur; ou bien, fi la partie a plufieurs parties de couleur differente, alors on ne colore point la piece. Et on met la couleur fur chaque partie après que la piece a ete fondue. Pendant que la cire fonde on prepare le moule, qu'on a le foin de bien huiller avec un pinceau. Enfuite on reffemble toutes les pieces du moule, qu'on retient unies avec des cordes ou de la ficelle, et pour que la cire ne paffe par les fentes ou les jointures des pieces du moule, on y met fur les jointures exterieurement, de la terre glaiffe. Le moule preparè ainfi, et ayant eu l'attention de y laiffer une ouverture, on verfe la cire dans le moule, et l'on à le foin de tourner le moule en tout fens, pour que la cire fe repande egalement par tout l'interieur du moule, jufques a ce qu'elle foit rufroidie. Si vous jugez que la piece ne foit pas affez epaiffe, vous remettez de nouveau de la cire, et vous faites comme ci deffus. Après quoi on laiffe rufroider la piece dans le moule, et enfuite on tire avec beaucoup de precaution les pieces du moule, l'une après l'autre. La piece etant entierement depouillée, on la repare. C'eft à dire qu'on ote de deffus.

the joinings of the pieces of the mould, which being entirely repaired, we then colour the different parts which compofe the piece with colours fuitable to each part, that the arteries may be coloured with vermillion; the veins with Pruffian blue; the mufcles with carmine; and fo of the other parts; *which finifhes the preparation.*

" *Note*, When we wifh to make the wax lefs brittle, we muft add fome fpermaceti to it; and fometimes a little of the fineft Venice turpentine that can be procured."

fus les portions èxcedentes de cire qui fe font glifsèes entre les jointures des pieces du moule. La piece etant entierement reparèe, on colore les differentes parties qui compofent la piece avec des couleurs convenables a chaque partie, en forte que les arteres feront colorées avec du vermillon; et les veines avec du bleu de Pruffe; les mufcles avec du carmin; ainfi des autres.

Nota que quand on veut rendre la cire moins caffante on y adjoute le blanc de baleine, quelque fois auffi un peu de terebentine de Venife, tout ce qu'il y a de plus fin.

N° XLIII.

Of a living Snake in a living Horfe's Eye, and of other unufual Productions of Animals. By JOHN MORGAN, *M. D. F. R. S. London, Profeffor of the Theory and Practice of Phyfic, Philadelphia.*

Read June 5, 1782. WHETHER there is fuch a thing in nature as equivocal generation, by which is to be underftood the production of any new animal independant of a parent ftock of the fame kind, has been a fubject of controverfy amongft philofophers; fome afferting the reality of this doctrine, whilft others, as the celebrated Harvey and his followers as ftrenuoufly reject it. The latter, which is now deemed the orthodox fide of the queftion, affirm that the young of all are produced from an egg, furnifhed by the female, and fœcundated by a male animal. From the light thrown upon this fubject, by the deep refearches of Hippocrates, Galen and Ariftotle,

among

among the antients; and amongſt the moderns by Mal-
phigi, De Graaf, and above all others by the beforementi-
oned renowned Harvey, phyſician to king Charles the
firſt of England, (the diſcoverer of the true circulation of
the blood) this induction ſeems to be eſtabliſhed upon an
induction of facts and experiments, carrying with them
the force of conviction, ſo far as that induction reaches.

The only room which ſome ſuppoſe there may be for
doubt of the univerſality of the propoſition is, that a variety of animals have been found, at different times, to exiſt
in the bodies of other animals, and in extraordinary places, which neither the diſcoverers of thoſe animals, nor
others have been able to trace, with clearneſs and certainty, to what mankind, in general, can deem a probable or
ſatisfactory origin.   Whether it be owing to an impati-
ence to arrive at ſome concluſion, which can ill brook the
difficulties of the inquiry, or to the rareneſs of the caſes
falling under the notice of perſons capable of making a
thorough inveſtigation, and the tedious progreſs of experimental knowledge; or whether it is that we are apt to
ſuppoſe the ſubject does not admit of mathematical certainty from the light of philoſophy, I know not; but ſome
men have had recourſe to the doctrine of equivocal generation, to account for thoſe productions, as Ariſtotle and
his followers had, in other caſes, to certain occult qualities; a term by which they have endeavoured to conceal
their ignorance of what they could not explain, but were
unwilling to confeſs.   Nor are there wanting, in the preſent day, many perſons, who will ſooner deny the teſtimo-
ny of their ſenſes, than allow the exiſtence of an animal
production, which they know not how to account for.

This I ſuppoſe to proceed from a falſe pride, or an appre-
henſion of being deemed credulous in a philoſophic and enlightened age; and becauſe, in times of ignorance, the
paſſions of illiterate men were wrought upon by fictions to
believe in prodigies, whereby they were led blindfold, into
opinions

opinions of religion and philofophy, which had no folid foundation, the race of fceptics I refer to deem it manly not only to with-hold their affent from truths they do not underftand, but to difown and difpute the reality of them. They do not confider that, by fuch conduct, they endeavour to diveft themfelves and others of their rational faculties, and of that natural curiofity implanted in man by his Creator, for the wifeft purpofe, as a guide for inveftigating facts, in order to lead him to knowledge, which has given birth to difcoveries of the greateft importance to mankind.

In anfwer to the cavils of minute philofophers, I would briefly remark the firft ftep to new difcoveries, is an exact attention to the phænomena of nature, unbiafed by preconceived hypothefes, and that it is as much a mark of a defective underftanding to admit too little for truth, upon evidence, as to believe too much from credulity.

I have been led into the above train of obfervations from a fingular phænomenon that may be now feen in this city, and which is worthy the infpection of the curious. It is advertifed in the public newfpapers, viz. the Pennfylvania Gazette, May 23d, as worthy of the attention and critical infpection of all curious perfons, whether philofophers or phyficians, and particularly the latter, as it may, for what they know, if properly examined into, throw fome ufeful light upon the functions and difeafes of the animal body.

What I refer to is an horfe with a fnake in its eye, to be feen in Arch-ftreet, between Sixth and Seventh ftreets, not only poffeffed of mere life, but endowed with a very brifk locomotive faculty. True philofophers will not treat the affertion as idle, fictitious or romantic, but fee and judge for themfelves.

The writer of this piece has undertaken the prefent tafk, on purpofe to excite every clafs of people to fatisfy themfelves of the reality of the fact, that when recorded in the very place where all have it in their power to determine its exiftence, on the teftimony of their own eyefight, they may not

not plead ignorance and unbelief. He profeffes, for his own part, to be as little credulous or liable to impofitions, from accounts of pretended miraculous appearances, as his neighbours, however learned. Indeed he has ever ftrenuoufly oppofed, and thinks he ever fhall, what he deems empty tales of vifionary fpeculatifts, bred by weak fancies, or raifed by defigning men, to amufe or deceive the vulgar; but he admires and reveres the unfearchable wifdom of the divine architect, who framed this fpacious univerfe, teeming with myriads of animal beings, as well in thofe inftances where his defign and footfteps are vifible, as in thofe which lay more remote from human comprehenfion. Upon the firft relation of this curious hiftory from others, unacquainted with the ftructure of the eye, and therefore more likely to pafs a wrong judgment; and, till he had an opportunity to examine it himfelf, he believed the appearance to be fome unufual difeafe, or a filimentary production on the cryftalline humour, from a ftroke or inflammation of the eye, and that a convulfion in the nerves of its coat might produce an irritation in that organ, and a tremulous motion, which might impofe upon thofe who, not knowing how to account for the appearance, fhould content themfelves with calling it a fnake in the eye, merely from its refemblance, on firft fight, to that animal. But from the clofeft ocular examination, with unwearied attention, repeated more than once, he conceives he is not miftaken, in afferting that there is a real fnake in the eye; which, from the vivacity and brifknefs of its motion, exceeds that of any worm, and equals that of any kind of ferpent he has ever feen.

To fatisfy the public in general, as well thofe who have now an opportunity of feeing it, as fuch who may happen never to fee it, I think it will not be amifs to defcribe its appearance, and to deliver what I have been able to collect of its hiftory.

The

The horfe in whofe left eye this extraordinary *lufus na-tura* is vifible, is of a forrel colour, nine years old; it belonged to Doctor Dayton near the lines at Elizabeth-town, and, I am told, appeared to have no uncommon appearance in either eye, till within a few months ago. The firft particular circumftance which excited the owner's attention was, that having lent him to a friend to take a ride in a chair, although it was not known to be vicious or unruly before, it could not now be kept under any government, but ran away with, and dafhed the chair to pieces. The right eye ftill continues in a found ftate.

Soon after, viz. about ten weeks ago, Mr. Richard Wells, merchant of this city, a gentleman of probity and of great philofophic knowledge, being at Elizabeth-town in company with Doctor Dayton, this gentleman told him he would fhew him a curiofity as great perhaps as he had ever feen, namely, a living fnake in a living horfe's eye. Mr. Wells then defiring to fee it, upon looking into the eye, difcovered the animal very plainly, in a conftant ferpentine motion, but neceffarily in a fomewhat convoluted form, as its length was equal, as nearly as he could judge, to two diameters and an half of the eye, which could not meafure lefs than between three and four inches. The head and tail, or if you pleafe, the two extremities of the animal were then vifible, and the horfe's eye ftill retained its tranfparency enough to admit feeing the whole of the fnake diftinctly.

The horfe was foon after purchafed by a free negro, on purpofe to bring to Philadelphia for fhow, in order to gratify the curiofity of the virtuofi of every clafs, by giving them an opportunity of feeing and contemplating fo curious a phænomenon, and of communicating the refult of their inquiries to the learned, for the information of the public at large.

At prefent, apparently from the brifk and almoft conftant motion of the animal, which is fomewhat increafed

in

in length, fince the infpection at Elizabeth-town, and which
is as thick as a knitting needle, or piece of common twine,
as nearly as can be determined through the intervening
medium, the aqueous and vitreous humours of the eye
are confounded (the fine cellular texture of the latter being broke down) and tinged with the fofteft part of the
cryftalline, fo as to affume fomewhat of a white milky appearance, bordering on the colour of a cataract. The Iris
appears to be greatly dilated, or rather wholly deftroyed.
For the feptum, or partition which feparates the anterior
from the pofterior chambers, in a found eye, muft be broken
down, as the animal, or, to fpeak like a fceptic, the animal
appearance of a fnake is continually receding into the
fundus and back part, and by times coming forward into
the anterior part of the eye, with a convoluted brifk motion. I cannot think a fnake of the fame fize moving
brifkly in a tumbler-ful of fair water, or of water dif-
coloured with a tea-fpoonful of milk, would be more
vifible; but the coats of the eye and humours have now
fomewhat of a milky appearance, or colour of an incipi-
ent cataract.

It may be juftly prefumed, that whatever might be the
ftate of vifion, at firft appearance of this furprifing phænomenon, that eye muft be now blind. The lids are
commonly clofed, probably owing to pain excited in the
eye by fo troublefome a gueft; but there is no bloodfhot
appearance on the cornea, though the furrounding parts,
namely, the palpebræ, are a little tumid. To get a view
of the eye, the keeper commonly ftrikes the horfe on its back
with an open hand, at which, as if frightened, it opens the
lid of the left, as well as widens the opening of the right
eye, which continues difclofed but a fhort time; however
this gives an opportunity for infpection for five or fix feconds of time together, and the blows muft be repeated
to keep the eye open, when a perfon wifhes to have a
longer time for infpection.

The

The milky appearance has for fome weeks grown gradually more opaque; from which circumftance it is probable the difeafe occafioned by the prefence of an extra-
neous body, or unnatural animal irritating the organ,
will gradually produce too great obfcurity to afford that
fatisfaction in viewing it, which hitherto it has done and
ftill continues to afford.

It has been my wifh, and I have expreffed my opinion
to feveral gentlemen that it would be worth while, to make
up a fum of money and purchafe the horfe for fake of diffecting the eye, whilft the animal is yet alive, but no notice has been yet taken of it: Perhaps the owner keeping
it for fhow places too high a value upon it. I have further defired, if that purchafe is not made, to have an opportunity of taking out the eye and diffecting it immediately after death, whenever that event takes place, if it
happens where I am.

The eye has been infpected by feveral gentlemen of the
faculty, who are aftonifhed, and at a lofs to account for the
appearance on common principles or from known difeafes;
a queftion then naturally arifes in the minds of moft who
have feen or heard of it, viz. If it be a real fnake or other
living animal, how it got there, or whether there are other
inconteftible hiftories to match it, in the annals of medical hiftory, of animals bred in man or other animals, as
difficult to be accounted for?

I anfwer, Facts are what I am more concerned to efta-
blifh than fpeculative opinions; therefore inftead of leading to theories that may be idle and groundlefs, I fhall be
fatisfied to refer all who doubt the reality of its being a
fnake in the eye, firft to the hiftory of the Guinea worm,
of which I have had more than one cafe falling under
my own care, and have feen others in the Pennfylvania hofpital, extracted from the leg, feveral yards in
length; fecondly, to the well known hiftory of a jointed
worm bred in the liver of Mrs Holt, in this city, about

D d d   thirty

thirty years ago, of about twenty inches long and near three in circumference, recorded in the medical essays of a society of physicians in London. This worm I have seen ten years after preserved in spirit, in the anatomical cabinet of the celebrated Dr. William Hunter of that place; and thirdly, I refer to the history and engraving of one exactly similar, as large as the life, inserted in the second volume of Edinburgh medical essays, plate fourth; and lastly, to autopsy, by examining the eye of the horse in question, which will afford ocular demonstration of the fact.

I shall add to these some observations of that prince of anatomists in his day, the famous Ruysch, who, as Dr. Haller attests, from a practice of dissection continued for near eighty years, with a diligence, skill and accuracy in examining into morbid bodies, and the niceness of his dissections and of his anatomical injections, exceeded all his cotemporaries; and in fine, whose testimony in those matters was looked upon by Boerhaave and Haller, and by every medical writer since, to be as incontestible authority as that of any other person whatsoever.

In his first volume, observation the 16th, he says, " daily experience proves that worms may be generated in all parts of the body. I strangled a dog that was very lively three hours after being fed, with a view to examine the lacteal or milk vessels. On opening the belly of it a live worm, at least two spans in length, skipped out. I could discover nothing amiss in the omentum, nor any solution of continuity of the parts; and both the mesentery and intestines were found."

Again he says, observation 54, " I have had room to doubt whether, as Harvey and his followers affirm, all animals are produced out of an egg, from worms being found in the arteries of living horses; as also from worms seen in the parenchyma, or the glandular substance of the liver, as it is now called, and also in the cystic duct and biliary pores of sheep, and very often in the gall-bladder.

I remember

I remember once to have seen them in the human kidneys, and such as are more frequently met with in the kidneys of dogs. That worms have been sometimes found in the brain, no body can deny who will be at the trouble of turning over the writings of authors of high repute."

By what passages those animals or their eggs were insinuated into the interior parts of the body, is not easy to determine. It does not seem probable that they could reach the forementioned places through the pores of the skin or the organs of respiration; much less that their eggs were taken in at the mouth, and from thence proceeded to their respective places; nor yet is it likely they could remain entire in the stomach, where, in the procefs of chylification, there is a remarkable fermentation and breaking down the parts of the food. Nor can the chyliferous or lacteal vessels afford a passage to the eggs in their rout; and lastly, no one alledges that he has ever seen exactly similar worms out of the body.

Were I so disposed, or did the design of this paper require it, I could to those observations add many extraordinary instances, of strange, rare, and surprizing productions of animals in the human body, from the works of the celebrated Bartholine, physician to the king of Denmark, and from other grave and learned authors of unexceptionable repute. But here I pause, to reverence the hand that framed not only our bodies, but those of the meanest reptiles, with an exuberance of skill, which proclaims that they are not the effect of chance; and acknowledging I am lost in wonder, I leave the fuller explanation of the uncommon productions, to some happy genius that may arise, if ever it should please God to produce such an one into the world, who by tracing out the footsteps of the Creator, shall be able to throw clearer lights than we yet have, upon these abstruse subjects.

N° XLIV.

Some Account of a motley coloured, or pye Negro Girl and Mulatto Boy, exhibited before the Society in the Month of May, 1784, *for their examination, by* Dr. JOHN MOR-GAN, *from the History given of them by their owner Monf. Le Vallois, Dentist of the King of France at Guadaloupe in the West Indies, as follows.*

ADELAIDE, the little girl now before the fociety, is aged two years and little more than one month, is of a clear black colour, verging to brown, except that fhe has a white fpot bearing fome refemblance to an aigrette; the point of which is at the root of the nofe, and it rifes into the hair, above the forehead, of which it occupies above an inch in width, from the margin to the fonte-nelle. In this part the colour of the hair is white, and it is curly like the hair of negroes in general, and thicker in that part than on any other part of its head. In the middle of its forehead and on the aigrette, is a large black fpot; on the external fide next to the temples, about one half of each eye-lid, both upper and under, is black, and the remaining half next to the nofe is white.

The eyes are black and lively, a little to the left and towards the middle of the chin a white fpot begins, which is long in proportion to its breadth, but of lefs magnitude than that of the forehead: It ftretches under the chin to the upper part of the throat. The neck, the upper and under part of the cheft, the fhoulders, the back, loins and buttocks to the junction with the thighs, and the puden-dum, are of the colour of her face, but the loins and the thicker part of the buttocks are of a deeper black.

The

The arms from the upper and middle part are white, and interfperfed with black fpots. There are fome fmaller and more numerous about her knees than elfewhere.

Upon the large black fpots there are alfo many fmaller and blacker which are very glaring. Many of thefe fpots divide into four, five and fix rays, refembling a ftar, which are not obferved but by a clofe infpection, and then they are very vifible. In feveral parts thofe fpots, being of different fhades, give an exact picture of lunar eclipfes, as they are commonly reprefented in the books of aftronomy. The hands, the middle part of the fore arms, the inferior and middle parts of the legs and feet are black, which have a pretty ftriking refemblance to gloves and to bufkins.

The white that prevails over the breaft, and over the belly, arms and thighs, has a lively appearance. The fkin is foft, fmooth and fleek.

Adelaide has fine features; we meet with few negroes of fo beautiful a form. In her temper fhe is cheerful, gay and fportful, and as tall as children of her age generally are, and hath evidently a very delicate temperament, yet enjoys pretty good health, neither hath fhe eyes, nor ears, nor any particularity in her features, or external conformation, like what may be feen at the firft infpection in thofe who are called white negroes, whofe fkin is altogether of a dead white colour, and whofe woolly white hair and features refemble thofe of their negro parents.

From this detail we may remark that the alteration of the natural colour of Adelaide, takes place over the fame parts of the body, for the moft part, as over the body of Maria Sabina, of whom Monf. Buffon gives an account; and confidering it as a well authenticated fact, from all the information that has been received of Adelaide, that fhe had a negro father and negro mother, we are led to believe, that the Englifh account under the portrait of Maria Sabina is exact, and not afferted merely for the

fake

fake of covering the honor of the mother, and of the fociety in which fhe was a flave.

' The pyed mulatto boy is named Jean Pierre. He is a
month younger than Adelaide; but from his figure, which
is robuft, he appears to be fix months older. He as well
as Adelaide both belong to Monf. le Vallois. He was born
at Grandterre, Guadaloupe, of a negro wench named Carolina and of a white man, an European, whofe name I
did not learn.

A certificate which Monf. le Vallois has with him, le-
gally authenticated by Monf. Blin, lieutenant judge, given
from under the hand of Monf. des Effart, king's phyfician, and of Monf. Cumin, king's furgeon, at Grandterre,
Guadaloupe, attefts that Adelaide was born at Gros-Iflet
in St. Lucia, that Bridget her mother is a negro of the Ibo
nation, and now reckoned to be about twenty-five years
old, and that her father, whofe name is Raphael, is a negro of the Mina nation. In this certificate it is farther
declared that the father of Jean Pierre has white fpots
(that is of a deeper white than his natural fkin) of the fame
fhape and in the fame parts of the body as the fon, and
that the mother and one of the brothers of this boy's European father have like white fpots, and in the fame parts
of the body.

However it may be in refpect to thofe obfervations concerning the fuppofed refemblance of the white fpots they
may bear about them, to thofe which mark Jean Pierre,
it fuffices to take notice here, that his body is entirely of
the colour of a mulatto, except that he has from nature a
white aigrette in his forehead like that of Adelaide. The
hair in that part is white mixed with black, which is not
fo in Adelaide. The ftomach, and the legs from two inches
above the ancles to the middle of the calf of the legs are
entirely of a beautiful lively white ; there is alfo a white
fpot in the upper part of the penis. Over the white parts
                                                        of

of the legs there is a light white down, longer and thicker than children commonly have at this age.

Such is the natural hiftory of thofe two extraordinary children; but what caufes have produced thofe furprifing phænomena and alteration of the natural colour of their fkin, are left for others to inveftigate and explain.

Monf. le Vallois relates that the mother of Adelaide, whilft pregnant with her, was delighted in laying out all night in the open air, and contemplating the ftars and planets, and that the great grandmother of Jean Pierre (a white lady) during the time of her being with child of her daughter, his grandmother by the father's fide, was frightened on having fome milk fpilled upon her. Whether this will account for her daughter and grandchildren being marked in the manner related, and for the fpots obferved on the mulatto boy defcending to him; or whether the ftrong impreffion made upon the mother of Adelaide, by the nightly view of the ftars and planetary fyftem, may be confidered as the caufe of the very extraordinary appearances in that girl, every one will determine for themfelves; there being many who difpute childrens being ever marked by the fears, longings, or impreffions made by mothers on the bodies of their children, at a certain time of pregnancy; for which they endeavour to account in different ways; whilft others who have known a variety of children born with different marks on them, (which have fallen under their particular notice) are equally confident of thofe marks proceeding from the caufes alledged.

Extract

N° XLV.

Extract of a Letter from BERNARD ROMANS, *of Penfa-
cola, dated Auguſt* 20, 1773.

THE common mariners compaſs has always appeared
to accurate obſervers as an imperfect inſtrument, but
in nothing has it proved to be more defective than in its
uſe in ſtorms, the heavieſt braſs compaſſes now in uſe are
by no means to be relied on in a hollow or high ſea.
This is owing to the box hanging in two braſs rings confining it to only two motions, both vertical, and at right
angles with each other, by which confinement of the box
upon any ſuccuſſion, more eſpecially ſudden ones, the card
is always put into too much agitation, and before it can
well recover itſelf, another jerk again prevents its pointing
to the pole, nor is it an extraordinary thing to ſee the card
unſhipped by the violence of the ſhip's pitching.

All theſe inconveniencies are remedied to the full by
giving the box a vertical motion at every degree and minute of the circle, and to compound theſe motions with a
horizontal one, of the box, as well as of the card. By this
unconfined diſpoſition of the box the effects of the jerks
on the card are avoided, and it will always very ſteadily
point to the pole. Experience has taught me, that the
card not only is not in the ſmalleſt degree affected by the
hollow ſea, but even in all the violent ſhocks and whirl-
ings the box can receive, the card lies as ſtill as it in a
room unaffected by the leaſt motion.

Lately a compaſs was invented and made in Holland,
which has all theſe motions. It is of the ſize of the common braſs compaſſes, the bottom of the braſs box inſtead
of being like a bowl, muſt be raiſed into a hollow cone,
like

like the bottom of a common glafs bottle; the vertex of the cone muft be raifed fo high as to leave but one inch between the card and the glafs; the box muft be of the ordinary depth, and a quantity of lead muft be poured in the bottom of the box round the bafe of the cone, this fecures it on the ftyle whereon it traverfes.

This ftyle is firmly fixed in the center of a fquare wooden box, like the common compafs, except that it requires a thicker bottom. The ftyle muft be of brafs about fix inches long, round and of the thicknefs of one-third of an inch, its head blunt, like the head of a fewing thimble but of a good polifh; the ftyle muft ftand perpendicular, the inner vertex of the cone muft alfo be well polifhed; the vertical part of the cone ought to be thick enough to admit of a well polifhed cavity fufficient to admit a fhort ftyle proceeding from the center of the card whereon it traverfes. The compafs I faw was fo conftructed, but I fee no reafon why the ftyle might not proceed from the center of the vertex of the cone, and fo be received by the card the common way. The needle muft be a magnetic bar blunt at each end; the glafs and cover is put on in the common way.

A compafs of this kind was given by the captain of a Dutch man of war to Capt. Burnaby of the Zephyr floop; this gentleman gave it to me to examine, and was very profufe in his encomiums thereon, faying that in a very hard gale, which lafted fome days, there was not a compafs but it of any fervice at all. Indeed to me it appears to deferve all the praife he gave it. My ftay is fo fhort here, as not to allow me time to have one made; but I intend to have one made for my own ufe, and fhall offer it to the fociety for infpection. I hope that this ufeful inftrument may become univerfal, as navigation certainly will be rendered more fafe through its means; and I fhall think myfelf highly honoured, if through the channel of this fociety it becomes public.

E e e   *Prefents*

Presents made to the American Philosophical Society, since its Revival and Incorporation in 1780, with the Names of the Donors.

DONORS.	PRESENTS.
1780, Apr. 7. Dr. *Coste*,	An analytic, etymologic, and argumentative treatise on the accent and pronunciation of the English language.
Dec. 15. Monf. *Chatilaux*,	His works de la felicité publique, 2 vol.
1781, Jan. 19. Monf. de *Marbois*,	A pamphlet in French, containing an account of, and proposals for printing a work of great merit, entitled voyages metallurgiques, &c. Par M. Jars.
Feb. 16. Gen. *Sullivan*,	Specimens of talc, from a large body of this fossil, lately discovered in New-Hampshire.
Mar. 16. *Sam. Adams*, Esq.	Copy of a Philosophical discourse delivered before the academy of arts and sciences at Boston, by their president James Bowdoin, Esq.
1783, Feb. 16. Assembly of the State of *Pennsylvania*,	One hundred and fifty pounds.
May 2. Mr. *J. M'Henry*,	A curious specimen of petrified pine.

Sept.

DONATIONS.

1783, DONORS.	PRESENTS.
Sept. 26. Dr. *Franklin*,	Natural hiſtory of the South of France, by Monſ. L'Abbé Soulavie, 2 vols.
Oct. 17. Mr. *John Hyacinth de Magellan*,	A collection of Philoſophical tracts, &c.
Mr. *Godfrey*,	A collection of prints, repreſenting ſome of the principal events during the late revolution in America.
Abbé de *Fontana*,	Four pamphlets on Philoſophical ſubjects, written by himſelf.
Dec. 5. Mr. *Van Berckel*,	Six volumes of the Tranſactions of the Batavian Philoſophical Society of Rotterdam.
Monſ. de *Etienne*,	On a cement impenetrable by water.
1784, Jan. 16. Mr. *John Felſted*,	A collection of ſpecimens of the ſeveral woods growing in the iſland of Jamaica.
Febru. 3. Mr. *Warder*,	A collection of animal calculi.
Mr. *Mandrillon*,	Voyageur Americain. An anſwer to the queſtion propoſed by the Academy of Sciences at Lyons, viz. Whether the diſcovery of America has been advantageous to mankind or not? both written by himſelf.

DONATIONS.

1784. DONORS.	PRESENTS.
Feb. 20. *Samuel Vaughan*, Efquire,	A 3½ feet acromatic telefcope, completely mounted on a mahogany ftand, with rack work to move it along the meridian, or parallel to the equator, made by Mr. Dolland.
	A Gunter's fcale improved, for navigation and aftronomy, by Mr. John Robertfon, with a defcription thereof by Mr. Mountaine.
	A magazine microfcope, confifting of a fingle, double, and folar microfcope.
Mr. *William Parker* by Mr. *S. Vaughan*,	A burning lens 11½ inches, with a fecond lens of 6¼ inches diameter, completely framed and mounted on a mahogany turned cone, with rack work, pillar, pinnion and apparatus for placing the whole in a proper fituation.
March 19. Dr. *Franklin*,	A treatife in French, on the fubject of air balloons.
Samuel Vaughan, Efq.	A copy in manufcript of Dr. Prieftley's experiments on phlogifton, and the feeming converfion of water into air.
Apr. 2. Mr. *J. Vaughan*,	Dr. Prieftley's works, complete in 33 volumes.
	Dr. Prieftley's biographical and hiftorical charts.

April.

DONATIONS.

1784. Donors.	Presents.
April 9. *Samuel Vaughan*, Efq.	Dr. Price on reverfionary payments, annuities, &c. 2 vols. Tranfactions of the fociety of arts, &c. 1783, 1784. Tracts publifhed by the fociety for conftitutional information, 1783. Proceedings at Quebec, 1773. Lind on difeafes incident to hot climates. Plinii fecundi hift. nat. Antiquitates Romanæ. Rowe's fluxions. Gregory's practical geometry. Hamilton on vapours and the aurora borealis.
April 16. Dr. *Cofte*,	Eight copies of his inaugural oration, delivered in the college of William & Mary, Virginia.
Oct. 15. Rev. *Jeremy Belknap*,	The firft volume of his hiftory of New-Hampfhire.
1784, Nov. 12. Dr. *M. Guthe*,	A filver medal in memory of the Rev. Chriftian Meyer of Heidelburg, late a member of this Society.
——19. Chev. d' *Armours*,	A pamphlet in manufcript, on the fubject of animal magnetifm, by Dr. P. Hervier, of the Sorbonne.
Dec. 9. Monf. de *Marbois*,	Report of the commiffioners appointed by the king of France, to examine into the merit of Dr.

DONATIONS.

DONORS.	PRESENTS.
	Dr. Mefmer's late difcovcries of animal magnetifm.
1785, Jan. 22. Mr. *Mandrillon*,	An elegant copy of his work entitled le fpectateur Americain.
Mar. 4. Mr. *W. Henry*,	The model of a wheel carriage, to run againft the wind by the force of the wind alone.
	Two very large pieces of chryftal found in Lancafter county.
	An exceedingly large tufk and one of the grinders of fome unknown fpecies of animals, brought from the neighbourhood of the Ohio.
Affembly of the State of *Pennfylvania*,	A lot of ground in the Statehoufe fquare, on which to erect a building for the accommodation of the Society.
Mrs. *Pauli*,	A horn of the Canada moofe deer of an extraordinary fize.
July 15. Rev. Mr. *Muhlenberg*,	A manufcript copy of his *Flora Lancaftrienis*.
Dr. *Noel*,	Three volumes of the proceedings of the Royal French Academy.
	An elegant electrical machine, with the neceffary apparatus.
Sept. 27. Dr. *T. Redman*,	Specimens of the Eaft-India manner of writing, on long ftrips of the leaves of the cocoa nut tree.
	Monf.

DONATIONS.

Mr.

DONATIONS.

DONATIONS.

The following Donations were received through the hands of Dr. FRANKLIN.

1786. DONORS.	PRESENTS.
June. Monf. the Count de *Buffon*,	His collection of birds, beautifully engraved and coloured. Supplement à l'hiftoire naturelle, 5 tome, 4°.
Dr. *Fothergill*,	Illuftratio fyftematis fexualis Linneæ, per Johannes Miller.
Lord *Stanhope*,	Roberti Simfon, M. D. opera reliqua. 4°.
Signior *Manini*,	Le lettere Americane, 3 vols. 12°.
Monf. *Grivel*,	L'ifle inconnue, ou memoires du Chev. des Gaftines, 4 vols. 12°.
Mr. *J. H. de Magellan*,	His collection, de differens traités fur des inftruments d'aftronomie, phifique, &c. Extrait d'une lettre de M. Magellan fur une pendule de fon invention. Defcription d'une machine nouvelle de dynamique, &c. Nouvelle conftruction d'alambic pour faire toute forte de diftillation en grande, avec le plus d'economie dans l'operation, et le plus d'avantage dans le refultat.
M. Court de *Gebelin*,	Monde primitif comparé avec le monde moderne, 1 vol. 4°.
The Author,	Le triomphe du nouveau monde, reponfes academiques, formant

DONATIONS.

mant un nouveau fyftême de confederation, fondé fur les befoins actuels des nations chrétiens-commercantes, et a-dapté à leurs diverfes formes de gouvernement, 2 vols. 8°.

June. M. *Elie de Beaumont*, Memoire pour Dame Marie Reine Petit de la Burthe, Marquife d'Anglure, contre le Sieur Pierre Petit.

Pere Berthier, Hiftoire de premiere temps du monde, 8vo.

Monf. *Mefmer*, Précis hiftorique de faits relatifs au magnetifme animal, 1 vol. 8vo. fix copies.

Monf. L'Abbé *Sans*, Guerifon de la paralyfie par l'electricité, 8°.

Dr. *Ingenhaufs*, Ingen-Haufz vermifchte fchriften, 1784, 2 vols. 8vo.
Obfervations fur la conftruction et l'ufage de l'eudiometre du M. Fontana,—both written by himfelf.

Marcus Lemort De-metigny, Tentamen ΨΥΧΟ-ΣΩΜΑΤΟ-ΙΑΤΡΙΚΟΝ feu confpectus thefiformis de naturâ animæ et corporis, &c. written by himfelf.

Monf. *Gerbier*, Lettres et obfervations de M. Gerbier, docteur en medicine, l'un des médicins de monfieur fervant par quartier, au fujét de deux nouveaux remedes, contre les maladies fquirrheufes, canccreufes, &c.

Pere

DONATIONS.

*Sundry other books, given by different perſons, will be men-
tioned in the liſt to be publiſhed in the next volume.*

END OF THE SECOND VOLUME.

www.ingramcontent.com/pod-product-compliance
Lightning Source LLC
Chambersburg PA
CBHW032259280326
41932CB00009B/628